BLAST TO FREEZE

BRITISH ART
IN THE
20TH CENTURY

This exhibition is under the patronage of the
Right Honourable Tony Blair M.P., Prime Minister of the United Kingdom,
and Gerhard Schröder, Chancellor of the Federal German Republic

sponsored by

VOLKSWAGEN BANK

BLAST TO FREEZE

BRITISH ART
IN THE 20TH CENTURY

kunst

KUNSTMUSEUM WOLFSBURG
Hatje Cantz Publishers

CONTENTS

THE SHORT CENTURY

1910–20 VORTICISM, FIRST WORLD WAR AND ITS AFTERMATH 25

1920–40 PRIMITIVISM, ABSTRACTION AND SURREALISM 57

1940–50 Second World War, Isolation and Existential Concerns 105

1950–60 Brave New Worlds, Abstraction and the Aesthetics of Plenty 130

MESSAGES FROM THE PATRONS OF THE EXHIBITION

I was delighted to be invited by the Kunstmuseum Wolfsburg to be the joint patron with Chancellor Gerhard Schröder of this exhibition.

Blast to Freeze. British Art in the 20th Century contains many of the most important works to have come out of Britain in recent times. It explores the main periods of experiment in British art of the last century, linking the developments and innovations in the art world with the historical and social events of the time, in a most original way.

It is easy to think of the twentieth century only as a time of great social, political and technological upheaval. But it was also a time of great change and development in the world of art. It was a time for thinking the unthinkable. It was an exciting time to be an artist, not least in Britain.

I have no doubt that this exhibition will be an enormous success. I congratulate the Kunstmuseum Wolfsburg and all those who have contributed to the planning.

Tony Blair
The Right Honourable Tony Blair M. P.,
Prime Minister of the United Kingdom

I am very pleased to join Prime Minister Tony Blair as a patron of the art exhibition *Blast to Freeze. British Art in the Twentieth Century* at the Kunstmuseum Wolfsburg.

The German and British organisers and sponsors have succeeded in putting together an excellent collection of important works of art. For the first time in many years, this exhibition offers the public in Germany a comprehensive survey of the complex development of British art of the twentieth century, with its many different facets and elements of continuity and change.

The list of exhibits alone, with names such as Francis Bacon, David Hockney and Richard Hamilton, is impressive and a sign of the variety in the exhibition, as a whole. But the exhibition also highlights the political and social background against which these works were created.

For me, the exhibition is also a clear sign of the excellent cultural relations between Germany and the United Kingdom. My special thanks go to all who have contributed to its realisation.
I wish the exhibition at the Kunstmuseum Wolfsburg great success, plenty of attention and numerous interested visitors.

Gerhard Schröder
Chancellor of the Federal Republic of Germany

SPONSOR'S FOREWORD

The Volkswagen Bank is pleased to support the exhibition *Blast to Freeze. British Art in the Twentieth Century*, as the main sponsor. This is the second exhibition of international rank at the Kunstmuseum Wolfsburg that we have undertaken to sponsor, following the success of the retrospective of the American video artist, Gary Hill. The Volkswagen Bank has a special connection to Great Britain within the framework of its international activities, since the Bank, like Volkswagen Financial Services UK, in Milton Keynes, belongs to Volkswagen Services AG in Brunswick. We should like to think that our support will enable people in the entire region and beyond to benefit to the full from the Kunstmuseum Wolfsburg's tried and tested programme of inter-national events. For this reason, one of the main features of our sponsorship is the special provision for schoolchildren in the region. Through the exhibition, they should be able to gain a vivid insight into the main developments in British art, which have culminated, most recently, in the work of the so-called "Young British Artists". The catalogue, too, which includes contributions by leading specialists in British art, will contribute to a better understanding of the culture of this neighbouring European country.

We should like to thank the Kunstmuseum Wolfsburg and its staff for organising international exhibitions of the quality of this retrospective of twentieth-century British art and wish all possible success to the exhibition in Toulouse, as well as in Wolfsburg.

Norbert M. Massfeller
Chairman of the Board
Volkswagen Financial Services AG

DIRECTOR'S PREFACE

Great Britain's relatively isolated geographical and cultural situation, between "Europe" or the "Continent" – as the English somewhat distantly call the mainland – and the United States of America, has had a decisive influence on the development of its own forms of modern art. It has also contributed in no small way to British artists' ability to define their own position and go their own way.

Every ten years or so London has regularly witnessed the emergence of distinctive new artistic trends and personalities (loners and eccentrics). However, for the first half of the last century most internationally orientated artists looked mainly to Paris for inspiration, and thereafter to New York, until London itself was elevated to the status of art metropolis, with the advent of so-called "Britart", at the beginning of the 1990s. The reason for the recent, dramatic shift in fortunes may be attributed to a new burst of energy emanating from Britain, which threatened to engulf the international art scene, as a form of postcolonial cultural revenge for the demise of the old political slogan, "Britannia rule the waves". The new "Britart" was a refreshing phenomenon, which caught on quickly in Germany, as elsewhere and achieved early recognition through the Kunstmuseum Wolfsburg's exhibition *Full House. Young British Artists* in 1996, which was staged in a setting inspired by the vulgar dereliction of London's East End. It was *Freeze*, organised by Damien Hirst and a number of his fellow students at Goldsmiths' College, that heralded the arrival of this newest wave of energy from England, at a time when Douglas Gordon and a number of other Scottish artists had also begun to lend their own distinctive flavour to the international scene, and this is what had sparked off our interest in exploring the history of British art, prior to its meteoric rise at the end of the twentieth century. In retrospect, we can now see that British art has been characterised by a succession of moments of extraordinary creativity. More often than not, these have left their mark on epoch-making exhibitions, which have perfectly captured the spirit of the time. However, these events have not always been able to generate sustained interest, at an international level. The opening shot was fired on the eve of the First World War, when Wyndham Lewis and a number of his Vorticist friends who had been productively engaged in coming to grips with the achievements of French Impressionsm and Post-Impressionism created a commotion with the launch of their magazine, *Blast*. If the first tidal wave of modern British art coincided with the first great world crisis of 1914, the series of climactic movements which followed at regular intervals throughout the century culminated in the greatest of them all, at the very moment which marked the end of the Cold War. These two key events, *Blast* and *Freeze*, span the entire period which the historian Eric Hobsbawm aptly defined as "The Age of Extremes". And it was against this background of historical landmarks and art historical movements that we settled on the exhibition's theme of British art in the "Age of Extremes" or, to put it another way, in the "short century" from 1914 to 1991. This theory of the ebb and flood of British art and of the constant interplay between tradition and innovation in an international context has been elaborated in close collaboration with the British art historian, Henry Meyric Hughes, who, in his capacity of former Director of the Visual Arts Department of the British Council and subsequently Director of the Hayward Gallery in London, has followed British art and studied it closely, in all its ins and outs, in addition to playing an active part in its development and promoting it in an international context. The close co-operation between the two of us, in the course of preparing this exhibition, has enabled us to develop a synthetic perspective or, as the case may be, a combination of views resulting from the fact that we were approaching our task from two different angles – that of the insider and that of the outsider – and aiming to offset one against the other. We believe that this dual perspective provided us with an ideal point of departure for our imaginary journey through the cosmos of twentieth century British art.

Like the exhibition itself, the exhibition design has evolved out of a dialogue between German and British partners. Against the background of the museum building, conceived and built by Peter Schweger as an urban loggia connecting the exterior with the interior, David Chipperfield has designed a veritable "museum inside a museum", whose succession of open spaces and enclosures provides the ideal supporting conditions for realising the basic idea of Blast to Freeze, with its contrasting moods of avantgardist rebellion and calm reassertion of traditional values. The crowning glory of it all is the especially developed light architecture, with monumental air wells surrounded by lofty air galleries, under the spacious glass roof of the museum.

The catalogue, which is being published in separate German and English editions, not only mirrors the exhibition in all its richness, but offers a commentary on the background of social and political change. The contributions on the various periods and tendencies in British art, written by leading specialists in the field, are thus placed in an historical and art historical context, to illustrate the complex relationship between art and history, society and politics. In addition, the catalogue includes detailed treatments and analyses of three of the principal force fields, which have had a decisive influence on the specific ways in which the British art system has tended to work in the past: the important role of the English art schools and the influence of academic education on the development of new trends in the twentieth century; the guidance and support which has been provided by publicly funded institutions such as the Arts Council and the British Council – and, at one remove, the Institute of Contemporary Arts – in the period after the Second World War; and, last not least, the pre-eminent role of the art critic. This, then, represents a first attempt at examining the complexity of Britain's individual position in the international art world, in context.

After Great Britain and Germany had twice fought wars against each other in the short century of extremes, British art was extensively exhibited and remarked upon in former West Germany. Indeed, the major survey exhibition of British Art in the 20th Century at the Royal Academy or Arts in London was given its only other showing at the Staatsgalerie in Stuttgart, in 1987. However, this event was held under the star of the painting revival in the 1980s, whereas the impetus for Blast to Freeze has been provided by the new sensibility and the new self-confidence of British art since Freeze. A special European dimension is added to this by the fact that this survey of British art will be shown, not only in Germany but in France, the country which has exercised such a profound influence on its development, over the years. That this should be possible, and that the exhibition will go on to the new Musée d'Art Contemporain Les Abattoirs in Toulouse, after its initial showing in Wolfsburg, is thanks to the spontaneous interest which that Museum's Director, Alain Mousseigne, has shown for the project. This exhibition could not have been realised without the contribution of many people, too numerous to list here, including all those artists who are still with us, and whose work is represented in the exhibition, and a large number of British art historians and critics, museum directors and curators, private collectors, gallery owners and art dealers, who have taken the time and the trouble to offer advice to Henry Meyric Hughes and me. Their active involvement has meant that some of the most powerful forces in British art have been mobilised in support of our enterprise. Our special thanks go to them all. I would also like to thank Henry Meyric Hughes, as well as the curators Holger Broeker and Annelie Lütgens, from this Museum, for furnishing the exhibition with a publication that is worthy of its ambitions.

I am very pleased that the Volkswagen Bank has seen fit once more to support our international exhibitions programme, in the wake of their generous commitment to the recent Gary Hill retrospective. This major cultural event could not have been realised without their support, and for this reason we owe them a mark of our deep appreciation and heartfelt thanks.

Gijs van Tuyl
Director

ACKNOWLEDGEMENTS

At an early stage in our plans, we held a series of valuable exploratory discussions with a number of eminent curators and art historians, some of whom have subsequently made illuminating contributions to the catalogue. These include Sir Alan Bowness, Professor Andrew Causey, Dr. Michael Compton, Richard Cork, Dr. Margaret Garlake, Professor Norbert Lynton, Professor David Alan Mellor, and Sir Nicholas Serota, Director of Tate. Among these we particularly wish to single out the late David Sylvester, who gave us strong encouragement from the beginning, and spurred us on with his wit and incisive judgements.

We should like most warmly to thank all the artists who have contributed to the exhibition, many of them with works from their own collections, and many others with valuable advice about possible loans from other sources; also, the members of the families of Adrian Heath, Kenneth Martin and Patrick Heron. At the planning stage, we also held wide-ranging discussions with a number of artists, including Michael Craig-Martin, Gilbert and George, and Richard Hamilton, and are particularly grateful to them for the insights with which they provided us. Further along the way, we received advice and practical help of all kinds from each one of the catalogue authors, many of whom went well beyond the normal courtesies, by helping us with contacts to other specialists in the field, and even with loans. It seems invidious to single out individuals, but we should particularly like to mention David Curtis, Dr. Penelope Curtis, Professor Robert Hewison, Dr. James Hyman, Richard Shone and Dr. Andrew Wilson, in this respect.

Our colleagues in the museum world were unfailingly helpful in offering us the benefit of their experience. Among those in Britain, we should particularly like to mention Stephen Deuchar, Jeremy Lewison, Sandy Nairne, Sarah Fox-Pitt and Catherine Clement, at Tate Britain, and Lewis Biggs, formerly at Tate Liverpool; Richard Calvocoressi, Alice Dewey, Keith Hartley and Philip Long, at the Scottish National Gallery of Modern Art, Edinburgh; Tim Llewellyn, the late Robert Hopper, David Mitchinson, Anita Feldman and Robin Airley, at the Henry Moore Foundation, together with Dr. Penelope Curtis at the Henry Moore Study Centre; Robert Crawford, Angela Weight and Roger Tolson, at the Imperial War Museum; Corinne Miller and Alex Robertson, at the Leeds City Art Gallery; Michael Harrison and Sebastiano Barassi, at Kettle's Yard Gallery, Cambridge; Godfrey Worsdale and Tim Craven at Southampton City Art Gallery; Sir Christopher Frayling and Juliet Thorp, at the Royal College of Art; John Murdoch, Dr. Joanna Selbourne and Julia Blanks, at the Courtauld Institute Gallery; Mark Hayworth-Booth at the Victoria and Albert Museum; Penny Johnson, at the Government Art Collection; Pamela Roberts, former Director of the Royal Photographic Museum in Bath; Robert and Lisa Scott, of the William Scott Foundation, London; and Antony Penrose, of the Lee Miller and Roland Penrose Foundation, Chiddingly, Sussex. In addition, we should mention all those colleagues with whom the contact was at a longer distance but who unfailingly offered us whatever help they could.

A number of museums in Germany and farther afield have substantial holdings of British art and we should like to individually thank the representatives of a number of these for their personal support, including Kasper König and Evelyn Weiss, at the Museum Ludwig, in Cologne; Vicente Todoli, lately Director of the Museu Serralves, in Porto; Jorge Molder and Ana Vasconcelos e Melo, at the Fundação Calouste Gulbenkian Centro de Arte Moderna José de Azeredo Perdigão, in Lisbon; and Jacek Ojrzynski and Maria Morzuch, of the Muzeum Sztuki, in Łódz.

We owe a special debt of gratitude to our friends at the British Council and at the Arts Council, who have helped us, not only with a generous amount of loans but with the use of their facilities, including their invaluable library and archival resources – namely, at the British Council: Andrea Rose, Director of the Visual Arts Department and Diana Eccles, who are in charge of the British Council's collection, together with Brett Rogers, Clive Philpott and Richard Riley, and, at the Arts Council Collection: Susan Ferleger Brades, as Director of the Hayward Gallery, together with Marjorie Allthorpe-Guyton, Director of Visual Arts at the Arts Council itself; Dr. Isobel Johnstone, Curator of the Arts Council Collection and her assistant, Jill Constantine and the Librarian, Pamela Griffin.

We thank the art historian Victoria Walsh and Andrew Hunter, Curator of Gainsborough's House, in Sudbury, Suffolk, for their valuable advice and for allowing us to borrow their special reconstruction of the Independent Group's exhibition, *Parallel of Life and Art* (1953). We are likewise grateful to Cosme Barragnano and Ana Valls at the IVAM Centre d'Arte Moderna Julio Gonzales, in Valencia, for lending us their reconstruction of the celebrated *Fun House*, by Richard Hamilton and others, from the Independent Group's 1956 exhibition, *This Is Tomorrow*. Other individuals to whom we also wish to extend our thanks include Rosemary Butler, Eva Chadwick, Raymond Danowski, Andrew Dempsey, John Dewe-Mathews, William Feaver, Mary Moore and Andrea Tarsia.

Many individual collectors have been exceptionally generous with their time, as well as with loans of precious works from their collections, including some of the most important among them, who prefer to remain anonymous. The names of all the lenders to the exhibition are acknowledged farther down, but we should also particularly like to record here the pleasurable discussions we have had with a number of them, and the great contribution which they have made to the realisation of our goals – notably, the late Dr. David Brown, Professor Sir Colin St. John Wilson, Dr. Jeffrey Sherwin, Dr. and Mrs. W. T. Mason and Mr. Ken Powell. The artist, Ivor Davies, who acted as Secretary for the *Destruction in Art Symposium* in 1966, has lent us valuable material from his archive.

Dr. Jeffrey and Ruth Sherwin (major lenders in their own right), have also lent us important documents relating to the British Surrealist movement.

It is also a pleasure to record here the personal interest which has been shown in our project by a number of individual dealers, from among the longer list of those who have given us tangible evidence of their support – namely, Ian Barker and David Juda, at the Annely Juda Gallery, Ivor Braka, Jonathan Clark, Anne Faggionato, Gérard Faggionato, Dorothee Fischer, of the Konrad Fischer Galerie, Düsseldorf, Bernard Jacobson, Andrew Kalman, of the Crane Kalman Gallery, Nicholas Logsdail and his staff at the Lisson Gallery, Geoffrey Parton, of Marlborough Fine Art, James Mayor, Victoria Miro, Anthony and Anne D'Offay, Richard Salmon, Karsten Schubert and Leslie Waddington.

In addition we should like to thank Tony Andrews, until recently the British Council's Director in Berlin, together with its Head of Cultural and Public Affairs, Elke Ritt, for their encouragement. For the French showing of the exhibition, we have received generous support from Mr. John Tod, Director of the British Council's office in Paris and the Council's long-standing Arts Officer, Madame Catherine Ferbos-Nakov, who has done so much to promote the cause of British artists, over the years. We are deeply grateful to Alain Mousseigne, Director of Les Abattoirs in Toulouse, for his personal commitment to the project and wish him and his team all possible success with the second and final showing of the exhibition.

We wish to express our thanks to Remo Röntgen and nya nordiska for their support, which alone made it possible for us to realise the light and airy setting for the show.

Henry Meyric Hughes
Gijs van Tuyl

LENDERS TO THE EXHIBITION

Aberdeen Art Gallery, Aberdeen

National Library of Wales, Aberystwyth

Stedelijk Museum, Amsterdam

Cecil Higgins Art Gallery, Bedford

Ulster Museum, Belfast

Private Collection, Herentals, Belgium

Piessens Collection, Belgium

Galerie Thomas Schulte, Berlin

Kunsthalle Bielefeld, Bielefeld

Birmingham Museum and Art Gallery, Birmingham

Bury Art Gallery, Bury

S. Martin Mason, Cambridge

Dr. and Mrs. W. T. Mason, Cambridge

University of Cambridge, Kettle's Yard, Cambridge

Australian National Gallery, Canberra

Ivor Davies, Cardiff

National Museums of Wales, Trustees of the Estate of Derek Williams, Cardiff

Carlisle Museum and Art Gallery, Carlisle

Lee Miller Archive, Chiddingley, Sussex

Museum Ludwig, Cologne

Galerie Konrad Fischer, Düsseldorf

Towner Art Gallery and Local Museum, Eastbourne

Scottish National Gallery of Modern Art, Edinburgh

Martin Rewcastle, Exmouth

Stedelijk Museum voor Actuele Kunst, S.M.A.K. Collection, Ghent

Hamburger Kunsthalle, Hamburg

Rita Donagh, Henley-on-Thames

Kirklees Museums and Galleries, Huddersfield Art Gallery, Huddersfield

Ferens Art Gallery, Kingston upon Hull

Mulier Mulier Collection, Knokke-Zoute

Private Collection, Krefeld

Leeds City Art Gallery, Leeds City Council, Leeds

Dr. Jeffrey and Ruth Sherwin, Leeds

Fundação Calouste Gulbenkian/CAMJAP, Lisbon

National Museums and Galleries on Merseyside, Walker Art Gallery, Liverpool

Museum Sztuki, Łódz

Edward Allington, London

Arts Council Collection, Hayward Gallery, London

Blackburn Associates Limited, London

David Bowie, courtesy Kate Chertavian Fine Arts, London

Boyle Family, London

Collection B. P., London

Ivor Braka Limited, London

The British Council, London

Jonathan Clark Limited, London

The Courtauld Institute Gallery, London

Jessica Craig-Martin, London

Michael Craig-Martin, London

Crane Kalman Gallery, London

Anne Faggionato Gallery, London

Faggionato Fine Arts, London

Barry Flanagan, London

Gimpel Fils, London

Antony Gormley, London

Government Art Collection, London

Family of Adrian Heath, London

Family of Patrick Heron, London

Claire and James Hyman, London

James Hyman, London

Imperial War Museum, London

Bernard Jacobson Gallery, London

Annely Juda Fine Art, London

Anish Kapoor, London

Phillip King, London

Lisson Gallery, London

Conroy Maddox, London

Estate of Kenneth Martin, London

Estate of Mary Martin, London

Victoria Miro Gallery, London

Modern Collections, London

National Portrait Gallery, London

Collection Ken Powell, London

Royal College of Art, London

The Saatchi Gallery, London

Saatchi & Saatchi, London

Karsten Schubert, London

Scott Collection, London

Simmons & Simmons, London

Tate, London

William Turnbull, London

Victoria and Albert Museum, London

Waddington Galleries, London

Richard Wentworth, London

Stephen Willats, London

The St. John Wilson Trust, London

Bill Woodrow, London

Musée National d'Art et d'Histoire, Luxembourg

The Gallery of Costume, Manchester City Galleries, Manchester

Massimo Martino Fine Arts & Projects, Mendrisio

Keith Arnatt, Monmouth

The Henry Moore Foundation, Much Hadham

Nottingham City Museums and Galleries, Nottingham

Oldham Gallery, Oldham

Astrup Fearnley Collection, Oslo

Kröller-Müller Museum, Otterlo

Reading Museum, Reading

Private Collector, Saffron Walden

Sintra Museum of Modern Art, The Berardo Collection, Sintra

Southampton City Art Gallery, Southampton

Orkney, The Pier Gallery, Stromness

Lynn Chadwick, Stroud

The Henderson Estate, Sudbury

Swindon Museum and Art Gallery, Swindon

Les Abattoirs, Toulouse

Tyne and Wear Services, Laing Gallery, Newcastle-upon-Tyne

IVAM, Instituto Valenciano de Arte Moderno, Generalitat Valenciana, Valencia

The New Art Gallery, Walsall

and other lenders who wish to remain anonymous

INTRODUCTION

With *Blast to Freeze* we have tried, within a broadly chronological display, to evoke some of the periodic bursts of creativity which have characterised the innovative British art of the twentieth century, alongside the sustained achievement of a number of individuals. We have chosen works for their visual strength and historical significance, and for their ability to suggest links across barriers of style, medium, chronology and display.

Blast to Freeze opens and closes with two moments representing a decisive break with the past: at one end, the Vorticists' call to arms, under the leadership of Wyndham Lewis; at the other, the exhibition of students' work, organised by Damien Hirst and his friends, in a run-down area of London's Docklands. The first issue of the Vorticists' puce-coloured magazine, *Blast* (June 1914), set standards of aggression and modernity, against which subsequent artistic movements would have to be measured, whilst the exhibition *Freeze* (1988) heralded the arrival of an iconoclastic generation of young British artists who, like the Vorticists, marked a new point of departure and placed the media at the heart of their strategy for self-promotion.

The Vorticists' First Manifesto was directed at the aesthetes of Bloomsbury as much as at the philistines they identified with the forces of reaction: "We hear from America and the Continent all sorts of disagreeable things about England: the unmusical, anti-artistic, unphilosophic country. We quite agree." Vorticism demanded a revolution, not only in art, but in human behaviour. That revolution, when it came, was precipitated by the barbarism of industrialised warfare. Harsh reality took away the appetite for experiment and even the Vorticists lost their

stomach for the fight, though this did not prevent them from executing some remarkable images of dehumanisation and destruction.

In the 1920s British art went into abeyance. For Paul Nash in the 1930s Vorticism was the obvious point of reference, "half-remembered [...] chiefly literary in inspiration, not excluding many of the 'Cubist' paintings". Nash identified abstraction ("the pursuit of form") and Surrealism ("the 'psyche' in its devious flight") as the rival poles to which British artists were attracted. Henry Moore was more successful than most, in navigating a course through this magnetic field.

The period of the Second World War, like that of the 1920s, represented a fallow period in British art, while it was cut off from the Continent and turned in on itself. However, Moore, Nash and Graham Sutherland all produced memorable individual responses to the physical isolation and spiritual need of the time.

After 1945 a number of artists turned to abstraction, in the hope of developing a language that could be harnessed to the cause of social reconstruction, whilst a new generation of abstract painters in St. Ives sought inspiration (or was it escape?) in the Cornish landscape. Perhaps more characteristic of the decade to 1955 were the feelings of terror and apprehension generated by images of the Holocaust (to which Francis Bacon's paintings were widely perceived as a response), the rising tensions of the Cold War and the spectre of nuclear annihilation. At the same time, British artists began increasingly to look to the United States for inspiration and were among the first to register the impact of Abstract Expressionism. The members of the Independent Group – Richard

Hamilton and Eduardo Paolozzi, among them – who were grappling with the legacy of Dadaism and Surrealism, were invigorated by American popular culture and moved to dismantle the traditional hierarchies of subject and medium.

Colour returned into people's lives in the early 1960s, as a result of the boom in consumer spending and growth of the cultural industries. This was reflected, not only in the classic British Pop Art of David Hockney and his contemporaries at the Royal College of Art, but also in the bold "American style" abstract paintings of Robyn Denny and others. At the same time, Bridget Riley laid the basis for her own, very individual form of "optical" (or perceptual) painting, which she has continued fruitfully to explore, down to the present time. Finally, Anthony Caro and his

associates at St. Martin's School of Art broke with carving and modelling, abolished the plinth and (like the abstract painters) sought directly to involve the spectator in their work.

Richard Hamilton was a pioneer of installation, which became a favourite medium for the neo-minimalist and neo-conceptual, though as yet unbranded, young British artists of circa 1990. Standing in for so many works from this rich, transitional period in British art (of which Rachel Whiteread's ghostly plaster cast of a once inhabited interior and Anya Gallaccio's ten thousand tea roses, "their heads laid on a bed of thorns", are two further examples), Damien Hirst's *A Hundred Years* – like the exhibition itself – is a meditation on the cyclical nature of human activity and the processes which condition our chances of change and renewal.

Henry Meyric Hughes
Gijs van Tuyl

FOG IN THE CHANNEL

THE BRITISH DIALOGUE WITH MODERNISM

ROBERT HEWISON

The story goes that, some time in the early years of the last century, the following headline appeared in *The Times*: "Fog in the Channel: Continent Cut off".

Whether true or not, the anecdote captures the Anglo-centric view of the relationship between the

(fig. 1) Claude Monet Charing Cross Bridge, La Tamise 1899–1901, oil on canvas, 73 x 100 cm, Musée des Beaux-Arts, Lyon

British Isles and the continent of Europe and, by extension, the rest of the world. Not Britain, but "abroad" is isolated, a place of foreign influence obscured by the fog of British self-confidence – or complacency. Yet the fog that has at times made twentieth century British art seem cut off from international Modernism may also veil aspects and achievements of the native tradition from external view. This exhibition intends to dispel that fog.

Fog was an early British contribution to modernism. Claude Monet (fig. 1) came to London to make a series of studies of the Thames, with Charing Cross Railway Bridge, emblem of modernity, dissolving in the sooty vapour of what Charles Dickens had christened the "London particular". Fog softened the silhouettes on Whistler's canvasses (fig. 2), seeped into Joseph Conrad's fiction and wound itself round T. S. Eliot's poetry. That these early

(fig. 2) James Abbott McNeill Whistler Nocturne: Blue and Silver – Chelsea 1971, oil on wood, 50.2 x 60.8 cm, Tate, London

British modernists were two Americans and a Pole puts into question the nature both of Britishness and of modernism.

To begin with, though at the opening of the twentieth century Britain's imperial eye was on her far-flung dominions, the Continent never was cut off. There was constant two-way traffic, as Monet demonstrates, between London and Paris. There were natural affinities with northern Europe, and it was not until after the Second World War that the United States began to challenge the Mediterranean as a destination for British artists seeking a larger scale and a stronger light. Britain also gained by the westward flow of Jewish artists and writers, that began with the Russian pogroms of the 1880s' and accelerated in the 1930s, as creative life became impossible in Germany and Russia.

The art historian Charles Harrison has written: "Modernism requires cosmopolitanism."[1] London, a seaport, a seat of government, a place of trade, a refuge, was a cosmopolitan capital. Whatever Britain's apparent geographic and cultural isoation, it is not a case of either/or. Geography is about communications, economics about exchange: so with the cultural economy. We should not exaggerate the oppositions of modernism and the British tradition; rather, this exhibition explores the dialogue between them.

1 Charles Harrison, *English Art and Modernism 1900–1939*, London 1981, p. 250.

It is, however, fruitful to consider the opposition between modernism and modernity. The literary critic John Carey argues in *The Intellectuals and the Masses* (1992) that modernist art and literature were a hostile reaction to the philistine, materialist culture that became established by the end of the nineteenth century – hence the deliberate obscurity of much modernist writing. Hostility to a highly industrialised, mass society is summed up by the title of the literary critic F. R. Leavis' pamphlet *Mass Civilisation and Minority Culture* (1930). The international modernism of the 1930s, to which British artists made a significant contribution, was a socially committed, reforming movement.

The desire to change society is one of the roots of the argument for the "autonomy" of modernist art, as articulated by that archpriest of high modernism, the American art critic Clement Greenberg. He first made the case in his article, "Avant-Garde and Kitsch", published in Britain in 1940, where he wrote of the "avant-garde poet or artist" trying to create "something valid only in its own terms". [...] Content is to be dissolved so completely into form that the work of art or literature cannot be reduced in whole or in part to anything not itself".[2]

If modernism *is* to be defined as the drive for autonomy, then in visual terms it had been achieved through abstraction long before Greenberg started writing. The artist Ben Nicholson, whose purest abstracts in the 1930s reach almost total independence from any reference beyond themselves (pl. 38), has written of "wanting to get right back to the beginning and then take one step forward at a time".[3] The rediscovery of the primitive (in Nicholson's case the discovery of Alfred Wallis) was another important element in Modernism, not only allowing a formally fresh beginning, as in the Mexican-influenced sculptures of Henry Moore, but also licensing the exploration of the raw desires of the unconscious, through Surrealism.

Where Modernism, abstract or figurative, raw or sophisticated, was inevitably and logically to differ from traditional British painting was that it was essentially an international movement. It was pan-European, from Russia to Spain, and after European energies waned following the Second World War, its focus shifted from Paris to New York without losing its essential character. The language of modernism was international; none the less, wherever it travelled it had to enter into dialogue with local practice and tradition. As this exhibition demonstrates, the encounter with fogbound Britain modulated the language of Modernism in distinctive ways.

What defines the encounter is that British painting and sculpture create an art of place. This is true, in some sense, of the art of any nation, but in Britain, quintessentially, place has been interpreted in terms of landscape. In 1934 that key figure in British Modernism, Paul Nash, defined the "motive power" that animated British art as a spirit "of the land; *genius loci* is indeed almost its conception."[4] A contemporary artist like Richard Long would not disagree. British landscape painting has had an international pre-eminence. Constable and Turner (fig. 3) helped to inspire the French vision that returned to Britain at the beginning of the twentieth century to reinvigorate British painting through Impressionism and Post-Impressionism. The distinctive qualities of the British climate – especially its mists and fog – lent themselves to the watercolour tradition in which the British have excelled. Modernist abstraction flourished best in St. Ives, where the almost Mediterranean light is least likely to be occluded by the softening moderation of more typical British weather (fig. 4).

The British landscape is always more than subject matter. Britain was not only the earliest, but also one of the most heavily urbanised countries in the world, yet ironically landscape and the values of the pastoral are profoundly associated with national identity. Landscape in turn is a vehicle for both literary and painterly romanticism. Even in breezy St. Ives, at the close of the 1930s the pull of the landscape drew Nicholson back towards representation from the most radical phase of his abstraction. During the Second World War, when Britain really was cut off, the landscape, threatened, damaged, or enduring, acquired a special resonance. The horrific landscapes of modernity created on the Western Front generated the most significant British paintings of the Great War (fig. 5). Landscape is valued in Britain for its otherness to the city, a place of interlocking narratives

2 Clement Greenberg, "Avant-Garde and Kitsch", *The Collected Essays and Criticism of Clement Greenberg*, ed. J. O'Brian, Chicago 1986, vol. 1, p. 8.

3 Quoted in Harrison 1981 (see note 1), p. 250.

4 Herbert Read (ed.), *Unit One: The Modern Movement in English Architecture, Painting and Sculpture*, London 1934, p. 80.

(fig. 3) J. M. W. Turner HURRAH! FOR THE WHALER EREBUS! ANOTHER FISH! 1846, oil on canvas, 90 x 121 cm, Tate, London

(fig. 4) Victor Pasmore THE HANGING GARDENS OF HAMMERSMITH NO. 1 1944–47, oil on canvas, 78.7 x 109.2 cm, private collection

rather than solitary emotion. There is a parallel tradition of urban art, going back to William Hogarth (fig. 6) and sustained by the mid-Victorians (fig. 7), where romanti-

(fig. 5) Paul Nash WE ARE MAKING A NEW WORLD 1918 oil on canvas 71,1 x 91,4 cm The Trustees of the Imperial War Museum, London

cism is tempered by empiricism, and both art and literature bear a moral responsibility in the stories they naturalistically tell. Urban realism regularly resurfaces in the twentieth century, from the Camden Town Group and its successors to the Euston Road School in 1937 (fig. 8), to the "Kitchen Sink" painters of the 1950s, and aspects of contemporary art now. The mainstream of British drama and literature, cinema and television has been realist to the point that, until Salman Rushdie became an acknowledged voice of postcolonial Britain with *Midnight's Children* in 1981, anything else has been bracketed off as "experimental".

Yet in spite of the essential foundation of British art on the observation of place, in practice this is modified by associations that reach well beyond the purely visual. Their roots are in literary romanticism, in the ecstasies of the Sublime, the thrills and terrors of the

(fig. 6) William Hogarth GIN LANE 1751, engraving, 35.7 x 30.5 cm, Tate, London

Gothick, in the taste for fantasy. The tradition can be traced back beyond that most literary of painters, William Blake and his follower Samuel Palmer, whose numinous landscapes of the 1820s and early 1830s were rediscovered by Graham Sutherland and others a hundred years later (fig. 9). Palmer's work emblematises the "landscape feeling" that was to resurface in the neo-romanticism of the 1940s (pls. 68 and 89). This aspect of the British visual tradition has such a broad imaginative and emotional range that it has not been precisely

(fig. 7) William Powell Frith PADDINGTON STATION 1862, Royal Holloway and Bedford New College, London

labelled. It can be found in the violence of Vorticism, in the grotesque of Edward Burra, in the Expressionism of the painters of the School of London, in the religious impulse of Stanley Spencer and David Jones, and in the whimsy that breaks out in Peter Blake or David Hockney. The word to describe this enduring aspect is "metaphysical". This is not the Italian *pittura metafisica* of Giorgio de Chirico, though de Chirico was an important influence on Paul Nash. Rather, it is metaphysical in

the sense that T. S. Eliot used when he argued for the significance of certain English poets of the late sixteenth and early seventeenth centuries.

Eliot, the American so taken with Britain that he changed his nationality, argued in an essay of 1921 that these "metaphysical" poets – John Donne, especially – fused concepts and images in a way capable of "transmuting ideas into sensations, of transforming an observation into a state of mind".[5] Thus the modern poet must become "more and more comprehensive, more allusive, more indirect, in order to force, to dislocate, if necessary, language into his meaning".[6] Eliot established both the metaphysical poets, and literary modernism, as twentieth century orthodoxies. But his case was that allegory depended on clear visual images. To extend Eliot's reasoning: the speculations of metaphysics, however foggy, must have some parallel in physical fact. Hence the resistance to absolute abstraction in British art that has rarely, though on occasion triumphantly, been overcome.

It may be that the case for a distinctively "metaphysical" aspect to British art has not been made more strongly because, as the cultural historian Nikolaus Pevsner wrote in 1956, "the distaste of the English for carrying a thought or a system of thought to its logical extreme is too familiar to need comment".[7] Pevsner made the comment none the less, in the BBC's broadcast Reith Lectures, reprinted as *The Englishness of English Art*. The elision here in this essay from "British" to "English" is conscious. The aesthetic ideology it has been trying to characterise is strongest when it is most English. And the "Englishness" of English art significantly moderates modernism.

Pevsner, a German refugee in the age of extremes, was well placed to judge the virtues and vices of English art. His book, published at the halfway point of this exhibition's chronology, could not conceal the general mildness of the English cultural climate. While there were outbreaks of fantasy, its pervasive characteristics were "reasonableness", and "conservatism".

5 T. S. Eliot, "The Metaphysical Poets", reprinted in *The Norton Anthology of English Literature, vol. 2*, 6th ed., New York 1993, p. 2182.

6 Eliot 1993 (see note 5), p. 2181.

7 Nikolaus Pevsner, *The Englishness of English Art*, London 1956, p. 88.

(fig. 8) Graham Bell THE CAFÉ 1937–38, oil on canvas, 121.9 x 91.7 cm, Manchester Art Galleries

(fig. 9) Samuel Palmer THE HARVEST MOON: DRAWING FOR "A PASTORAL SCENE" c. 1831–32, pencil, ink and gouache on cardboard, 15.2 x 18.4 cm, Tate, London

ROBERT HEWISON

"Americans and Germans take it to be a sign of old age and tiredness" but conservatism had positive qualities: "trust in the tried out, distrust of experiment for experiment's sake, and – most important – faith in continuity".[8] "Reasonableness", however, is not a climate in which an avant-garde flourishes, and Pevsner concludes: "What English character gained of tolerance and fair play, she lost of that fanaticism or at least that intensity which alone can bring forth the very greatest in art."[9]

Many in Britain have had reason to be grateful for the lack of fanaticism, but the evident reasonableness and conservatism of British character and culture mean that, in the case of Britain, the view of world history taken by Eric Hobsbawm in his book *Age of Extremes* needs to be modified.[10] British cultural life has enjoyed a largely unbroken continuity precisely because it was able to avoid the worst in the age of extremes. Hobsbawm (like Pevsner a refugee) divides "The Short Twentieth Century" into three distinct periods: "The Age of Catastrophe" from 1914 to 1945, governed entirely by war or the anticipation of war; "The Golden Age" that followed when, paradoxically, the Cold War froze a balance between East and West allowing, in the West, a vast expansion of material and cultural wealth. Finally there followed "The Landslide", when the contradictions within the prosperity of the previous period were exposed by the oil shock of 1973, and the century closed in instability and crisis.

While not disputing this masterly periodisation as a framework that matches the cultural shifts between the modernist, high modern and postmodern eras, the extent to which Britain avoided both catastrophe and landslide, while enjoying but a modest golden age, must affect our assessment of British culture. As might be said of much British painting, the British experience was less extreme.

Following the Great War, a catastrophe for all combatants except America, the 1920s and 1930s for Britain were an "Age of Appeasement", as the country began the long process of coming to terms with its economic and imperial decline. Conflict with totalitarianism was avoided for as long as possible – hence Britain's neutrality during the Spanish Civil War. 1940 opened an "Age of Consensus", where the enforced recognition of the need for social reform and a managed economy allowed, post-war, a now post-imperial power to enjoy prosperity without capitalist excess. This consensus began to break up in the mid 1970s, and was self-consciously followed by an "Age of Privatisation", when capitalist individualism was unleashed in an attempt to revitalise an economy and a culture rapidly changing from one of production to one of consumption. There was social slippage rather than landslide, but Britain experienced *fin-de-siècle* instability and crisis, as the close to this exhibition shows.

Britain's dialogue with Modernism began with a quarrel. Vorticism was in dispute both with the native (if deeply Frenchified) avant-garde of Bloomsbury, and with Italian Futurism, from which it borrowed its propagandist techniques. Though *Blast* no. 1, published in June 1914, declaimed in large type "BLAST First (from politeness) ENGLAND. CURSE ITS CLIMATE FOR ITS SINS AND INFECTIONS", this was an attempt to establish a decidedly un-watered-down avant-garde that was both modern and distinctly English.[11] "BLESS ENGLAND, industrial island machine, pyramidal workshop."[12] In its short life, Vorticism achieved everything a thoroughgoing modernist avant-garde could. That is partly due to its international character. Wyndham Lewis had an American father and studied in Munich and Paris. Jacob Epstein was born in New York of Russian-Jewish parents and studied in Paris before becoming a British citizen. Henry Gaudier-Brzeska was French. David Bomberg was the son of Polish-Jewish immigrants. Apart from Lewis, the literary element was supplied by Ezra Pound, an American, who developed the idea of the "vortex" from his earlier association with the French and Japanese influenced poetry of imagism. Eliot contributed to the second number of *Blast*. The decidedly English Edward Wadsworth had studied engineering and art in Munich, and made the translations from Wassily Kandinsky's *Über das Geistige in der Kunst* for *Blast* no. 1.

Vorticism certainly achieved autonomy, as the first English art movement to practise abstraction, but it could not achieve autonomy from history, as the movement and its members were sucked into the greater vortex of the First World War. Paul Nash, who respected, rather than imitated, the achievements of Vorticism, translated the landscape feeling that he had inherited from Samuel Palmer into the modernity of war with the appropriately titled *We Are Making a New World* (fig. 5).

8 Pevsner 1956 (see note 7), p. 61.

9 Pevsner 1956 (see note 7), p. 192.

10 Eric Hobsbawm, *Age of Extremes: The Short Twentieth Century, 1914–1991*, London 1994.

11 Percy Wyndham Lewis, *Blast!* (issue no. 1), London 1914, p. 11.

12 Lewis 1914 (see note 11), pp. 123f.

The shock of war imposed a "return to order"; weary and impecunious artists were unwilling to go once more into battle for the values of the avant-garde. Literary Modernism survived better, partly because its writers had been non-combatants. In Virginia Woolf's *To the Lighthouse* (1927) the war occupies *a caesura* in the action of the novel. The broken landscape crying out for redemption and renewal in Eliot's poetic masterpiece, *The Waste Land* (1922), made sense in the new world that had been created. But the caution with which a new exhibiting society introduced itself in 1920 demonstrates the reluctance of English artists to follow an idea too far: "The 'SEVEN & FIVE' are grateful to the pioneers, but feel that there has been of late too much pioneering along too many lines in altogether too much of a hurry, and themselves desire the pursuit of their own calling rather than the confusion of conflict. The object of the 'SEVEN & FIVE' is merely to express what they feel in terms that shall be intelligible, and not to demonstrate a theory nor to attack a tradition."[13]

In spite of the aesthetic pacifism of the original seven artists and five sculptors, with changes of personnel the group sustained a progressive, anti-academic art during the 1920s. Before its dissolution in 1935, David Jones, Ben Nicholson, Winifred Nicholson, Christopher Wood, Barbara Hepworth and Henry Moore were all members. In the 1920s artists like Edward Wadsworth, Nash, and Mark Gertler were able to resume their intercourse with France, while David Bomberg travelled extensively. But this was a period of artistic and economic recession, characterised, as the art historian David Corbett argues, by "retreat, evasion, and concealment of modernity's impact [...] direct registration of the modern seemed for over a decade to be all but impossible in English painting".[14]

It was not until the 1930s that another concerted effort was made to express a British response to Modernism. The critic Herbert Read recalled that: "From 1930 onwards Henry Moore, Ben Nicholson, Barbara Hepworth, and several other artists were living and working together in Hampstead. [...] There was an unusual degree of mutual sympathy and understanding, an unusual intensity of effort and feeling, and the formation of a 'front' vis-à-vis the indifferent public."[15]

13 Quoted in Harrison 1981 (see note 1), p. 164.

14 David Peters Corbett, *The Modernity of English Art 1914–1930*, Manchester 1997, p. 1.

15 Herbert Read, *Contemporary British Art*, revised ed., London 1964, p. 28.

Herbert Read's use of the contemporary metaphor of a political "Popular Front" shows the changed conditions. While totalitarianism was making its ominous rise in Italy and Germany, the Wall Street crash of 1929 put democracies under strain. Eric Hobsbawm argues that the Soviet Union's apparent immunity from this economic and social disaster made communism seem a viable alternative. He also argues that the strength of Britain's political conservatism meant that there was no chance of fascism making headway. He comments that the leading British artists of the 1930s, Henry Moore and the composer Benjamin Britten "give the impression that they would have been quite ready to let the world crisis pass them by, had it not intruded. But it did".[16] For them, as for a poet like W. H. Auden or a novelist like Christopher Isherwood, the only possible position was to be "left", and so it was with the artists and architects who formed Unit One in 1933.

Under the auspices of Paul Nash, Read, as editor of Unit One's single, but influential publication, deployed a suitably military image: "The aims of the Unit are strategical: to form a point in the forward thrust of modernism in architecture, painting and sculpture, and to harden this point in the fires of criticism and controversy."[17] The new consciousness was international: "Whatever happens in England will be part of what is happening in Europe and America."[18] What was happening in Europe was the flight westwards of Modernist artists and designers. Walter Gropius arrived in London, following the dissolution of the Bauhaus in 1933. László Moholy-Nagy and Naum Gabo followed in 1935 and 1936. Piet Mondrian arrived from Paris in 1938.

Unit One was part of an overlapping series of "fronts" formed to promote the cause of Modernism by linking artists and art forms. The Unit One architect Wells Coates was a founder member of the Modern Architectural Research Group in 1933. In 1932 the avant-garde in the performing arts coalesced around Rupert Doone's Group Theatre, which produced works by Auden, Isherwood, Stephen Spender and Louis MacNeice, and employed Moore, John Piper and Britten. The most specifically political of such formations was the British section of the Artists' International Association, launched in 1933. In 1937 the publication *Circle*, edited by Gabo, Nicholson and the architect Leslie Martin, presented the creative and social ideals of Constructivism.

16 Hobsbawm 1994 (see note 10), p. 190.

17 Read 1934 (see note 4), p. 12.

18 Read 1934 (see note 4), p. 13.

ROBERT HEWISON

British Modernism began to resolve into two streams: abstraction and Surrealism. Both were represented by international exhibitions in London in 1936, and Henry Moore contributed to both. Ben Nicholson and Barbara Hepworth, who had joined the Paris-based Association Abstraction-Création in 1933, led the drive for pure abstraction with missionary zeal. The *Abstract and Concrete* exhibition of 1936 marks the most intense moment of Britain's dialogue with this aspect of European modernism.

The 1936 *International Surrealist Exhibition* in London revealed the affinity between the native British metaphysical tradition and Surrealism, licensing as it did artists' use of fantasy and symbol. Pre-war works by Francis Bacon (now destroyed) and early paintings by Lucian Freud show in the one case the figurative distortion and the other the estrangement of Surrealism. But it was the late works of Paul Nash that made the most interesting accommodation with English themes (pls. 64 and 91).

That these were produced in wartime is a reminder that once again history intervened to rupture the links between Britain and the international discourse of Modernism, forcing artists and writers either into military service and war work, or into a form of internal exile, manifested in "apocalyptic" poetry and neo-romantic painting. The leaders of the *Circle* group, Gabo, Nicholson, Hepworth, withdrew in 1939 to St. Ives. Their Constructivist aesthetic was to interact fruitfully with local tradition and local subject matter, so that by the end of the 1950s St. Ives was to be recognised as a centre of Modernist landscape painting.

When the fog of the Second World War lifted from a broken and exhausted Europe, the reconfiguration of cultural power followed a similar pattern to that of the world political and economic system. A global capitalist economy centred on the United States was created, and in the West a cultural economy developed around the same axis, while the East, from Peking to partitioned Berlin, was excluded. Art followed science to the United States.

During the war, art – like science – had been recruited for national service, and it continued to be deployed as a propaganda weapon in the Cold War that followed. As private patronage shrank, official sponsorship grew; in Britain the Arts Council promoted a progressive Modernist consensus at home, while the British Council did the same abroad. There was also a signifi-cant expansion in art teaching. The art historian Margaret Garlake argues: "The art support system, which underpins production, was so deeply modified in the post-war years that it changed the status of art in society as well as the way art functioned as a profession."[19] The number of private galleries dealing in contemporary art doubled between 1950 and 1960.

19 Margaret Garlake, *New Art New Worlds: British Art in Postwar Society*, New Haven 1998, p. 4.

This institutional development made London less a satellite of Paris; increasingly, its artists joined in an international movement that drew its energy from New York. Modernism became mainstream, losing the oppositional, anti-fascist edge of the 1930s as it was absorbed into an international style. Abstraction in the visual arts and modernism in architecture became attached to ideas of "Western values" and freedom. In Britain mature artists associated with a distinctly English – though formally abstracted – concept of place, Henry Moore, Barbara Hepworth, Ben Nicholson, Graham Sutherland, Ivon Hitchens (fig. 10), became an "official" avant-garde with institutional support.

(fig. 10) Ivon Hitchens Damp Autumn 1941, oil on canvas, 40.6 x 74.3 cm, Tate, London

Younger artists – notably Eduardo Paolozzi, William Turnbull, and Nigel Henderson – headed for Paris as soon as the exchange allowance permitted. There, together with the young art critic David Sylvester, they discovered the former Surrealist Alberto Giacometti who pointed a way round the giant figures of Henri Matisse and Pablo Picasso, whose joint exhibition at the Victoria and Albert Museum had made such a daunting impression in London in 1945. In spite of fashionable, black-sweatered, posturing, exemplified by Colin Wilson's best-seller *The Outsider* (1956), Parisian Existentialism did not gain much of an intellectual foothold in Britain, but the anguish, despair and grubby austerity of the immediate post-war period encouraged an existentialist mood where the suffering body became the vehicle of expression. Francis Bacon (as interpreted by David Sylvester) was its chief exponent. As the art historian David Mellor has written: "the still potent residue of Surrealist *hazard* informed the interest of Bacon and others in painterly contingency, accident and chance".[20]

20 David Mellor, "Existentialism and post-war British Art", in F. Morris (ed.), *Paris Postwar: Art and Existentialism 1945–1955*, London 1993, p. 54.

It was not until the beginning of the 1960s that New York finally established its hegemony over international modernism. During the 1950s the split between abstraction and figuration was cross-divided by the tensions of the Cold War and the issue of "commitment". In the field of abstraction the pre-war tradition of Constructivism was continued by Victor Pasmore (who had abandoned his earlier style in 1947), Anthony Hill, and Kenneth and Mary Martin. Their geometric and proportional "Constructionism", though visually non-referential, implied the desire for a better world, as expressed in Pasmore's contribution to the design of Peterlee New Town from 1955 onwards. For others, the Parisian influence of *art informel* and the *tachisme* of Nicholas De Staël, who had a well-received exhibition in London in 1952, encouraged a gestural abstraction suited to the expression of an asocial, existential *Angst*.

Similarly, those artists who did not practise abstraction found themselves divided – at least in the competing writings of critics David Sylvester and John Berger – into two camps. Though Berger was careful to distinguish the politically committed social realism that he detected principally in a group of young artists – Jack Smith (fig. 11), Edward Middleditch, Derrick Greaves and John Bratby – from official Soviet Socialist Realism, the climate of the Cold War, especially after the Hungarian Uprising in 1956, discouraged both critic and artists. Sylvester, however, who had a stronger stable to back, was able to promote what the art historian James Hyman has characterised as a Modernist or "nihilist" realism that reflected contemporary psychological realities without making overt political statements.[21] It was from this group of figurative artists – Bacon, Freud, Michael Andrews, Frank Auerbach and Leon Kossoff – that the so-called School of London, a term used by the critics David Sylvester and Patrick Heron in the late 1940s, and relaunched by the London-based American artist R. B. Kitaj in his selection of artists for *The Human Clay* in 1976, was to emerge.

In 1956 the reality of Britain's post-imperial condition was confirmed by the humiliating failure to regain control of the Suez Canal, and the West's impotence in

21 James Hyman, *The Battle for Realism: Figurative Art in Britain during the Cold War 1945–1960*, New Haven 2001, p. 37.

(fig. 11) Jack Smith MOTHER BATHING CHILD 1953, oil on wood, 182.9 x 121.9 cm, Tate, London

the face of Russia's suppression of the Hungarian Uprising. Yet both events had a liberating effect on intellectual life. The moral collapse of the declining British Communist Party led to the emergence of a self-styled "New Left" that found in Suez and then the Campaign for Nuclear Disarmament a focus for the "anger" that had been articulated by John Osborne's play *Look Back In Anger* at the newly opened Royal Court Theatre in 1956. A new, post-war generation of playwrights, film makers, novelists and poets presented, with unromantic realism, a new meritocratic society that challenged the class-bound, mandarin values of conventional high culture. Ironically, both conservative and New Left intellectuals such as Raymond Williams and Richard Hoggart were deeply suspicious of the "shiny barbarism"[22] of contemporary American culture, yet it was American vigour, combined with rising affluence, that was to bring colour and light into their earnestly grey world.

22 Richard Hoggart, *The Uses of Literacy*, (1957), London 1990, p. 193.

British artists had been aware of American Abstract Expressionism since at least 1948, when the painter Alan Davie saw Peggy Guggenheim's collection in Venice. The ground for the acceptance of "action painting" was also prepared by Parisian *tachisme*, and individual visits to America, but in the pivotal year of 1956 the final room of the Tate Gallery's *Modern Art in the United States*, showing sixteen New York abstract expressionists, had a powerful, proselytising effect, reinforced by the Tate's exclusively abstract Expressionist show the following year. A number of individual conversions to American-style abstraction followed, but the most important indication of the shift in orientation from Paris to New York came with the artist-organised *Situation* exhibition in 1960. Curated by the English critic most committed to American art, Lawrence Alloway, *Situation* showed English abstract paintings made on an American scale. In the catalogue, the critic Roger Coleman declared the artists' new direction: "The change in the definition of what a picture could be, that was brought about by American painting in the 1940s, is only the second, counting cubism as the first, fundamental reorientation in the history of modern art."[23]

23 Quoted in Robert Hewison, *In Anger: Culture in the Cold War 1945–60*, London 1988, p. 192.

This reorientation, however, was not confined to abstract art. Throughout the 1950s, American popular, consumer culture had an energising effect on its British counterpart, while air travel narrowed the Atlantic. As early as 1952, a group of artists, architects and critics had come together at the recently-founded Institute of Contemporary Arts to discuss aspects of mass production, communication and design, with American examples very much in mind. These concerns with the urban scene were expressed in a series of environmentally self-conscious exhibitions that, as in the case of *This Is Tomorrow* in 1956, engaged with popular culture. The writings and paintings of Richard Hamilton, especially, prepared the way for what was to emerge as Pop Art.

By 1960, as the *Situation* show demonstrated, there was a new atmosphere of affirmation, expansiveness and colour. New techniques, such as spraying, and new technologies, in the form of acrylic paint and colour-saturated plastics, were part of a stimulating visual economy informed by a revolution in graphic design. A new generation of sculptors, led by Anthony Caro, shared in this revolution, as the *Angst* of the 1950s sculptors whose work had been shaped, in Read's famous phrase, by "the geometry of fear" gave way to the exuberance of the 1960s.[24] Abstract sculpture got off its plinth and danced across the floor.

As Caro said at the time: "America certainly was the catalyst."[25] In 1963 he arranged for a group of sculptors at St. Martin's School of Art to pay for a visit to London by Clement Greenberg. A group of Royal College of Art students, Derek Boshier, Peter Blake, Allen Jones, David Hockney, Patrick Caulfield, Peter Phillips, mentored by their American colleague R. B. Kitaj (pl. 131) and encouraged by the example of Richard Smith, who had first visited New York in 1957, began to celebrate the urban scene as it became animated under the influence of American popular culture. In 1961 they emerged with media *éclat* as "Pop Artists". A fresh crop of galleries opened to deal in the new art, floating on a rising tide of affluence and optimism that coincided with the election in 1964 of a Labour government that spoke, not of austerity, but the "white heat" of technological innovation. The popular equivalent to Greenberg's approving visit came in April 1966 when *Time* magazine published its mythologising feature on "London: The Swinging City". In December 1966 Patrick Heron tried to counter this reverse colonialism with his article "The Ascendancy of London in the Sixties" in the hitherto conservative and nationalist *Studio*, which that year had emblematically become *Studio International*.

24 Quoted in Susan Compton (ed.), *British Art in the 20th Century: The Modern Movement*, London 1987, p. 100.

25 Quoted Hyman 2001 (see note 21), p. 34.

The economic bubble supporting the new hedonism did not last, and the Swinging Sixties revealed a disturbing de Sadeian side. 1966 was also the year of the *Destruction In Art Symposium*, which brought German, Austrian and American exponents of a shocking, body-based expressionism to London. America's underground led the emerging international counter-culture, but the increasing violence of her involvement in Vietnam produced hostility, too. In 1968 the contradictions created by educational privilege and bourgeois guilt, enhanced by generational conflict and "repressive tolerance", spilt over internationally in student revolt. London was not Paris, but it is significant that the tensions were felt most strongly in art schools, notably Brighton, Guildford, and Hornsey in North London.

The students' defeat marked the opening of a new phase of institutional retrenchment, matched by a radical refusal that took the form of a revived politicisation and what the American critic Lucy Lippard characterised in 1968 as "the dematerialisation of art".[26] Minimalism – the last stage before the dematerialisation of conceptual art – was promoted by two international shows in London in 1969, *The Art of the Real* at the Tate, and *When Attitudes Become Form* at the ICA which included Richard Long, Barry Flanagan and Victor Burgin. In the same year conceptual art marked its arrival with the first issue of *Art-Language*.

Minimalism had its roots in America, but conceptual art, by its very immateriality, denied location – hence the movement's paradoxical obsession with maps (pl. 177). The music-hall humour of performances by Bruce McLean (fig. 12), or Gilbert and George (fig. 13), did, however, have a whimsical British flavour. The Art & Language Group was self-consciously international, until doctrinal disputes divided the British and American sections. The British branch saw this as a declaration of indpendence, but what was really happening was the dissolution of the very idea of territorially defined identity. Notions of centre and periphery collapsed in the face of the globalising sweep of international capitalism and

26 Lucy Lippard, *Changing: Essays in Art Criticism*, New York 1971, p. 255.

(fig. 12) Bruce McLean
POSE WORK FOR PLINTHS I
1971, photograph, Tate, London

(fig. 13) Gilbert and George
THE SINGING SCULPTURE 1973,
National Gallery of New South Wales
(in the background
THE SHRUBBERIES, 1972)

the rapid circulation of commodities and ideas. The artist who most successfully parlayed personal, local experience into international influence and reputation was Joseph Beuys, much respected in Britain.

For British artists the conditions, rather than place, of production were of concern. Inflation and the global oil crisis of 1973 ended the expansion of public patronage long before the election of Mrs Thatcher in 1979 brought to power a government committed to reducing the expenses of the state. What Hobsbawm calls the international landslide of the 1970s triggered a crisis of national identity, as the post-war British consensus broke down in an atmosphere of class conflict and racial disharmony. The economy began a painful transformation from the production of things to the supply of services and ideas, and modernist progressivism surrendered to post-modern pessimism. Cultural certainties were supplanted by a de-centred relativism that suited the hedonistic, individualistic, entrepreneurship that the Thatcherite privatisation of the economy unleashed. In the 1980s British artists found themselves in a contradictory position. As a commodity, art saw the biggest international boom it had ever known. Established members of the School of London found international acceptance and commanded high prices from patrons grown rich on the bubble economies of the media and advertising. Almost more important than any of the artists he collected was the advertising magnate Charles Saatchi, who, with his American first wife Doris, opened his ever-changing and expanding collection to the public in 1985, and who, after the Wall Street crash of 1987, increasingly shifted his investment to younger artists. Public patronage, however, remained weak, though paradoxically the dematerialisation of art had made museums more, not less important, for they created a context in which the ephemeral, the performance-based and the three-dimensional could be presented and, just as importantly, curated.

Towards the close of the 1980s, with the conventional career path of part-time teaching and commercial gallery shows more difficult to negotiate than ever, emergent artists, including those shrewdly taught by an older generation of conceptually-oriented artists, notably Jon Thompson and Michael Craig-Martin at Goldsmiths' College, became entrepreneurs and advertisers on their own behalf. Taking advantage of the massive reconfiguration of industrial space in London's East End, they began to mount shows for themselves, using the new patronage of business sponsorship and media attention, and being used by it.

The students who gathered under the leadership of Damien Hirst in 1988 to show their work in an abandoned gym in docklands under the title *Freeze* had no explicit manifesto in the manner of *Blast*. It was their future patron, Saatchi, who branded them as Young British Artists in 1992. Yet, confidently international in a multicultural milieu, they showed contempt for the conventional niceties of England and Englishness that recalls Wyndham Lewis's curses. Promiscuous in their use of materials, from video to gloss paint to their own blood, urban in reference, exploiting eroticism and popular culture, theirs was a tabloid conceptualism that discovered Duchampian ready-mades in the detritus of social change. They dislocated the language of objects into meaning, and in spite of their provocative anti-intellectualism – an echo of that reluctance to push an idea to its conclusion – they carried on the metaphysical tradition: much of their work is a speculation on the ephemeral pleasure of life, and the inevitability of death.

This tragic hedonism caught the spirit of Hobsbawm's pre-millennial landslide and has propelled contemporary British art towards a national and international popularity that it has never enjoyed before. From the land of irony and moderation, where native fogs allow nothing to appear as it is, has emerged an art that thrives on that ultimate extremity, the death of art.

ROBERT HEWISON

1910–20

VORTICISM, FIRST WORLD WAR AND ITS AFTERMATH

This chronology as well as the following have been compiled by Robert Hewison

1910

Events: Liberals win two General Elections with Asquith as Prime Minister; death of Edward VII, accession of George V

Contemporary Art Society founded by Roger Fry and others; Filippo Tommaso Marinetti lectures in London

Artists: Paul Nash, William Roberts, Ben Nicholson enter Slade School; David Jones enters Camberwell School of Art; Julian Trevelyan born

Exhibitions: MANET AND THE POST-IMPRESSIONISTS at Grafton Galleries in London

Publications: Filippo Tommaso Marinetti, MANIFESTO OF FUTURIST PAINTERS

1911

Events: Suffragettes conduct campaign of civil disobedience; industrial unrest

Diaghilev Ballets Russes at Covent Garden; Camden Town Group formed

Artists: Henri Gaudier-Brzeska settles in London; Frederick Etchells leaves Royal College of Art, moves to Paris; David Bomberg enters, Ben Nicholson leaves Slade School of Art; Eileen Agar arrives in England from Buenos Aires; Roger Hilton born

Exhibitions: Paul Cézanne, Paul Gauguin at Stafford in London; first and second Camden Town Group shows at Carfax Gallery, London

1912

Events: Political unrest in Ireland as Liberal Government attempts to introduce Home Rule

Madame Strindberg's Cabaret Theatre Club The Cave of the Golden Calf opens; Jacob Epstein completes TOMB OF OSCAR WILDE at Père-Lachaise cemetery, Paris

Artists: Stanley Spencer, Edward Wadsworth, Christopher Nevinson leave Slade School of Art; Conroy Maddox born

Exhibitions: WORKS BY THE ITALIAN FUTURIST PAINTERS at Sackville Gallery in London; SECOND POST-IMPRESSIONIST EXHIBITION. BRITISH, FRENCH AND RUSSIAN ARTISTS at Grafton; last Camden Town Group show, at Carfax; Percy Wyndham Lewis exhibits KERMESSE at Allied Artists' Association Salon, Royal Albert Hall; Paul Nash at Carfax

Publications: Ezra Pound, RIPOSTES

1913

Events: London Group formed; Roger Fry, Duncan Grant, Vanessa Bell establish Omega Workshops; Filippo Tommaso Marinetti given celebratory dinner by English artists in London

Artists: Christopher Nevinson studies in Paris; William Roberts leaves Slade; Reg Butler, William Scott born

Exhibitions: Gino Severini at Marlborough Fine Art Ltd., London; POST-IMPRESSIONIST AND FUTURIST EXHIBITION at Doré Galleries, London; THE

CAMDEN TOWN GROUP AND OTHERS AT BRIGHTON PUBLIC ART GALLERY; Jacob Epstein at Twenty-One Gallery, London; Paul Nash at New English Art Club, London
Publications: Harold Gilman and Charles Ginner, "Neo-Realism", NEW AGE

1914

Events: First World War breaks out (August)
Filippo Tommaso Marinetti visits London; Percy Wyndham Lewis opens Rebel Art Centre
Artists: Paul Nash enlists; Henri Gaudier-Brzeska joins French Army; Christopher Nevinson joins Red Cross as a driver; Lynn Chadwick born
Exhibitions: FIRST EXHIBITION OF WORKS BY MEMBERS OF THE LONDON GROUP at Goupil; MODERN GERMAN ART; EXHIBITION OF THE WORKS OF ITALIAN FUTURIST PAINTERS AND SCULPTORS; TWENTIETH CENTURY ART. A REVIEW OF MODERN MOVEMENTS at Whitechapel; Rebel Art Centre stand at Allied Artists' Association Salon at Holland Park Hall, London; Bomberg at Chenil Gallery, London
Publications: Filippo Tommaso Marinetti and Christopher Nevinson, "Futurist Manifesto: Vital English Art" in THE OBSERVER; Percy Wyndham Lewis (ed.) BLAST, no. 1; Clive Bell, Art, Michael Sadler English translation of Wassily Kandinsky's ÜBER DAS GEISTIGE IN DER KUNST as THE ART OF SPIRITUAL HARMONY; Ezra Pound (ed.), DES IMAGISTES. AN ANTHOLOGY; Ezra Pound, "Vorticism", FORTNIGHTLY REVIEW

1915

Events: Military stalemate in France; Gallipoli campaign; Italy enters war against Austria and Germany
Artists: Henri Gaudier-Brzeska killed in France; Edward Wadsworth joins Royal Navy; David Jones, David Bomberg enlist; Stanley Spencer joins Royal Army Medical Corps; William Gear born
Exhibitions: VORTICIST EXHIBITION at Doré; Jacob Epstein exhibits original version of THE ROCK DRILL at second London Group show
Publications: Percy Wyndham Lewis (ed.), BLAST, no. 2, War Number July 1915

1916

Events: Battle of Jutland; Siege of Verdun; Somme offensive; Lloyd George replaces Asquith as Prime Minister; Easter Rising in Ireland crushed
Artists: Percy Wyndham Lewis, David Roberts join Royal Artillery; Stanley Spencer serving in Greece and Macedonia; Kenneth Armitage born
Exhibitions: Christopher Nevinson at Leicester Galleries

1917

Events: Russian Revolution (March); United States enter war (April); German army occupies Hindenburg Line T. E. Hulme killed in France
Artists: Edward Wadsworth invalided out of Navy, supervises camouflage painting of ships; Paul Nash serves in France, becomes Official War Artist; Percy Wyndham Lewis, David Bomberg become Official War Artists; Jacob Epstein, Henry Moore enlist, Nigel Henderson born
Exhibitions: Jacob Epstein at Leicester; EXHIBITION OF THE VORTICISTS at Penguin Club, New York
Publications: D'Arcy Wentworth Thompson, GROWTH AND FORM

1918

Events: Ludendorff offensive fails; Armistice ends First World (November); civil war in Ireland
Canadian War Memorials Fund commissions David Bomberg, Frederick Etchells, Percy Wyndham Lewis, Christopher Nevinson, David Roberts and Edward Wadsworth
Artists: Stanley Spencer demobilised; Peter Lanyon born
Exhibitions: Henri Gaudier-Brzeska memorial exhibition at Leicester
Publications: Percy Wyndham Lewis, TARR; Eric Gill, SCULPTURE. AN ESSAY ON STONE-CUTTING. WITH A PREFACE ABOUT GOD

1919

Events: Treaty of Versailles; post-war economic boom in Britain; Seven and Five Society formed; Omega Workshops close
Artists: Paul Nash, William Roberts demobilised; Henry Moore demobilised, enters Leeds College of Art; David Jones demobilised, enters Westminster School of Art; John Tunnard studies design at Royal College of Art; Stanley Spencer given commission for TRAVOYS ARRIVING WITH WOUNDED by Ministry of Information
Exhibitions: Matisse at Leicester; FRENCH EXHIBITION at Heal's Mansard Gallery, London; Edward Wadsworth at Adelphi Gallery, London; David Bomberg at Adelphi; Percy Wyndham Lewis at Goupil
Publications: Percy Wyndham Lewis, CALIPH'S DESIGN. ARCHITECTS! WHERE IS YOUR VORTEX?; James Joyce begins publication of ULYSSES in THE EGOIST

BLAST, ARMAGEDDON AND AFTERMATH

RICHARD CORK

In November 1910 the art critic Roger Fry, whose own paintings displayed a growing debt to his new hero Paul Cézanne (fig. 1), mounted a landmark exhibition that forced every artist in Britain to acknowledge the profound transformation of modern French painting. *Manet and the Post-Impressionists* was a large survey, focusing on the triumvirate of Paul Cézanne, Vincent van Gogh and Paul Gauguin but also including Fauvist painting and pre-Cubist work by Pablo Picasso. Many visitors to the show, at the Grafton Galleries in London, were horrified. The "Art-Quake of 1910"[1] created a furore so prolonged and well-publicised that Post-Impressionism entered the national consciousness at last.

1 Desmond MacCarthy, "The Art Quake of 1910", *The Listener*, 1 February 1943.

(fig. 1) Roger Fry, RIVER OF POPLARS, c. 1912, oil on wood, 56.5 x 70.8 cm, Tate, London

Young painters who had yet to establish themselves were profoundly impressed. And some of them became even more elated when an equally controversial *Exhibition of Works by the Italian Futurist Painters* invaded London in March 1912. But the Francophile Fry hated Filippo Tommaso Marinetti (fig. 2) and his belligerent Milanese cohorts for their love of aggression, speed and machine-age power. Soon afterwards, he gave the bewildered metropolis another chance to become acquainted with the forces he had unleashed. In October 1912 his *Second Post-Impressionist Exhibition* opened, with British and Russian artists supplementing the representation of French painters like Henri Matisse. Although Vanessa Bell (pl. 9) and Duncan Grant (pl. 7) were the two British contributors most closely in sympathy with Fry's critical standpoint, Clive Bell's introduction to the "English Section" of the catalogue spoke for other par-

ticipants as well – young men as restless as Frederick Etchells (pl. 22), Wyndham Lewis (pl. 1) and Edward Wadsworth (pl. 21), who shared Fry's appetite for renewal. "The battle is won", Bell wrote triumphantly. "We all agree, now, that any form in which an artist can express himself is legitimate [...]. We have ceased to ask, 'What does this picture represent?' and ask instead, 'What does it make us feel?'. We expect a work of art to have more in common with a piece of music than with a coloured photograph."[2]

For a moment, at least, the new generation of avant-garde British artists seemed united by a common determination to find an emancipated alternative to what Bell described as "traditional forms". The solidarity, if it ever really existed, proved short-lived. But a memorable coming-together of diverse young painters and sculptors did occur in the summer of 1912, when Madame Frida Strindberg, the Swedish playwright's former wife, unveiled London's first artists' cabaret – The Cave of the Golden Calf.[3] This exuberant night-club, situated in a basement off Regent Street and dedicated to profane delight, broadcast the new spirit in art with uninhibited *élan*. Spencer Gore, in overall charge of the ambitious decorative scheme, executed immense wall-paintings of brazen jungle scenes influenced by Wassily Kandinsky (fig. 3). So did his close friend Charles Ginner, a fellow-member of the Camden Town Group founded

(fig. 2) Filippo Tommaso Marinetti and Benedetta in their house at Piazza Adriana in Rome, in the background portraits by Marinetti of Zatkova and Depero, photograph by Luxardo, 1932.

2 Clive Bell, "The English Group", in: *Second Post-Impressionist Exhibition*, exh. cat. Grafton Galleries, London, 1912, unpaginated

3 For a detailed account of The Cave of the Golden Calf, see Richard Cork, *Art Beyond The Gallery in Early 20th Century England*, New Haven and London 1985.

the previous year to promote an English form of Post-Impressionism. They were joined by Wyndham Lewis, who painted a colossal and explosive canvas called *Kermesse* for the staircase. The first large-scale British painting convincingly to demonstrate an awareness of Cubism, Futurism and even Expressionism, it catapulted Lewis to the very forefront of his generation.

(fig. 3) Spencer Gore, sketch for the wall decoration in The Cave of the Golden Calf, 1912, oil on paper, 30.5 x 60.3 cm, Tate, London

The sculpture in the Cave was equally remarkable. Jacob Epstein, a Jewish New Yorker who had settled in London, carried out brilliantly painted plaster reliefs on the columns supporting the low ceiling. And Eric Gill made gilded images of the calf itself for the entrance and a pedestal in the central room. The two men shared a fervent desire to revolutionise British sculpture. Inspired by African and Indian cultures rather than the traditional classical or Renaissance sources, they adopted a radically simplified approach stressing the importance of primal themes: birth, virility, motherhood and erotic ecstasy. All these subjects had appeared in Epstein's earlier sequence of statues for the British Medical Association headquarters in the Strand, and soon afterwards he collaborated with Gill on a visionary scheme for a temple in Sussex, "a sort of 20th century Stonehenge".[4] The project was never realised, but surviving fragments suggest that the two allies intended it as a monument to the principle of "carving direct". Close manual engagement with the sculptor's material, letting the stone play a crucial role in determining the shape of the final image, became their *modus operandi* for a while. It reached a climax when Epstein, who had befriended Constantin Brancusi and Amedeo Modigliani in Paris, completed his great winged figure on the *Tomb of Oscar Wilde* (fig. 4). Installed at Père-Lachaise cemetery in 1911, the carving's severe simplification and brazen anatomical frankness provoked vandalism and a widespread feeling of outrage.

4 Eric Gill to William Rothenstein, 25 September 1910, Walter Shewring (ed.), *Letters of Eric Gill*, London 1947, p. 32.

(fig. 4) Jacob Epstein, TOMB FOR OSCAR WILDE at the Père-Lachaise cemetery in Paris, 1912

By the summer of 1913, Roger Fry's Omega Workshops had become fully active. The project was primarily conceived as a source of patronage for young experimental artists, who could subsidise their own work by producing, part-time and under a cloak of anonymity, decorative commissions for private houses and restaurants. Fry, who relied on the irrepressible vitality of his Bloomsbury friends Vanessa Bell and Duncan Grant, also saw the Omega as a testing-ground for his latest theories. He told a friend in 1913 that "all the essential aesthetic quality has to do with pure form",[5] a radical concept that received its definitive English defence in Clive Bell's 1914 book *Art*. Lewis, Etchells, Wadsworth and Cuthbert Hamilton – who had been Lewis' student contemporary at the Slade around the turn of the century – joined the Bloomsbury artists at the Omega. The Workshops' concentration on rugs, textiles, inlaid trays or desks, screens, lampshades and tables gave their work a sense of liberation, encouraging them to dispense with figurative references altogether. Design after design reflects the exuberance they all shared, and a fascination with the freedom of abstract form. Bell and Grant thrived on the stimulus of decorative ventures, and their work at this time is alive with a brilliantly sustained spirit of boldness and infectious exhilaration.

5 Roger Fry to Lowes Dickinson, 18 February 1913, Denys Sutton (ed.), *Letters of Roger Fry*, London 1972, p. 362.

But the Omega honeymoon did not last long. Accompanied by Etchells, Hamilton and Wadsworth, Lewis marched out of the Workshops in October 1913 after angrily accusing Fry of stealing an important commission. The rebels then issued a ferocious "Round Robin" accusing Fry of shark-like dishonesty. The split between the Bloomsbury group and the nascent Vorticists proved irrevocable. Lewis and his friends were momentarily fascinated by Italian Futurism, a movement that Fry continued to abhor. They wanted young English artists to explore the dynamic of the machine age, and joined the young C. R. W. Nevinson in honouring the Futurists' leader Marinetti at a special London dinner in November. Lewis

(fig. 5) Christopher R. W. Nevinson, COLUMN ON THE MARCH, 1915, oil on canvas, 63.8 x 76.6 cm, Birmingham Museum and Art Gallery, Birmingham

was for the moment impressed by Marinetti's headlong aggression and declamatory power, although Nevinson was the only English artist to become a member of the Futurist movement (fig. 5).

Marinetti's insistence on conveying the speed and energy of the new mechanised century also played a part in the evolution of Epstein's most important early sculpture *Rock Drill* (pl. 17). He began it in late 1913 by developing the idea of a totemic male figure, who would embody not only phallic strength but the thrusting dynamism of a world dominated by machine power. Epstein was encouraged to pursue mechanistic metaphors by his new friend T. E. Hulme, a poet, philosopher and critic who was convinced that "the new 'tendency towards abstraction' will culminate, not so much in the simple geometric forms found in archaic art, but in the more complicated ones associated in our minds with the idea of machinery".[6] Ezra Pound, another innovative poet fascinated by the new art, also supported the *Rock Drill* project. With astonishing audacity, Epstein purchased a second-hand American rock drill mounted on a tripod, and modelled a white plaster figure straddling the machine. The combination of man-made driller and ready-made implement was revolutionary, paralleled at that time only by Marcel Duchamp who announced that an ordinary *Bicycle Wheel* was a work of art.[7] Epstein considered setting his *Rock Drill* in motion with pneumatic power, but then discarded the plan. He was, after all, sufficiently removed from Futurism to dislike the representation of motion in art, and his stark drawings for *Rock Drill* of 1913–15 (fig. 6) are more closely allied with the vision defined in Wyndham Lewis' contemporaneous work.

Deciding to adopt a cooler and more detached viewpoint than the Futurists, with their rhapsodic celebration of the modern world, Lewis aimed at arriving at a unique synthesis of blurred Futurist vitality and Cubist formal grandeur (pl. 15). He wanted to involve himself in modern urban clangour, yet deal with it in a stringent, analytical and multi-layered manner. His own Vorticist images may be volcanic in their implications, but their restless and often vertiginous forms are all contained within clearly defined boundaries. However complex his aims may have been, Lewis always opted for lucidity, and his drawings and watercolours of the archetypal 20th century city are controlled by a whiplash emphasis on line. Although he had not yet visited New York, it seems to have shaped his image of the

modern metropolis. One of his finest Vorticist watercolours is entitled *New York*, and in 1913 Alvin Langdon Coburn exhibited some outstanding photographs of Manhattan in an influential London exhibition. Coburn subsequently became interested in Vorticism, collaborating with his fellow-American Pound on some innovative abstract experiments called Vortographs – a fascinating attempt to parallel Vorticism in photographic terms.

It was surely no accident that so many of the people associated with Vorticism came from outside England. Lewis had himself been born near Amherst in Nova Scotia, and, towards the end of 1913, his burgeoning friendship with Pound prompted them to think about founding a revolutionary movement of their own. They shared an impatient dissatisfaction with established British culture. Pound gave Vorticism its name, and explained its meaning by announcing that the Great English Vortex was "a radiant node or cluster [...] from which, and through which, and into which, ideas are constantly rushing".[8] Lewis preferred to emphasise the centrality of the Vorticists' endeavour, telling a friend to think "at once of a whirlpool [...]. At the heart of the whirlpool is a great silent place where all the energy is concentrated. And there, at the point of concentration, is the Vorticist".[9] Impelled by the fierce hope that England would produce a truly radical movement, he wanted its young artists to recognise the harsh, disturbing and yet dynamic reality of modern industrial life. The British, claimed Lewis, "are the inventors of this bareness and hardness, and should be the great enemies of Romance".[10] Epstein was too sturdily independent ever to become a member of the movement whose arrival was announced in July 1914 by *Blast*, a witty, irreverent and eruptive magazine edited with tireless panache by Lewis (fig. 7). But Epstein did contribute two drawings to *Blast*, and there is no doubt that *Rock Drill* can be related to many of the Vorticists' concerns. With its hard-hitting typography and headlong denunciation of the Victorian legacy, *Blast* confirmed the arrival of a rumbustious new force in British art. The multi-talented Lewis wrote many of its belligerent articles, but the magazine also included

6 T. E. Hulme, "Modern Art and its Philosophy", Herbert Read (ed.), *Speculations*, London 1924, p. 104.

7 For an extended discussion of the rock drill as a mechanised invention, see Richard Cork, *Vorticism and Abstract Art in the First Machine Age*, London 1976, vol. 2, pp. 470–472.

8 Ezra Pound, "Vorticism", *Fortnightly Review*, 1 September 1914.

9 Douglas Goldring, *South Lodge*, London 1943, p. 65.

10 Percy Wyndham Lewis, *Blast*, no. 1, London 1914, p. 41.

(fig. 6) Jacob Epstein, Study for ROCK DRILL, 1913, black chalk on paper, 53.3 x 64.1 cm, Ivor Braka Ltd., London

(fig. 7) Percy Wyndham Lewis, cover of BLAST no. 2, 1915

written contributions and illustrations by many of the liveliest new painters and sculptors in London. Outstanding among them was the very young French sculptor Henri Gaudier-Brzeska, who had settled in London three and a half years earlier. Although he could be eclectic, moving from classicism to primitivism with virtuoso assurance, Gaudier did formally identify himself with the Vorticists. He signed their manifesto in *Blast*, wrote a defiant credo for the magazine, and introduced to carvings like *Red Stone Dancer* (1914) an interest in geometrical rigidity that became fused with his innate response to organic vitality. *Bird Swallowing a Fish* (1914) reveals the strength of Gaudier's ability to turn these complex concerns into convincing sculptural form (pl. 20). The action of the bird's predatory impulse is arrestingly defined, and Gaudier also succeeds in transforming both the combatants' bodies into eerily mechanistic components.

The painters associated with Vorticism were likewise remarkably young. Both Wadsworth and William Roberts had recently left the Slade, but they made impressive contributions to the Vorticists' harsh, clean-cut and often bitingly coloured vision of the modern world. Like Malevich and the Suprematists in Russia, Wadsworth was exhilarated by the new visual possibilities opened up by air travel and photography taken from aeroplanes. The images of flight helped him to define a fresh way of looking at Britain's great northern industrial centres, some of which he had known since his Yorkshire childhood (pl. 21). Roberts, by contrast, was a Londoner, and based most of his Vorticist work on life in the metropolis: street games, boatmen and dancing were among the subjects he tackled, in large near-abstract canvases, all subsequently lost.

Many of the major paintings shown at the *Vorticist Exhibition*, held in June 1915 at the Doré Galleries, London, have likewise failed to survive. Little can now be found of the work produced by Lawrence Atkinson (pl. 8), and the same fate befell the art of the three talented women associated with the Vorticist cause: Jessica Dismorr, Helen Saunders (pl. 24) and Dorothy Shakespear, who married Pound. But enough of their drawings and watercolours remain to prove that they all helped to make Vorticism a vital attempt to define the rapidly changing pulse of 20th century existence. The brutal advent of the First World War gave the movement far too brief a time to establish itself, and

RICHARD CORK

the second issue of *Blast* in July 1915 proved to be the last. Before they left for active service in France, though, the Vorticists and their allies produced an art with a fiercely independent identity. And within its tightly defined contours, their work enclosed a prophetic awareness of the capacity for destruction that mechanised armaments would unleash during the four-year slaughter.

Enlistment in the armed forces halted the careers of many young artists caught up in the conflict, and tragically terminated Gaudier's life when he died in the trenches at the age of twenty-three. But the war also generated some impressive paintings. Nevinson's first-hand experience of the soldiers' suffering while he worked in the ambulance service forced him to reject the Futurists' callow enthusiasm for the violence of battle. Invalided home from France, he started painting an uncompromising series of images that stressed the futility and despair of war (pl. 30) – anti-heroic work courageously at odds with the jingoism of the patriotic propaganda produced by the government's enlistment drive. *Returning to the Trenches* (fig. 5) is among the earliest and most powerful of these canvases, with its marching soldiers caught up in a relentless, dehumanised process over which they have no control.

It was, inevitably, a difficult time for painters who had pushed their work to the greatest extreme in the pre-war period. David Bomberg, a prodigious young artist from a Jewish émigré background in London's East End, found the transition especially agonising. The paintings he produced around 1913–14 were among the most impressive and adventurous of the period, drawing on an intelligent understanding of Cubism, Futurism and Vorticism while asserting an independent alternative of his own. Fascinated by the energy of "a great city, its motion, its machinery",[11] Bomberg transformed the spectacle of men working on a ship in dockland, or bodies exercising at a Whitechapel Steam Baths, into spare, jagged and exuberant images. *In the Hold* of 1913–14 and *The Mud Bath* of 1914 (fig. 8) are among the most enduring canvases in early Modernist art, and Bomberg's pared-down vision of life made his 1914 one-man show in London an outstanding event. It proclaimed the emergence of a major new British painter, and in the catalogue Bomberg declared that "I look upon *Nature*, while I live

11 David Bomberg, interview with *The Jewish Chronicle*, 8 May 1914.

(fig. 8) David Bomberg, *Study for* Mud Bath II, 1914, gouache, 45 x 68 cm, Ivor Braka Ltd., London

in a *Steel City*".[12] The figures who jerk, leap and fling their limbs across the surface of *The Mud Bath* are purged images of the mechanistic energy in modern life. Bomberg carves them into tense, stripped-down amalgams of white and blue, so that their angular bodies jut against the blaring red rectangle of water. Half human and half machine, they are reminiscent of the plaster figure who bestrode the first version of Epstein's *Rock Drill*, and T. E. Hulme gave Bomberg's solo show an enthusiastic review.[13]

By 1916, however, the artists' attitude to machine power had changed irrevocably. Too many young men were being annihilated by 20th century weaponry, and when Epstein displayed the second, drastically altered version of *Rock Drill*, all its former *machismo* had disappeared. *Torso in Metal from the Rock Drill*, as he now renamed it, is an elegiac image. Shorn not only of his phallic machine but of legs and hands as well, the driller seems powerless. His mask-like head projects forward at a plaintive angle, as he seeks to anticipate the prospect of danger. But his body has become so crippled and abject that he is no longer capable of defending himself or the embryonic form lodged within his ribs. He has no hope of dominating the world as he once did on his mighty machine. This truncated victim is as forlorn and pathetic as the severely wounded soldiers who were returning from the Front in ever more horrifying numbers, testifying through their broken bodies to the nightmarish carnage in the trenches.

Near the end of the war, several of the Vorticists received official commissions to produce monumental paintings of the conflict. Lewis' *A Battery Shelled* (1919) and Roberts' *The First German Gas Attack at Ypres* (1918), commissioned by the British and Canadian governments respectively, achieve the difficult feat of reconciling their earlier avant-garde concerns with the more documentary demands of memorial image-making. So did Wadsworth, when he used his own experience of applying hard-edge camouflage patterning on war-time vessels, to paint *Dazzle-Ships in Drydock at Liverpool* (1919). All these artists were aided in their tasks by a genuine desire to retreat from near-abstraction and forge a more figurative art which nevertheless retained the formal tautness they had developed during their Vorticist period. Bomberg's gruelling experiences in the trenches,

12 David Bomberg, foreword to the catalogue of his exhibition at the Chenil Gallery, London, July 1914, unpaginated.

13 For a detailed account of early Bomberg's relationship with Epstein and Hulme, see Richard Cork, *David Bomberg*, New Haven and London 1987.

where conditions became so terrible that they drove him to administer a self-inflicted wound, left a permanent mark on his outlook. On his return from the war, he could no longer deal with machine-age life in such a forceful spirit. Having once identified it with the dynamism of construction, he now saw it as the agent of annihilation. Far too many soldiers had been slaughtered at the Front, including friends like Gaudier, Hulme and Bomberg's boyhood friend, the poet and painter Isaac Rosenberg. Bomberg began to regard mechanisation as a sinister development, which threatened to dehumanise and alienate. His first version of *Sappers at Work* (fig. 9), commissioned by the Canadian government in 1918, was a brave attempt to reconcile his previous style with a greater awareness of figurative priorities. But it was scornfully rejected by the committee. Epstein suffered even greater humiliation. No government was prepared to commission him to make a war memorial. After suffering a severe nervous breakdown towards the end of the war, he continued to work on a radically different image that heralded the direction his work would take in the post-war world. He called this attenuated bronze *Risen Christ* (1917–19), as if to signify his hope that human existence would itself experience a resurrection after the trauma and waste of conflict. But no facile optimism can be found in this reticent and sombre figure, who emerges from death with resigned stillness rather than joy. And Epstein's modelling displays a new interest in figurative elaboration, which contrasts with the stripped-down austerity of his pre-war work.

(fig. 9) David Bomberg, Study for Sappers at Work: A Canadian Tunnelling Company, Hill 60, St. Eloi, c. 1918–19, oil on canvas, 304.2 x 243.8 cm, Tate, London

Many of the former Vorticists shared this urge to redefine their standpoint and negotiated and altered relationship with tradition. But the immediate post-war years proved an uneasy period. Although the prominent Manhattan collector John Quinn had organised an *Exhibition of the Vorticists* at the Penguin Club in New York as recently as January 1917, Lewis' subsequent plans for a third issue of *Blast* came to nothing. When he organised a London exhibition containing many of his earlier Vorticist allies in 1920, the non-committal label *Group X* was finally chosen for an event proposing "no theory or dogma that would be liable to limit the development of any member".[14]

14 Percy Wyndham Lewis, preface to the catalogue of *Group X*, an exhibition held at Heal's Mansard Gallery, London 1920, unpaginated.

In common with many initiatives elsewhere in Europe, there was a widespread desire to "return to order" and revalue the classical past. As a result, abstraction played little part in their work during the 1920s, and most former adherents of the Vorticist cause decided to concentrate above all on the human figure during this period of retrenchment. But the rigour and ambition of pre-war experimentation continued to inform their finest post-war painting and sculpture, while the explosive energy of the Vorticist insurrection can now be seen as a seminal moment in the history of modern British art at its most inventive, stimulating and audacious.

RICHARD CORK

1 | Percy Wyndham Lewis THE VORTICIST 1912

W Lewis.
1912.

6 | Duncan Grant FEMALE DANCER 1913–14

8| Lawrence Atkinson Vorticist Composition circa 1914–15

9 | Vanessa Bell ABSTRACT PAINTING circa 1914

10a | David Bomberg   COMPANY HILL 60, ST. ELOI   1914

10b | David Bomberg   STUDY FOR MUD BATH II   1914

11 | Jacob Epstein   ONE OF THE HUNDRED PILLARS OF THE SECRET TEMPLE   circa 1910

12 | Vanessa Bell o. Duncan Grant   PAMELA   1914

14 | Percy Wyndham Lewis BATTERY POSITION IN A WOOD 1918

13 | Nina Hamnett VIEW OF OMEGA INTERIOR 1917

15 | Percy Wyndham Lewis ABSTRACT DESIGN 1912

16 | Helen Saunders VORTICIST COMPOSITION IN BLUE AND GREEN circa 1915

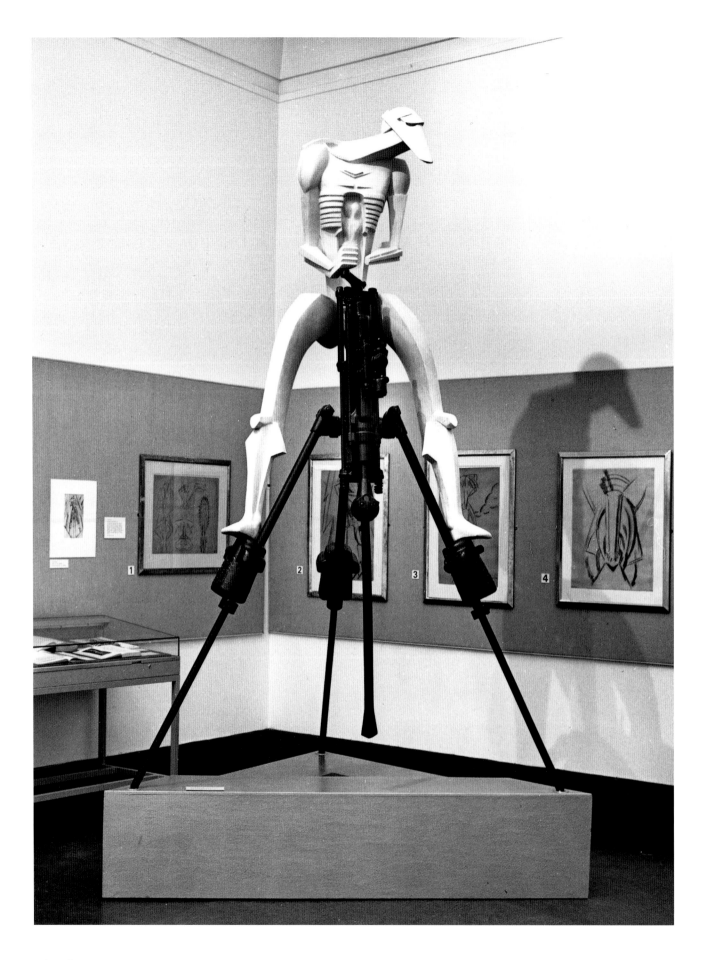

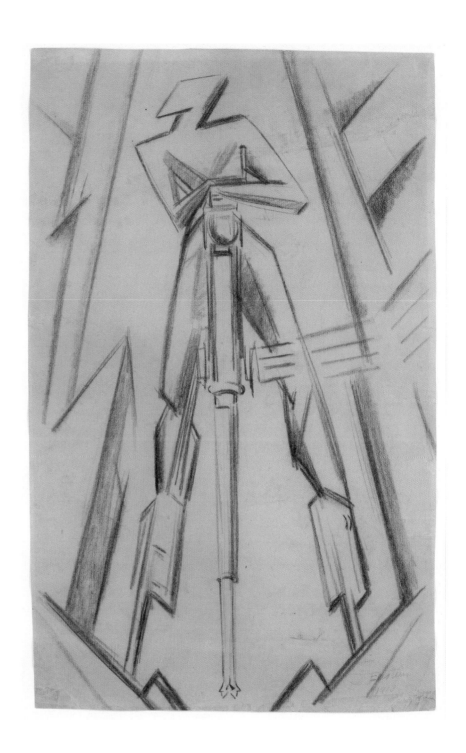

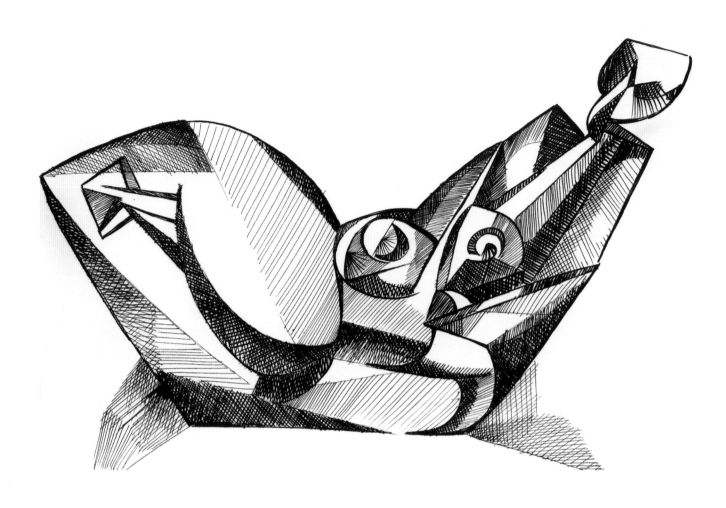

Henri Gaudier-Brzeska STUDY FOR BIRD SWALLOWING A FISH 1914

23 | Percy Wyndham Lewis THE CROWD (REVOLUTION) 1915

24 | Helen Saunders VORTICIST DESIGN (MAN AND DOG) circa 1915

25 | Christopher Nevinson COLUMN ON THE MARCH 1915

26 | Percy Wyndham Lewis DRAWING OF THE GREAT WAR NO. 1 (THE MENIN ROAD) circa 1918

27 | Percy Wyndham Lewis DRAWING OF GREAT WAR NO. 2 circa 1918

1920–40

PRIMITIVISM, AbSTRACTION ANd SURREALISM

1920

Events: Society of Wood Engravers founded
Artists: Barbara Hepworth enters Leeds School of Art; Alan Davie, Patrick Heron born
Exhibitions: Group X at Mansard; first Seven and Five at Walker Art Gallery, London
Publications: Roger Fry, *Vision and Design; Seven and Five; Manifesto*

1921

Events: Post-war boom in Britain turns to slump, unemployment rises, art market shrinks
Artists: Henry Moore and Barbara Hepworth win scholarships to Royal College of Art; Edward Burra enters Chelsea Polytechnic; Graham Sutherland enters Goldsmiths' College; David Jones received into Roman Catholic Church, joins Eric Gill and so-called Ditchling Community, John Latham born
Exhibitions: Picasso at Leicester; African carving at Goupil; Lawrence Atkinson at Eldar Gallery, London
Publications: Ludwig Wittgenstein, *Tractatus Logico-Philosophicus*; D. H. Lawrence, *Women in Love*

1922

Events: Partition of Ireland; Conservatives win general election following split in Liberal Party, Bonar Law becomes Prime Minister; Mussolini takes power in Italy
Artists: Roland Penrose settles in France; Lucian Freud born in Berlin; John Tunnard leaves Royal College of Art; Richard Hamilton, William Turnbull born
Publications: T. S. Eliot, *The Waste Land* in first issue of *The Criterion*

1923

Events: Stanley Baldwin succeeds Bonar Law as Prime Minister, defeated at General Election; first Labour government under Ramsay MacDonald; French occupation of the Ruhr area

Redfern Gallery opens in London
Artists: Edward Burra enters Royal College of Art

1924

Events: General Election returns Conservatives to power under Stanley Baldwin
Artists: Henry Moore appointed Instructor in sculpture at Royal College of Art; Ben Nicholson joins Seven and Five Society; Barbara Hepworth leaves Royal College of Art, travels in Italy; Eduardo Paolozzi, Anthony Caro born
Publications: T. E. Hulme (ed. Herbert Read), *Speculations. Essays on Humanism and the Philosophy of Art*

1925

Events: Locarno Treaty confirms Germany's post-war frontiers
Tate opens Modern Foreign Gallery in London
Artists: Stanley Spencer marries Hilda Carline; Barbara Hepworth marries John

Skeaping in Rome; Edward Burra leaves Royal College of Art; Eileen Agar enters Slade; Ian Hamilton Finlay born
Publications: first issue of *Apollo*; Virginia Woolf, *Mrs Dalloway*

1926
Events: General Strike (May); Germany joins League of Nations
Artists: Winifred Nicholson joins, Ben Nicholson becomes chairman of, Seven and Five Society; Eileen Agar leaves Slade; Leon Kossoff born; Gustav Metzger born in Nuremberg
Publications: Roger Fry, *Transformations*; Sidney Hunt (ed.), *Ray 1*

1927
Events: British Broadcasting Corporation (BBC) established by Royal Charter
St. Ives Society of Artists founded
Artists: Stanley Spencer commissioned to decorate Burghclere Chapel; Christopher Wood joins Seven and Five Society
Exhibitions: Stanley Spencer at Goupil; Barbara Hepworth studio show in St. John's Wood, London
Publications: R. H. Wilenski, *The Modern Movement in Art*; Sidney Hunt (ed.), *Ray 2*; first issue of *Close Up*; Virginia Woolf, *To The Lighthouse*

1928
Artists: David Jones joins Seven and Five Society; Ben Nicholson encounters Alfred Wallis; F. E. McWilliam enters Slade; Francis Bacon visits Berlin and Paris; Alison Smith (née Gill), Michael Andrews, Joe Tilson born
Exhibitions: Giorgio de Chirico at Tooth's; Henry Moore at Warren Gallery, London; Barbara Hepworth at Beaux-Arts Gallery, London
Publications: D. H. Lawrence, *Lady Chatterley's Lover*

1929
Events: Labour wins General Election, Ramsay MacDonald becomes Prime Minister; Wall Street Crash, Depression begins
Artists: Roger Hilton enters Slade; Mary Martin (née Balmford), Kenneth Martin enter Royal College of Art; Peter Joseph born
Exhibitions: David Jones show with Eric Gill at Goupil; Duncan Grant at Paul Guillaume Gallery, London
Publications: T. E. Hulme (Herbert Read ed.), *Notes on Language and Style*; Virginia Woolf, *A Room of One's Own*; first issue of *The Listener*

1930
Events: Allied troops withdraw from Rhineland
J. B. Manson becomes director of Tate
Artists: Mary and Kenneth Martin marry; Gillian Ayres, Keith Arnatt, Robyn Denny, Anthony Hill born
Publications: Sigmund Freud, *Civilization and Its Discontents*; F. R. Leavis, *Mass Civilization and Minority Culture*; W. H. Auden, *Poems*

1931
Events: World Economic Crisis; Labour government collapses, replaced by "National Government" dominated by Conservatives; devaluation by abandoning the Gold Standard for sterling
Artists: Barbara Hepworth joins Seven and Five Society; Henry Moore resigns from Royal College of Art; Bill Brandt arrives in London; Roger Hilton, F. E. McWilliam leave Slade; William Scott enters Royal Academy Schools; Bridget Riley, Richard Smith born; Frank Auerbach born in Berlin; Lawrence Atkinson dies
Exhibitions: *Room and Book* at Zwemmer Gallery, London; *Recent Developments in British Painting* at Tooth's
Publications: Herbert Read, *The Meaning of Art*

1932
Events: Government introduces protectionist trade measures; British Union of Fascists founded
Group Theatre founded
Artists: Ben Nicholson and Barbara Hepworth visit Paris and Provence; Henry Moore becomes first head of sculpture at Chelsea School of Art, joins Seven and Five Society; David Jones has nervous breakdown; Edward Wadsworth joins Abstraction-Création; Julian Trevelyan studies in Paris; Mary Martin, Kenneth Martin leave Royal College of Art; Peter Blake, Howard Hodgkin born; R. B. Kitaj born in America
Exhibitions: Paul Nash at Venice Biennale; Ben Nicholson at Tooth's; Francis Bacon in mixed show at Mayor Art Gallery, London
Publications: Aldous Huxley, *Brave New World*

1933
Events: Hitler becomes Chancellor; failure of World Disarmament Conference
Unit One formed; Artists' International Association formed; Modern Architectural Research Group (MARS) formed; General Post Office Film Unit formed; dissolution of Bauhaus in Germany
Artists: Ben Nicholson, Barbara Hepworth join Abstraction-Création in Paris; Lucian Freud arrives in Britain; Stuart Brisley, Bernard Cohen born
Exhibitions: Ben Nicholson at Lefevre Gallery, London; John Tunnard at Redfern; Stoop Bequest at Tate; Francis Bacon at Sunderland House
Publications: Herbert Read, *Art Now*; Eric Underwood, *A Short History of British Painting*; T. S. Eliot, *The Use of Poetry and the Use of Criticism*; last issue of *Close Up*; first issue of *New Verse*

1934

Events: Britain begins to rearm and modernise military and naval forces; British Council founded
Walter Gropius arrives in London; Kenneth Clark appointed director of National Gallery
Artists: Mark Boyle, Phillip King, John Hoyland, Bob Law born; Roger Fry dies
Exhibitions: Unit One at Mayor; *Objective Abstractions* at Zwemmer
Publications: Herbert Read (ed.), *Unit One. The Modern Movement in English Architecture, Painting and Sculpture*; Adrian Stokes, *The Stones of Rimini*, first issue of *Left Review*

1935

Events: General Election brings in second "National Government" under Stanley Baldwin; Italy invades Abyssinia
Naum Gabo and László Moholy-Nagy arrive in Britain; Benjamin Britten and W. H. Auden collaborate on Basil Wright's documentary *Coal Face* for GPO Film Unit
Artists: Roland Penrose returns to Britain; William Scott leaves Royal Academy Schools; Roger Hilton re-enters Slade; William Tucker born
Exhibitions: *Last Seven and Five* at Zwemmer, Ben Nicholson at Lefevre; Julian Trevelyan at Lefevre
Publications: David Gascoyne, *First Manifesto of English Surrealism* and *A Short Survey of Surrealism*; first issue of *Axis*; W. H. Auden and Christopher Isherwood, *The Dog Beneath the Skin*; Christopher Isherwood, *Mr Norris Changes Trains*

1936

Events: Death of George V; Edward VIII provokes Abdication Crisis, succeeded by George VI; Germany reoccupies Rhineland; Spanish Civil War begins (July); The British Council established by Royal Charter

Benjamin Britten and W. H. Auden collaborate on Harry Watt's and Basil Wright's documentary *Night Mail* for GPO Film Unit
Artists: Roger Hilton leaves Slade; David Annesley, Patrick Caulfield born
Exhibitions: *International Surrealist Exhibition* at New Burlington Galleries, London; *Abstract and Concrete* at Lefevre
Publications: André Breton (translated by David Gascoyne), *What Is Surrealism?*; Bill Brandt, *The English at Home*; Alfred J. Ayer, *Language, Truth and Logic*

1937

Events: Coronation of George VI; Stanley Baldwin succeeded as Prime Minister by Neville Chamberlain
Mass Observation founded; Artists' International Association holds *First British Artists' Congress*; László Moholy-Nagy, Walter Gropius leave Britain for America
Artists: Stanley Spencer divorces Hilda Carline and marries Patricia Preece; Conroy Maddox works with Surrealists in Paris; Alan Davie enters Edinburgh College of Art; Kenneth Armitage, Patrick Heron enter Slade; Derek Boshier, David Hockney, Allen Jones, Tim Scott born
Exhibitions: Artists' International Association; *Constructive Art* at London
Publications: Ben Nicholson, Naum Gabo and Leslie Martin (eds.), *Circle – International Survey of Constructive Art*; David Jones, *In Parenthesis*; last issue of *Axis*; Myfanwy Evans (ed.), *The Painter's Object*; Adrian Stokes, *Colour and Form*; W. H. Auden, *Spain 1937*; George Orwell, *The Road to Wigan Pier*

1938

Events: Germany annexes Austria; Munich Crisis (September)
British Council art collection begins; John Rothenstein becomes director of Tate; Euston Road School opens; Sigmund Freud, John Heartfield, Oscar Kokoschka arrive in Britain

Artists: Barbara Hepworth and Ben Nicholson marry; Piet Mondrian arrives in Britain accompanied by Winifred Nicholson; Bill Brandt starts work for *Picture Post*; Lucian Freud enters Central School; Richard Hamilton enters Royal Academy Schools; Pauline Boty, Paul Huxley born
Exhibitions: Picasso *Guernica* at New Burlington, Whitechapel and tour; *Twentieth Century German Art* at New Burlington; Paul Nash at Venice Biennale
Publications: R. G. Collingwood, *The Principles of Art*; Bill Brandt, *A Night in London*; first issue of *The London Bulletin*

1939

Events: Germany occupies Czechoslovakia (March); Russo-German Non-Aggression Pact (August); Germany occupies Poland, Britain declares war on Germany (September)
War Artists Advisory Committee established by Kenneth Clark, director of National Gallery; National, Tate and other gallery and museum collections put into store for security reasons
Artists: Naum Gabo, Barbara Hepworth and Ben Nicholson move to St. Ives; Frank Auerbach, Gustav Metzger arrive in Britain; Stanley Spencer commissioned by War Artists Advisory Committee to paint ship-building on the Clyde, resulting in the cycle *Shipbuilding on the Clyde;* Lucian Freud moves to East Anglian School, Denham; Kenneth Armitage leaves Slade, joins army; Roger Hilton joins army, Anthony Donaldson born
Exhibitions: Artists' International Association *Art for the People* at Whitechapel; *Living Art in England* at London Gallery
Publications: Graham Bell, *The Artist and His Public*; last issue of *The Criterion*; first issue of *Poetry London*

DIRECT CARVING

AND THE NOTION OF A "MODERN BRITISH SCULPTURE" INTERNATIONAL OR INSULAR? MODERN OR TRADITIONAL?

PENELOPE CURTIS

PREFACE

The notion of the "tradition of carving" has shackled British sculpture and its historiography, as has the notion of "truth to materials". While attempts have been made in the last ten or fifteen years to show that "truth to materials" is in fact a concept that spreads both backwards (to Ruskin and Arts and Crafts), and sideways (to, for example, German *Jugendstil* and *Bauhaus*), both concepts are still invariably attached to the idea of something especially "British", and especially "Modernist". Artists in other countries practised direct carving (referred to as "*la taille directe*" in France and Germany), but only in Britain did this come to be equated with the way to be modern. Because of this, the canonical story of Modern British Sculpture is entirely premised on direct carving. It runs from Jacob Epstein and Henri Gaudier-Brzeska, through Eric Gill, to Henry Moore and Barbara Hepworth. There have been occasional attempts, in other fori, to show that direct carving need not necessarily have been Modernist.[1] Plenty of sculptors, of many kinds, employed direct carving in the 1920s and 1930s, to the extent that it became something of an orthodoxy. Nevertheless, this wider story has not yet been embedded in the history of British sculpture, and we continue to encounter chapters on "direct carving" written in largely modernist terms.

1 See Charles Harrison, "Sculpture and the New 'New Movement'", in Sandy Nairne and Nick Serota (eds.), *British Sculpture in the Twen-tieth Century*, exh. cat. Whitechapel Art Gallery, London 1981, ch. VIII, pp. 103–111. See also Penelope Curtis, "Barbara Hepworth and the Avant Garde of the 1920s", in *Barbara Hepworth; A Retrospective*, Liverpool and Ontario 1994, pp. 11–28.

All carving is, at face value, direct. When we talk about direct carving, we are, in effect, dismissing a large amount of carving which we do not consider to have been made by artists. To understand the narrower art historical definition of direct carving we need to recognise its inherently self-limiting (and class-ridden) definition, in its narrow art historical sense, as carving by one kind of artist rather than another. It means carvings made by artists for themselves, and not for others, to their own designs, and not those of others.

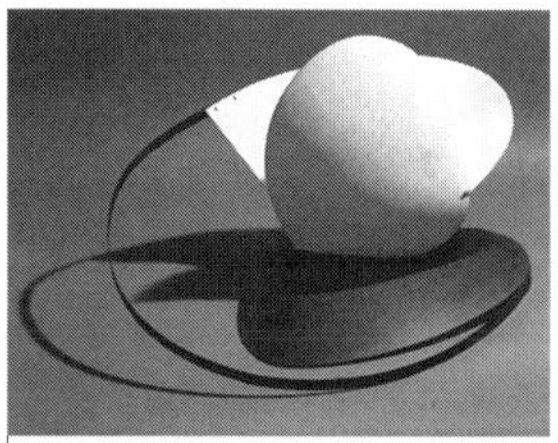

(fig. 1) Naum Gabo CONSTRUCTION: STONE WITH A COLLAR 1933, stone, ivory, brass, slate plinth, c. 40 x 72 cm, Private Collection

It is another accepted truth that artists such as Epstein (pl. 4) and Gaudier-Brzeska, but more especially Moore (pl. 33) and Hepworth (pl. 42), did their best work when they themselves were carving directly. This owes something to the strength of their own early protestations, but it is a narrow view which does not help to illuminate the nature of their creativity.

"Truth to materials" has a religiosity about it, well illustrated by views of the work which Naum Gabo made while he was in Britain, which included carved stone for the first time (fig. 1). These composite pieces, often combining stone with the early Plexiglas for which Gabo is better known, have been viewed as having a humanism which is absent from his truly Constructivist (or non-British) pieces.

(fig. 2) Charles Wheeler LEVERHULME FOUNTAIN GROUP, PORT SUNLIGHT bronze, Leeds Museums and Galleries Collection (Henry Moore Institute Archive)

The talismanic "truth to materials" has run through twentieth century British sculpture well beyond the years when direct carving was first "rediscovered". A belief in its essential "rightness" must lie behind the favours bestowed not only on other direct carvers (notably Peter Randall Page in the last two decades), but on sculptors who have uncovered the truth of their materials by working them themselves. This allows sculptors as diverse as the welders of the late 1950s and 1960s – from Reg Butler (pl. 106) to Anthony Caro (pl. 154) – to Richard Long (pl. 181) in the 1970s and Richard Deacon (pl. 199) and Anish Kapoor (pl. 201) in the 1980s, to be included within the same national story. It is a tradition which would only appear to have moved to the margins in the last decade or so.

(fig. 3) Aristide Maillol VENUS 1918–28, bronze, height 176 cm, Kunsthalle Bremen

The concentration on truth to materials has put a straitjacket on sculpture in Britain in a way it never did to British art in general. The concentration on this one true path has meant that we have neglected not only those artists who continued to use skilled artisans to carve their work, but, more especially, that we have neglected a whole alternative strand: modelling.

(fig. 4) Gerhard Marcks SEATED YOUTH 1937, bronze, 44.7 x 31.1 x 19.7 cm, Museum of Modern Art, New York

There certainly are modellers to be found in Britain, even if they have been dropped from the standard story of British sculpture. Among them, Francis Derwent Wood, Alfred Drury, Alfred Gilbert, John Tweed, Reid Dick, George Frampton, Gilbert Bayes, Sargeant Jagger, J. Havard Thomas and Charles Wheeler (fig. 2). Most of the artists who won the conventional plaudits of the establishment modelled, and the archives of the British School at Rome (for example) are full of photographs of sculptures which are not simply modelled, but also show how these sculptors were looking to an international sculpture which did not interest most of the direct carvers.

(fig. 5) Gilbert Ledward carving a Portland stone sculpture for the Adelphi building, London, c. 1937, vintage photograph, Henry Moore Institute Archive, Leeds

Many modelled works are notable for seeking to render movement in a manner opposite to the "stasis" engendered by direct carving. "Stasis" is indeed a key word found in the writings and statements of many Modernist carvers and stands in marked opposition to the very attempts by European figurative sculptors to capture movement in such a way as to give their sculpture an outwards expansion, a beat, the sense of being held in suspense.

In France what is known as *art indépendant* embraced a range of sculptors who were not in the far vanguard, but whose work was nevertheless understood to be "modern". In Germany "modern sculpture" was very much premised on a subtle and knowledgeable refashioning of figurative modelling. Artists such as these – Aristide Maillol (fig. 3), Charles Despiau, Georg Kolbe, Gerhard Marcks (fig. 4) – or, in other countries, Paul Manship, Carl Milles or Simone Martini – enjoy very little status in Britain. The most powerful modeller, Epstein, has tended to have the modelled part of his *oeuvre* described as that which was driven by largely commercial imperatives. The concentration on direct carving has separated Britain off from European sculpture and did indeed, for better or for worse, make of British sculpture something that was different and more insular.

(fig. 6) Eric Gill MOTHER AND CHILD 1910, Portland stone, 62.2 x 20.3 x 17.1 cm, Leeds Museums and Galleries

(fig. 7) Jacob Epstein standing next to his sculpture NIGHT 1928–29, Portland stone, for the Underground Electric Railways building, 55 Broadway, London

A BRIEF HISTORY OF DIRECT CARVING

Direct carving was only officially integrated into fine art practice in the English academies in the 1930s. Prior to this, it had been available, but as a secondary skill, taught to those who were training to be monumental masons or architectural sculptors. In the 1920s direct carving featured in two quite distinct *milieux*: on the facades of buildings (fig. 5), and in the domestic interior. While the former was associated with tentative moves in modern architecture, the latter was linked to growing connoisseurship in non-western sculpture, and led sculptors to carve in similarly exotic materials. By the 1930s, direct carving

(fig. 8) Frank Dobson TWO HEADS 1921, Mansfield sandstone, 48.3 x 27.9 x 30.5 cm, Courtauld Institute Galleries, London (Courtauld Collection)

was much more clearly established as a modernist or-thodoxy, with a corresponding shift to native materials. This is in line with my argument, which will propose that direct carving has been effectively linked with something especially English. With this shift came the links to the English landscape.

(fig. 9) Gertrude Hermes BABY 1932, carved from chalk pebble, this version in terracotta, LM & G Collection (HMI Archive)

Eric Gill made his first "sculpture" in 1910 (fig. 6). It was executed by the artist who had carved it directly, using the technique he had hitherto used for lettering. Gill's reintegration of art and craft had its roots, as we might suspect, in the distrust shown by John Ruskin and William Morris of industrialisation and the fragmentation of the worker's production. In 1918 Gill published *Sculpture*, subtitled *An Essay on Stone-Cutting, With a Preface About God*. The position which links direct carving with morality – in which English post-Reformation Puritanism resurfaces – is found again to some extent in Moore, but more particularly in Hepworth.

(fig. 10) Maurice Lambert MAN WITH A BIRD 1929, stone, 89 x 20.3 x 19 cm, Tate, London

However, at the beginning of the 1920s those British artists – Eric Gill, Alfred Turner, Harold Parker, Ernest Cole, A. G. Walker – who were known as direct carvers were largely those who worked on monumental projects on the surface of the building. Epstein and Gaudier-Brzeska have been singled out from this group, but Epstein, too, followed the convention of doing his carved work on monumental or architectural projects (fig. 7). Perhaps only Gaudier-Brzeska was completely different, in making carved and modelled works on the same scale, and in the same context (pl.20).

(fig. 11) John Skeaping FISH 1929–30, iron stone, 14.4 x 27.4 x 4.1 cm, Tate, London

By the end of the decade, the scale had shifted. Those British sculptors who were known for their direct carving by the end of the 1920s include Richard Bedford, Alan Durst, Frank Dobson (fig. 8), Barbara Hepworth, Gertrude Hermes (fig. 9), Maurice Lambert (fig. 10), John Skeaping (fig. 11) and Leon Underwood. Their works were mostly small and essentially decorative. In their reflection of Art Deco they, too, indicate a context which is less purely British.

Their supporters – the critics Stanley Casson and, more guardedly, Kineton Parkes, alongside W. H. Wilenski and Eric Underwood – were, by 1930, beginning to acknowledge their doubts about the increasing hold of direct carving. Given that these authors had a Europe-wide knowledge of modern sculpture, it is not too much to suggest that they express (though not explicitly) a nervousness about the developing insularity which direct carving would bring with it.[2]

In 1931 Barbara Hepworth was asking her dealer if she could have a separate contract from her husband, John Skeaping, because her work was becoming increasingly abstract (pl. 32). This is one of several signals marking out the next wave in British direct carving. Another signal is that, from 1930, the artists become increasingly involved in writing about their own practice: writing directly, carving directly. Moore and Hepworth published important statements in 1930, 1934 and 1937.[3] The 1930s also saw the emergence of professional writers – notably Herbert Read[4] and Adrian Stokes[5] – who were fascinated by the rich potential (and analogies) within the discipline of direct carving for the genesis and development of prose.

Henry Moore held his second solo show in 1931. This was also the year in which Herbert Read first wrote about him, some two years after they had first met in the Director's office of the Victoria and Albert Museum. The article which Read had written for the BBC magazine *The Listener* was reprinted in *The Meaning of Art*, a canonical book published by Faber & Faber later that year. In order to appreciate Moore, Read asked his readers to go back to first principles. What was sculpture? Sculpture was carving. So far, so good. But Moore looked also to stone as a material which bears the marks of wind and water (pl. 31). And then he looked to translate his idea into stone. Lastly, Read describes

2 An important event and example in Britain was the 1915 exhibition of the work of Ivan Meštrović which opened at the Victoria and Albert Museum to great success and confirmed him as a carver of great facility. Stanley Casson saw Meštrović as exemplifying Vasari's dictum "that a sculptor sees in his block of marble an idea that has already grown in his mind" (Stanley Casson, *Some Modern Sculptors*, London 1928, p. 59). As Casson goes on to assert, Eric Gill's warnings that "Carvers in stone must have in their minds before they begin a complete and perfect knowledge of the forms they wish to create" are "simple and clear but not original", having been prefaced by Vasari, "Rodin, Meštrović and all the great sculptors" (pp. 88 ff.). The difference then, is surely that Gill has been seen to form part of a distinctively British heritage. Casson praised Gaudier-Brzeska for his bronze work and described him as an independent-minded sculptor, who "as is obvious [...] worked direct upon the stone" (p. 96). At the very end of his book, Casson lamented Epstein's loss of maturity in his modelled work: "So great is the loss of style and technique to a sculptor who abandons stone" (p. 116).

3 Henry Moore in the *Architectural Association Journal* of 1930, Barbara Hepworth in *The Studio* of 1932, *Unit One* of 1934 and *Circle* of 1937.

4 Herbert Read wrote the preface to the catalogue of Hepworth's exhibition at the Tooth Galleries in November 1932.

5 Stokes reviewed *Miss Hepworth's carvings*, shown at the Reid & Lefèvre Gallery, in November 1932.

Moore's process as four-dimensional: growing out of a conception which inheres in the mass.

"Form is then an intuition of surface made by the sculptor imaginatively situated at the centre of gravity of the block before him. Under the guidance of this intuition, the stone is slowly educated from an arbitrary into an ideal state of existence."[6]

The praise of stone was developed by the critic Adrian Stokes, especially in his *Stones of Rimini* of 1934, which begins "I write of stone", in a first chapter entitled "Stone and Water". Like Read, Stokes talks of time in the form of weather, of "days and nights", of "'warmth and wet'". He goes on to develop "The Pleasures of Limestone", introducing his notion of "the 'stoniness' of stone". Stokes demands that a "basic distinction be made between what is carving conception and what is plastic or modelling conception [...]".

"In view of the Germans and their horrid noun *Plastik*, one cannot emphasise too strongly that sculptural values are not synonymous with plastic values."[7]

This is a point worth remembering, in the current discussion of carved sculpture, as is the point which Stokes goes on to make, which is that photography favours modelling over carving.[8]

Stokes' elaboration of the creed would appear to have encouraged the increasing interest in polish and surface finish. His idiosyncratic book conjured up a new comprehension of what it might mean to work stone, a notion that had less to do with resistance and more to do with caressing. In line with this is a deeper comprehension of the sculpture as an intimate and inalienable product of the sculptor. At the same time, links with the continental debate in painting also led to a greater focus on the surface and graphic qualities of the carved line.

Stokes helped Hepworth to write her contribution for *Unit One*; Read helped Moore. While Stokes' vocabulary worked well in tandem with Hepworth's in terms of the "stone-shape", Read's developing interest in "vitality" was ultimately to serve Moore much better. In the longer run, Hepworth's carvings tended towards the quiescent (fig. 12), whereas Moore's provided the liveliness which Read – as the

6 Herbert Read, *The Meaning of Art*, London 1931, p. 153.

7 Adrian Stokes, *Stones of Rimini*, 1934, new ed. New York 1969, pp. 107 f.

8 A point which I wished to make in my recent exhibition of German modelled sculpture from the Third Reich, which photographed very well then, and still does. See *Taking Positions*, exh. cat. Henry Moore Institute, Leeds 2001.

(fig. 12) Barbara Hepworth CARVING 1932, grey Cumberland alabaster, height 25.5 cm, Mrs Irene Brumwell

pre-eminent international art critic of the immediate post-war period – did so much to foster (fig. 13). Moore's swift rise to fame did much to assert the importance of direct carving, and Read's monographs on Moore (1944) and then Hepworth (1952) asserted their importance, and with it, the importance of carving.

A POST-WAR HISTORIOGRAPHY: HOW MODERN BRITISH SCULPTURE CAME TO MEAN CARVED

We have sketched the outlines of direct carving in the twenties and thirties and the principal authors associated with its development. But this story is well known, even if some of the writers are no longer read. More useful, perhaps, will be to look at how carving has come to be so indissolubly associated with "modern British sculpture", and to do this we need to look at how the story of sculpture has been told in the last fifty years.

Moore was unusual in being the single English sculptor who was also incorporated into international histories of modern sculpture. On these occasions, he was normally positioned alongside Constantin Brancusi and Jean Arp in making "organic abstract sculpture" inspired by his materials.[9]

The story of Moore's place within a national school, and of English sculpture *per se*, is told rather differently, and rather infrequently. Although the story of English Modernism is, in a sense, all about attaining interaction with the Continent by the mid 1930s, it is ultimately an internalised story with only brief moments of internationalism, largely centred upon Paris.

In 1949 E. H. Ramsden, a notable and active critic in the post-war period, proposed that "it is as carvers rather than as modellers that English sculptors have

9 A. C. Ritchie, *Sculpture of the Twentieth Century*, exh. cat. MOMA, New York 1952, p. 24, and Herbert Read, *Modern Sculpture*, London 1964. Alan Bowness, in his *Modern Sculpture* of 1965, also credits modern sculpture with the revival of direct carving (p. 114).

(fig. 13) Henry Moore RECLINING FIGURE 1929, Hoptonwood stone, 84 x 57 x 38 cm, Leeds Museums and Galleries

excelled".[10] Like Read, Ramsden believed that "such was the level of mediocrity to which sculpture had fallen by the end of the last century that it is probable that without the regaining of a primitive vitality and a return to the direct method sculpture as an art would scarcely have survived".[11] Writers seem to conjoin carving and Modernism within a story which is English rather than British.

Ramsden occupies an unusual place as a critic, Renaissance art historian and artist. She was British, but her book was international in scope. Abraham Marie Hammacher, on the other hand, is more straightforwardly a professional critic, but unusual for writing a history of "English sculpture" from a continental viewpoint. His 1967 account sets the scene in insular terms which differ very little from those of Eric Underwood in his *A Short History of Sculpture*, thirty years earlier.[12]

Hammacher: "Throughout her history, England had failed to come forward with sculpture of importance. There had been anonymous Anglo-Norman carving; a vigorous sculpture in stone and wood in and outside the cathedrals and a charming production of panels and images in alabaster which became an industry and lasted into the fifteenth century. Up until the present no English critic or historian has written a more or less complete survey of the amazing phenomenon that in this country in the twentieth century, within less than fifty years, a sculpture came into being which not only held its own beside continental European sculpture, but which even determined to an important extent the aspect of twentieth-century sculpture [...].
[...] the English history of sculpture, in the important context of a characteristically local artistic life, is still awaiting its English exposition."[13]

To what extent was Hammacher's understanding of English sculpture premised upon direct carving as it was for Underwood in 1933?
"Gill is almost certainly the greatest carver in the world today; his work is in the purest English tradition; in it can be seen again the dramatic quality of Saxon sculpture, the grace of Nottingham alabasters, the austere formalisation of the Romanesque – this especially, the simplicity of the best Gothic and even something of these earlier and better times which still lingers in the Tudor and Stuart tombs."[14]

(We might note that though Casson, too, at around the same time, saw Gill's carving as being "as English as the faces and forms of the Nottingham alabaster carvings of the fourteenth and fifteenth centuries" [fig. 14], he defines Gill's Englishness in terms of being "neither an inventor nor an innovator".)[15]

Hammacher goes on to delineate this "peculiar insular life", naming Leon Underwood and Frank Dobson, and moving on to Moore's promotion of "truth to materials" and the "direct carving idea". Though Hammacher acknowledges the "corrections" which this idea has undergone – partly by means of sculptors' own practice (including Hepworth's move away from a "puritan clinging to 'direct carving' in wood, marble or stone"), and partly by means of the discussion of Moore's contemporary work opened up by the critics David Sylvester and John Russell after 1951 – he nevertheless develops his discussion of Hepworth in terms of the tradition of wood, stone and marble and the very old English tradition of carving in alabaster.[16]

Thirty years after Hammacher, we find Daniel Abadie, in his *Un siècle de sculpture anglaise*, making a similar bid for an English sculpture, founded, he asserts, on Epstein's *The Rock Drill* (pl. 17), and developed by Moore, Hepworth and Ben Nicholson in terms of their unison of pure form and direct carving.

The 1981 Whitechapel catalogue of *British Sculpture in the Twentieth Century* does not specifically devote a chapter to direct carving, although apparently ready to accept it as received wisdom. In that catalogue Charles Harrison interestingly highlights the two: "It has generally been considered that a commitment to carving – as against modelling – and to 'truth to materials' was the principal pointer to modernist ambition among sculptors, but this is to underestimate both the extent to which carving was practised among exhibitors in the Academy and the persistence of monumental and ecclesiastical carving as means of employment even for many with modern interests."[17]

In the same year, Harrison published his own book, *English Art and Modernism 1900–1939*, with a chapter devoted to "The Development of Modernism in Sculp-

(fig. 14) Eric Gill CRUCIFIX c. 1913, Hoptonwood stone, 45.2 x 17.1 x 4.1 cm, Tate, London

10 E. H. Ramsden, *Twentieth Century Sculpture*, London 1949, p. 17.
11 Ibid., pp. 16 ff.

12 London 1933.

13 Abraham Marie Hammacher, *Modern English Sculpture*, London 1967, p. 5.

14 Eric Underwood, *A Short History of English Sculpture*, London 1933, p. 156.
15 Casson 1928 (see note 2), p. 88.
16 Hammacher 1967 (see note 13), p. 28.

17 In his essay "Sculpture and the New 'New Movement'", p. 103.

ture". Harrison emphasises the importance of writers in establishing the importance of direct carving (singling out T. E. Hulme for Epstein and Ezra Pound for Gaudier-Brzeska), and stresses that, through the writings of Reginald Wilenski, among others, Epstein's Modernism was seen to reside entirely in his carved work. On the other hand, by the time Epstein was published in monographic form, his writers concentrated on the modelled work which dominated the post-war period.

In the Royal Academy's 1987 survey of *British Art in the 20th Century*, Richard Cork entitled his essay "The Emancipation of Modern British Sculpture". How was sculpture emancipated? And from what? There is here, I think, an unwritten assumption that it was emancipa-

ted by means of direct carving, and emancipated from the thrall of statuary.[18] Cork's story is a familiar one, largely fashioned in a monographic sequence such as we see here. This abbreviated story is the story of direct carving, and, as it moves into Reg Butler, Anthony Caro and Richard Long, the story of truth to materials. But there are other stories to tell, not least that direct carving can be as regressive as progressive, not only in the beginning of the century, but also at the end. Telling these stories might allow us to not only to break away from this well known cast of characters, but also to cut loose from our Island Story.

18 See also the 1998 exhibition *Carving Mountains. Modern Stone Sculpture in England 1907–37*, arranged by Kettle's Yard, 'Cambridge, which singled out Dobson, Epstein, Gaudier-Brzeska, Gill, Hepworth, Moore, Nicholson and Skeaping, in terms not only of their sculpture, but also of their writing.

GOING MODERN AND BEING BRITISH

THE CHALLENGE OF THE 1930s

JEREMY LEWISON

The 1920s had been a period of reconstruction, recovery and mourning in England following the devastation of the First World War. The impression of political stability and recovery was consistently undermined by strikes and there was a widespread feeling that the war had been a watershed in which the pre-war order had disintegrated and been replaced by something more fluid and unstable. The Great Crash at the end of the decade was proof that the recovery had been merely illusory, as the British economy was thrown into turmoil.

The belligerent attitudes of the Vorticists and the dilute experimentalism of the artists associated with Bloomsbury had been replaced in the early 1920s by a renewed interest in Paul Cézanne, André Derain, the Italian "primitives" – particularly Piero della Francesca and Fra Angelico – and a growing interest in the late Cubist work of Georges Braque and Pablo Picasso. Landscape became a dominant motif in the work of younger artists, as they sought to reconstruct the devastated landscape of war and retrieve a memory of a prelapsarian idyll. Still life was another, as artists evoked a domestic harmony that excluded the changing nature of the world outside.

At the end of the decade, the art market was severely affected by the economic slump, and younger artists with pretensions to avant-garde practice were particularly badly hit. There were few exhibiting opportunities and very few collectors interested in modernist art. Indeed, in 1932 Paul Nash could ask, in a now celebrated article, whether it was "possible to 'Go Modern' and still 'Be British'".[1] Responding to a series of articles in the conservative *Studio* magazine, Nash bemoaned the fact that artists were being asked "to abandon all research, all experiment; to close our eyes to the vital art of other lands – in short to be British". Nash optimistically maintained that this was a patronising misreading of the English public. In the early 1930s there was a crisis of confidence in the ability of English artists to match their foreign counterparts for interest, experimentalism and genius. Herbert Read, who was to become the leading art critic in the world through a succession of best-selling books written in the 1930s – *The Meaning of Art* (1931), *Art Now* (1933), *Art and Industry* (1934), *Surrealism* (1936) (fig. 1) and *Art and Society* (1937) – as well as a prodigious number of articles published in English and foreign magazines, wrote in 1930: "We have talent in plenty, but no outstanding genius – no Picasso or Matisse, for example." But worse than that, he identified that English artists were individualists: "[...] we have no cohesion; our artists do not make a programme, do not present a united front or generate a common intensity of any kind".[2] Read regretted that there had been no schools or movements in England during the 1920s to match those in Germany or France. Vorticism had disappeared after an abortive revival in Percy Wyndham Lewis'

(fig. 1) Cover of Herbert Read's SURREALISM (1936), collage of Roland Penrose

1 Paul Nash, "'Going Modern' and 'Being British'", *The Week End Review*, 12 March 1932, p. 322.

2 Herbert Read, "Art in Two Countries", *The Listener*, vol. 4, 22 October 1930, p. 660.

Group X in 1920, the Seven and Five Society was no more than a genteel exhibiting group masquerading as avant-garde, the London Group had no bite and Bloomsbury had retreated to rural pursuits in Sussex and the South of France. All this was to change in the 1930s, as English artists made regular contact with their foreign and, in particular, Parisian counterparts leading to the formation of groups, magazines, in which English art was seen alongside continental art, and rapid shifts of alliances and allegiances. By 1933 John Piper was able to write, somewhat ahead of actuality: "Twenty years ago artistic London was a long way behind Paris: today the distance between the two capitals is small indeed."[3] Paris was the measure of artistic originality and success.

3 John Piper, "Young English Painters 1", *The Listener*, vol. 9, 22 March 1933, p. 450.

In the late 1920s a handful of English artists had settled in Paris, among them Anthony Gross and Stanley William Hayter. Gross befriended Balthus and made paintings consciously in the tradition of the *flâneur*, concentrating on scenes from urban life as well as rural idylls, while Hayter became involved in Surrealism (fig. 2). In 1927 Hayter set up an *atelier* in Paris to carry out research into the techniques of engraving, a medium to which he had been introduced by Joseph Hecht. In 1933 Hayter moved to 17, rue Campagne-Première and it was from this address that Atelier 17, as it came to be known, took its name. More than simply a teaching studio, it was a place where artists of all nationalities would gather to make prints and experiment with the medium, and as such it was a meeting place for artists of diverse artistic inclinations living in Paris. Among those with whom Hayter associated were Jean Arp, André Masson, Alexander Calder, Joan Miró, Alberto Giacometti, Picasso, Max Ernst and Oskar Kokoschka, most of whom, at various times, made use of his facilities. As an Englishman in Paris he also became the first port of call for his countrymen. Thus, when Ben Nicholson arrived in Paris to visit his estranged wife Winifred and their children at Christmas 1932, one of the first people with whom he made contact was Hayter, an artist with whom he had had no direct contact before. Through Hayter he also encountered Julian Trevelyan, who had moved to

(fig. 2) Stanley William Hayter
DELIQUESCENCE 1935, oil on wood, 99.1 × 200 cm, Tate, London

Paris in the previous year (pl. 60). Hayter became a conduit for information about Parisian art in the 1930s.

Nicholson had been a frequent visitor to Paris between 1921 and 1923 and was there again in 1930, when he held a show jointly with Christopher Wood at Galerie Georges Bernheim. The French considered his paintings charmingly naïve but somewhat out of the mainstream. His frequent sojourns in Paris from 1932 to 1938, when Winifred was in residence there, had a dramatic effect on his art. Arriving in 1932 his heroes were Braque and Picasso, both of whom he met early on. By 1933 he had made his way to the studios of Arp, Constantin Brancusi (fig. 3), Auguste Herbin and Jean Hélion and discovered a strong interest in the work of Miró and Calder. Alongside his still life paintings indebted to the late Cubism of Braque and Picasso, Nicholson developed the practice of carving reliefs in which the imagery of Miró and Calder was allied with the playful qualities of Giacometti's carvings. During the period when Nicholson's works were at their most austere, when he purged his reliefs of colour and painted them white (pl. 38), he still admired Giacometti above all other artists in Paris (fig. 4),[4] notwithstanding his admiration for Piet Mondrian, whom he met in 1934.

4 Letter to Herbert Read, dated 24 January 1936. For a discussion of the impact of Giacometti on Nicholson see Jeremy Lewison, *Ben Nicholson*, exh. cat. Tate Gallery, London 1993, p. 41.

(fig. 3) Constantin Brancusi self-portrait in the studio, 1933

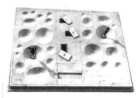

(fig. 4) Alberto Giacometti ON NE JOUE PLUS 1932, marble, wood, bronze, 4.1 × 58 × 45.1 cm, National Gallery of Art, Washington, D. C., Gift of Patsy R. and Raymond D. Nasher Collection, Dallas, in Honour of the 50th Anniversary of the National Gallery of Art

Nicholson's appropriation of different approaches to making art – the automatism of Surrealism in paintings of 1932 and 1933, geometric abstraction in the paintings and reliefs of late 1933 and succeeding years, the Cubist depiction of domestic objects from the mid 1920s onwards – was evidence of an artist intent on not only catching up with continental developments, but wanting to fight on the front line (fig. 5). In 1933 Nicholson, together with Barbara Hepworth (pl. 32), was invited to become a member of Abstraction-Création, an exhibiting society which brought together artists allegedly *non-figuratifs*, although it made no distinction between geometric, constructive or biomorphic abstraction. They were not the first British artists to be invited in: Edward Wadsworth (pl. 21) and Marlow Moss joined in 1932, while Paule Vézelay became a member in 1934. It had become the practice of the French avant-garde to form societies and groups. The Surrealists had gathered under the leadership of André Breton, the Purists under the wing of *L'Esprit nouveau* and, in 1930, the abstract artists had joined either Cercle et Carré, led by Michel Seuphor, or Art Concret under Jean Hélion and Theo van Doesburg. When Read bemoaned the non-existence of groups or movements in Britain, he undoubtedly had some of these models in mind.

(fig. 5) Ben Nicholson c. 1936 (SCULPTURE) c. 1936, painted wood, 22.8 x 30.5 x 24.1 cm, Tate, London

The formation of Unit One in London in 1933 had half an eye to the Continent. In an exchange of letters between Paul Nash, its founding chairman, and the Canadian architect resident in London, Wells Coates, who initially took on the role of secretary, Nash suggested that the group be called English Contemporary Group because it was "simple and sufficiently explanatory – especially for foreigners".5 Nash and Coates consulted Henry Moore and Wadsworth, in selecting artists to join the "unit", and eventually determined on John Armstrong (pl. 63), Edward Burra (pl. 57), John Bigge, Barbara Hepworth (pl. 34), Tristram Hillier, Ben Nicholson and the architect Colin Lucas, in addition to the original quartet. Unit One was an uneasy alliance of painters, sculptors and architects with the intention of forming a united front against the English distaste for the avant-garde and Modernism and continuing devotion to Cézanne and Derain. It was both a market ploy and a bid to assert the importance of modernism in England. As Nash explained it in a letter to the *Times*, published on 12 June 1933, the group stood "for the expression of a truly contemporary spirit, for the thing which is recognised as peculiarly *of today* in painting, sculpture and architecture". He intimated that its origins and counterpart were to be found abroad.

5 Letter from Nash to Coates dated 19 January 1933, Tate Archive.

Nash stated that Unit One artists rejected "the great Unconscious School of Painting" but in fact the group manifested a number of different tendencies, including that of Surrealism. It represented a melting pot of continental influences harnessed to the idioms of English art. Nash's paintings of the English landscape were enlivened by the unexpected and dislocated appearance of familiar objects (fig. 6); Nicholson's geometric reliefs retained a memory of the Arts and Crafts movement (pl. 38); Moore's Picassoesque sculptures were made from English stone; Wadsworth's biomorphic images, painstakingly painted in tempera, displayed a considerable debt to Arp, while Burra's decadent images were redolent of Neue Sachlichkeit painting but laced with a particularly English sense of irony (pl. 40).

(fig. 6) Paul Nash EVENT ON THE DOWNS 1934, oil on canvas, Leeds City Art Gallery

At the end of the first year, after holding a successful touring exhibition in London and the regions, Unit One disbanded following elections to its membership that resulted in only Moore and Nash being reelected. Nash, together with Wadsworth, Coates and Moore, attempted, with the wise counsel of Read, to reformulate the Unit along the lines of the Bauhaus, but it never got off the ground. The exhibition had been well attended – over 30,000 people visited the Liverpool showing in four weeks – and had shown that there was an appetite among the public for modern art. But the strains within the group, which divided more or less along lines of interest in either Surrealism or abstraction, were too great for it to continue to cohere.

Unit One had little impact abroad. Nicholson tried unsuccessfully to interest Christian Zervos in Paris to hold an exhibition and to give the movement some publicity in *Cahiers d'Art*. However, Read's article on British art, published in that magazine in 1938, was the product of Nicholson's persistence. In fact Nicholson became one of the principal conduits for information about art in Paris, as he travelled back and forth to visit his children. He provided introductions to Paris-based artists for his British colleagues and regularly showed photographs of the work of his English contemporaries to his foreign friends. When French artists came to London – for example Hélion, Braque and Fernand Léger in 1934 – Nicholson guided them around or invited them to his and Hepworth's residence in Hampstead. But Nicholson was not the only conduit for information and introductions. Roland Penrose, artist, writer and collector, was also based in Paris and was fully integrated into the circle of Surrealists. He, too, became a port of call for visiting English artists.

JEREMY LEWISON

Among one of Nicholson's most effective introductions was that of Myfanwy Evans to Jean Hélion. Hélion urged and inspired her to found a magazine that was to be published as *Axis*. It set out to be a periodical supporting the abstract movement, in which English artists would be discussed side by side and on an equal footing with their continental counterparts. Alongside its British contributors, among whom were Read, Piper and Geoffrey Grigson, it ranged, among others, Jan Tschichold, Anatole Jakovski, Wassily Kandinsky, Will Grohmann, Herta Wescher and Hélion himself. However, it always expressed a certain unease with being a journal exclusively supporting abstraction. In the first issue Grigson wrote: "Abstract art at this time needs […] to be bodied out in such a way; to be penetrated and possessed by a more varied affective and intellective content. Only so can it answer to the ideological and emotional complexity of the needs of human beings with their enlarged knowledge of the widened country of self."[6] Grigson was never happy with pure or geometric abstraction and soon declared his allegiance to the Romantic revival, in the form of Neo-Romanticism. As far as the English contribution to international abstraction was concerned, he remarked: "I see in [it] a small history of English ideas, English hesitancy, English error and English performance."[7] *Axis* was important, however, in raising the level of debate within Britain. Whereas in the first issue Read would regret that "we have reached a stage at which the everyday vocabulary of criticism is proving inadequate and therefore confusing" to the task of discussing contemporary art, by the time *Axis* ceased publication in 1937, the modern movement had become familiar to the public and its discussion more sophisticated.[8] In spring 1936 Evans had devoted issue number five to the promotion of the *Abstract and Concrete* exhibition organised by Nicolete Gray, which opened in Oxford in February and toured to Liverpool, Cambridge and London. Advised by Nicholson, Gray selected a range of international abstract artists and showed them alongside English artists. It was, in some respects, an English equivalent to the exhibitions of Abstraction-Création, for the exhibition refused to promote a coherent approach to abstraction. It included artists as various as Nicholson, Hepworth, Arthur Jack-

son, Piper and Moore from the British contingent, and Léger, Kandinsky, Miró, Mondrian, Naum Gabo, Giacometti and Hélion from Paris.

This lack of focus was immediately apparent when certain artists exhibited simultaneously in the *International Surrealist Exhibition* at the New Burlington Galleries, London. It opened in the same month as the London showing of *Abstract and Concrete*, thus providing the public with the opportunity to see Calder, Moore, Miró and Giacometti in two different contexts. The Surrealists and the advocates of abstraction each claimed these artists as their adherents, in a period when turf wars were being waged. As Evans put it in an article titled "Order, Order!": "The battle has been pitched between abstract painting and sculpture and Surrealist painting and sculpture; but there it cannot flourish. It is a silly battle. There are too many painters who do not paint in the name of either (though they have been claimed by one of the two or by both). […] [Artists] reserve the right to alter according to their inclination and nature, and not according to a group-programme."[9]

The *International Surrealist Exhibition* was the culmination of a growing interest in Surrealism in Britain. First encountered through such magazines in the 1920s as *Transatlantic Review* and *Transition*, all available from Zwemmer's bookshop in London, the advent of *Cahiers d'Art*, and *Minotaure* in the 1930s had perhaps the greatest impact. Surrealism in Britain began principally as a literary movement, with poems and texts by David Gascoyne and Hugh Sykes Davies among others, and penetrated the corridors of academe, particularly Cambridge University, where Humphrey Jennings held court. It was there that Julian Trevelyan was first introduced to the concept of modernity and where Jennings judged art by whether or not it had "1931ness" or not. By the mid 1930s, however, with Penrose, Trevelyan, John Banting and Eileen Agar all at various times in Paris, it penetrated painting and sculpture.

English artists never adopted the rebellious or highly politicised stance of continental Surrealism but adapted it to an English idiom. Disruption was one of their key strategies, whether it was the depiction of a Swiss roll in the sky (Jennings, in the manner of René Magritte) or a group of geometric megaliths standing in the English countryside (Nash, with reference to Giorgio de Chirico and Brancusi). There was also consider-

6 Geoffrey Grigson, "Comment on England", *Axis*, no. 1, January 1935, p. 8.

7 Grigson 1935.

8 Herbert Read, "Our Terminology", *Axis*, no. 1, January 1935, p. 6. There were eight issues of *Axis*. The last appeared in early winter 1937.

9 Myfanwy Evans, "Order, Order!", *Axis*, no. 6, summer 1936, p. 8.

able emphasis, as in France, on eroticism, violence and desire, particularly in the work of Penrose (pl. 53), F. E McWilliam (fig. 7) and Edith Rimmington, but somehow this was very un-English. In the main, it was as though the puritan tradition prevented English artists from delving into the subconscious, for fear of releasing the uncontrollable. They stayed with perceived reality but heightened it to create a sense of the super-real.[10] Thus, Wadsworth did not regard himself as a Surrealist but as a painter of still lifes, where objects were disconcertingly depicted with a sharpened sense of realism. Nash, too, never deviated from the depiction of real objects, although he sometimes placed them in unexpected contexts. To that extent, Nash's approach was akin to that of a *collagiste*. His was an art of insertion.

10 I do not use this word in the sense implied by Herbert Read, who tried to insert it in the place of surreal. Rather I imply a distinction between the super-real, as something more than real, and the surreal which, being based on fantasy, is less than real.

(fig. 7) F. E. McWilliam LONG ARM (FIST RAISED IN REPUBLICAN SALUTE) 1939, lime wood, painted, 188 x 7 x 17 cm, Dr. Jeffrey and Ruth Sherwin, Leeds

The publication of Gascoyne's *First Manifesto of English Surrealism* in 1935 was followed shortly after by his *Short Survey of Surrealism* (fig. 8). Gascoyne thus became a spokesman. He was not, however, the instigator of the *International Surrealist Exhibition*. That fell to Penrose and Read. André Breton and Paul Eluard, friends of Penrose, had planned to visit London to initiate talks. Penrose set up an organising committee consisting of himself, Read, Nash, Moore, Rupert Lee and Hugh Sykes Davies. They were joined at a later stage by Gascoyne, Man Ray and Jennings, among others. There was little problem in choosing the continental artists, many of whom were already well known – some had even previously shown in London in such galleries as the Mayor Gallery – but the representation of British artists proved more problematic, simply because Surrealism in Britain was not only a new phenomenon, but impure. The result was a selection of artists such as Edward Burra, Cecil Collins (fig. 9), Merlyn Evans (fig. 10) and Paul Nash, who might not have been recognised by their Parisian counterparts as Surrealist.

The exhibition was a resounding success and was visited by more than 23,000 visitors. In terms of public impact it had considerably more than *Abstract and Concrete*, not least because of the programme of events

and lectures that took place, including talks by Breton and Read, and by Salvador Dalí in a diving suit in which he nearly suffocated. There were also idiosyncratic "interventions" by Sheila Legge, who wandered around at the opening dressed in a long white satin dress, her face covered in roses, and the poet Dylan Thomas, who walked around offering teacups filled with boiled string enquiring "do you like it weak or strong?"[11]

Disconcerted by the popularity of Surrealism and determined to offer some countermeasure, Nicholson, Gabo and the architect, Leslie Martin, plotted to produce a magazine to replace *Axis*, that was to be known as *Circle*.[12] It appeared a year later in 1937, as an international survey of Constructive art, bringing together painting, sculpture, design, architecture, science and the performing arts in a blueprint for a utopian, integrated, modernist society of cleanliness, clarity and fine design, where art and life would bind seamlessly together. While Surrealist fantasy dwelt on the grotesque and erotic, Constructivist fantasy concentrated on the pure and platonic. With contributions from Mondrian, Gabo, Le Corbusier, Léonide Massine, Sigfried Giedion, Marcel Breuer and Walter Gropius, among others, it was every bit as international as the Surrealist exhibition of the previous year. Its optimism and utopian outlook were mistimed, however, given the background of the Spanish Civil War and the impending annexation of Eastern Europe by the Nazi regime in Germany.

The rivalry between the Surrealist and Constructivist camps did not endure indefinitely. Indeed, as the international crisis worsened, they came together in their affiliation with the Artists' International Association that mounted exhibitions in aid of such causes as the Republican forces in Spain. They also found themselves side by side in the *London Bulletin*, a magazine established in 1938. This was edited by E. L. T. Mesens, who had first arrived in

11 See Michel Rémy, *Surrealism in Britain*, Aldershot 1999, p. 76.
12 In the event, *Circle* only had one number. The outbreak of war in 1939 rendered it impossible to print a second number. Moreover, the optimism enshrined in *Circle* had been overtaken by events.

(fig. 8) Cover of David Gascoyne, A SHORT SURVEY OF SURREALISM (1935), design by Max Ernst

(fig. 9) Cecil Collins OBSEQUIES OF TIME 1933, charcoal, pen, black ink, and gum on paper, 38 x 55.8 cm, Dr. Jeffrey and Ruth Sherwin, Leeds

(fig. 10) Merlyn Evans TYRANNOPOLIS 1939, oil on canvas, 33 x 44 cm, Dr. Jeffrey and Ruth Sherwin, Leeds

London to hang the *International Surrealist Exhibition*, but who was retained by Penrose and Anton Zwemmer to manage the London Gallery that they had taken over in April that year. The *London Bulletin* was a timely replacement for *Axis*, although less lavishly produced. It began life as an organ of the Surrealist movement with Jennings and then Penrose as editorial assistants but, within a year, was promoting the work of Nicholson and other Constructivist artists. Its outlook was decidedly international, to reflect the international centre that London had become. By the late 1930s London was home to many refugees from fascism including Breuer, Gabo, Gropius, Kokoschka, László Moholy-Nagy and Mondrian, to the extent that Read could write with pride in 1939 about the exhibition *Living Art in England*: "One of the objects of the present exhibition is to demonstrate the extent to which England, and more particularly London, has become what Paris has always been – an international art centre."[13] For a brief moment, London was an important centre for European modernism. The programme of exhibitions at the London Gallery, the Mayor Gallery, Guggenheim Jeune and Alex Reid and Lefèvre regularly promoted the work of continental artists and British artists on an equal footing, which had not been the case in London in the previous decade. In the 1920s the Parisian avant-garde had barely been visible and there had been precious few opportunities for younger British artists to show in the West End. By the late 1930s, London had come of age.

13 Herbert Read, *London Bulletin*, January/February 1939, p. 5.

(fig. 11) Dame Laura Knight
THE GIPSY before 1939, oil on canvas, 61 x 40.6 cm, Tate, London

(fig. 12) Meredith Frampton
PORTRAIT OF A YOUNG WOMAN
1935, Oil on canvas, 205.7 x 107.9 cm, Tate, London

Of course, the history of English art in this period is not simply that of a contest between Surrealism and abstraction. Still life and landscape continued to be painted with painstaking accuracy, as exemplified in the work of William Nicholson, Ben's father. At the Royal Academy the President, Alfred Munnings, continued to resist modernism and satisfied the upper class penchant for sporting art, while Laura Knight depicted gypsies and circus troops, the rural underclass (fig. 11). Among others, Meredith Frampton painted chillingly elegant portraits and allegories (fig. 12)

and Algernon Newton's intensely clear depictions of the streets and canals of London represented the pastoralisation of the inner city (fig. 13). Among British artists abroad, David Bomberg, based in Spain, executed brooding, expressionist landscapes, celebrating the unrelenting heat and dramatic forms of the Spanish landscape.

(fig. 13) Algernon Newton
THE SURREY CANAL, CAMBERWELL
1935, oil on canvas, 71.8 x 91.4 cm, Tate, London

The narrative tradition remained a potent force in the work of Stanley Spencer, who combined the allegory and attention to detail of the pre-Raphaelites with an idiosyncratic style of painting that owed much to the Italian "primitives", as well as to an appreciation of his English forebears, William Blake and Samuel Palmer. Rooted in Cookham, Berkshire, Spencer's paintings were as much about a sense of place as Nash's, although his principal subjects were domestic: his unconsummated marriage with Patricia Preece (pl. 49) and his fantasy of living in a domestic paradise with Hilda Carline (his first wife). Spencer's work, however, was no more naturalistic than Ben Nicholson's still lifes or Moore's female figures (pl. 31). Each of these artists started from close observation, before subjecting their motifs to abstraction and distortion, in pursuit of a personal expression of an inner reality.

In response to this flight from naturalism, Graham Bell and William Coldstream established the Euston Road School to which they attracted Claude Rogers, Victor Pasmore, Geoffrey Tibble and Rodrigo Moynihan. Believing, as did many, that art had lost touch with its public and was closeted in an ivory tower, their programme was based on the depiction of everyday life in a gritty, realistic manner.[14] Bell and Coldstream, as well as Trevelyan, had been together in Bolton, in the north of England, in connection with Mass Observation, a programme to chart the lives of the working classes in the finest detail. For the Euston Road affiliates, art had to have a commitment to realism and to craftsmanship, and both had to be readily evident to the public. Above all, they sought contact with the public through their art.

14 Read and the critic Anthony Blunt were among those who held polarised views on this matter. Read argued that the separation of the artist from society was determined by the conditions in which he found himself. He suggested that the artist should carry on with his experimentation, honing his skills, until such time as society was in a condition to make best use of him. Blunt, on the other hand, writing from a communist point of view, was out of sympathy with what he regarded as art for art's sake and claimed that art should have a public purpose and be readily intelligible.

Among the antecedents of the Euston Road School was Walter Richard Sickert, who, towards the end of his life, turned away from reality observed to the depiction of people and places mediated through photography and reproductive prints. His indirect engagement with the motif paralleled his withdrawal from the world, following a breakdown in 1926 and the onset of ill-health. Sickert effectively abandoned direct speech for translation, at the same time returning to the reproduced object its "aura" and uniqueness, its hand-made quality.[15]

15 For a discussion of this topic see David Peters Corbett, *Walter Sickert*, London 2001, p. 61.

By the time Sickert died in 1942, Britain had closed its borders to the world and was engaged in a fight for survival. In the late 1930s, as continental Europe was swept into political turmoil, Britain became a country of appeasement, in effect turning a blind eye to fascism to ensure its own peace. It became increasingly inward-looking. At the same time certain British artists, for example Graham Sutherland (pl. 68) and John Piper (fig. 14), began to paint the British landscape, in effect reasserting their national identity and the primacy of the British tradition of landscape painting. Piper abandoned his Hélion-inspired abstraction to make landscape collages, where the fragmentary, torn pieces of paper appeared to reflect the fractured and unstable times in which they were made. Sutherland's Palmeresque Arcadian view of life was displaced by a disturbing vision of gnarled forms in a darkened landscape, ominously expressive of the impending cataclysm.

(fig. 14) John Piper ABSTRACT 1 1935, oil on canvas over wood, 91.4 x 106.7 cm, Tate, London

By 1940 the utopian spirit had been swept away on the tide of war. Aspirations to build a better society had been replaced by a desperate bid to maintain the basic right of freedom – political, personal and cultural. The London art world had more or less dispersed as Nicholson, Hepworth and Gabo moved to Cornwall, Read was already installed in Beaconsfield, Moore moved to Hertfordshire, Nash was in Oxford and Mondrian, Gropius and Breuer had moved on to the United States.

In a decade framed by two seismic events – the Great Crash and the Second World War – British artists rose to the challenge laid before them by Paul Nash. They embraced cosmopolitanism without losing their regional accents, but as the decade drew to a close there was a significant failure of nerve. Piper and Sutherland made picturesque views of bomb-damaged England laced with the nostalgia of the Gothic revival (fig. 15). Moore was in the London Underground drawing families sheltering from the Blitz (pls. 74–77, 82), returning to the classical theme of Madonna and child to express the human condition. Even Nicholson returned to the landscape, confining his modernist abstraction to small projects. As isolation set in and the country came under the threat of damage and extinction, not only was there a felt need to record the nation but there was a strong desire to identify and preserve a link with the national past. Romantic sentiment took precedence over the urge to be modern.

(fig. 15) Graham Sutherland FOUR STUDIES OF BOMB DAMAGE 1941, chalk, ink, and pencil, washed, on paper, 25 x 19.2 cm, Arts Council Collection, Hayward Gallery, London

JEREMY LEWISON

Barbara Hepworth LARGE AND SMALL FORM 1934

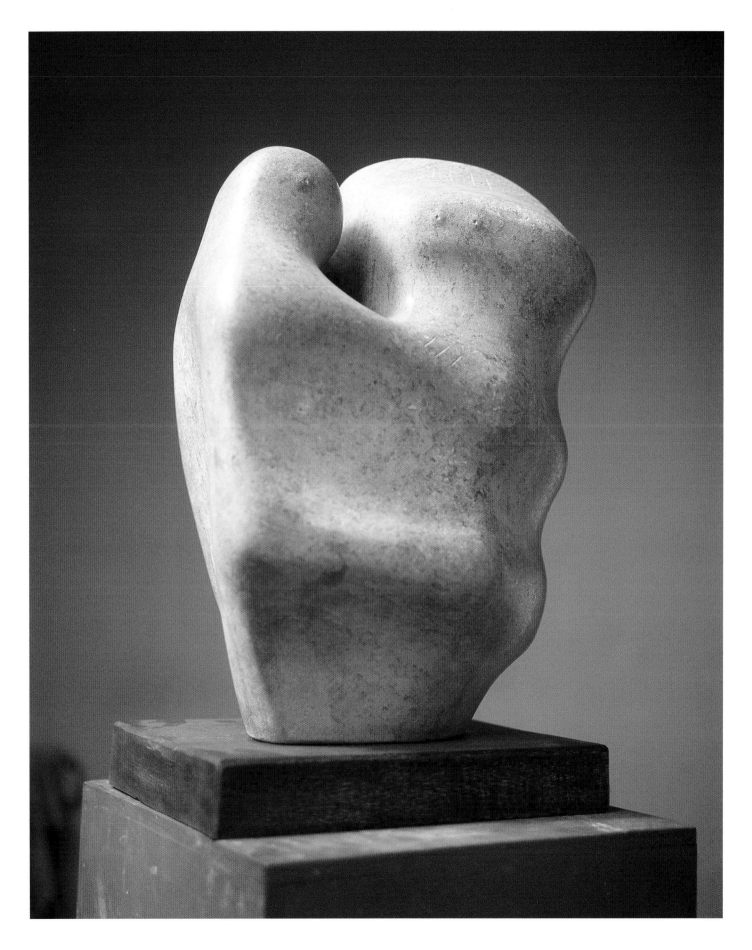

33 | Henry Moore THE MOTHER AND CHILD 1936

34 | Barbara Hepworth HELICOID IN SPHERE 1938

38 | Paul Nash Landscape of the Megaliths 1934

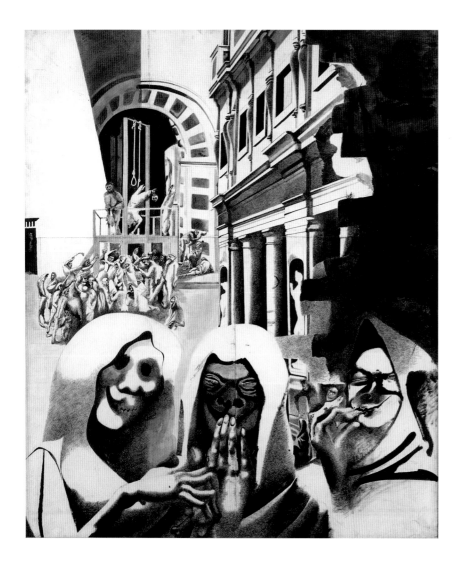

40 | Eduard Burra THE THREE FATES circa 1937

41 | Barbara Hepworth TWO FORMS 1934–35

42 | Barbara Hepworth TWO FORMS 1934–35

43 | Henry Moore HEAD AND BALL 1934

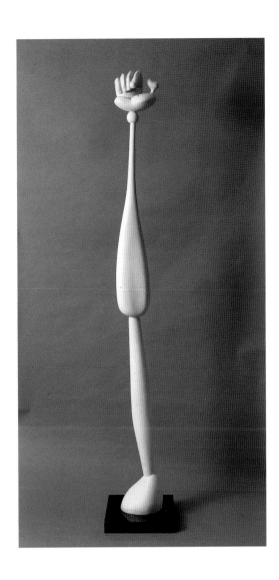

45 | Grace Pailthorpe   October 3 and 4 (Wind)   1935

44 | F. E. McWilliam   The Long Arm (Fist Raised in a Republican Salute)   1939

46 | Ceri Richards   Drawing for a Relief   1936

47 | Lee Miller   Portrait of Space, nr. Siwa, Egypt   1937

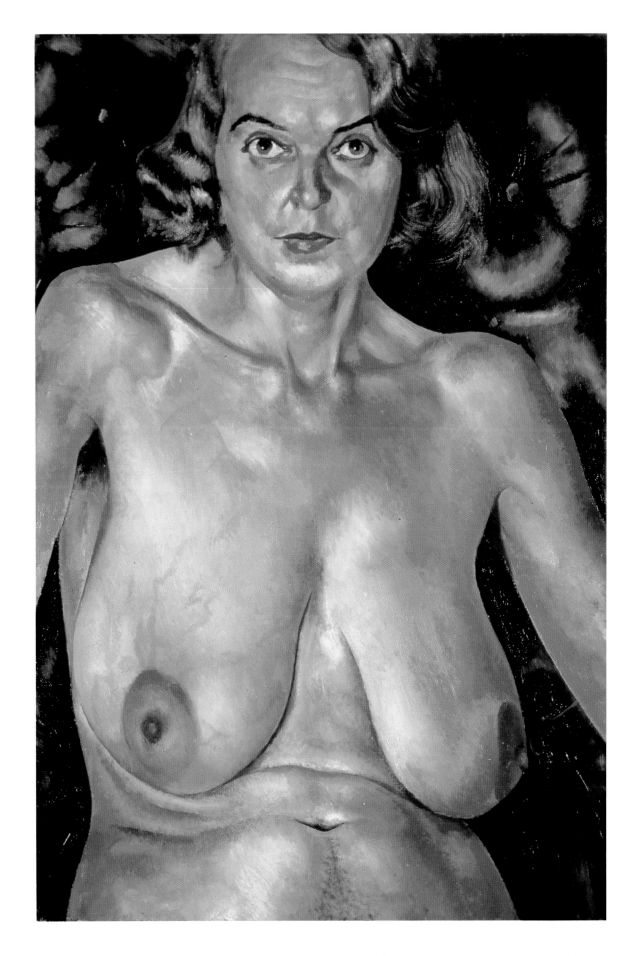

49 | Stanley Spencer Nude, Portrait of Patricia Preece circa 1935

David Jones Llys Ceimiad: La Baissée Front, 1916 1937

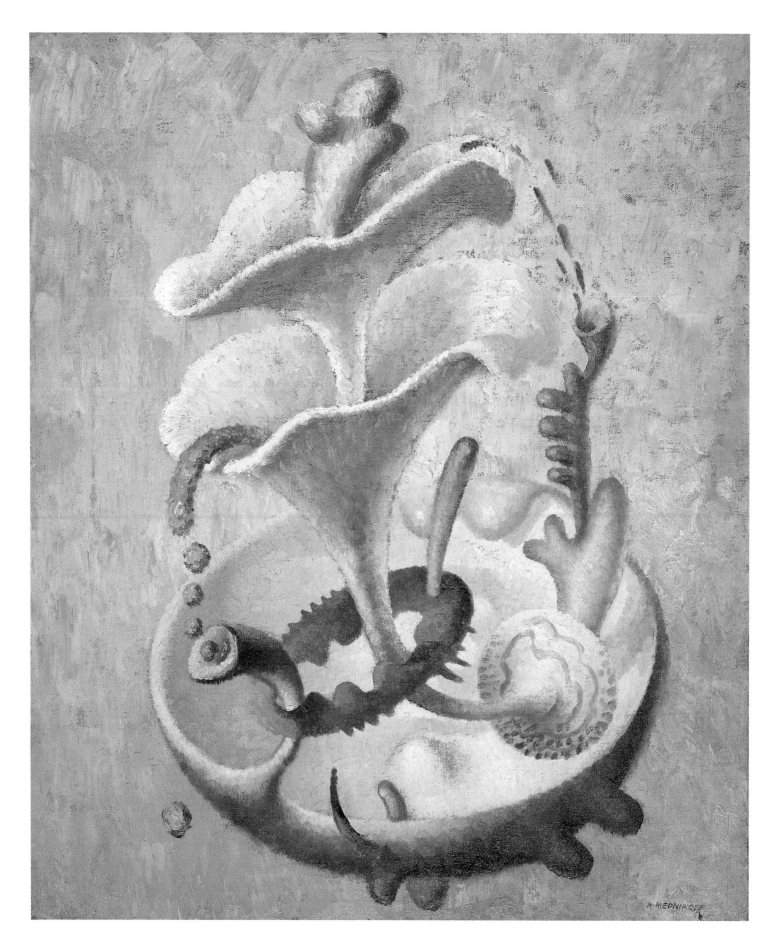

53 | Roland Penrose OCTAVIA 1939

54 | John Banting THE COUPLE circa 1933

55 | Alfred Wallis   HARBOUR WITH TWO LIGHTHOUSES AND MOTOR VESSEL   circa 1932

56 | Alfred Wallis   ST. IVES HARBOUR AND GODREVY YACHT, PINK AND GREEN   circa 1934–38

Humphrey Jennings COMMODE WITH SWISS ROLL 1936

63 | John Armstrong Unit One Composition 1933

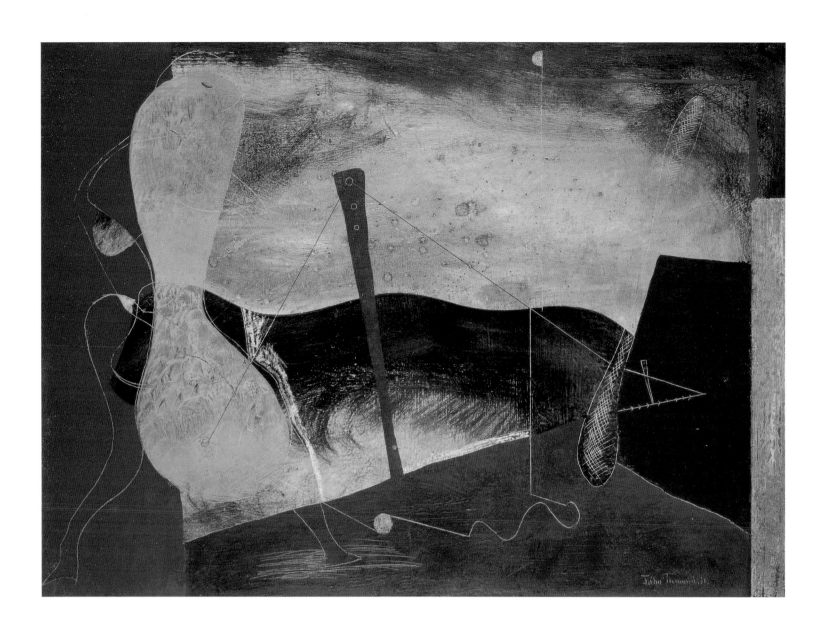

67 | Graham Sutherland Gorse on Sea Wall 1939

69 | Grace Pailthorpe Composition (April 22, 1940) 1940

1940–50
Second World War, Isolation and Existential Concerns

1940

Events: Fall of France; wartime coalition government formed under Winston Churchill; Italy joins war; male "enemy aliens" interned; London Blitz begins

Council for the Encouragement of Music and the Arts formed; Tate Gallery badly damaged by bombing

Artists: Paul Nash appointed Official War Artist; Graham Sutherland joins War Artists scheme; Henry Moore makes shelter drawings, moves to Perry Green, Hertfordshire; Lee Miller joins London War Correspondents Corps; Francis Bacon joins Civil Defence, invalided out; Richard Hamilton begins war service as draughtsman; Patrick Heron registers as conscientious objector; William Gear enlists; Peter Lanyon, F. E. McWilliam join Royal Air Force; John Tunnard joins Coastguard; Piet Mondrian leaves for New York; Kurt Schwitters arrives in Britain

Exhibitions: *Surrealism Today at Zwemmer*; Paul Nash and Graham Sutherland War Artists Advisory Committee commissions at National Gallery

Publications: Last issue of *The London Bulletin*; first issues of *Horizon* and *Penguin New Writing*; Clement Greenberg, "Avant-Garde and Kitsch", *Horizon*

1941

Events: Germany invades Russia (June), air raids on Britain lessen; Anglo-Russian alliance; United States and Japan enter war (December)

Artists: Henry Moore appointed Official War Artist; Alan Davie leaves Edinburgh College of Art, joins army; William Turnbull joins Royal Air Force; Lynn Chadwick joins Fleet Air Arm; Reg Butler begins war service as blacksmith; Victor Burgin, Barry Flanagan born, Michael Craig-Martin born in Ireland

Exhibitions: *Euston Road School* at Ashmolean, Oxford; *Britain at War*, Museum of Modern Art, New York

Publications: Ben Nicholson "Notes on Abstract Art", Horizon

1942

Events: Battle of El Alamein; Beveridge report on social welfare published

Artists: William Scott enlists; Lucian Freud joins Merchant Navy, invalided out; Roger Hilton made prisoner-of-war; Victor Burgin, George (Passmore) born; Alfred Wallis dies

Exhibitions: *New Movements in Art. Contemporary Work in Britain* at London Museum; *Imaginative Art Since the War* at Leicester

Publications: Geoffrey Grigson, *The English Romantics*; John Piper, *English Romantic Art*

1943

Events: Allies invade Italy, Italian government surrenders

Artists: Henry Moore *Madonna and Child*, St Matthew's Church, Northampton; Gilbert (Proesch) born Italy; Stephen Willats born

Exhibitions: Henry Moore at Buchholz Gallery, New York; first *Recording Britain* at National Gallery; Artists International Association *For Liberty* at John Lewis store, London

Publications: F. D. Klingender, *Marxism and Modern Art*; T. S. Eliot, *Four Quartets*

1944

Events: D-Day Landings in Normandy (June); V1 and V2 rockets on London; Ardennes Offensive (December); Butler Education Act
Council for Industrial Design founded
Artists: Anthony Caro joins Royal Navy; Lynn Chadwick demobilised; Bruce McLean born
Exhibitions: Lucian Freud at Lefevre
Publications: Theodor W. Adorno and Max Horkheimer, *Dialectic of Enlightenment*; Herbert Read, *Henry Moore* and *Paul Nash*; Henry Moore, *Shelter Drawings*

1945

Events: War in Europe ends (May); atomic bombs on Hiroshima and Nagasaki, war in East ends (September); Labour wins General Election, Clement Attlee becomes Prime Minister
Arts Council of Great Britain, chairman designate Maynard Keynes, succeeds Council for the Encouragement of Music and the Arts; War Artists Advisory Committee dissolved
Artists: Roger Hilton, Peter Lanyon, F. E. McWilliam demobilised; Richard Long born
Exhibitions: Picasso and Matisse at Victoria and Albert Museum, London; Paul Klee at National Gallery; War Artists Exhibition at Royal Academy; Francis Bacon *Three Studies for Figures at the Base of a Crucifixion* (1944) at Lefevre; Henry Moore at Museum of Modern Art, New York
Publications: George Orwell, *Animal Farm*

1946

Events: Winston Churchill makes "Iron Curtain" speech at Fulton, Missouri

Tate reopens; Gimpel Fils Gallery opens in London
Artists: Naum Gabo leaves England for America; Percy Wyndham Lewis returns from America, becomes art critic for *The Listener*; Anthony Caro enters Regent Street Polytechnic; John Latham enters Chelsea College of Art; Gustav Metzger enters Borough Polytechnic; William Turnbull enters Slade; Paul Nash, Christopher Nevinson die
Exhibitions: Braque and Rouault at Tate; Henry Moore retrospective at Museum of Modern Art, New York

1947

Events: Severe winter contributes to economic crisis in Britain; America launches Marshall Plan for economic revival of Europe
Institute of Contemporary Arts (ICA) founded by Herbert Read, with Roland Penrose and others; first Edinburgh International Festival
Artists: David Jones suffers second nervous breakdown; Lee Miller and Roland Penrose marry; Eduardo Paolozzi moves to Paris; Frank Auerbach naturalised, studies at Borough Polytechnic; Anthony Caro enters Royal College of Art; Richard Hamilton rejoins Royal Academy Schools, expelled; Anthony Hill enters St. Martin's School of Art; Richard Wentworth, Bill Woodrow born; Kurt Schwitters dies
Exhibitions: Victor Pasmore at Redfern

1948

Events: Soviet blockade of West Berlin; "Cold War" sets in; Britain introduces National Health Service
Hanover Gallery opens in London; Robin Darwin becomes Rector of Royal College of Art
Artists: Henry Moore wins International Prize for Sculpture at Venice Biennale; Peter Smithson enters

Royal Academy Schools; Frank Auerbach, Richard Hamilton enter Slade; William Turnbull leaves Slade, moves to Paris; Alan Charlton born
Exhibitions: First *London County Council Open-Air Exhibition of Sculpture*, Battersea; ICA *40 Years of Modern Art* and *40,000 Years of Modern Art* at Academy Cinema; Paul Nash retrospective at Tate; William Gear at Gimpel
Publications: David Sylvester "The Problems of Painting: Paris–London 1947", *L'Age Nouveau* (Paris); first issue of *Art News and Review*

1949

Events: Russia tests atomic bomb; Britain joins NATO; devaluation of sterling
Penwith Society founded in St. Ives; William Coldstream becomes Slade Professor at University College, London; Sir Alfred Munnings, President of Royal Academy attacks Picasso and Henry Moore
Artists: William Scott demobilised; Michael Andrews enters Slade; Eduardo Paolozzi returns from Paris; Peter Smithson leaves Royal Academy Schools, marries Alison Smithson; Tony Cragg, Richard Deacon born; Edward Wadsworth dies
Exhibitions: Henry Moore British Council show tours 1949–50 to Belgium, France, Holland, West Germany and Switzerland; Francis Bacon at Hanover; Reg Butler at Hanover
Publications: Patrick Heron, "The School of London", *New Statesman and Nation*; Victor Pasmore, *Abstract Art*; last issues of *Horizon* and *Poetry London*; Richard Crossman (ed.), *The God that Failed: Six Studies in Communism*; George Orwell, *1984*

APOCALYPTIC VISIONS

BRITISH ART IN THE 1940s AND 1950s

DAVID ALAN MELLOR

Perhaps the most formative factor in the development of British art in the 1940s was a governmental one – The War Artists' Advisory Committee (WAAC), under the Chairmanship of Sir Kenneth Clark. From November 1939 this official body was given a national mandate to produce a form of reportage, to produce "an artistic record of the war in all its aspects"[1] (fig. 1). The WAAC was intimately linked to the wartime Ministry of Information (MoI); hence a form of state-sponsored and directed pictorial documentary flourished, with 3,000 paintings and drawings being produced by the fifth year of the conflict. But, in the hands of artists such as Stanley Spencer, Henry Moore and Paul Nash, this dynamic towards State Realism was often transformed into something both fantastic and romantic; into "apocalyptic visions",[2] as Stanley Spencer described his records of shipbuilders of 1941–42 (pl. 70). This sublime register was detected, in Stanley Spencer's mural-sized Glasgow shipbuilding paintings, as being Dante-esque: "[His] riveters and welders work with a grotesque intensity reminiscent of primitive paintings of the Inferno."[3] This Italianate turn – Spencer's earliest influences had been trecento and quattrocento Italian art –

1 Anon., *War Pictures at the National Gallery*, London 1944, unpaginated.
2 Stanley Spencer writing to the WAAC in 1942, in Tom McGrath "Foreword", *Stanley Spencer: War Artist on Clydeside, 1940–45*, Glasgow, undated, unpaginated.
3 Anon. (but probably Sir Kenneth Clark), *War Pictures at the National Gallery*, London 1944, unpaginated.

(fig. 1) Cover of the catalogue *War Pictures at the National Gallery*, 1944

was echoed in the monumentalism of Moore's "shelter" and mining studies, as well as the lurid, Blakean drawings of tin miners by Graham Sutherland (pl. 79). Eventually, this neo-romantic, apocalyptic religiosity would also surface in Sutherland's *Thorn Tree* allegory of the crucifixion (pl. 93). Sutherland – a practising Catholic within the heavily secularised Anglican state – extended that vector which had originated in the Pre-Raphaelites' bright and flat *faux-naïf* citation of "Italian Primitives" space (which was present in Spencer's visual imagination, too). This was renovated in a painting such as *Thorn Tree* of 1945–46 by the annexation of Pablo Picasso's and Alberto Giacometti's Post-Cubist sombre and '*désagreables*' morphologies of visceral distentions – a vocabulary which would go on, in less than a decade, to underpin both the brutalism and biomorphism of a sculptor such as Reg Butler,

(fig. 2) Reg Butler ARCHAIC HEAD 1952, bronze, width 26.5 cm, Collection Ken Powell, London

in his decidedly Giacometti-esque *Archaic Head* (1952; fig. 2) and the abject assemblage of body tissue and teeth composing the physiognomy of Francis Bacon's *Head II* (1949).

There was something foundational for British art of the 1940s and 1950s about the epic series of Tube shelterers which Moore produced (pls. 74–77, 82): his activity down in the London Underground became memorialised within a couple of years by a recreation of his actions for the MoI propaganda film, *Out of Chaos* (1942),4 for which stills were shot by Lee Miller (fig. 3).

On celluloid, like this, Moore became a compassionate demiurge, descending into the limbo of the suffering London proletarians, a profile which, with its transcendent philanthropic humanism, would colour his appearance and role in post-war British culture. As with other documentary projects of the time – Mass Observation, for instance – the existential protocols of observation and notation were carefully marked: in the texts coupling his drawings with the shelter photographs of Bill Brandt in the magazine *Lilliput*, Moore is presented as a discrete inscriber (fig. 4), a compassionate prose-poet, in his observation: "He says he would have been ashamed to intrude on private suffering. It was his habit to wander round from midnight until dawn, watching and remembering the people and the patterns he saw. On his way home he would make little word pictures to remind him [...]."5

But Moore also created, in the Tube shelterer drawings, a counter-image to this model of transcendental populist welfareism, a powerful iconography of anxiety and oblivion, in the age of total war: "He has painted a terrifying vista of recumbent shapes, pale, as all underground life tends to be pale; regimented, as only fear can regiment; helpless yet tense, safe yet listening, uncouth, uprooted, waiting in the tunnel for the dawn to release them. This is not the descriptive journalism of art. It is imaginative poetry of the highest order."6 That Clark realised the cleavage and contradictions around the demands for a "descriptive journalism of art" speaks eloquently of his outstandingly sensitive cultural management of the WAAC from 1939 to 1945. These shelter drawings were seminal to British art of the 1940s and 1950s, in the sense that they delineated a new existential compass, which could address the anxieties around pressures towards the totalitarian shaping of society. The mortified informalism of those line-bound sleepers would give a sort of pictorial sanction to the art of Bacon, of Butler and of

Eduardo Paolozzi and opened that imaginative space which, a little more than a decade later, would be dubbed "The Geometry of Fear".

Just as the documentation of Moore, with that of Bill Brandt, became re-located to photo representations of them working *sur le motif* in magazines and film, so the efforts of Stanley Spencer were inventorised in *Picture Post*, the leading documentarist weekly, incorporating the artist within the larger war effort and its propagandising. Where, in the case of Henry Moore, the nervous network of barbed lines and wax-resistant watercolour metaphorised the archaic and ruinous aspect of bodies under siege from Nazi aerial bombardment,7 Spencer's representations of shipbuilders had a secure corporeal integrity. These were highly formalised and locked into the larger technological forms of metal plates and ducts: in the centre panel of *Shipbuilding on the Clyde – Riveters*, the riveters are circumscribed within the circles of the vast metal tubings; similarly, in *Shipbuilding on the Clyde – Burners* their compressed bodies are laid out on irregular pre-fabricated sections of parts for ships' hulls (fig. 5). The effect is to frame *naïf* figures which have a kind of kinship to contemporary animated cartoons from Hollywood and share a contemporary cinematic sense of Technicolor and Kodachrome colour codes. This compartmentalising of seeing by space frames, which demarcated the bodies' placement, had run, in Spencer, from his earliest work until the 1940s. Just as Moore insisted, in his shelter drawings, on the topic of the body withstanding, by its self-absorption, an external threat, so Spencer concentrated on reveries of domains of intimacy, repose and security, within a *heimlich* zone. The iron sections of merchant and naval ships provided spatial supports for bodies, augmented by the rhetoric of frames or flattened planes or niches.

While Spencer and Moore found a *locus* for the struggles and strains of war embodied in troglodytic civilians of the Home Front, Paul Nash located it – as he had in the First World War – in the vast patternings of panoramic aerial landscapes. Massive, and baleful, *Battle of Germany* of 1944 (pl. 92), was intended by him to be a sequel to his large oil, *The Battle of Britain* (1941).

4 Directed by Jill Craigie.

5 Uncredited caption "One of the Great Artists of our Day – Henry Moore in his Studio«, *Lilliput*, 1943, pp. 473–482, p. 477.

6 Anon. (see note 3).

(fig. 3) Film still by Lee Miller from *Out of Chaos*, produced by the Ministry of Information (MoI) in 1942

(fig. 4) Double page in *Lilliput Magazine* showing TUBE SHELTER and FOUR GREY SLEEPERS, 1943, between p. 472 and p. 473

7 "It seemed to him (Moore) [...] its inhabitants had been sleeping and suffering for hundreds of years.« Uncredited caption: "One of the Great Artists of our Day – Henry Moore in his Studio«, *Lilliput*, 1943, pp. 473–482, p. 475.

(fig. 5) Stanley Spencer SHIPBUILDING ON THE CLYDE – BURNERS 1940, oil on canvas, triptych, centre 106.7 x 153.4 cm, sides 50.8 x 203.2 cm, Imperial War Museum, London

Linked to Nash's personal and late *symboliste* mythologies of aerial metaphysics, but sourced from combat photographs, *Battle of Germany* resembles a late Paul Cézanne, catastrophically militarised, or an extension of Franz Marc's *Kämpfende Formen [Fighting Forms]*, 1914 – an abstraction for the culture of high altitude bombing and photo-reconnaissance (fig. 6). This may also be, from a wilfully formalist perspective, the most comprehensively modernist painting which Nash ever performed, as its flattened paint segments hug the ground, while also maintaining its function as a late-imperial battle panorama, with its foreground itemising of air-crew or paratroop parachutes, as surface "discs".[8]

(fig. 6) Royal Air Force over Dunkirk, 1941

Sir Kenneth Clark had ascribed the category of "poetry" to Moore's shelter drawings. Moore's own imagistic mnemonics direct us, historically, to that section of contemporary neo-romantic art which concentrated on subjective states and private realms; a poetic register of the fantastic. The immediacies of the public and political realm, of surveillance and propaganda, gave way to versions of private mythologies, or the idiosyncratic nuancing of a larger ideology such as Catholicism, in the hands of Graham Sutherland. Paul Nash managed to straddle both the mandate for painted public record, with *Battle of Germany*, and the private displacements of a revived and renovated Blakean world, in paintings such as *Eclipse of the Sunflower* (1946; fig. 7). Combined with paintings such as *Solstice of the Sunflower* (1945), a world of cosmic analogies is displayed through close-ups of painterly, if estranged, vegetal forms – some, gathered from that album of global tribal myths of fertility, Sir James George Fraser's *The Golden Bough* (1922). Nash's final paintings suggested a universe of ritual signs filling the picture plane in an abrasive and rough-hewn painterly mode, often using watercolour in a bold fashion, reminiscent of Emil Nolde.

(fig. 7) Paul Nash ECLIPSE OF THE SUNFLOWER 1945, oil on canvas, 71.1 x 91.4 cm, The British Council

Fraser's compendium of fertility narratives had been a resource for T. S. Eliot, in *The Waste Land* (1922), and organic, abstracted images of primitivised rituals were also crucial for the Scottish ex-bomber pilot,

painter and sculptor, William Turnbull. In *Head 2* (1955) and *Drumhead* (1955), Turnbull employed that weathered, archaic rhetoric of ruined volumetrics which Moore had initiated, and deployed, as an overlay to the elemental forms of Constantin Brancusi. A pictorial rhetoric of distressing suggested an immemorial antiquity, of lost civilisation's lacerated objects. The advent of a nuclear horizon to history, in August 1945, given added significance by the detonation of the first U.S. hydrogen bomb, in 1954, and Britain's own thermonuclear weapon, in 1957, was a factor which could not be escaped. Like Max Ernst's deserted cities, Turnbull's *Heads*, with their derelict signs fabrication – particularly, the corrugated patternings on the carapace of *Drumhead* – were evidence of an encroaching entropy in a culture reduced to an elemental state, a theme elaborated by his colleagues, Nigel Henderson's and Eduardo Paolozzi's post-apocalyptic lean-to garden shed in the 1956 exhibition, *This is Tomorrow*. Corporeal vulnerability, discovered in female fertility and martial male roles,[9] was a prime iconography of a modernising Britain, and one which Moore condensed in *Helmet* (1940) and *Falling Warrior* (1956/57). Still reflecting upon the epochal implications of the spatial revolutions of the "men of 1914", and especially Jacob Epstein's *Rock Drill* of 1913–15 (pl. 17), Moore's *Helmet* probed dialectics of foetal internalities and defensive exteriorities, while *Falling Warrior* toppled (albeit in an archaistic manner) the imperial heroics found in the martial formats of artists such as George Frederick Watts,[10] which had already been discredited by the Great War, and which awaited a final erasure at the hands of the contemporary Angry Young Men and the Cambridge satirists.[11] The collapse of certain idealising ideological paradigms – Anglican state religion, unquestioned imperial patriotism and deference to vertical hierarchies of class – in post-war British society, found a visual metaphor in the host of grounded, de-idealised formats and brute forms of sculpture from the period. The about-to-be-stretched-off horizontalising of the transcendent hero, in Moore's *Falling Warrior*, predicted not only the culture of the revisionist secularising of Anglicanism in the influential tract by the Bishop of Woolwich, *Honest to God* (1963),

8 Paul Nash "Picture History«, cited in *Paul Nash*, exh. cat. Tate Gallery, London 1975, p. 100.

9 Heavily inflected by the First World War identification of the pathology of "male hysteria« – Shell Shock. Cf. Elaine Showalter, *The Female Malady*, London 1988.

10 Cf. Watts' monument to the colonist Cecil Rhodes, *Physical Energy* (c.1900).

11 The group associated with Beyond the Fringe, who emerged at the Edinburgh Festival in 1960, also de-sanctified British martial heroics of the Second World War in their stage and cabaret acts.

but also the formalist horizontalising of Moore's assistant, Anthony Caro. Caro's sculptures, made before his switch to the emphatically grounded, factualised and colourised geometries of post-1960, had already started to extend Moore's engagement with universal bodily states. *Baby with a Ball* (1955) belongs to that charting of engrossment with the lived body in its primordial existence, advancing into potential and, in Maurice Merleau-Ponty's terms, lived space, which was also to be discovered in Lynn Chadwick and Kenneth Armitage. In the latter's bronze, *Figure Lying on its Side* of 1957 (fig. 13), the phenomenology of the body's weight, and its paroxysmic instability in the world, tip over into a horizontality which seems almost like an oblique allusion to the predicament of Gregor Samsa in Franz Kafka's celebrated short story, *Metamorphosis*[12] which enjoyed wide circulation in post-war British literary culture. That frontal display of ritual signs which Nash had pioneered in his paintings of 1943–46 – segmented across the picture's field – anticipates the much more informalist and post-Surrealist, painterly signs of Alan Davie. Davie's vitalism, like that of William Gear, is utterly resolved into highly abstracted, dramatised and rhapsodic pictorial dithyrambs. Resembling, in many aspects, the contemporary smeared ideographic writing of Cy Twombly, Davie's art, like David Hockney's, two decades later, can be said to have been inspired by paradigms of American poetry, such as the lyricism of Walt Whitman and the modernist ideograms of Ezra Pound. Pound's crucial intervention at the first moment of modernism in London, through his participation in vorticism, forecast, in his collaborations with Henri Gaudier-Brzeska, a kind of condensed sculptural and calligraphic image. (Again, it should be remembered that the leading theorist of art in 1940s Britain, Herbert Read, like Henry Moore, emerged from this Poundian matrix in the early 1920s). Beginning at the end of the 1940s, Davie expanded the ideographs of Gaudier-Brzeska into a colourism overlaid by inscriptions, announcing "I love the calligraphic filling of pages with luscious scribble".[13] To this end, Davie's lyrical improvisations were massively

12 This motif is elaborated in ways comparable to the concerns of other post-war British artists, such as Michael Andrews, whose painting, *Man Who Suddenly Fell Over* (1952) concentrated on the male body in an existential crisis, and Lucian Freud, whose illustrations for William Sansom's novel, *The Equilibriad* (1948) drew attention to the self-same topic.

13 Alan Davie, cited in Michael Horovitz, *Alan Davie London*, London 1963, unpaginated.

(fig. 8) Alan Davie IMAGE OF THE FISH GOD 1956, oil on plywood, 122 x 153 cm, The British Council

influenced by his encounter with the art of Robert Motherwell and Jackson Pollock, in Venice in 1948. Residues of the chiaroscuro, the compartmentalised space and the incantatory animations of Pollock of circa 1943, visible in Davie's extraordinary *Altar of the Blue Diamond* of 1950 (pl. 103), were further developed and transformed by the time he painted the runic and sculptural interlocking in *Image of the Fish God* of 1959 (fig. 8).

Where Nash had sketched a future for the English landscape tradition in an age of catastrophe, the Scots artist William Gear accelerated this radicalised turn in the pastoral. He achieved this by a more integral and professionalised process of abstraction, learned alongside German abstractionist such as Carl Buchheister and Karl Otto Götz: "In touch with European painting, he had a drive and confidence that nobody could match."[14] In a kind of mirror image of the activities and location of Moore and Sutherland during the Blitz on London, in 1940–41, Gear was heavily impressed by his surroundings of *human* privation and devastation, during his work for the Monuments, Fine Arts and Archives section of the post-war Allied Control Commission in West Germany, from 1946–47. Out of the abject vistas of post-war Hanover, with the population reduced, like Moore's Tube shelterers, to wasteland inhabitants, Gear's painting bodied forth charred dislocations of the pastoral genre, like *Autumn Landscape* of 1950 (fig. 9), which was the sole abstract canvas in the large painting exhibition accompanying the Festival of Britain, in 1951, *60 Paintings for '51* (fig. 10). The Festival of Britain suggested a national polity and welfareist civic culture that was leaving behind the last structures Victorian Imperialism. Commanding paintings from this officially festive gathering of art, such as *Autumn Landscape* and Lucian Freud's *Interior in Paddington*, outlined a contrary and melancholy future – one that was informed by a disconsolate "Age of Anxiety", of subjectivities and cultural pessimisms.

14 Lawrence Alloway, 1958, cited in Sarah Wilson, *Cosmopolitan Patternings: The Painting of William Gear*, exh. cat. Redfern Gallery, London 1990, pp. 5–12, p. 12.

(fig. 9) William Gear AUTUMN LANDSCAPE 1950, oil on canvas, 44 x 41 cm, Tyne and Wear Museums, Newcastle-upon-Tyne

(fig. 10) Cover of the exhibition catalogue *60 Paintings for '51* for the Festival of Britain 1951, organised by The Arts Council

DAVID ALAN MELLOR

This bleak and elementally figured mental landscape found its epitome in the British entries for the international sculpture competition to fund a monument which would crystallise resistance to the encroachment of totalitarian dread: *The Unknown Political Prisoner* of 1952 (fig. 11).[15] The constraining enclosures of Henry Moore's 1942 drawings of *Figures in a Setting*, which placed biomorphic figures in ambiguously prison-like public situations (fig. 12), infected by an ambience of dread, were a crucial base reference for the British entries, just as they had been more immediately critical for Francis Bacon's *Three Studies for Figures at the Base of a Crucifixion* (1945), which had already circulated a coupled iconography of modernised martyrdom and modernist spatial relations. Eduardo Paolozzi's *Maquette for Unknown Political Prisoner International Sculpture Competition* (1952), deployed Moore's bleak civic enclosures, but replaced their minimal geometric patternings with markings suggesting playground gamechalkings, and substituted for Moore's disconcerted biomorphic protagonists/martyrs, a black, domino-like slab. Paolozzi, as with his later, mid 1950s, monumental junk personages, such as *The Philosopher* (1957; pl. 121), advanced a battered architectural frame. For the 1952– 53 competition, Butler sculpted a small group of schematised humanoids: pin-headed, stretched and bulky faceted torsos with stick limbs-outlines which are recognisably aligned to the re-codings of the human figure effected by his "Geometry of Fear" associates, Kenneth Armitage (fig. 13) and Lynn Chadwick (pl. 105). Butler carefully surveyed the proposed location for his winning design; when complete, the open steel work would have stood more than 120 metres high on the Humboldthöhe hill at Wedding, West Berlin (fig. 14), a resonant site which would have signified the sculpture's unparalleled symbolic place as a cultural counter of the Cold War, crowning the bastion of Western democracy and outpost of the Free World.

15 For the most detailed accounts of the contexts for this competition and Reg Butler's winning entry, see Robert Burstow, "Butler's Competition Project ...]«, *Art History*, vol. 12, no. 4, December 1989, pp. 472–496, and Richard Calvocoressi, *Reg Butler: The Man and the Work*, exh. cat. Tate Gallery, London 1983, pp. 9–33.

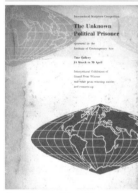

(fig. 11) Cover of the publication for the competition *The Unknown Political Prisoner*, organised by the ICA, 1953

(fig. 12) Henry Moore FIGURES IN A SETTING 1942, pen, watercolour on paper, 40.6 x 53.3 cm, private collection

Butler placed his political martyr and superintending observers in an open arena – once again, the sadomasochistic scene reiterated by Bacon through the post-war decades. This visual imagination depended upon the existentialist texts of Albert Camus and Arthur Koestler; that cellular world of total illumination and visibility consequent upon totalitarian social terror which George Orwell used as the climax of *1984* (1949). This new textual universe can be thought of as a context for, and precondition of, the art of Lucian Freud. At the close of the 1940s, Herbert Read regarded Freud as "The Ingres of Existentialism",[16] and by the time of Freud's first published statement, in *Encounter*, in 1954, the charged political currency of visual regimes of oppressive surveillance was well established. Freud metaphorised this pictorial strategy with a figure of portraiture functioning as a form of interrogation, a trope from that prison cell imagination of the mid-century "Age of Anxiety", where the sitter possessed secrets which must be prised out of them: "The subject must be kept under closest observation: if this is done, day and night, the subject – he, she or it – will eventually reveal the all without which selection itself is not possible [...]."[17] He had put himself through just this gruelling process of threatening visual interrogation: his self portraits from the late 1940s show a shocked, hysterically frozen head and shoulders: in *Man with a Thistle* of 1947 the devious head of the heretic Pharaoh, Akhenaten, erased from history, of *damnatio memoriae*, the original source for Jewish identity in the account of his grandfather's last historical romance, *Moses and Monotheism* (1939), is re-imagined as a performing self under observation. Freud incarnated another narrative as the displaced, *émigré* Jewish stranger within British post-war culture; having a photo of Kafka fantastically standing in for his presence in Francis Bacon's *Portrait of Lucian Freud* (1951).

Lucian Freud's patent anxiety, in his 1940s self-portraits, leaps catastrophically towards a sense of total mastery, with power given over to the artist to force out hidden secrets which must be divulged. When,

(fig. 13) Kenneth Armitage FIGURE LYING ON ITS SIDE (No. 5) 1957, bronze, width 82.5 cm, The British Council

(fig. 14) Reg Butler photomontage of his contribution for the monument *The Unknown Political Prisoner* on Humboldthöhe, Berlin

16 Quoted by Robert Hughes, *Lucian Freud Paintings*, London 1988, p. 17.

17 Lucian Freud, "Some Notes on Painting«, *Encounter*, July 1954, p. 23.

in 1963, Freud made another short statement in *Cambridge Opinion*, it was clearly under the shadow of Cold War exterminism, but it centred, as in 1954, on the illuminating omnipotence of the artist, in the face of the nuclear horizon: "[...] this new dimension, having the end in sight can give the artist supreme control, daring and such an awareness of his bearings in existence that he will (in Nietzsche's words) create conditions under which 'a thousand secrets of the past crawl out of their hiding places – into his sun'".[18] To this end, Freud transcended the attenuated linearities and the fetishised and fascinating Magic Realist surfaces of his 1940s art. Similarly, he erased the surrealist melodramatics of dead animals which had so distressed Sir Kenneth Clark when he had paid a studio visit to Freud and found rabbit and bird corpses on a floor covered with broken glass. His Sutherland-derived anxiety-emblems of spiky vegetation, such as *Gorse Sprig* (1944) and the cursive neo-romantic mortifications of *Cock's Head* (1951), all give way to a kind of painterly realism, as the 1950s progressed. Stanley Spencer's paintings, especially the *Leg of Mutton Nude* (1937), have an especial resonance alongside Freud's representations of nakedness from the beginnings of the 1960s, but the example of Francis Bacon's painting, around the time of their friendship in the early 1950s and again in the mid 1960s, was functionally compelling to Freud, as a model for the pictorial construction of a nervous, painterly monumentality.

Bacon passed from the Fuseli-like monstrousness and grotesquery of his late 1940s paintings – such as *Head II* – to a cultural strategy of restoration. It was the English pictorial dream, at least since the time of Sir Joshua Reynolds and his protocols for a Grand Manner, to restore the Michelangelesque Sublime Body. But Bacon's project, which was evident in his monumental figures of male nudes of 1949 and 1950, was more than an antiquarian exercise: it was intimately linked to an appropriation of photographic accounts of the body. Bacon had encountered the time-based photographs of the showman and experimenter, Eadweard Muybridge, at the Victoria and Albert Museum in London, and these positivist documents from late-nineteenth century California sat squarely with Bacon's perverse reckonings of the naturalism of Edgar Degas. Memory, the sanction of the Grand Manner, documentary photography and a

18 Lucian Freud, "Statement«, *Cambridge Opinion*, no. 37, 1963, p. 47.

strong homo-erotic reading, were placed into an extraordinary matrix by Bacon, who insisted on the role of the vulgar medium, besides sanctified Old Master drawings: "Actually", Bacon said, "Michelangelo and Muybridge are mixed up in my mind together, and so perhaps I could learn about positions from Muybridge and learn about the ampleness of form from Michelangelo, and it would be very difficult for me to disentangle the influence of Muybridge and the influence of Michelangelo."[19] In *Study from the Human Body* (1949) and *Painting 1950* (1950), Bacon figured a version of masculinity which was not eroded and victimised, like that of many of his contemporaries. Enigmatic, but Hellenistically bulky and massive, these images may have lain in Lucian Freud's mind, together, perhaps, with Bacon's *Two Figures in the Grass* (1954), which he owned, up to his own, magisterial but also carnivalesque, assumption of the Grand Manner, in his late 1980s paintings of Leigh Bowery. With these male nudes, on the cusp of the 1950s, Bacon had also invented a hybrid art which could acknowledge modernist autonomies of colour – *Painting 1950* is staged in a profoundly Matisse-ian format of planar colour fields – and the impure mass media of social modernisation, as well. A decade later, at the Royal College of Art, David Hockney was carefully to note Bacon's revolution (as well as retrieving Stanley Spencer's figuration as a preferred model of painting). By 1950, Bacon had, with his annexation of popular photography and film, returned to that unfinished agenda from the German culture of the Neue Sachlichkeit, with which he had become familiar, during his stays in Berlin in the late 1920s yet Bacon also looked forward to the advent of Pop Art, more than a decade later. The new world, which Orwell believed to be a more likely outcome than the horrendous tyrannies of totalitarianism that had overshadowed the 1940s, was that of James Burnham's *The Managerial Revolution*, which the author of *1984* reviewed as the Second World War ended. The smartly blue-besuited, anonymous figure, portrayed in Bacon's *Man in Blue II* (1954; fig. 15), is a paragon of the glossy magazine corporate world and its modernised interior *décors*: an executive or a politician, a Hollywood entertainer or a well-groomed psychopath.

19 David Sylvester, *Interviews with Francis Bacon*, London 1975, p.14.

(fig. 15) Francis Bacon MAN IN BLUE II 1954, oil on canvas, 152.5 x 117 cm, private collection

DAVID ALAN MELLOR

71 | Ben Nicholson 1942 (two forms) 1942

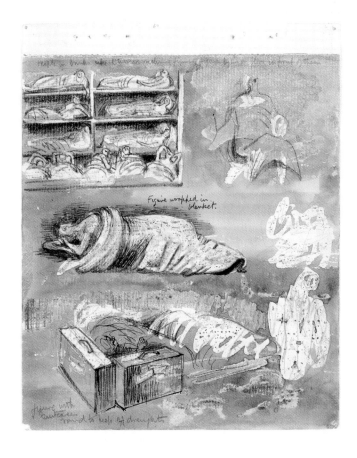

80 | Lucian Freud GIRL WITH FIG LEAF 1947

81 | Francis Bacon FIGURE STUDY II 1945–46

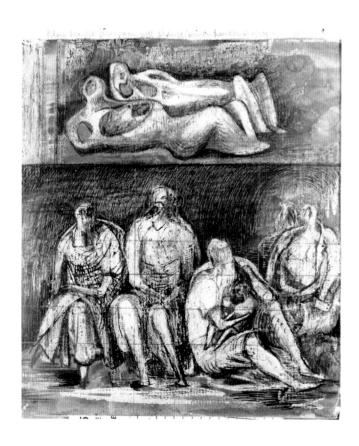

82 | Henry Moore STUDY FOR GROUP OF SHELTERERS DURING AN AIR RAID 1941

83 | Graham Sutherland FOUR STUDIES OF BOMB DAMAGE 1941

84 | Graham Sutherland SLAG LADLES 1942

85 | Graham Sutherland OPENCAST COAL PRODUCTION:
DRAGLINE DEPOSITING EXCAVATED EARTH 1943

86 | Victor Pasmore POSTER FOR THE LONDON GROUP 1948

87 | Eduardo Paolozzi COLLAGE 1950

89 | Graham Sutherland Red Landscape 1942

90 | Ben Nicholson November 11–47 (Mousehole) 1947

91 | Paul Nash Eclipse of the Sunflower 1945

92 | Paul Nash BATTLE OF GERMANY 1944

95 | Francis Bacon MAN KNEELING IN GRASS 1952

The nihilism of the "Image World", with its surfaces of consumption, meshed with Bacon's own deep immersion in Nietzsche and suggested a cultural turn which equally abandoned the tortured authenticities of existentialist culture and consensus State Welfareism. The Vincent van Gogh who was heroised by Bacon's paintings exhibited at the Hanover Gallery was much the same as the van Gogh spectacularised in Vincent Minelli's film *Lust for Life*, as the martyr of high modernist hagiography.

1950

Events: Labour majority severely reduced in General Election; outbreak of Korean War (June) ICA opens premises in Dover Street; Picasso visits Britain for Sheffield Peace Conference
Artists: William Turnbull returns from Paris; John Heartfield leaves for East Germany; Howard Hodgkin enters Corsham School of Art; Leon Kossoff begins evening classes at Borough Polytechnic; Antony Gormley born
Exhibitions: Renato Guttuso at Hanover; *Modern Italian Art* at Tate; Alan Davie at Gimpel, Lynn Chadwick at Gimpel; *London–Paris* at New Burlington, *Aspects of British Art* at ICA
Publications: Ernest Gombrich, *The Story of Art*; last issue of *Penguin New Writing*

1951

Events: Festival of Britain; Conservatives win General Election under Winston Churchill (October) First *Young Contemporaries exhibition*; London art market begins to revive
Artists: Percy Wyndham Lewis loses sight; Barbara Hepworth and Ben Nicholson divorce; Richard Hamilton leaves Slade; Anthony Hill leaves St. Martin's School of Art
Exhibitions: Edward Wadsworth retrospective at Tate; *60 Paintings for '51* Arts Council tour;

Graham Sutherland at ICA; *Growth and Form* at ICA; British Abstract Art at Gimpel
Publications: Herbert Read, *Contemporary British Art; The Philosophy of Modern Art*; Bill Brandt, *Literary London*; John Berger starts contributing art criticism to *New Statesman*

1952

Events: Death of George VI, accession of Elizabeth II; Britain tests atomic bomb; United States elect President Dwight D. Eisenhower Independent Group formed at ICA, Eduardo Paolozzi illustrated "lecture", *Bunk*; Lawrence Alloway becomes assistant director at ICA; Victor Musgrave opens Gallery One
Artists: Anthony Caro leaves Royal College of Art; Frank Auerbach, Bridget Riley enter Royal College of Art; Leon Kossoff ends evening classes at Borough Polytechnic
Exhibitions: *Looking Forward* at Whitechapel; *Recent Trends in Realist Painting* at ICA; Nicolas de Staël at Mathiesen Gallery, London; Kenneth Armitage at Gimpel; first Constructivist Group studio show; *The Mirror and the Square* at New Burlington; *New Aspects of British Sculpture* at Venice Biennale
Publications: David Jones, The *Anathemata; Broadsheet*, no. 2; Herbert Read, *Barbara Hepworth*, "Geometry of Fear"

essay in *New Aspects of British Sculpture* catalogue

1953

Events: Death of Joseph Stalin; coronation of Elizabeth II; end of Korean War
The Unknown Political Prisoner, International Sculpture Competition at Tate; Borough Bottega formed; Bryan Robertson becomes director of Whitechapel; Lindsay Anderson directs Free Cinema documentary *Oh Dreamland*
Artists: Anthony Caro begins teaching at St. Martin's School of Art; Richard Hamilton begins teaching at Newcastle-upon-Tyne University; Michael Andrews leaves Slade; Peter Blake, Leon Kossoff enter Royal College of Art
Exhibitions: Graham Sutherland retrospective at Tate; *Opposing Forces, Wonder and Horror of the Human Head*, and *Parallel of Life and Art* at ICA; *Space in Colour* at Hanover
Publications: first issue of *Encounter*, with David Sylvester as arts editor

1954

Events: End of rationing in Britain Alison and Peter Smithson complete Hunstanton School; John Latham co-founds Institute for the Study of Mental Images
Artists: Howard Hodgkin leaves Corsham School of Art; Robyn Denny, Richard Smith

1950–60
Brave New Worlds, Abstraction and the Aesthetics of Plenty

enter Royal College of Art; Anish Kapoor born Bombay
Exhibitions: David Jones retrospective at Tate; Barbara Hepworth retrospective at Whitechapel; *Cubism, Abstractionism, Sur-Realism, Formalism* at Redfern; *Collages and Objects* at ICA; Ben Nicholson, Francis Bacon and Lucian Freud at British Pavilion, Venice Biennale
Publications: David Sylvester, "The Kitchen Sink Painters", *Encounter*; Lawrence Alloway, *Nine Abstract Artists*
First issue of *The London Magazine*; Kingsley Amis, *Lucky Jim*

1955
Events: Winston Churchill resigns as Prime Minister, succeeded by Anthony Eden
Tate becomes formally independent of National Gallery; English première of Beckett's *Waiting for Godot*
Artists: Victor Pasmore becomes design consultant to Peterlee New Town; Peter Blake, Frank Auerbach, Bridget Riley, Joe Tilson leave Royal College of Art; Tim Scott enters St. Martin's School of Art
Exhibitions: Stanley Spencer retrospective at Tate; Ben Nicholson retrospective at Tate; *Man, Machine and Motion*, Hamilton Gallery, Newcastle-upon-Tyne; *Four French Realists* at Tate; Jean Dubuffet at ICA; Mondrian at Whitechapel; Bacon at ICA; *Nine Abstract Artists* at Redfern;

Publications: Patrick Heron, *The Changing Forms of Art*; Reyner Banham, "The New Brutalism", *Architectural Review*; first issue of *ARK*

1956
Events: Kruschev attacks Stalin at 20th Congress of Soviet Communist Party; Nationalisation of Suez Canal and Anglo-French invasion; Hungarian Uprising
Royal Court Theatre opens; Lorenza Mazetti directs film *Together*, featuring Michael Andrews and Eduardo Paolozzi; film *Rock Around the Clock* released in Britain
Artists: Lynn Chadwick wins International Sculpture Prize at

Venice Biennale; Roger Hilton first visits St. Ives; Patrick Heron settles in Cornwall; R. B. Kitaj joins US Army; Stuart Brisley enters Royal College of Art; John Hoyland enters Royal Academy Schools; Leon Kossoff leaves Royal College of Art;
Exhibitions: *This Is Tomorrow*, at Whitechapel; Frank Auerbach, Leon Kossoff at Beaux-Arts; *Modern Art in the United States* at Tate; Nicholas de Staël at Whitechapel; Georges Matthieu demonstrates tachiste painting at ICA; *Looking Forward 2* at South London Gallery; Jack Smith, Edward Middleditch, Derrick Greaves, and John Bratby at British Pavilion, Venice Biennale
Publications: Nikolaus Pevsner, *The Englishness of English Art*; Colin Wilson, *The Outsider*; John Osborne, *Look Back in Anger*

1957
Events: Harold Macmillan becomes Prime Minister, warns "Most of our people have never had it so good"; formation of European Economic Community (EEC); Russia orbits Sputnik
Ken Russell TV film of William Green *Painting an Abstract Painting*
Artists: Robyn Denny, Richard Smith leave Royal College of Art, visits New York; Phillip King enters St. Martin's School of Art; R. B. Kitaj enters Ruskin

School, Oxford; Bob Law moves to St. Ives; David Bomberg, Percy Wyndham Lewis die
Exhibitions: Yves Klein at Gallery One, London, *Statements* at ICA; *Metavisual Tachiste Abstract, Paintings in England Today* at Redfern; *Dimensions, British Abstract Art 1948–57* at O'Hana Gallery, London; Sam Francis at Tooth's; *Eight American Artists* at ICA; *Paintings from the Solomon R. Guggenheim Museum* at Tate
Publications: Richard Hoggart, *The Uses of Literacy*

1958
Events: Campaign for Nuclear Disarmament launched
Victor Waddington Gallery opens in London; John Moores Painting Competition established in Liverpool; Clement Greenberg visits London
Artists: Ben Nicholson leaves Cornwall for Switzerland; Henry Moore *Reclining Figure* for UNESCO, Paris; David Annesley enters, Phillip King leaves St. Martin's School of Art; Julian Opie born
Exhibitions: Alan Davie at Whitechapel; Kurt Schwitters at Lords' Gallery, London, Bernard Cohen at Gimpel; Robyn Denny at Gimpel; David Bomberg retrospective at Tate; Jackson Pollock retrospective at Whitechapel
Publications: John Berger, "The Art of Assassination", *New*

Statesman; Lawrence Alloway, "The Arts and the Mass Media", *Architectural Design*; Harold Pinter, *The Birthday Party*

1959
Events: Conservatives increase their majority in General Election; Obscene Publications Act eases literary and artistic censorship
Grabowski Gallery opens in London; Clement Greenberg visits London
Artists: Anthony Caro travels to New York; Derek Boshier, David Hockney, Allen Jones, R. B. Kitaj enter Royal College of Art; Stuart Brisley leaves Royal College of Art, enters Akademie der Bildenden Künste, Munich; Tim Scott leaves St. Martin's School of Art, goes to Paris; Richard Smith scholarship to New York; Stanley Spencer, Jacob Epstein die
Exhibitions: *Place* at ICA; Duncan Grant retrospective at Tate; Kenneth Armitage retrospective at Whitechapel; *The New American Painting* at Tate
Publications: Lawrence Alloway, "The Long Front of Culture", *Cambridge Opinion*; Harold Rosenberg, *The Tradition of the New* (New York, UK 1962); Gustav Metzger, *Auto-Destructive Art*; first issue of *X* magazine; Isaiah Berlin, *Two Concepts of Liberty*

WE ARE THE MASTERS NOW

MODERNISM AND RECONSTRUCTION IN POST-WAR BRITAIN

CHRISTOPHER STEPHENS

"We are either the fathers of a new hopeful but austere and courageous world or we are the lost generation." Peter Lanyon, Italy 16 May 1945

For a long time, the 1940s was seen as a period of nationalistic, neo-romantic reaction in British art, a time when, against the background of the jingoistic fervour of the war, artists abandoned modernist ideas of progress and looked back to British cultural traditions and more permanent values. Most prominently, Henry Moore's "shelter drawings" (pls. 74–77,82) and sculptures such as the *Madonna and Child* for St. Matthew's Church (fig. 1), Northampton, aided in his transformation from a leading avant-garde figure to a popular humanist. Conversely, Ben Nicholson and Barbara Hepworth were seen in this view as marginalised, quietly keeping the modernist flame alight at the end of the country in Cornwall. In fact, the Constructivist ideals espoused by Nicholson, Hepworth and their close colleague Naum Gabo were not in complete abeyance. It is true that in his 1947 review of *British Painting Since 1939* Robin Ironside (himself a neo-romantic artist) could describe Nicholson as increasingly isolated, but it is also the case that Lillian Somerville, the influential Director of Fine Arts at the British Council,

(fig. 1) Henry Moore MADONNA AND CHILD 1943, bronze, height 14 cm, Henry Moore Foundation, Leeds

would apologise to Nicholson and assure him the statement would be excised from the second edition.[1] During the war began the movement that would see them, their circle and their values drawn into the heart of the process of reconstruction of the blasted physical and social fabric of Britain.

The immediate post-war years were a time for re-evaluation, revision and recuperation. It was then that an oscillation between hopes for a better future and despair at the state of humankind was established as the key cultural condition. During the conflict, the Left's demands for more social and environmental planning gathered an unstoppable momentum that ensured a sense that the war's end marked the beginning of a brighter, better, more just world. At the same time, the revelation of the Holocaust and the advent of the nuclear age gave credence to the idea that humankind was hopeless and irredeemable. One view placed society over the individual, while the other saw that same individual as absurd and alone. In the context of these two extremes, people had to recover from the physical and psychological damage of the war. For younger artists, whose careers had been violently interrupted, the creative process could offer a form of recuperation. For some, the situation led to a return to what was perceived as a more natural way of living and working. For

1 Robin Ironside, *Painting Since 1939*, The British Council, London 1947, republished in *Since 1939: Ballet; Film; Music; Painting*, London 1948; Lilian Somerville, letter to Ben Nicholson, 27 July 1948, Tate Archive 8717.1.2.2342.

many, it demanded a review of their activities and of the development of modern art, in general. More optimistically, the fate of Paris presented the opportunity for London (or Britain) to cast itself as the new art capital of the world.

Only a few days after the signing of the Nazi-Soviet pact on 23 August 1939, Nicholson and Hepworth left London, where they had established themselves as the leaders of a British Constructivist movement, for the Carbis Bay home of the writer Adrian Stokes, close to the established artists' colony of St. Ives, Cornwall. They were soon followed by Naum Gabo and his wife, Miriam Israels; Piet Mondrian was also invited, but stayed in London. In Cornwall, despite the privations of war and restrictions on income, space and time, they sought to advance the modernist cause. Nicholson was particularly aware of the importance of maintaining a propaganda campaign and continued with what Stokes's wife, the painter Margaret Mellis, termed his obsession with "the Movement". While maintaining contact with important colleagues, critics and collectors in Britain and America, they even gathered around them a group of young followers: Mellis, who began a series of Constructivist-inspired collages, John Wells and Peter Lanyon, both of whom made reliefs and three-dimensional constructions clearly influenced by all three senior artists and, especially, by Gabo.

Nicholson's 1941 essay "Notes on Abstract Art" in the widely-read journal, *Horizon*, was an uncompromising and defiant statement of modernist idealism. It was certainly audacious to assert: "this liberation of form and colour is closely linked with all the other liberations one hears about. I think it ought, perhaps, to come into one of our lists of war aims".[2] He ensured his group was included in several exhibitions, most notably *New Movements in Art*, in a review of which Read observed that "as far as constructivism is concerned [...] the column is advancing".[3] Their work appeared in magazines, not least in the American *Partisan Review* and in *World Review*, in a series of articles on art edited by Nicholson. *World Review* was owned by Edmund Hulton, one of the influential members of the 1941 Committee campaigning for a policy of social reconstruction. Another series of essays, *This Changing World*, effectively explained how the cultural revolu-

tionaries of the 1930s would set about changing the social and intellectual fabric. Edited by the Hepworth-Nicholsons' close friend Marcus Brumwell, the series included essays on science, art and sociology by the likes of J. D. Bernal, C. H. Waddington, Karl Mannheim and Lewis Mumford. Like Nicholson's views on art, Read's introduction was a reassuringly optimistic rallying call: "The individuals in whom the spirit of modernism is embodied still survive, still work, still create [...] When the cloud of war has passed, they will re-emerge, eager to rebuild the shattered world [...] They will say: our world is in ruins [...] Let us direct your work and we promise you that out of the ruins a better world will emerge."[4]

Thus, as the war carried on, the modernists quietly established a link between their work and the dominant discourse in domestic politics: the reconstruction of Britain, once the fighting ended.

After the war, the presence of these artists helped to attract a large number of modern-minded younger artists to west Cornwall. For many, the area, with its rugged landscape and apparently simple way of life, offered an escape from violence and a chance for recuperation. As had happened after the First World War, the natural world offered a welcome retreat from a threatening and murderous modernity. St. Ives and its environs became "Bohemia's sea coast".[5] The painter Bryan Wynter chose to live isolated on top of the moors in a half-derelict cottage, with no modern conveniences. This became the stereotypical view of the "St. Ives" artist; like all stereotypes, it has some truth and is wildly inaccurate. In a now-famous letter to Sven Berlin, John Wells echoed William Blake in his articulation of how attempts to address nature through abstract art provided a chance to contemplate one's own sense of being: "how can one paint the warmth of the sun, the sound of the sea, the journey of a beetle across a rock, or thoughts of one's own whence or whither".[6] Peter Lanyon, a native of St. Ives returning to Cornwall after four years' active service, discovered a deep attachment to the place. The Cornish landscape and the history of it and its occupants provided what he described as a "personal myth". His return to, and immersion in, it was seen as more of a rebirth than a recovery. Similarly, Berlin's description of his hor-

2 Ben Nicholson, "Notes on Abstract Art", *Horizon*, vol. 4, no. 22, Oct. 1941, p. 272.

3 *New Movements in Art: Contemporary Work in England*, exh. cat. London Museum, London 1942; Herbert Read, "Vulgarity and Impotence: Speculations on the Present State of the Arts", *Horizon*, vol. 5, no. 28, April 1942, p. 267.

4 Herbert Read, "Threshold of a New Age: Renaissance of Decadence?", *World Review*, June 1941, p. 29.

5 John Heath-Stubbs, *Hindsights: An Autobiography*, London 1993, p. 150.

6 John Wells, letter to Sven Berlin, 8 April 1945, Tate Archive 8718.

rific experience of the invasion of Normandy, subsequent breakdown and return to Cornwall, *I am Lazarus*, made clear the reparative role of nature and of art.[7]

So it was that in the late 1940s Constructivism in Cornwall evolved more organic forms invested with psychological significance. Even during the war, Gabo had explained how the forms of his abstract, Perspex sculptures originated in his observation of such natural phenomena as "a torn piece of cloud carried away by the wind [...] the green thicket of leaves and trees [...] the naked stones on hills and roads [...] the bends of waves on the sea"[8] (fig. 2). At the same time, Hepworth's sculptures of the last years of the war were characterised by their enfolding forms, the tension between inside and outside being heightened by the application of paint to the internal spaces (fig. 3). Lanyon, Wells and Wilhelmina Barns-Graham (a Scottish painter in St. Ives since 1940) all produced works with similarly involuted forms. Titles such as *Generation* and *Embryonic* made it clear that the womb-like character of these images, dubbed "Gaboids" by Wells, was not the fruit of art historians' imaginations. Stokes' view of art was determined by his experience of analysis with Melanie Klein, a pupil of Freud. It seems likely that her theory that art was part of the adult desire to repair fantasied attacks upon the mother influenced the development of this imagery.

Lanyon came to combine such imagery with the motif of landscape, so that the land became a protective, maternal form enfolding, perhaps, a germinating seed (fig. 4). Such notions of the landscape as regenerative were common and can be discerned in British art beyond St. Ives, not least in Henry Moore's conflation of the nurturing female figure and landscape. Lanyon's personal engagement with the land of Cornwall would become increasingly politicised with such works as *St. Just* of 1953, which he saw as both a crucifixion and an act of atonement for generations of workers killed in the tin mines of the area. In a bitter secession from Hepworth and Nicholson, he would contrast his approach with the distanced views of Nicholson. In his works of the late 1940s, such as *November 11–47 (Mousehole)* (fig. 5), Nicholson combined schematised still life groups with relatively representational landscapes. Such views through windows implied a landscape for aesthetic enjoyment which was in sharp contrast to Lanyon's historicised engagement with a place validated by his local attachment. This polarity echoed the current debate over land use as a resource for its inhabitants or an amenity for the wider population. In part, Lanyon's work was a protest at the demise of local industry in the face of Cornwall's increasing reliance on tourism.

A renewed humanist concern among artists was reflected in the success of two exhibitions of senior modernists. The recent work of Georges Braque, shown at the Tate Gallery in 1946, presented a rooted, integrated development of Cubism that offered a welcome alternative to the fractured anxiety of Pablo Picasso's wartime work. Similarly, it is significant that an artist such as Hepworth should have been more anxious to see the exhibition of Paul Klee's work than that of Picasso. This, too, was seen as a less austere, more affective kind of art than the tradition of Mondrian and Nicholson. The new humanism was seen most dramatically in a series of figurative paintings that Hepworth made in tandem with her abstract sculptures. Images of surgical operations, these used pictorial composition to emphasise the co-operative work of the surgical teams. As such, they suggest how the concern in her sculpture with the harmonious deployment of forms might be seen as a symbol of human interaction. The relationship of people with each other and with their environment became the dominant theme of her work. The shift in values was, perhaps, reflected in the fact that for a period she seemed to enjoy more success than Nicholson, whose work still appeared too austere to ration-bound Britain.

Despite their peripheral location and, in many cases, self-fashioned Bohemianism, St. Ives artists were not outside the metropolitan art world. The younger artists were signed on to London dealers and, with Nicholson and Hepworth, had their works acquired by national collections and enjoyed state promotion,

7 Sven Berlin, *I am Lazarus*, London 1961.

8 Naum Gabo and Herbert Read, "Constructive Art: An Exchange of Letters", *Horizon*, vol. 10, no. 55, July 1944, p. 61.

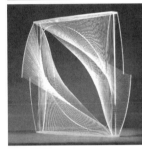

(fig. 2) Naum Gabo LINEAR CONSTRUCTION IN SPACE NO. 1 (VARIATION) 1942–43/c. 1957–58, Perspex, nylon, 62.9 x 24.2 cm, Patsy R. and Raymond D. Nasher Collection, Dallas

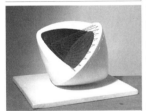

(fig. 3) Barbara Hepworth SCULPTURE WITH COLOUR – DEEP BLUE AND RED 1940–43, wood, painted white and dark blue, with red cords, 25.4 x 27.9 x 30.5 cm, private collection

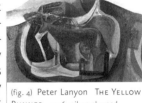

(fig. 4) Peter Lanyon THE YELLOW RUNNER 1946, oil on plywood, private collection

(fig. 5) Ben Nicholson NOVEMBER 11–47 (MOUSEHOLE) 1947 oil on canvas, mounted on wood, 46.5 x 58.5 cm, The British Council

especially through the British Council's international touring exhibitions. Hepworth represented Britain at the 1950 Venice Biennale and she and Nicholson were commissioned to produce major works for the Festival of Britain in 1951.

The organic images of late 1940s St. Ives were not the only offspring of pre-war Constructivism in Britain. In 1951, another group emerged, for whom Hepworth

(fig. 6) Victor Pasmore POSTER FOR THE LONDON GROUP EXHIBITION 1948, Collection Ken Powell, London

and Nicholson were again senior points of reference. This group, which became known as the Constructionists, was dominated by Victor Pasmore and included Kenneth and Mary Martin, Anthony Hill, Robert Adams and Adrian Heath. Pasmore was an established painter, who had worked in a range of Post-Impressionist styles. In 1948, however, following a review of the development of art through the century, he had dramatically converted to a wholly non-figurative style, producing collages based on the Golden Section and influenced by Picasso and Klee (pl. 97). The others also started by making two-dimensional abstract works but the Martins, Hill and Pasmore soon departed into constructed reliefs and, in the case of Kenneth Martin, fully three-dimensional constructions (pl. 109).

The group's identity was established through a series of exhibitions. They first showed together, along with several others, as a sub-section of the annual *London Group* exhibition (fig. 6) in February 1951 and, that May, in *Abstract Paintings, Sculptures, Mobiles* at the Artists' International Association Gallery. In 1952–53 they also showed in three exhibitions held at Heath's Fitzroy Street studio in London in 1952 which, though simple in presentation, were significant and caught the attention of the art world hierarchy. In returning to the methods of the pre-war Constructivists, these artists also adopted their aims for an art with a social function that was integrated with architecture. A tradition was proposed by Heath, in his historical account of *Abstract Painting*. There he argued that abstract art was not "pure decoration, or the work of men who have chosen to retreat within themselves from the world's chaos", as many seemed to think, but that "the pioneers of abstract art were the only artists to adapt themselves to the thought and the rapidly changing social and technical conditions of our world".[9]

9 Adrian Heath, *Abstract Art: Its Origins and Meaning*, London 1953, p. 6.

For Pasmore, this was the next stage in the search for an "objective" art that had led him to co-found the realist Euston Road School, in 1937. Kenneth Martin explained that their art was "a construction or concretion from within. [...] Not painting which imitates the illusory nature and transient aspects of nature, but which copies nature in the laws of its activities".[10] Pasmore reiterated: "art imitates nature in its manner of operation".[11] As well as geometrical formulae, the Constructionists drew upon theories of organic growth, specifically D'Arcy Wentworth Thompson's proposal that the forms of natural organisms were determined by their growth patterns.[12] This theory stimulated works made up of forms of inter-related proportions, such as Pasmore's *White Relief* and, often, with a compositional dynamic, as each component led to the next, in imitation of growth – for example Mary Martin's *Spiral Movement* (fig. 7). The compositions of Kenneth Martin's *Chance and Order* series were established through a logical progression, started at a point chosen at random.

In 1952, Kenneth Martin associated his work with a social collectivism as opposed to art's "old individualist humanism". For him, as for Gabo before him, the space within and created by his art was an embodiment of this democratisation: "Concepts of the space around man [...] of the relation of man to society, develop towards a new humanism".[13] This was most clearly signalled in his mobiles which, in their movement, define and extend space (fig. 8). As such, he saw them as "both architecture and machine".[14] The comparison with architecture was common: the reliefs made by many of these artists imitated architectural form and, in the work of Pasmore, elements extend to draw the supporting wall into the work itself. Several of the constructionists produced large-scale works for architectural settings and collaborated with architects on such projects as the exhibition *This is Tomorrow* in 1956

10 Kenneth Martin, "Abstract Art", *Broadsheet No. 1: Devoted to Abstract Art*, London 1951.

11 Victor Pasmore in Lawrence Alloway (ed.), *Nine Abstract Artists*, London 1954, p. 35.

12 D'Arcy Wentworth Thompson, *On Growth and Form*, 2nd ed., Cambridge 1942.

13 Kenneth Martin, "An Art of Environment", *Broadsheet No. 2*, London 1952, unpaginated.

14 Kenneth Martin, "On Architecture and Mobile", *Architectural Design*, vol. 26, July 1956, p. 234.

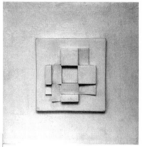

(fig. 7) Mary Martin SPIRAL MOVEMENT 1951–72, multiple made of fibreglass, 29.1 x 29.4 cm, Collection Ken Powell, London

(fig. 8) Kenneth Martin SCREW MOBILE in the studio 1953, brass and steel, 82.5 x 20.3 cm, Drs. J. M. and M. Morris

CHRISTOPHER STEPHENS

(fig. 9), where different teams presented imagined future environments. Pasmore literally extended his activity into architecture, when he became design consultant for Peterlee New Town, in the north of England (fig. 10). He produced plans for part of the

(fig. 9) Mary and Kenneth Martin environment for the exhibition *This is Tomorrow*, Whitechapel Art Gallery 1956

town as well as designs for individual dwellings, both of which resembled his constructed reliefs. At the centre of the scheme was a pavilion (recently saved from demolition) that crosses a lake and is made up of horizontal and vertical slabs; it is both architecture and sculpture.

In the book *Nine Abstract Artists*, the aims of the constructionist group were set out in essays by each artist and an introduction by Lawrence Alloway. These nine were a loose affiliation, and Alloway pointed up the contrast between what he saw as two factions: the logical, system-derived, geo-

(fig. 10) Houses in Peterlee New Town designed by Victor Pasmore

metric abstraction of the Constructionists (Pasmore, the Martins, Hill, Heath and Adams) and the "irrational expression by *malerisch* means" of Roger Hilton, William Scott and Terry Frost.[15] In fact, Frost employed many of the compositional devices of Heath and Pasmore, both of whom had taught him. Based in St. Ives, however, and close to Nicholson and Lanyon, his paintings were inspired by external realities, by moments in front of nature (fig. 11). For Alloway, this bore a lingering whiff of Romanticism. Hilton and Scott both saw themselves as followers of a painterly school associated with Paris and with the Dutch-

(fig. 11) Terry Frost   M17   1962, oil on canvas, 180.7 x 180.7 cm, The British Council Collection, London

based CoBrA movement (pls. 102 and 113). Though around 1953 their paintings were as severe in the abstraction of their forms as they would ever be, they were, nevertheless, based on the figure or still-life and demonstrated the artists' love of paint. Theirs was a painterly art, which, at that time, was framed by existential ideas of the artists' subjectivity and the immediacy of the gesture. Such work came to dominate the art of St. Ives – in the work of Lanyon, Heron, Frost and others – and bore close comparison to Parisian *Tachisme* (notably to the work of Nicolas de Staël and Sam Francis) and would be emboldened by the influx of American Abstract Expressionism, in the middle of the 1950s.

The American painters were first shown in London in any depth in January 1956, as the final room of a survey of *Modern Art in the United States*.[16] Much has been made of this event; though the first-hand experience of major works by Jackson Pollock, Willem de Kooning, Mark Rothko and others undoubtedly had a profound effect on younger painters, for the artists who would soon be known as "the middle generation" this work seemed more to confirm what they already knew. Several of them had seen such work before. Having seen Peggy Guggenheim's collection of Pollocks at the 1948 Venice Biennale, the Scottish painter Alan Davie had developed a similarly improvisational method and style (pl. 103); Lanyon had seen the mature work of de Kooning and others at the Venice Biennale two years later; in 1953 Pollock's *One (No.31)*, 1950, was shown at the Institute of Contemporary Arts; in the same year, Scott visited a number of the American artists in New York, reported his findings to friends in Britain and concluded that he remained, at heart, a European.

It was not the size of the American paintings that impressed (only one was over eight feet and paintings of such stature were not uncommon in Britain), but their expansiveness. Their lack of incident – the resistance to figure/ground relationships – and their shallow space were in accordance with the abstract values espoused by Patrick Heron (pl. 100). Indeed, Heron's criticism was almost indistinguishable from that of the chief apologist for the Americans, Clement Greenberg. Reviewing the Tate exhibition, Heron was appreciative but warned against further experimentation.

Perhaps encouraged by the American painting, the work of many "middle generation" artists changed around 1956. Heron abandoned overt representation for, initially, paintings based upon the foliage of his Cornish garden that are close to the work of Sam Francis, and then a series of striped paintings which he described as non-representational, but which invited inevitable comparisons with sunsets (fig. 12). Lanyon's work became increasingly loose in application and expressive in style, as he based it upon his observation of

15 Lawrence Alloway, Introduction, *Nine Abstract Artists*, London 1954, p. 3.

16 *Modern Art in the United States: A Selection from the Collections of the Museum of Modern Art, New York*, exh. cat., Tate Gallery, London 1956.

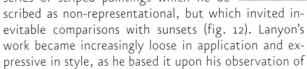

(fig. 12) PATRICK HERON BLUE PAINTING (SQUARES AND DISC) 1958–59, oil on canvas, 152 x 122 cm, Collection Ken Powell, London

weather conditions and, from 1959, on his experience of gliding. More than the history of a place, they were concerned with his own bodily experience. Davie's compositions became more deliberate in conception, and their titles identified sources in mythology and ideas of the unconscious (pls. 114 and 104). As much as the forms of their work, British artists shared common thematic concerns with their American contemporaries: myth, Jungian analytical psychology, theories of the self. Perhaps this was less a question of influence than of a common response to a *Zeitgeist*. The work of British artists bore a resemblance to painting in America, but also to art in France, Italy, Spain and elsewhere. The theoretical confusion of that time was reflected in the Redfern Gallery's 1957 exhibition *Metavisual Tachiste Abstract*, the catalogue of which described "action painting" as "the hybrid child of the Frenchman Dubuffet, the German Ernst, the American Jackson Pollock".[17]

17 Denys Sutton, "Preface", *Metavisual Tachiste Abstract*, exh. cat., Redfern Gallery, London 1957.

Despite public support, there was an innate resistance to the American art, which echoed broader British cultural anxieties about Americanisation. Attachments to place, or to old Bloomsbury values of taste, rendered the new art "vulgar". In time, this would make the St. Ives artists appear conservative: on the one hand, younger painters such as Robyn Denny and John Hoyland responded enthusiastically to the Greenbergian aesthetic of flat colour, and, on the other, the interest in American mass culture espoused by the Independent Group led on to the development of Pop Art. Pop's celebration of the brash, the urban, the commercial and the transitory in modern life was anathema to the more eternal values sought in nature in the years immediately following the war. In the early 1960s, changes in the work of Heron, Frost, Davie, Lanyon and others reflected these shifting values, but these artists would not regain the dominance they had enjoyed during the 1950s.

CHRISTOPHER STEPHENS

FORBIDDEN CONVERSATIONS

THE INDEPENDENT GROUP, MODERNISM, URBAN REALITY AND AMERICAN MASS CULTURE

ANNE MASSEY

The Independent Group represents a decisive moment in the revolt against prevalent taste in twentieth century British art; the type of revolt which forms the main theme of this exhibition.[1] This revolt took the form of three, interlocking conversations: with the dominant British understanding of Modernism; with urban reality; and with American mass culture. The Independent Group took its inspiration from these areas of contention and generated an exciting and challenging aesthetic understanding that overturned the dominant ideology of the post-war British art world. And like all good conversations, the traffic was two-way. The Independent Group also made a long-lasting impact on the British understanding of Modernism; on urban reality; and on the British understanding of American mass culture.

But what was the Independent Group? Currently, as a historical phenomenon it is regarded as the precursor of Pop Art, a group of male artists, or The Fathers of Pop, who begat The Sons of Pop.[2] However, the Group was about much more than this; it was concerned with a subtle, challenging and intellectual project. The Independent Group was a loose collection of like-minded artists, designers, architects and critics that met informally at the Institute of Contemporary Arts (ICA), London, from 1952 to 1955. At its nucleus was a group

of creative couples. There were the architects, Alison and Peter Smithson, who had designed the Modernist Hunstanton School, Norfolk, in 1949. There was the artist Eduardo Paolozzi and his wife Freda, who worked in the gallery at the ICA. The anthropologist Judith Henderson was a contributor, along with her husband, the photographer Nigel Henderson (fig. 1). The artist Richard Hamilton, along with his wife Terry, were stalwart members, as were the critic Reyner Banham and the art historian Mary Banham. The art critic Lawrence Alloway made a substantial contribution to the Independent Group, supported by his wife, the feminist painter Sylvia Sleigh (fig. 2). The Hungarian abstract painter Magda Cordell was another member, along with her first husband, Frank, who was a musical director for EMI. (She was to later live in the USA with the art critic John McHale, who was another key theorist in the Independent Group). The dynamic created by this rich collection of young and hungry creatives was nurtured at their informal meetings at the ICA during the grim and gloomy post-war years. Whilst the Group met officially between 1952 and 1955, their lives were interconnected well beyond that cut-off date.

(fig. 1) Smithsons, Henderson and Paolozzi, from the exhibition catalogue *This is Tomorrow*, 1956

(fig. 2) Sylvia Sleigh ELEANOR ANTIN 1968, oil on canvas, 114.3 x 152.4 cm, Lerner-Misracki Gallery, New York

1 For a fuller account of the history of the Independent Group see Anne Massey, *The Independent Group: Modernism and Mass Culture, 1945–59*, Manchester 1995.

2 See Anne Massey and Penny Sparke, "The Myth of the Independent Group", *Block* 10, 1985, pp. 48–56.

RETHINKING MODERNISM

The first important topic of conversation which the Group engaged with was the re-evaluation of Modernism. This took place within the context of a new Welfare State culture, which played a vital part in the construction of a national identity during the late 1940s and 1950s. This national identity drew on national tradition, combined with a muted form of Modernism. New official bodies such as the Council of Industrial Design and the Arts Council of Great Britain promoted a gentle mix of traditional British form and Modernism. For example, the Arts Council gave support to Neo-Romanticism, which drew heavily on traditional British sources. Neo-Romanticism ignored the formalist experiments of Modernism and retracted into an approachable form of soft landscape painting and humanistic sculpture. Representative artists included Henry Moore, John Piper, Prunella Clough and Graham Sutherland, as evidenced at the *Festival of Britain* in 1951 (fig. 3).

This national cultural identity in art and design was challenged during the early post-war years by the creation of the ICA. Roland Penrose, Herbert Read and E. L. T. Mesens were the founders of the ICA, the roots of which linked back to the *International Surrealist Exhibition* at the New Burlington Galleries in 1936. Another important source of inspiration was the Museum of Modern Art in New York. The Institute's founders aimed to provide a venue for the exhibition and debate of international Modernism, which they hoped would attract the general public and inspire a younger generation of British artists. Early events to be staged by the ICA included the exhibition *40,000 Years of Modern Art* in 1948–49, which included Modernist classics such as Pablo Picasso's *Les Desmoiselles d'Avignon* (1906–07), on loan from the Museum of Modern Art, New York (fig. 4). This exhibition took place in the basement of the Academy Cinema in Oxford Street, London. However, with the support of the Arts Council the ICA moved to its own premises in 1950. This was not an ideal exhibition space,

(fig. 3) Cover of the magazine *The Illustrated London News* from 12 May 1951, showing the exhibition site

(fig. 4) Ewan Phillips and Roland Penrose hanging Picasso's LES DEMOISELLES D'AVIGNON in the ICA's exhibition *40.000 Years of Modern Art*, London, 1949

situated as it was in a former dressmaker's studio on the first and second floors of a terrace in the West End of London, just near the Ritz Hotel (fig. 5). However, the ICA's Managing Committee[3] succeeded in organising an impressive array of events and exhibitions, which informed the work of the Independent Group and, at times, included them. Richard Hamilton and Eduardo Paolozzi contributed to a series of discussions entitled *Points of View*, at which contemporary art exhibitions were examined and these two artists, together with William Turnbull, contributed to the exhibition *1950: Aspects of British Art*.

(fig. 5) Installation view of the exhibition *1950: Aspects of British Art* at the ICA in Dover Street in December 1950

The roots of the Independent Group in an enthusiasm for modernism informed by the activities of the ICA has tended to be overlooked, mainly because the emphasis has been on their supposed influence on British Pop Art, or more recently, on their links to Post-Modernism.[4] However, the Group had an in-depth knowledge of Modernism, which they then used to re-evaluate its importance as a direct challenge to the approach of the ICA's founders. One key example of this was Richard Hamilton's exhibition, *Growth and Form*, staged in 1951 at the ICA (fig. 6). *Growth and Form* (1917) by D'Arcy Wentworth Thompson was a scientific text which Hamilton used to launch an attack on Aristotelian philosophy, as extolled by Herbert Read, supported by the work of Sigfried Giedion and Ernst Gombrich.[5] Read had argued in 1951:
"There is no phase in art, from the Palaeolithic cave paintings to the latest developments in construction that does not seem to me to be an illustration of the biological and teleological significance of the aesthetic activity in man."[6]

The Independent Group rejected Read's metaphysical analysis of visual culture by adopting a more inclusive, empirical approach. The exhibition *Growth and Form* was the first of the Group's shows to use a radical approach to exhibition design. It did not consist of art objects displayed on the wall, on a plinth or in a glass

3 Jacques Brunius, Edward Clark, E. C. (Peter) Gregory, G. M. Hoellering, E. L. T. Mesens, Roland Penrose, Herbert Read and Peter Watson.

4 See David Robbins (ed.), *The Aesthetics of Plenty*, Cambridge/Mass. 1990.

5 Sigfried Giedion, *Mechanization Takes Command*, New York 1948, and Ernst H. Gombrich, "Meditations on a Hobby Horse or the Roots of Artistic Form" in: Lancelot W. Whyte (ed.), *Aspects of Form*, London 1951.

6 Herbert Read, *The Philosophy of Modern Art*, London 1951, p. 13.

(fig. 6) Installation view of the exhibition *Growth and Form* at the ICA, 1950

ANNE MASSEY

case. It consisted of an entire environment constructed from panels decorated with biological images, blown up microphotographs and films showing crystal growth and the maturation of a sea urchin.

The Independent Group also re-evaluated Modernism during discussions. The first meeting of the Group took place early in 1952 and consisted of Eduardo Paolozzi displaying a series of coloured images taken from contemporary American magazine advertising by means of an epidiascope (fig. 7). These images are frequently cited as the first examples of British Pop Art, but they linked back to the heritage of Dada collage, exercised during the 1920s and 1930s by Hannah Höch, Raoul Hausmann and Max Ernst – also by Kurt Schwitters, who had moved to Britain in 1940 to escape persecution by the Nazis (fig. 8). The Group certainly identified with the Dadaists as an alternative form of early Modernism, which challenged the idealist aesthetic of Herbert Read.

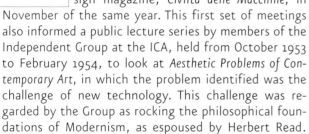

(fig. 7) Eduardo Paolozzi EVADNE IN GREEN DIMENSION 1952, silk screen in 13 colours, collage in 5 parts, 21 x 30 cm

(fig. 8) Kurt Schwitters MR. CHURCHILL IS 71 1945–47, collage, 19.5 x 16 cm, Dr. Jeffrey and Ruth Sherwin, Leeds

The first full session of the Independent Group started in September 1952 and lasted until June of the following year and focused on the challenge of new technology for art and design. The sessions were convened by Reyner Banham, who was studying for his higher degree at the Courtauld at the time. The thesis was eventually to form the basis of his vital reappraisal of the modern movement: *Theory and Design in the First Machine Age* (1960). These fertile discussions also gave rise to an important set of influential magazine articles, including "Machine Aesthetic" in *Architectural Review* in April 1955 and "Industrial Design and Popular Art" in the Italian design magazine, *Civiltà delle Macchine*, in November of the same year. This first set of meetings also informed a public lecture series by members of the Independent Group at the ICA, held from October 1953 to February 1954, to look at *Aesthetic Problems of Contemporary Art*, in which the problem identified was the challenge of new technology. This challenge was regarded by the Group as rocking the philosophical foundations of Modernism, as espoused by Herbert Read.

The Group argued that no everlasting notion of "good design" could exist, no form of painting was aesthetically purer than any other form. The concept of timelessness was anathema to the Group.

The Independent Group's re-evaluation of Modernism also encompassed the work of the Abstract Expressionists, who were beginning to make an impact beyond the USA in the early 1950s. The work of Jackson Pollock and Sam Francis was exhibited at the ICA in January 1953 as part of the *Opposing Forces* exhibition, the first London showing of what was to be the most important movement in painting in the 1950s (fig. 9). Herbert Read and Roland Penrose were unimpressed by the work, but for the Independent Group it represented a radical challenge to dominant notions of a Eurocentric Modernism. Reyner Banham observed of Pollock's work in 1955: "[...] not so much as a painter but for his images [...] because the drip paintings appeared to be examples of disorder and yet contained as works of art. I think that meant quite a lot to Eduardo and ideologically to a lot of us".[7]

(fig. 9) Invitation to the exhibition *Opposing Forces* at the ICA, 1953, designed by Toni del Renzio

7 Peter Reyner Banham, "The New Brutalism", *Architectural Review*, December 1955, p. 356.

The Independent Group enriched Modernism with a new aesthetic understanding, which was empirical and inclusive. The members of the Group were among the earliest admirers of the work of the American Abstract Expressionists, and its impact on Lawrence Alloway was one of the factors influencing his decision to migrate to New York, where he later worked as a curator at the Guggenheim Museum. The work of Jackson Pollock, in particular, inspired some of the Group's radical conversations with urban reality.

TALKING DIRTY: CONVERSATIONS WITH URBAN REALITY

The work of Jackson Pollock was one component of a pivotal exhibition organised by members of the Independent Group, *Parallel of Life and Art*, held at the ICA from September to October 1953. A tightly knit circle of young architects and artists had emerged from the Central School of Arts and Crafts, London, during the early 1950s, and it overlapped with the membership of the Independent Group. Among the first to belong were Eduardo Paolozzi, Victor Pasmore and Peter Smithson, who were all teaching there part-time. Paolozzi then introduced the Smithsons to Judith and Nigel Henderson at his home in Bethnal Green in the East End of London during 1952, and the idea of an exhibition, which should focus on the mess of ordinary, everyday life was born.

8 See Victoria Walsh, *Nigel Henderson: Parallel of Life and Art*, London 2001.

9 See Claude Lichtenstein and Thomas Schregenberger (eds.) *As Found: The Discovery of the Ordinary*, Baden 2002.

10 See Anne Massey, *Hollywood Beyond the Screen: Design and Material Culture*, Oxford, 2001 for more background on material culture.

Nigel Henderson lived in Bethnal Green from 1948 to 1952, as his wife, Judith, was an anthropologist and was based there as part of a project led by the sociologist J. L. Peterson.[8] The shop fronts which Henderson photographed are grubby and the advertising displays set in this working-class area of London are chaotic (fig. 10). This was the mess of ordinary, everyday life. Henderson was photographing these scenes "As Found",[9] as the everyday, as the material culture of his surroundings.[10]

Unlike those older Modernists linked with the ICA from its inception in 1946, who continued to dominate during the 1950s, the Independent Group did not come from traditional, upper- or middle-class, South of England, white backgrounds. The Group was more diverse, if we think of Paolozzi's Italian parentage, Magda Cordell's Central European origins or Hamilton's, Banham's and Alloway's lower-middle-class background. Members of the Independent Group used things and images of things from their everyday culture in their creative work – advertising images, Hollywood cinema, detective novels, comics – which were anathema to the older generation British Modernists at the ICA.

This approach can be found in the Art Brut work of Eduardo Paolozzi from this period, including *Forms on a Bow* of 1951 (fig. 11). It also informed *Parallel of Life and Art* – like *Growth and Form*, a radical departure for exhibition design. The exhibition consisted of a total environment. Here again, everyday images of everyday life were taken and represented as coarse,

(fig. 10) Nigel Henderson, photograph of BETHNAL GREEN ROAD, EAST END, LONDON 1950–51

(fig. 11) Eduardo Paolozzi FORMS ON A BOW 1949, bronze, 55.5 x 64.8 x 26.7 cm, Tate, London

grainy, black and white photographs, in a jumbled environment. Microscopic views of tumours, X-rays and images of non-western habitats were thrown together. The exhibits were drawn largely from scientific and technical sources, including diagrams and photographs of radio valves, televisions and space suits. The exhibition was organised by four members of the Independent Group: Alison and Peter Smithson, Nigel Henderson and Eduardo Paolozzi. Paolozzi, who was working with Peter Smithson at the Central School of Arts and Crafts, had introduced the Smithsons to Nigel Henderson at his home in Bethnal Green, in the East End of London, during 1952. They discovered that they shared a common obsession with everyday material culture, with images found in newspapers and on the street, in scientific books and popular magazines. *Parallel of Life and Art* was a direct result of this fascination with urban grime and challenged existing orthodoxies. Original photographs and sculptures by Henderson

(fig. 12) Installation view of *Parallel of Life and Art*, 1953, photographed by Nigel Henderson

and Paolozzi were not shown in their own right, but as images in a photograph. The images shared a crudeness and vulgarity. The microphotographs were not of attractive snowflakes, but of benign tumours and rats. There were images of George VI's funeral and a burnt-out forest (fig. 12).

A discussion about the exhibition, which took place at the Architectural Association in Bedford Square on 2 December 1953, confirmed the Group's fascination with the everyday and with material culture. It was led by the show's curator, Reyner Banham. He referred subsequently to the debate in his article on "New Brutalism" which showcased the work of the Smithsons: "[...] students at the Architectural Association complained of the deliberate flouting of the traditional concepts of photographic beauty, of the cult of ugliness and denying the spiritual in man'".[11]

Subsequently the Smithsons interacted with urban reality by designing architectural commissions for dwellings – for example, the Robin Hood Lane housing in London (1964–70). Henderson continued to work with his Bethnal Green images before concentrating on a more inward looking series of images based around the human head,[12] and Paolozzi went on to create public sculptures, and even murals, for the London Underground.

11 Banham 1955 (see note 7), p. 356.

12 Walsh 2001 (see note 8).

ANNE MASSEY

CAN YOU SPEAK AMERICAN?

The third controversial topic of conversation for the Independent Group was with American mass culture. In the gloomy post-war years of rationing and food shortages, colourful advertising images emanating from the USA made a tremendous impact on society and on the members of the Group. Whilst they were summarily dismissed by the traditional art establishment, the Independent Group embraced all aspects of culture and proposed arranging them along a continuum, such that every experience was eligible for further examination and analysis. For the Independent Group, things were of interest, whether they were traditionally categorised as high culture or low culture. The central focus for the Group's overturn of cultural hierarchies was American popular culture. The Group admired Hollywood cinema, mass produced design, advertising and popular music, and this admiration fed into their creative practice. For example, the works of Richard Hamilton, such as *Hommage à Crysler Corp.* (1957) and *$he* (1958–61) showcased snippets from adverts for American cars and adverts for domestic appliances, rendered in oils.

In many ways the culmination of the Independent Group's work was the exhibition *This is Tomorrow* at the Whitechapel Art Gallery in 1956. This consisted of twelve, distinct areas which were then filled with a particular environment, specially designed by a team of three – one architect, one sculptor and one painter. Part of the exhibition consisted of a British Constructivist celebration, whilst other areas celebrated an Art Brut approach to urban reality. The latter is illustrated by the area created by the *Parallel of Life and Art* team – Henderson, the Smithsons and Paolozzi – and was entitled "Patio and Pavilion". The area was dominated by a roughly assembled, quasi-garden shed (fig. 13), filled with disparate objects and a large photocollage by Nigel Henderson entitled *Head of a Man* of 1956 (pl. 120). This consisted of photographic fragments of organic substances suggesting the image of a head at the moment of natural decomposition. The "Patio" area surrounding the shed was covered in sand and littered with ceramic

(fig. 13) Installation view of the exhibition *This is Tomorrow* at the Whitechapel Art Gallery, London 1956

tiles, collages by Henderson and sculpture by Paolozzi. This was like an archaeological excavation or a scene following an atomic explosion. As Reyner Banham observed: "One could not help feeling that this particular garden shed with its rusted bicycle wheels, a battered trumpet and other homely junk, had been excavated after an atomic holocaust."[13] The group created a symbolic environment, intended to be read by the audience as an interactive exhibit.

Another interactive exhibit was created by a team comprising Independent Group members Lawrence Alloway, Toni del Renzio and John Holroyd. This exhibit relied heavily on a recent trip to America by Holroyd, who had met the designers Charles and Ray Eames and seen their film, *A Communication Primer*. The academic discipline of communication studies was developing at this time, particularly at Yale University, and the Independent Group seized upon the academic framework, as a means of understanding and explaining the ways in which all forms of visual culture operate. In the exhibition catalogue the Group used simple diagrams borrowed from American communication theory to demonstrate that cultural boundaries could be overcome by the application of such theory. The exhibit consisted of a pinboard filled with random images related to palmistry, the Dead Sea Scrolls and Doris Day plus an interactive tackboard with sheets torn from magazines, which were changed during the exhibition.

The third of the areas to involve Independent Group members was "The Fun House" – an environment created by John Voelcker, Richard Hamilton and John McHale. Here American mass culture played a central role in overturning existing values and assumptions, as did the Group's concentration on perception. The space was adorned with a cardboard cut-out of Marilyn Monroe from *The Seven Year Itch* and Robbie the Robot from *Forbidden Planet*, a jukebox played contemporary popular music in the background and a print of Van Gogh's *Sunflowers* hung there. The space also incorporated material referring to sensory perception, with soft floors, fluorescent paint and optical illusions. McHale was in the United States on a two-year Yale Fellowship and sent material back to Richard Hamilton, which was then used in the exhibition. In one case, the discs on one wall were taken from images given to McHale by Marcel Duchamp.

13 Peter Reyner Banham, *The New Brutalism: Ethic or Aesthetic?*, London 1966.

Hence, this part of *This Is Tomorrow* encapsulates perfectly the importance of the Independent Group – it re-used concepts from modernism, it revelled in urbanity and it represented a conversation with American popular culture. The Independent Group was a radical collection of young intellectuals who succeeded in challenging existing orthodoxies and enriching our understanding of both art and the everyday. As such the Group forms a significant part of the history of twentieth century British art and its radical nature is a vital component of this exhibition.

ANNE MASSEY

96 | Adrian Heath CLIMBING COMPOSITION GREEN AND BLUE 1950

97 | Victor Pasmore RECTANGULAR MOTIF IN BLACK AND WHITE 1949

PEARS

TRANSPARENT

SOAP

MADE IN
GREAT BRITAIN

99 | Peter Lanyon WHEAL OWLES 1957–58

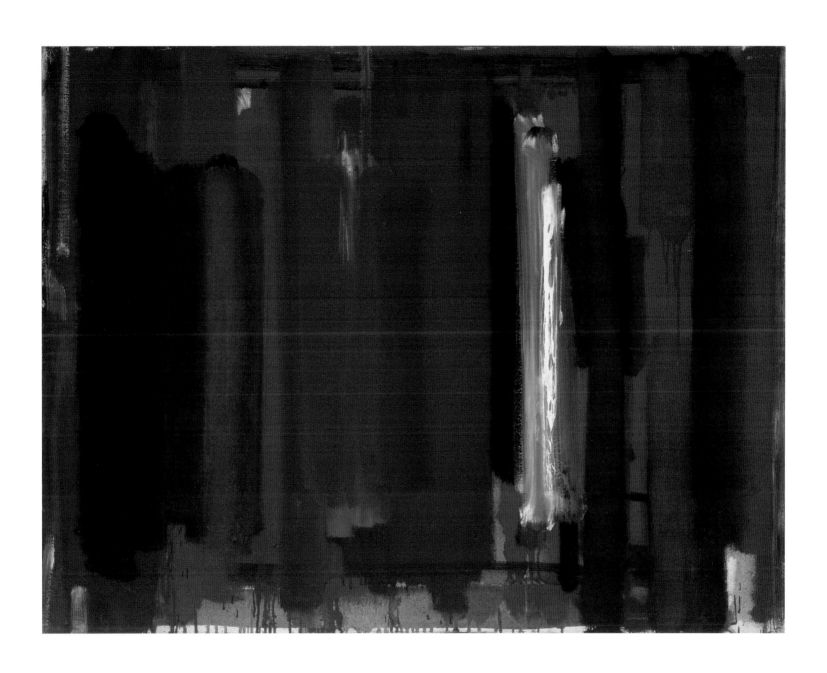

101 | Patrick Heron Big Grey – With Disc: June–September 1959 1959

103 | Alan Davie ALTAR FOR THE BLUE DIAMOND 1950

107 | Bernard Meadows THE BLACK CRAB 1953

108 | Lucian Freud OWL 1952

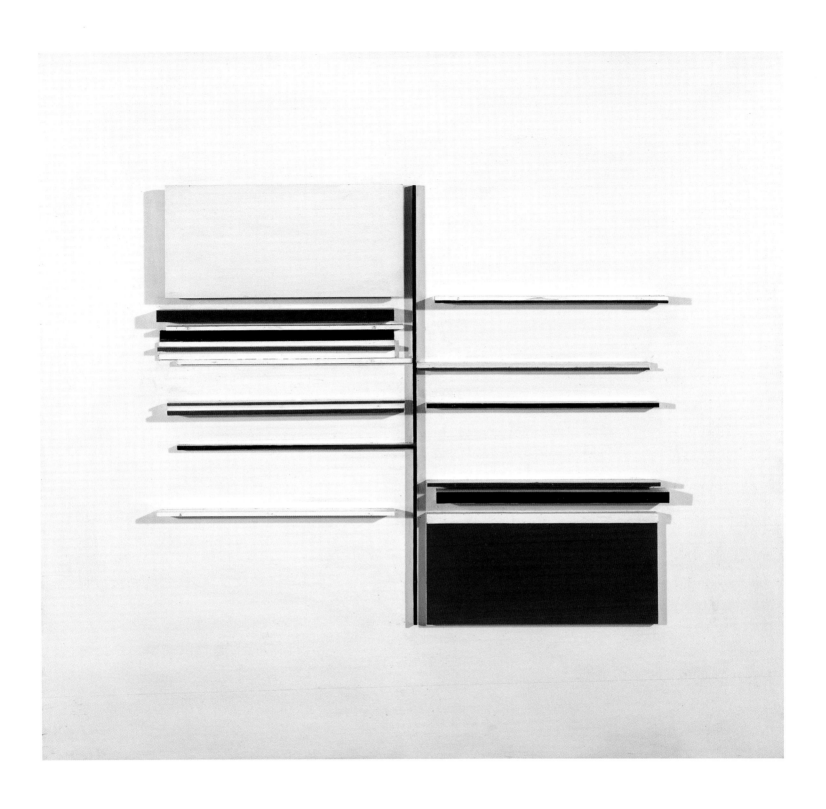

109 | Victor Pasmore RELIEF IN WHITE, BLACK, BROWN AND LILAC 1957

110 | Kenneth Armitage FIGURE LYING ON ITS SIDE (No. 5) 1957

111 | Nigel Henderson VERTICAL STATUE 1952

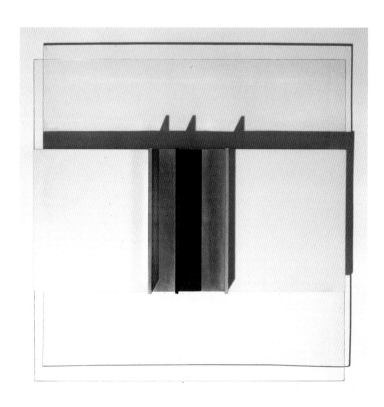

112 | Anthony Hill RELIEF CONSTRUCTION 1955–56

113 | Roger Hilton OCTOBER '56 (BROWN, BLACK & WHITE) 1956

114 | Alan Davie THE ALCHEMIST 1958

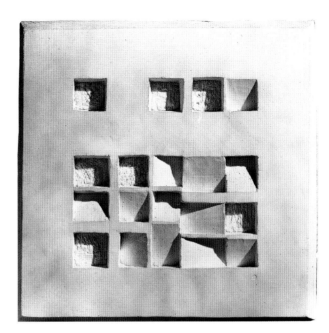

115 | Mary Martin COLUMBARIUM 1951

116 | Eduardo Paolozzi THE CAGE 1951

117 | William Turnbull HEAD 1955

120 | Nigel Henderson HEAD OF A MAN 1956–61

121 | Eduardo Paolozzi THE PHILOSOPHER 1957

124 | Nigel Henderson, Eduardo Paolozzi STUDY FOR PARALLEL OF LIFE AND ART 1952

126 | Richard Hamilton et al. Fun House 1956

1960–65
Pop, Op and Hard Edge

1960

Events: America elects President John F. Kennedy; direct American military aid to South Vietnam begins; Britain ends National Service

Coldstream Report on art education; *Lady Chatterley* trial exonerates Penguin Books

Lawrence Alloway resigns from ICA and moves to New York

Artists: Anthony Caro returns from New York; Eduardo Paolozzi begins teaching at Hochschule für Bildende Künste, Hamburg; John Latham animated film Speak, David Annesley enters St. Martin's School of Art; Patrick Caulfield enters Royal College of Art, Allen Jones expelled; John Hoyland leaves Royal Academy Schools, Stuart Brisley leaves Akademie der Bildende Künste, Munich; Henry Lamb dies

Exhibitions: Situation: *An Exhibition of British Abstract Painting* at Royal Society of British Artists (RBA); *Construction – England 1950–60* at Drian Galleries, London; Victor Pasmore at Venice Biennale; Picasso at Tate; Gustav Metzger *Auto-Destructive Art Lecture/demonstration* at Temple Gallery, London; *West Coast Hard Edge* at ICA

Publications: Clement Greenberg, *Art and Culture*; John Berger, *Permanent Red. Essays in Seeing*; Reyner Banham, Theory and *Design in the First Machine Age*; R. D. Laing, The *Divided Self*

1961

Events: Berlin Wall built

Young Contemporaries launch British Pop Art

Artists: Ian Hamilton Finlay founds Wild Hawthorn Press; Tim Scott returns from Paris; Richard Smith returns from New York; David Hockney first visits America; Peter Blake wins John Moores Prize; Vanessa Bell dies

Exhibitions: Epstein at Tate; Max Ernst at Tate; *New London Situation* at Marlborough; Bridget Riley at Gallery One; Richard Smith at Green's Art Gallery, New York

Publications: Bill Brandt, *Perspective of Nudes*; Raymond Williams, *The Long Revolution*; Gustav Metzger manifesto *Auto-Destructive Art Machine Art Auto-Creative Art*

1962

Events: Cuban Missile crisis (October); Consecration of new Coventry Cathedral; first *Sunday Times* colour supplement; Robert Fraser Gallery opens in London; Ken Russell TV film *Pop Goes The Easel*; first Fluxus event at ICA; Lawrence Alloway settles in America

Artists: David Hockney graduates from Royal College of Art with Gold Medal; Derek Boshier, R. B. Kitaj leave, Victor Burgin enters Royal College of Art; Gary Hume born

Exhibitions: Francis Bacon retrospective at Tate; Barbara Hepworth retrospective at Whitechapel; Fluxus *Festival of Misfits* at Gallery One; Mark Rothko at Whitechapel; Jackson Pollock at Marlborough; Derek Boshier at Grabowski Gallery, London; Bernard Cohen at Molton Gallery, London; Joe Tilson at Marlborough; William Tucker at Grabowski

Publications: Lawrence Alloway, "Pop Art since 1949", *The Listener*; Ian Hamilton Finlay, *Poor. Old. Tired. Horse.*

A. Alvarez (ed.) *The New Poetry*; Doris Lessing, *The Golden Notebook*

1963

Events: Britain refused entry to European Community; Profumo scandal rocks Conservative Government, Harold Macmillan succeeded as Prime Minister by Alec Douglas-Home; President Kennedy assassinated (Nov)

Kasmin Gallery opens in London; Gustav Metzger founds Centre for Advanced Creative Studies; Clement Greenberg visits London at British artists' expense; Beatles top all recording sales charts

Artists: David Hockney moves to Los Angeles; Richard Smith returns to New York; Patrick Caulfield leaves Royal College of Art; Bruce McLean enters St. Martin's School of Art; Anya Gallaccio, Michael Landy, Rachel Whiteread born; Helen Saunders dies

Exhibitions: *British Painting in the Sixties* at Whitechapel and Tate; R. B. Kitaj at Marlborough; Mark Boyle at Woodstock Gallery, London; Kenneth Noland at Kasmin; Archigram *Living City* at ICA

1964

Events: Tonkin Bay incident brings America openly into Vietnam War; Labour wins General Election under Harold Wilson; Jennie Lee appointed first ever Minister for the Arts

Alison and Peter Smithson complete Economist Building; Norman Reid becomes director of Tate; Signals Gallery opens in London; Peter Brook "Theatre of Cruelty" season and production of Peter Weiss' *Marat/Sade*

Artists: Roger Hilton wins UNESCO prize at Venice Biennale; Allen Jones moves to New York; John Latham first Skoob-Tower ceremony; Barry Flanagan enters St. Martin's School of Art; Peter Lanyon dies

Exhibitions: Robert Rauschenberg at Whitechapel; Joan Miro at Tate; *'54–'64 Painting and Sculpture of a Decade* at Tate; *Between Poetry and Painting* at ICA; Richard Hamilton at Hanover; Phillip King at Rowan Gallery, London

Publications: *The Studio* becomes *Studio International*; first issue of *Archigram*; Herbert Marcuse, *One-Dimensional Man*; Gustav Metzger, "On Random Activity In Material/Transforming Works of Art", *Signals*

1965

Events: America increases military commitment to South Vietnam

International Festival of Poetry, Royal Albert Hall; Peter Whitehead documentary *Wholly Communion; Sigma* installation at Better Books; Anthony d'Offay Gallery opens in London; Lessore Gallery closes in London

Artists: Roger Hilton settles in Cornwall; Victor Burgin leaves Royal College of Art, enters Yale; John Latham begins teaching at St. Martin's School of Art; Damien Hirst born

Exhibitions: *British Sculpture in the Sixties* at Tate; *New Generation Sculpture* at Whitechapel; Victor Pasmore retrospective at Tate; Alberto Giacometti at Tate; Bridget Riley at Richard Feigen, New York, and in *The Responsive Eye*, Metropolitan, New York

Publications: Government white paper *A Policy for the Arts*; Edward Bond, *Saved*; Bryan Robertson, John Russell, Lord Snowdon, *A Private View*, Gustav Metzger, *Auto-Destructive Art*; Mario Amaya, *Pop as Art*

OPEN SITUATIONS

BRITISH ABSTRACTION IN THE 1960s

TIM MARLOW

In 1965 the influential director of the Whitechapel Art Gallery Bryan Robertson teamed up with the critic John Russell and photographer Anthony Armstrong-Jones to produce a book which charted – as its subtitle put it – "the lively world of British art". *A Private View* was remarkable in its emphasis as much on the visual image as on the written word, particularly in a country where the cultural establishment was still predominantly a literary one. But the climate was changing and *Time* magazine's swinging city was beginning to see itself as "one of the world's three capitals of art". Instead of the "sectarian interests" that had dominated the London art world for much of the twentieth century and rendered British art largely a parochial adjunct to that of continental Europe, Russell and Robertson felt able to proclaim that "today we have an open situation" where "everything is allowable if it is done well enough".[1]

The most obvious manifestation of openness in British culture through the 1960s came from the blurring of boundaries between "high" and "low" art and the flourishing of Pop across the spectrum from music and fashion to painting and graphic design. But perhaps the most under-rated area, and certainly neglected in the historical surveys of the period conducted over the past two decades, was abstraction in both painting and sculpture, which seemed critically and creatively central to the perceived mainstream. Of course, abstraction had been of primary importance in the unfolding saga of modernism throughout the century, but it only became an established part of British art in the 1950s. This was partly because of the achievements of sculptors like Henry Moore and Barbara Hepworth as well as painters associated with the West Cornish peninsula, but also because of a change in the curriculum in art schools, which finally saw the Bauhaus – or aspects of its teaching methods – adopted, with the emphasis shifting from realism to a tighter focus on materials, basic skills and the idea – as one young sculptor from St. Martin's School of Art put it in 1960 – that "suddenly anything seemed possible".[2] Above all, though, there was the monumental impact of equally monumental abstract painting, which had emerged in the post-war period not in Europe but, like so much else on the cultural agenda, in America.

"During those years", according to John Hoyland who graduated in London in 1960, "we were regularly bombarded by American Art and we awaited each new installment like food parcels to a half-starved community."[3] The food parcels had begun to arrive in 1956, when Jackson Pollock and Mark Rothko (fig. 1) provided the

1 Bryan Robertson, John Russell, Lord Snowdon, *A Private View*, London 1965.

2 Tim Scott, interview with the author, April 1989.

3 John Hoyland, "An Appreciation", *Hans Hofmann: Late Paintings*, exh. cat. Tate Gallery, London 1988.

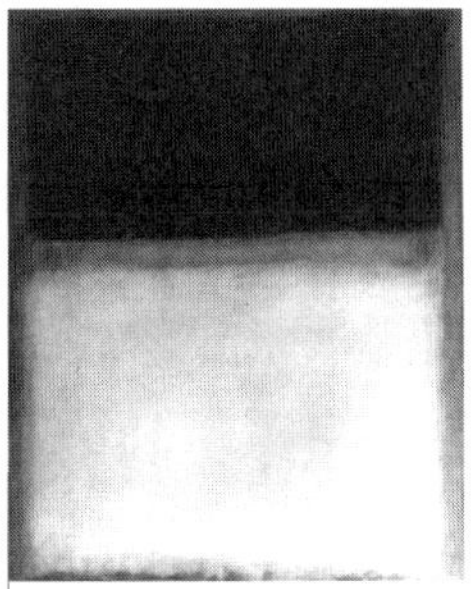

(fig. 1) Mark Rothko VIOLET AND YELLOW ON ROSE 1954, oil on canvas, 211 x 170 cm, Panza di Biumo Collection

rousing finale to an otherwise restrained exhibition at the Tate called *Modern Art in the United States*. Two years later Pollock (fig. 2) had a retrospective at Robertson's Whitechapel and then in 1959 was once again a star attraction at the Tate, in *New American Painting*. But aside from the visceral expressiveness of Pollock and the New York "action" painters, interest was growing in both Rothko and "colour field" and in an altogether cooler, detached, hard-edged form of abstraction practised at first by Barnett Newman (fig. 3), who was only seen for the first time in London in 1959, and by a younger generation, including Ellsworth Kelly and Kenneth Noland. In turn, a younger generation of London-based painters began to take up what was tantamount to a transatlantic challenge and by 1960 they were ready – as the critic Lawrence Alloway put it – "to make public what the public has not been seeing". [4]

Situation was staged at the RBA Galleries in London and was seen by very few people, but it is still seen as "one of a handful of exhibitions of twentieth century British painting that have profoundly re-shaped the direction and expectation of art in Britain"[5] (fig. 4). With assistance from Alloway and the writer Roger Coleman, it was mainly organised by artists with Bernard Cohen, Robyn Denny, Gordon House, Henry Mundy and William Turnbull forming the core group, who then selected a further fourteen painters to show work that was "abstract [...] and not less than 30 square feet".[6] The show had numerous sub-texts but perhaps the most striking was the idea of making size matter: first by using it as a political device, both to show work too big for most commercial galleries and to preclude the involvement of St. Ives painters, a point reinforced by the committee's definition of abstraction as being "without explicit reference to events outside the painting – landscape, boats, figures"; second, to suggest what Coleman described as "a new conception of space in painting" which enveloped the spectator and effectively re-defined the experience of confronting a painting as an environmental one; third, to emphasise the idea of the artist's direct physical engagement with the canvas which, as the American critic Harold Rosenberg put it, "was not a picture but an event"; finally, to reinforce the view initially articulated by Rosenberg's compatriot Clement Greenberg, that a work of art was an autonomous, self-contained object, in and of itself, and not a representation or simulation of reality.

Within these broad parameters there was massive scope for diverse style and practice and although Sylvia Sleigh painted a portrait of what she called *The Situation Group* in 1961 (fig. 5), the artists involved denied anything more than a loose affiliation. William Turnbull, the oldest participant, worked as both a painter and a sculptor. In 1957 he had visited New York and begun to use paint in thick swathes applied rapidly with a palette knife, but which were also the result of a long process of meditation which came from an interest in Eastern mysticism (pl. 118). He was also an influential teacher at the Central School of Art, four of whose students were selected for *Situation*: Peter Coviello, John Epstein, Peter Hobbs (who later withdrew) and Brian Young.

The most explicitly expressive painting in *Situation*, full of energy and dynamic painterly gestures, came from Gillian Ayres, whose work had initially been inspired by the rhythmical processes of Pollock. Ayres became equally absorbed in the stuff of paint and in the choreography of applying it, but whereas the American had painted on the floor, she worked on a vertical canvas, clambering about on ladders, stretching as far as her body could extend and thereby making her body the measure of all things painterly (fig. 6). Her surfaces shimmered as increasingly dense applications of paint caught the light and drew the eye of the spectator across the entire canvas, conveying a sense of vitality and, over the ensuing decade, of the joy of colour itself.

John Hoyland was producing tauter paintings with clearly delineated forms of darker tones split by angular wedges of brightness (pl. 162). Paint was applied

(fig. 2) Jackson Pollock retrospective at Whitechapel Art Gallery 1958

(fig. 3) Barnett Newman ACHILLES 1952, oil on canvas, 243.8 x 200.6 cm, National Gallery of Art, Washington D.C.

(fig. 4) Installation view of *Situation* at the RBA Galleries, London 1960

(fig. 5) Sylvia Sleigh PORTRAIT OF THE SITUATION GROUP 1961, oil on linen, 122 x 183 cm, Artist's Collection

(fig. 6) Gillian Ayres CUMULI 1959, oil on canvas, 304 x 320 cm, Artist's Collection

4 Lawrence Alloway, "Size Wise", *Art News and Review*, September 1960.
5 David Mellor, *The Sixties Art Scene in London*, exh. cat. Barbican Art Gallery, London 1993. This was produced as the catalogue for an exhibition curated by Mellor at the Barbican Art Gallery in London and remains the most perceptive and interesting survey of the art and culture of the period.
6 Roger Coleman, introduction to *Situation*, exh. cat. RBA Galleries, London 1960.

TIM MARLOW

in saturated areas and, although the canvas was precisely organised, there remained scope for optical ambiguity; forms jostled for attention one with another, sometimes laterally and othertimes in a push-pull dynamic, as if through the surface of the work. Soon after his precocious appearance in *Situation*, Hoyland discovered the work of Hans Hofmann, which liberated the young painter's belief in the expressive power of colour: "He opened up the whole spectrum of colour in painting and blew various conventions about tonal values in American art wide open."[7]

More detached, less painterly but emblematic of the broader framework in which painting was now being created was the work of Gordon House, Harold and Bernard Cohen and Robyn Denny. House was a graphic designer (fig. 7) as well as a painter, and the elegance of his compositions and the ensuing optical flicker had a distant relationship to the later work of one of the most original talents in British art over the next few decades, Bridget Riley. But hers was an art almost impossible to hold fixed by the eye, and although confronting the idea of visual perception it de-stabilised the process of looking (pls. 149 and 150). Riley's work also became increasingly concerned with the distillation of memory and experience, full of intense feeling and with strong metaphorical overtones, too.

Both Denny and Cohen produced more static images which both affirmed the flatness of the canvas, but which were also allusive in their references to lintels and doorways, windows and portals, all of which suggested the idea of a threshold ultimately rebuffed by the emphatic presence of the canvas itself (pl. 153). Standing in front of a work like Bernard Cohen's *Painting 96* (fig. 8), you feel both pulled into the yellow rectangular opening or frame towards a bright blue void, but ultimately repelled by the yellow targets which stare out as if returning the gaze in a crazily boggle-eyed manner. And yet, as you look again, the fact reasserts itself that this is a carefully composed, largely geometric, two-dimensional painting.

7 John Hoyland, interview with the author, May 1993.

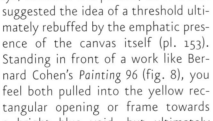

(fig. 7) Gordon House cover design for the exhibition catalogue *Situation*, London 1962

(fig. 8) Bernard Cohen PAINTING 96 in the exhibition *Situation*, RBA Galleries, London 1960

The formal elements in Cohen's *Painting 96* were remarkably similar to those in the first abstract welded steel sculpture ever produced by Anthony Caro. *Twenty Four Hours* was made in March 1960 (fig. 9), immediately after Caro had returned from a visit to America. For much of the previous decade, Caro had worked as an assistant to Henry Moore and his own work was figurative, modelled in clay and plaster and cast in bronze. But he increasingly felt constrained and expressed the desire "to make sculpture more real". Having met Clement Greenberg in London and then in New York, the young sculptor was told "if you want to change your art, change your methods". So, taking the critic's advice, Caro "decided to find a new material and I immediately went down to the docks when I got back to London and found some steel".[8]

Caro's methods owed a good deal to Constructivist sculpture, to the collage technique of Pablo Picasso and the work of the American David Smith, but his most potent inspiration came from painting – notably that of a generation of American artists whom he had met; including Helen Frankenthaler, Kenneth Noland and Jules Olitski. "It was better to go to painting than to old sculpture", Caro observed, "because it gave one ideas what to do but no direct instructions on how to do it".[9] By the end of the year, he had begun to paint his work (pl. 154), partly as a way of repudiating Moore's former interest in "truth to materials", but mainly as a way of articulating mood and expressiveness and creating what he described as "the abstractness of feeling that you got in painting". This affinity with painters led to Caro's inclusion in the *New London Situation* exhibition in 1961.[10]

Caro also inspired a group of younger sculptors whom he taught, and then taught with, at St. Martin's School of Art and who were subsequently hailed as producing "a revolution in British sculpture"[11] when their work was shown together in the *New Generation Sculpture* exhibition at the Whitechapel in 1965. David Annesley, Michael Bolus, Phillip King, Tim Scott,

8 Anthony Caro, interviewed by Phyllis Tuchman, 1980, quotes by Tim Hilton, *Anthony Caro Sculpture 1960–84*, exh. cat. Arts Council, London 1984. All other Caro quotes from interviews with the author, published in *Anthony Caro*, exh. cat. Openluchtmuseum voor Beeldhouwkunst Middelheim, Antwerpen 1997.

(fig. 9) Anthony Caro TWENTY-FOUR HOURS 1960, painted steel, 138.5 x 223.5 x 89 cm, Tate, London

9 Caro 1980 (see note 8).
10 *New Situation: An Exhibition of British Abstract Art*, exh. cat. New London Gallery, London. 1961. The following year, the Arts Council produced a touring exhibition also called *Situation* which turned out to be the last in an impromptu series.

William Tucker and Isaac Witkin all produced abstract, coloured sculpture, which did away with the plinth and stood on the floor in the most direct relationship possible with the spectator. But each began to develop his own dialect of what Caro called "the language of sculpture". Aside from steel, they used aluminium, plastic, Perspex, fibreglass and glass. King made perhaps the most iconic works; which deconstructed the form of the cone. *Rosebud* of 1962 (pl. 157) was an early and pivotal piece, where the sculpture seemed to be breaking out of its own skin, and where the soft sensual pink seemed integral to the form rather than being a late, essentially decorative element. *Through* (1965) was the grandest of the cone pieces, sliced into sections to reveal both inside and out but still charged with a mysterious, hieratic presence which aimed to inspire a certain sense of wonder: "I want people to stand aghast for a second", King commented, "and I hope they'll do it again and again with my best work".[12]

Scott, the youngest of the sculptors, had trained as an architect and although his work became more environmental in scale and impact towards the end of the decade, initially he worked on a smaller, denser scale, using simple forms which he then rotated or almost refracted in a piece like *Peach Wheels* (1961–62). Here, two painted wooden structures (looking a little like dumbbells) are separated but paradoxically bound together by a sheet of glass which seems to have caused a drop in scale from one form to another. It is a work which seems to reveal itself totally on first viewing, but ultimately it feels elusive, full of unexpected connections and disjunctions.

Although Tucker acknowledged the importance of painting, both his writing and his own work sought to emphasise the essential nature of what sculpture was and ought to be (pl. 156). Over the decade, he formulated a series of rules, which attempted to define *The Condition of Sculpture* and later formed the basis of an exhibition at the Hayward, which he selected.[13] It was symptomatic of Tucker's analytical mind and his acute intellect; it was also brave, but motivated increasingly by the desire to attack a new form of art which was emerging internationally but whose development in Britain came strongly from the sculpture department at St. Martin's School of Art. There are two ways of viewing the development of what is loosely called Conceptual Art in London: one is the Freudian killing of the father figure, with Barry Flanagan, Gilbert and George, Richard Long and others effectively doing to Caro and the New Generation what they had done to Moore; the other is of an ongoing evolution of sculpture into what Rosalind Krauss called "an expanded field".[14] This perhaps comes closest to the experimental spirit, ambition and energy which characterised the "open situation" in British art at the beginning of the decade, even if many of those involved came to repudiate the direction that art took towards the end of the 1960s.

11 The term "revolution" seems to have first been proclaimed by Bryan Robertson in *The Times*, 9 March 1965, but it was widely used in the press subsequently and also by Robertson and Russell, in *A Private View* (see note 1).

12 Phillip King, quoted by Norbert Lynton in "Latest Developments in British Art", *Art and Literature*, no. 2, 1964.

13 *The Condition of Sculpture*, exh. cat. Arts Council, London 1975. The exhibition was curated by William Tucker and staged at the Hayward Gallery. It sparked off a heated debate in both the art press and the national media.

14 Rosalind Krauss, "Sculpture in the Expanded Field", first published in *October*, no. 8, spring 1979, republished in Krauss' collection of essays *The Originality of the Avant-Garde and Other Modernist Myths*, Boston 1985.

TIM MARLOW

POP ART

MARCO LIVINGSTONE

Daily life in Britain was drab and grey for some years after the War. Rationing of food came to an end only in 1952, and the benefits of the capitalist system enjoyed by Americans – abundant consumer goods, television, increased leisure time – only gradually began to become reality for the British in the early 1960s. When Prime Minister Harold Macmillan proclaimed in 1957 that "Most of our people have never had it so good", it was still for many a case of wishful thinking.

British Pop Art, particularly in the forms that emerged in the work of painters studying together at the Royal College of Art in London during the early 1960s, was largely the invention of working-class men, whose early years coincided with the deprivations of the Second World War. It was perhaps this common experience, rather than pure serendipity, that explains why the intake of students in autumn 1959 included so many who were to become important figures in the movement by the time they completed their postgraduate course three years later: David Hockney, Allen Jones and Derek Boshier, all born in 1937, Peter Phillips, born in 1939, and the American R. B. Kitaj, born in 1932, who had settled in England in 1957 and was studying there under the terms of the G. I. Bill. Patrick Caulfield, born in 1936, arrived at the College in 1960, and Pauline Boty, born in 1938, studied in the Stained Glass department (1958–61), before becoming the only female Pop painter in the few years before her death from cancer in 1966 (pl. 139) Compulsory military service, or National Service as it was known, was phased out in the UK in 1960, and of the artists listed here only Boshier and Hockney (who, as a conscientious objector, spent two years working as a hospital porter) had their studies interrupted. A new hedonistic atmosphere beckoned.

Earlier in the 1950s, other British artists had paved the way. Two prominent members of the Independent Group, Richard Hamilton and Eduardo Paolozzi, had put into practice many of the group's theoretical interests in product design, advertising, science fiction and the cinema. The word "pop" itself had first been used in a fine art context at their meetings, and its first published appearance in this sense was in a 1958 article by Lawrence Alloway, one of the critics at the heart of the group. Much of the material to which Hamilton and Paolozzi had recourse was American in origin, in particular the glossy magazines which they plundered for collage material and which they used as a repository of exotic, alluring images of a prosperous way of life. When Hamilton made paintings such as *Hommage à Chrysler Corp.* (1957), it was American rather than British cars that he chose to celebrate.

As early as the late 1940s, while working in Paris under the spell of Surrealism, Paolozzi had produced a series of collages in scrapbook form that retrospectively appeared to be harbingers of Pop; in 1972 he published a portfolio of facsimiles of these as *Bunk*, using the title of a rapid-fire lecture he had given to the IG in 1952, in which he had first shown these works with the aid of an epidiascope. The collage aesthetic was essential, also, to Paolozzi's sculpture: the mythical figures he produced during the 1950s, redolent of science-fiction "B" movies, were brutalist works encrusted with the traces of found objects, which he had embedded into the maquettes from which the bronzes were cast. By the time he came to make works such as *Diana As an Engine* of 1963–66 (pl. 132), his longstanding obsession with the marriage of classical mythology to science fiction was manifested in his adoption of the robot as a central point of reference.

Like Paolozzi, Hamilton was a key figure in the early development of Pop, though his brilliant investigations in this idiom mostly postdate the arrival of the younger artists. The success in the early 1960s of the Royal College painters and of American Pop artists such as Andy Warhol and Roy Lichtenstein appears both to have cemented his position as a pioneer and to have inspired him, for it was only in the mid to late 1960s that he reached his peak as a Pop artist in such works as *My Marilyn* (1965) – a personalised response to the screen goddess already immortalised by Warhol and others – and the *Swingeing London 67* series (1968–69), a set of variations on the screenprinted portrait of rock singer Mick Jagger and art dealer Robert Fraser being driven away on drugs charges. These latter works perhaps encapsulate more vividly than any others the contradictions, glamour and excesses of the period. Yet it is a single tiny collage of 1956, *Just What Is It That Makes Today's Homes So Different, So Appealing?*, that still holds pride of place as the key work to which all later explorations of Pop Art can be traced. Made for reproduction as a poster and for the catalogue of the IG's final thematic show, *This Is Tomorrow*, at the Whitechapel Art Gallery, it is crammed full of every image and theme later to be explored by Hamilton and other artists: muscle-man and pin-up girl; space exploration; canned and processed food (including a huge lollipop prominently labelled "POP"), cars, domestic appliances and other modern conveniences made possible by the assembly line; and new technologies, popular entertainments and forms of communication, recording and image-making, including the cinema, television, tape recorders and comic strips.

The Royal College of Art artists were too young, and the IG discussions too closed to non-members, for the IG to have had a direct influence on their art. They had seen a few reproductions of works by American artists, such as Jasper Johns, Robert Rauschenberg and Larry Rivers, who were influential figures on the development of Pop on both sides of the Atlantic, but it was only in 1961/1962, by which time they had developed

their own idioms, that they first heard of Lichtenstein, Warhol, James Rosenquist and other seminal Pop artists from the USA. There was little awareness, too, of works by the French Nouveaux Réalistes, a group of artists (mostly sculptors) who had banded together in 1960 and who were exploring notions of mass production and the found object akin to those being examined by the American Pop artists. Closer to home, however, was the work of Peter Blake, who had studied at the Royal College of Art a few years before them (in the company of two other future Pop artists, Richard Smith and Joe Tilson) and who, as a visiting tutor, took an immediate interest in their paintings. As early as 1952, Blake had been making paintings that expressed directly (and without recourse to the irony characteristic of the IG) his affection for the popular entertainments of his youth in Dartford, Kent (the movies, circuses, wrestling matches, amusement arcades), as well as pin-up images, packaging and other printed ephemera. *Children Reading Comics* of 1954 (pl. 105) is one of the earliest works to feature the frames of a comic strip so prominently, prefiguring Lichtenstein's comic strip paintings by seven years, although the technique of transposing the source could still be described as traditional or old-fashioned. By the end of the decade, Blake had devised more daring ways of using such material: *Girlie Door* (1959) is one of a series of works in which found photographs or printed images are simply pasted onto surfaces identified as functional objects, coated in bright household enamel paint. In their raw "hands-off" presentation of found motifs, they rival Warhol's adoption of photo-screenprinting in autumn 1962.

The investigations into popular culture that characterised the work of the Royal College painters, and their reliance on pictorial strategies from advertising, game boards and other consumer items, photography and the cinema, were stated by them with a particular forcefulness, gusto, playfulness, humour and youthful exuberance. Some of their immediate predecessors, such as the "Kitchen Sink" painters or the Expressionist disciples of David Bomberg, or even, for that matter, Francis Bacon and Lucian Freud, emphasised the harshness of life in deliberately bleak and drab hues. These Pop artists, by contrast, favoured high-keyed primary colours that spoke of optimism and energy. They pushed aside the emphasis on nature promoted by the St. Ives painters during the 1950s in favour of an aggressively

128 | David Hockney Going to Be a Queen for Tonight 1960

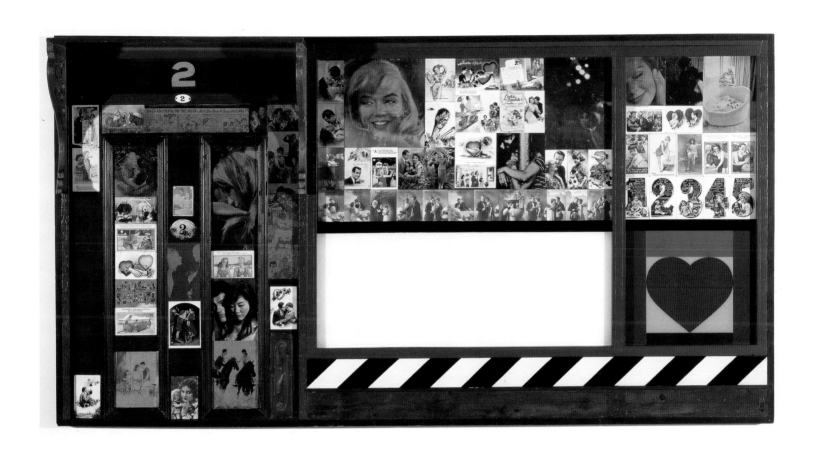

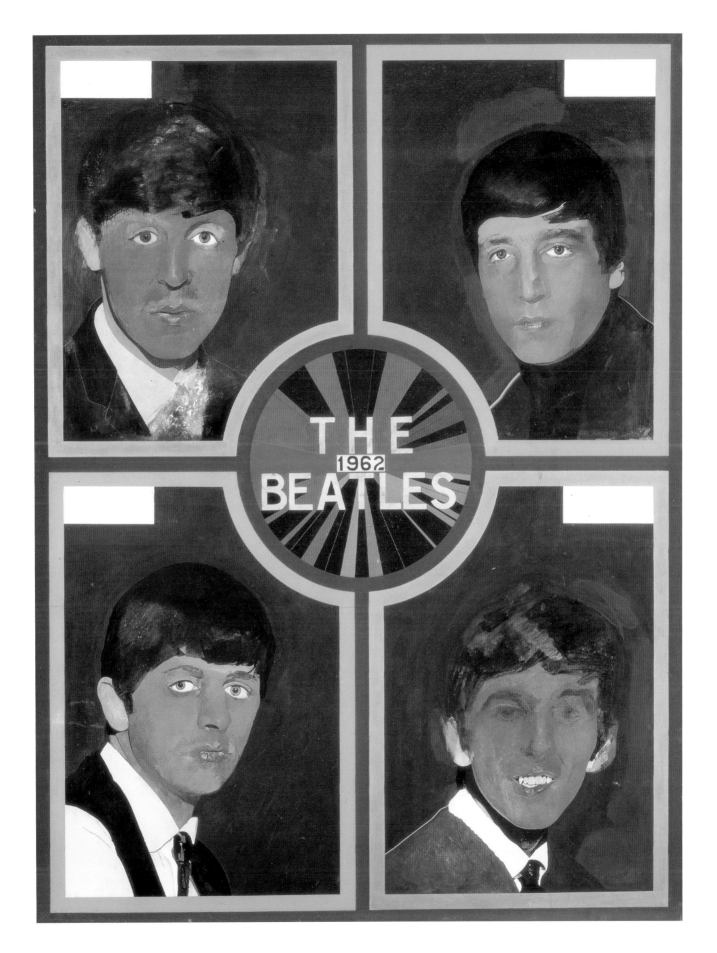

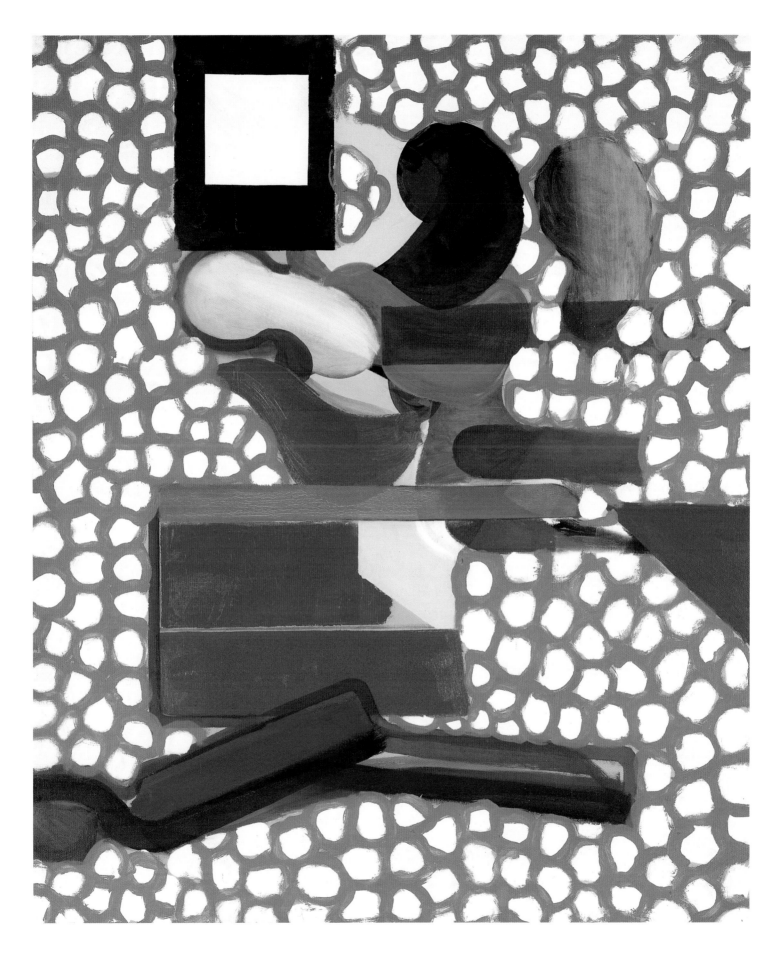

135 | Howard Hodgkin ANTHONY HILL AND GILLIAN WISE 1963–66

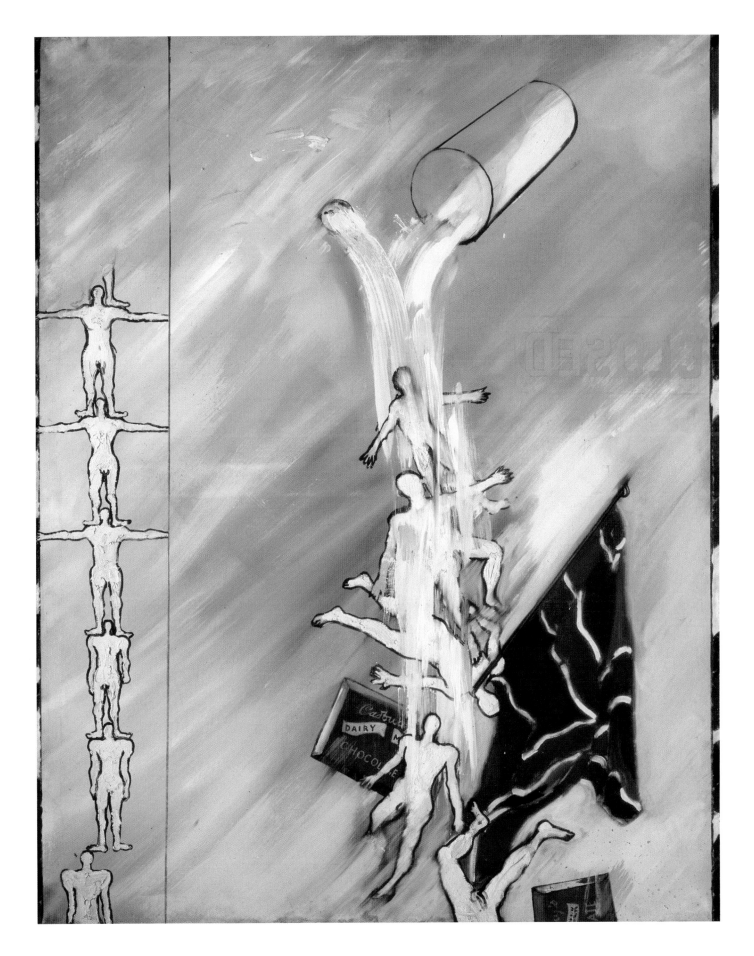

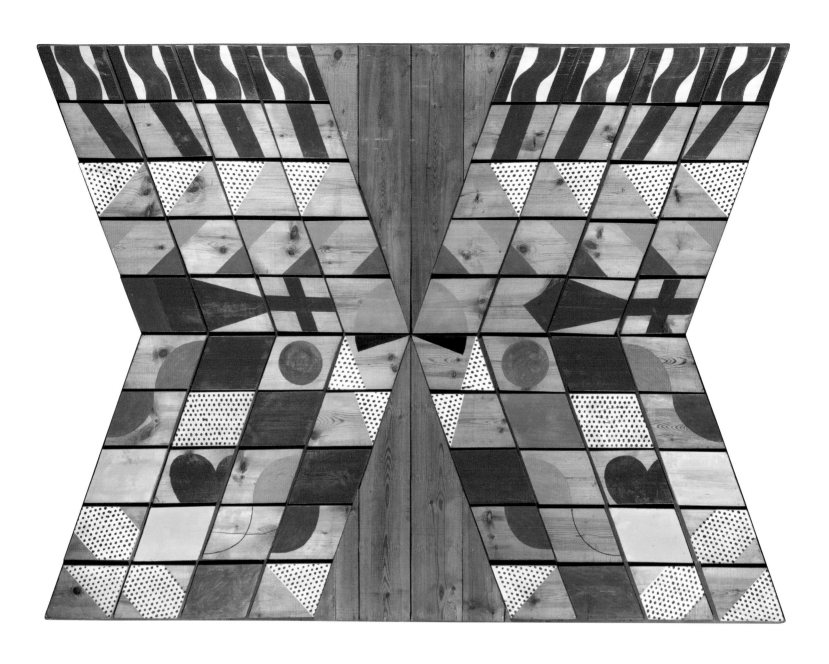

THIS IS MY BOOK AN UNUSUAL BOOK THIS IS MY COLOURING BOOK

these are the eyes that watched him as he walked aWay
colour tHem grey

this is the heart that thought he would alWays bE TRuE   Colour IT

BLUE

THESE are the arms that Held Him and Touched Him & lusT
HIM Somehow COLOUR Them empty noW

these are the beads I wore until she came
BETWEEN COLOUR THEM GREEN

this is the room I sleep in and walk in and
weep in and hide in that nobody sees   colour it lonely please

IS THE BOY THE Boy
PENDED BROK

140 | Richard Hamilton WHITLEY BAY 1965

141 | Richard Hamilton ᴇᴘɪᴘʜᴀɴʏ 1964/89

143 | Michael Andrews THE COLONY ROOM 1962

142 | Robyn Denny SLOT 1961

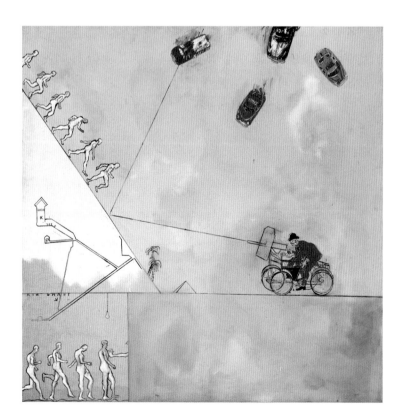

144 | Derek Boshier MAN VERSES LOOK VERSES LIFE VERSES TIME VERSES MAN ABOUT 1962

145 | Frank Auerbach STUDY AFTER DEPOSITION BY REMBRANDT II 1961

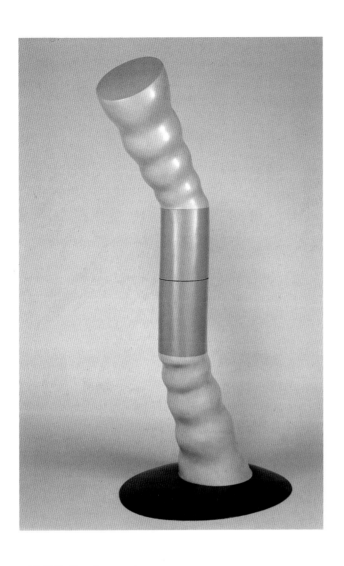

146 | Phillip King Ripple 1963

147 | Mary Martin White Diagonal 1963

148 | Allen Jones 9th Bus, Yellow Ochre Lady 1962

149 | Bridget Riley Crest 1964

150 | Bridget Riley Cataract 3 1967

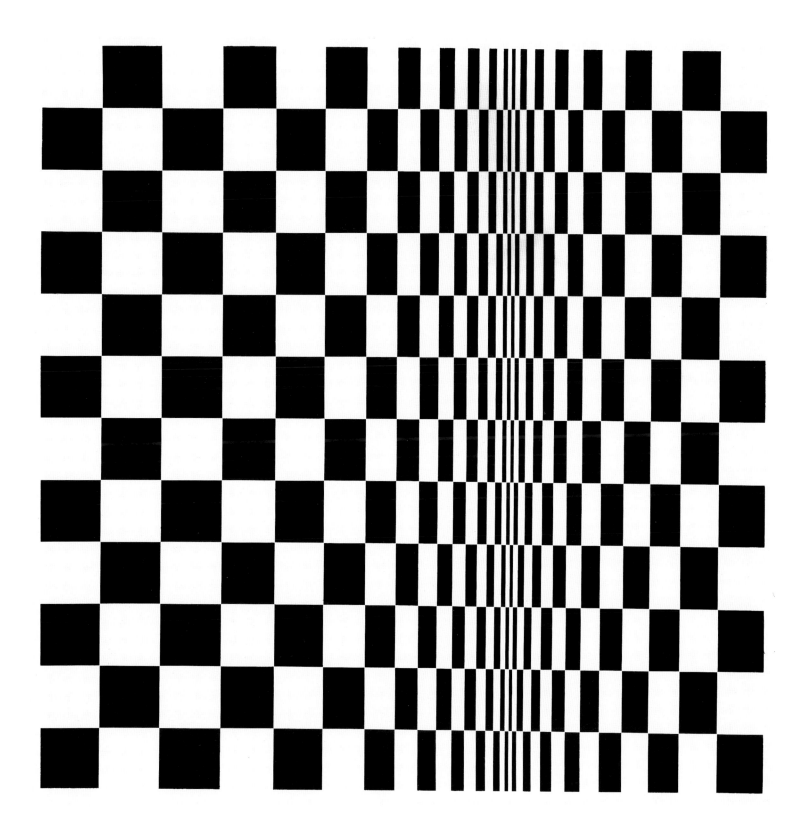

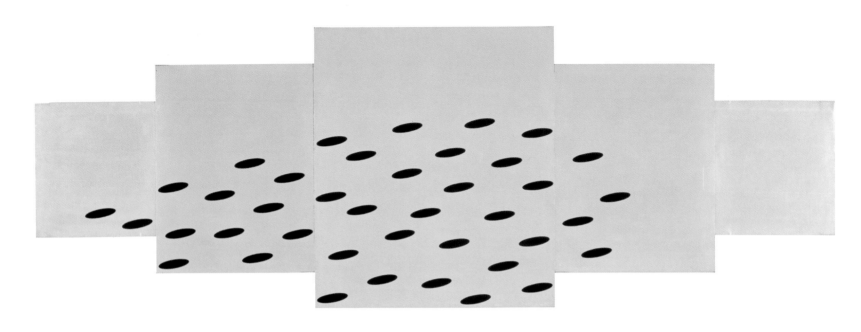

152 | Jeremy Moon Concord 1964

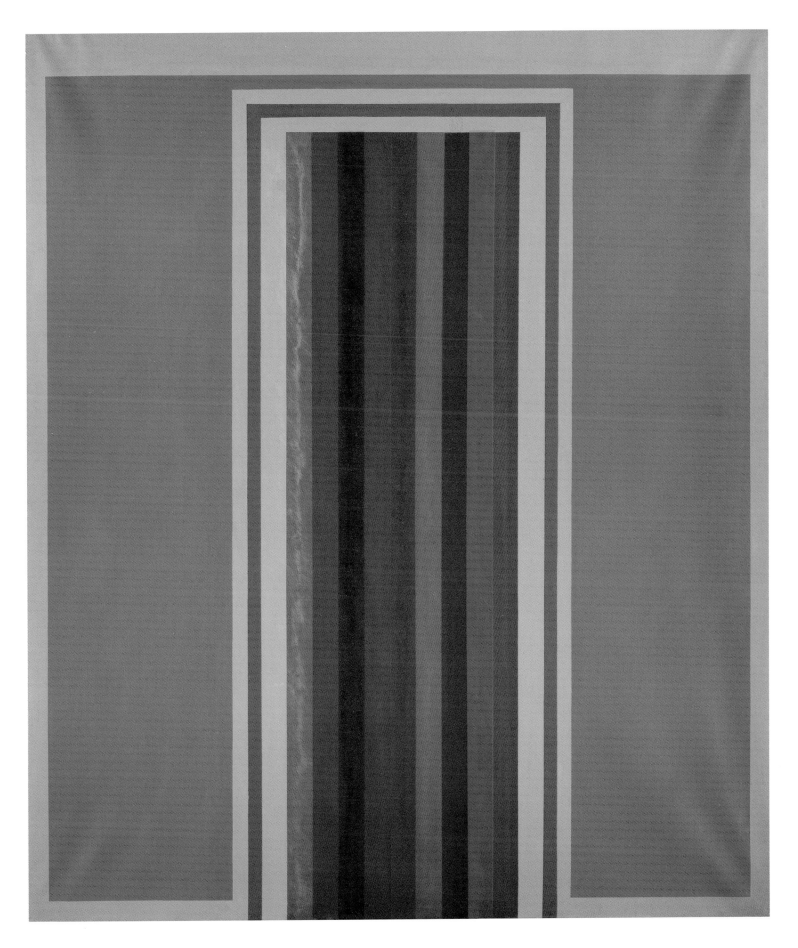

154 | Anthony Caro SCULPTURE SEVEN 1961

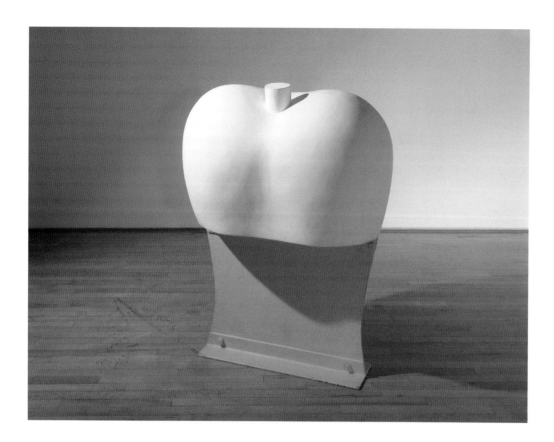

156 | William Tucker Florida 1962

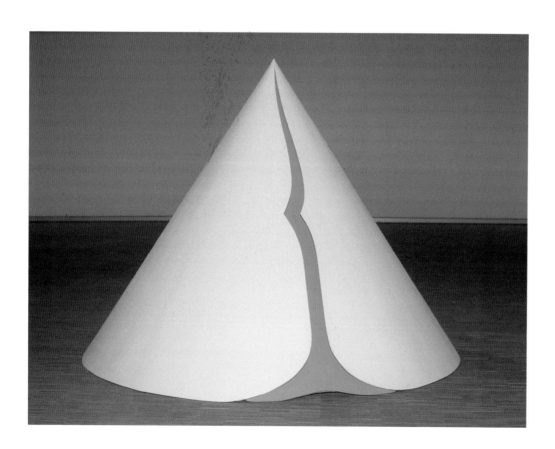

157 | Phillip King Rosebud 1962

158 | Richard Smith FLAP TOP 1962

159 | Paul Huxley UNTITLED No. 36 1964

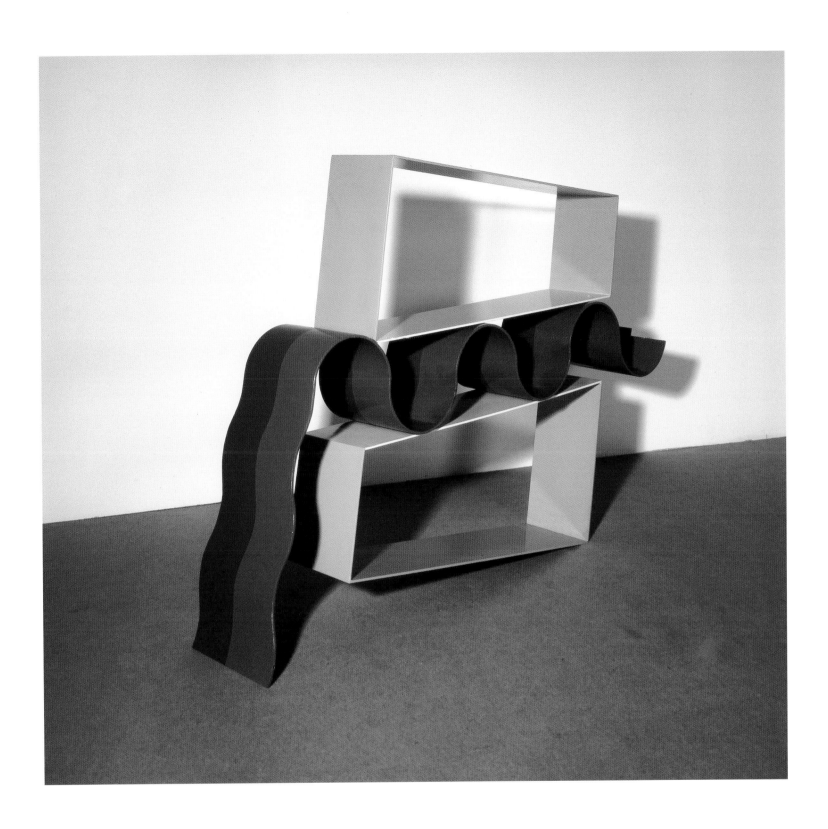

161 | William Turnbull 25-1959 1959

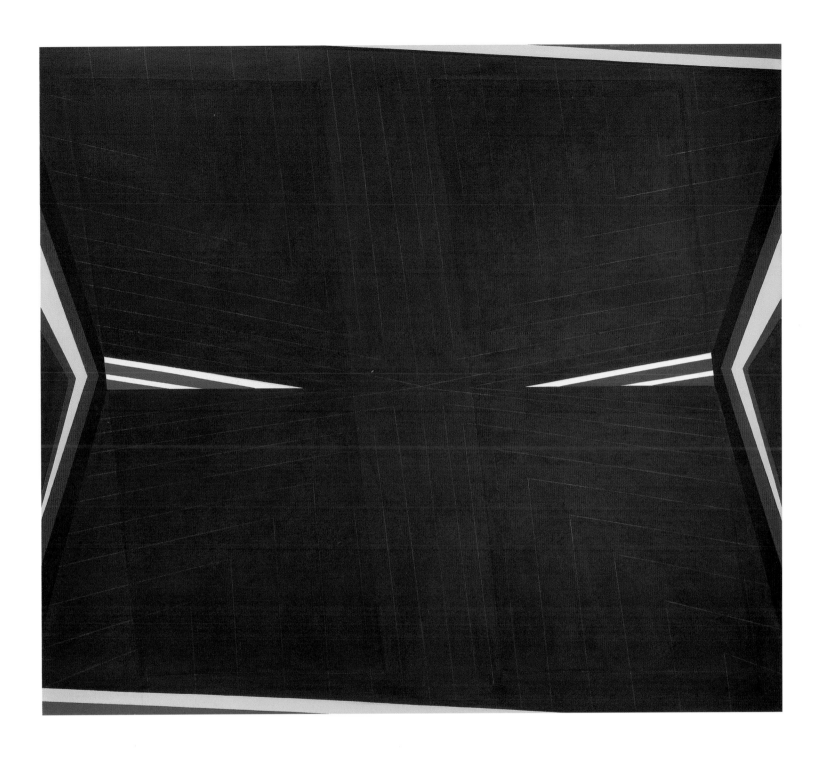

163 | Bob Law BLACK PAINTING # 48 1966

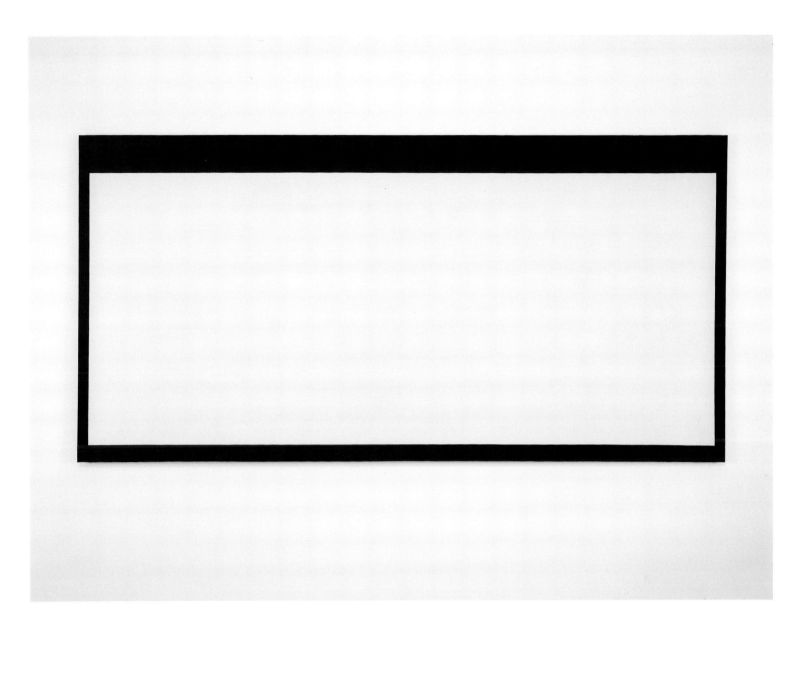

164 | Peter Joseph CREAM COLOUR WITH BLACK BORDER 1970

165 | Alan Charlton Double Channel Painting 1972

urban stance, just as surely as they countered emerging forms of abstraction with immediately recognisable imagery conveyed as directly as possible. Nevertheless they shared with the abstract painters, particularly with those who banded together in the *Situation* exhibitions of 1960 and 1961, a concern with strong colour, bold formal design and large scale. In any case, the divide between the formalist abstract painters and the Pop artists was not always clear-cut. One particular *Situation* painter, Richard Smith, was a leading innovator in both camps: the cinema screen, billboard advertisements and the colour photography of mass-circulation magazines were all important reference points for paintings such as *Flap Top* (pl. 158), *Package* and *Product*, all 1962, and for three-dimensional shaped canvases which took on a more overt Pop appearance.

The reliance by the Royal College painters on commonplace contemporary motifs previously regarded as unworthy of the attention of fine artists was symptomatic of the newly forged teenage culture, then just in the process of being defined (most ostentatiously in the form of rock'n'roll music and the new concept of youth fashion). These painters, much younger than most of their Pop counterparts in New York and Los Angeles, were all barely in their twenties when they created the works that defined the new movement. The courage and confidence, even the recklessness and effrontery, of their youth, were all important factors in the production of the fresh and vibrant art they were to create before they had even finished their courses. These same qualities were also evident in the lengths they took to present themselves as a force to be reckoned with in the student exhibitions known as *Young Contemporaries*. In February 1961, Peter Phillips (the organising committee's president) and Allen Jones (its secretary) hung their work in the same room as that of Boshier, Caulfield, Hockney and Kitaj, making for a powerful and coherent statement of intent that could not fail to be noticed. As a marketing strategy for their careers, it anticipated by nearly thirty years the *Freeze* exhibition, through which Damien Hirst and his fellow students first unveiled "BritArt" to an unsuspecting public.

One of the remarkable aspects of the work produced at the Royal College of Art in the early 1960s was the speed and clarity with which each painter defined himself in relation to his peers. Phillips, who by the end of the decade was the most extreme British

exponent of Pop in huge airbrushed canvases on which floating images of cars and machine parts collided with dazzling geometric patterns, was producing some of the largest and most formally impressive paintings of any student by the time he was 21. *Gravy for the Navy* of 1963 (fig. 1), painted after he had completed his course but a year before his departure for New York and later Switzerland, typifies his early production: his interests in heraldic patterns and emblematic imagery, game-board design and the formal structure and axial symmetry of pre-Renaissance paintings are effortlessly fused into a vividly coloured surface that communicates on a purely formal abstract level, as well as through its sexy and nostalgic imagery.

(fig. 1) Peter Phillips GRAVY FOR THE NAVY 1963, oil on canvas and hardboard, 240 x 259 cm, Oldham Gallery

The most overtly political of the Royal College painters, Boshier, was also the one who most revelled in the contemporaneity of his references to advertising, world events (such as the Cuban missile crisis) and the space race between America and the USSR. His reading of Marshall McLuhan, Vance Packard and other writers brought to his work a critical and even satirical edge that was markedly at odds with the more celebratory or neutral stance of the Americans.

Caulfield's *Santa Margherita Ligure* of 1964 (fig. 2), like his *Engagement Ring* of the previous year, conveys the chosen image with an extreme economy of means. In each case, the severity of the reduction of the motif to its essential linearity, filled in by a flat coat of gloss paint, yields improbably to the power of a barely repressed emotion. This is particularly the case when the motif seems both impossibly corny or romantic, as with the picture-postcard view of a Mediterranean scene, and luscious in colour. Caulfield's mastery of such paradoxes and contradictions encouraged him to favour perverse choices of subject matter often drawn from the Romantic tradition, and to reject the popular contemporary imagery used by some of his colleagues. While he rejected the appropriateness of the Pop label to his own work, his fascination with pushing his work towards different forms of banality made him one of the movement's most original and challenging painters.

(fig. 2) Patrick Caulfield SANTA MARGHERITA LIGURE 1964, oil on board, 122 x 244 cm, private collection

Jones, who was expelled from the Royal College of Art in 1960 as an example to his year, demonstrated early on that he was one of the great colourists of his generation. His true allegiances as a student were to early twentieth-century pioneers of abstraction, such as Robert Delaunay, Wassily Kandinsky and Paul Klee, who retained references to the visible world and used colour as an essential expressive tool. In his early work, Jones came closest to Pop in a series of shaped canvases referencing the double-decker red buses of London. Although the choice of subject conveyed his experience of urban life, his concern was more with the resolution of a pictorial problem, specifically in the expression of movement through the shape of the canvas support. It was only in the mid 1960s, while living for a short time in New York, that he adopted a more overt Pop mode in paintings and sculptures derived from fetish magazines. The exaggeration and directness with which such illustrators portrayed the female body proved an enduring inspiration, particularly for the "furniture" sculptures such as *Table* (1969), his most provocative statements.

Kitaj and Hockney were quick to deny their identity as Pop artists. Kitaj, whose greater experience and first-hand knowledge of American art made him an important mentor to his fellow students, had virtually no interest in popular culture (with the exception of Hollywood films and baseball, both of which were to appear as subject-matter in his paintings). It was, rather, his freewheeling approach to style – as an expressive element that could be chosen or parodied at will – and his transcriptions of found motifs that were to prove so influential on his younger colleagues. He demonstrated that all that was required to make disparate elements cohere were pictorial and thematic links that could unify them conceptually in the mind of the spectator.

Hockney made only passing reference to pop culture, invariably from a very personal perspective as a young gay man fighting to express his identity at a time when homosexual acts between consenting adults were still illegal. His "homosexual propaganda" paintings, such as *Going to Be a Queen for Tonight* of 1960 (pl. 128), and the paintings he made a few years later such as *Man Taking Shower in Beverly Hills* (1964), which expressed the much more relaxed acceptance of gay relationships that he found on his move to Los Angeles in 1964, did much to create the more liberal climate that led to the

law being changed in 1967. His great originality lay in the effortlessness with which he moved from one idiom to another, taking what he needed and adapting it to his own purposes.

As with the selection of works in this exhibition, so in this essay limited space necessarily precludes discussion of all the artists who made an important contribution to the development of Pop in Britain. For example, Joe Tilson's single work in this show, *For Jos* of 1961 (pl. 138), cannot adequately convey even that early formalist phase of his art, which combined aspects of sculpture and painting in brightly coloured wooden constructions suggestive of children's toys. By the end of the decade, when Tilson was on the point of abandoning Pop and leaving London for rural Wiltshire, he had explored a variety of forms including images screenprinted onto canvas and a large body of graphic work derived from collage principles. Other painters not trained at the Royal College, such as Anthony Donaldson (born 1939 and a student at the Slade) and Gerald Laing (born 1936 and trained at St. Martin's), made vital early contributions that were recognised in the early accounts of the movement. In their marriage of form and content both were closer in some respects to the "pure Pop" of the Americans than to the work of other British artists: Donaldson with graphic, simplified images such as *To Blue Films* of 1963 (fig. 3), reliant on rhythmic repetitions, and Laing with oil paintings such as *Brigitte Bardot* (1963), in which his use of dot patterns suggestive of newspaper photographs came close to the technique employed by Lichtenstein.

(fig. 3) Anthony Donaldson
To Blue Films 1963, oil on canvas, 152.4 x 152.4 cm, Alex Hood Collection

(fig. 4) Clive Barker Newspaper 1967, chrome-plated brass, 35.5 x 47 x 5.1 cm, Rupert E. G. Power Collection , London

Nicholas Monro (born 1936), who studied at Chelsea School of Art in the late 1950s with Caulfield, and the largely self-trained Clive Barker (born 1940) each produced sculptures as highly distinctive and original as those by Paolozzi: Barker favouring direct casting and chrome-plating of existing objects (fig. 4), Monro modelling his fantastic and humorous concoctions, such as *Martians* in 1965, and then casting them in fibreglass before painting them in vivid colours (fig. 5). It is perhaps Colin Self (born 1941 and a student at the Slade), however, who most powerfully demonstrates the seemingly endless possibilities offered by Pop and the difficulty of encompassing some of its most astonishing inventions within conventional accounts. Devoting himself largely to works on paper,

in the form of drawings and graphic works, Self surveyed the world around him with the innocent curiosity of a child and the caustic intelligence of a world-weary and sophisticated adult obsessed by the possibility of the planet's imminent destruction. In etchings such as *4th Monument* of 1964 (fig. 6), printed from individually inked pieces of metal and other found objects, he played with the iconography of Pop while undermining some of its standard assumptions.

(fig. 5) Nicholas Monro MARTIANS 1965, painted fibreglass, 120 x 60 x 30 cm, Rupert E. G. Power Collection , London

The classic Pop years, according to purists, were between 1961 and 1964. While it was during that period that the movement gained currency and produced some of its acknowledged masterpieces, its origins in Britain were too varied for its starting date to be labelled with such certainty: the first stirrings of Pop had been manifested throughout the previous decade. By the same token, Pop continued to evolve and to maintain its position at least to the early 1970s, notwithstanding the increasing fragmentation of art into other directions including conceptual, Minimal, performance and video art. With the resurgence of representational painting and sculpture in the 1980s came a renewed wave of influence from Pop on a variety of artists working in Britain including Lisa Milroy, David Mach, Julian Opie and even such established artists as Michael Craig-Martin. By then the language of Pop – with its stylistic playfulness, reference to the mass media, investigations of modern technology and methods of communication, reliance on found imagery and accessibility – had become so accepted as to become part of the vocabulary to which any artist could make recourse. Constantly renewed and reinterpreted, Pop has survived in mutated form right into the twenty-first century, proving its longevity and perhaps surprising even its inventors by its refusal to mimic the ephemerality of its sources.

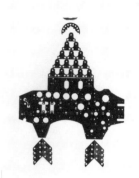

(fig. 6) Colin Self 4TH MONUMENT 1964, etching from found metal plates laid together, one of six unique variations, 77.6 x 57.2 cm, private collection

1966

Events: Labour increases majority in General Election, economic crisis follows
Encounter revealed to be indirectly funded by American CIA; *Destruction In Art Symposium*; first *People Show* performance at Better Books; *Festival of the New Moon* at Royal Albert Hall; John Latham and Barbara Steveni establish Artist Placement Group; London Film Makers Co-Operative formed; Indica Bookshop opens; Leslie Waddington Gallery opens in London; Molton Gallery, Signals Gallery close in London; Robert Fraser prosecuted for showing Jim Dine collages
Artists: Ian Hamilton Finlay settles in Dunsyre, Scotland ("Little Sparta"); Michael Craig-Martin settles in Britain; Richard Long enters St. Martin's School of Art, Bruce McLean leaves; Richard Wentworth enters Royal College of Art; Pauline Boty dies
Exhibitions: *The Almost Complete Works of Marcel Duchamp* at Tate; Richard Smith at Whitechapel; Mark Boyle and Joan Hills at Indica Gallery, London; Barry Flanagan at Rowan; Tim Scott at Waddington Gallery, London
Publications: *Time Magazine* "Swinging London" feature; Susan Sontag, *Against Interpretation*; Patrick Heron, "The Ascendancy of London in the Sixties", *Studio International*; Bill Brandt, *Shadow of Light*; first issue of *Art and Artists*; first issue of *IT (International Times)*

1967

Events: Devaluation of sterling; liberalisation of laws on abortion and homosexuality; first demonstration against America's London Embassy
Arts Lab opens; Dialectics of Liberation Conference; Beatles release *Sergeant Pepper* album; Lisson Gallery opens in London; Indica, Zwemmer Gallery close in London
Artists: Victor Burgin leaves Yale; Gilbert and George meet at St. Martin's School of Art; John Latham dismissed from St. Martin's School of Art
Exhibitions: John Hoyland at Whitechapel
Publications: first issue of

Oz magazine; R. D. Laing, *The Politics of Experience and the Bird of Paradise*; George Steiner, *Language and Silence*

1968

Events: Tet-Offensive in Vietnam; Paris *évènements*; Russian invasion of Czechoslovakia; America elects President Richard Nixon
Abolition of theatre censorship; Student anti-American demonstrations and occupations, including Hornsey, Guildford and Brighton art schools; London Anti-University founded; Arts Council opens Hayward Gallery in London; ICA moves to Royal Mall; Bryan Robertson leaves directorship of Whitechapel; Artists Information Registry founded; Welfare State International founded
Artists: Bridget Riley wins International Prize for Panting, Venice Biennale; Mark Boyle and Joan Hills begin *Journey to the Surface of the Earth*; Bill Woodrow enters, Richard Long leaves St Martin's School of Art,
Exhibitions: Henry Moore retrospective at Tate; Barbara Hepworth retrospective at Tate; Roy Lichtenstein at Tate; Phillip King at Whitechapel; Richard Long at Konrad Fischer, Düsseldorf
Publications: Jeff Nuttall, *Bomb Culture*; Lucy Lippard "The Dematerialisation of Art", *Art International*

1969

Events: British troops sent to Northern Ireland
Kenneth Clark TV series *Civilisation*; SPACE begins work; London Anti-University collapses; Arts Lab, Robert Fraser close in London
Artists: Peter Blake moves to Avon; Mary Martin dies
Exhibitions: *The Art of the Real* at Tate; *When Attitudes Become Form* at ICA; *Pop Art Redefined* at Hayward; Ben Nicholson retrospective at Tate; Anthony Caro retrospective at Hayward; Peter Blake retrospective at Bristol City Art Gallery; Gilbert and George *Our New Sculpture (Underneath the Arches)*; Mark Boyle at ICA; Michael Craig-Martin at Rowan
Publications: Kenneth Clark, *Civilisation*; first issue

of *Art-Language*; Joseph Kosuth "Art after Philosophy", *Studio International*

1970

Events: America takes Vietnam war to Cambodia; Conservatives win General Election under Edward Heath; inflation in Britain Art market in recession; Arts Council opens Serpentine Gallery in London; Second Coldstream Report on art education; Jon Thompson reorganises fine art teaching at Goldsmiths' College; Charles and Maurice Saatchi found advertising agency, Charles and Doris Saatchi begin collecting
Artists: Joe Tilson moves to Wiltshire; Richard Wentworth leaves Royal College of Art; Joseph Beuys performance at Edinburgh Festival
Exhibitions: Claes Oldenburg at Tate; Richard Hamilton retrospective at Tate; David Hockney retrospective at Whitechapel; *Idea Structures* at Camden Central Library
Publications: Ted Hughes, *Crow*; Germaine Greer, *The Female Eunuch*

1971

Events: Prosecution of *Oz* magazine
Artists: Bruce McLean founds Nice Style; Bill Woodrow enters Chelsea School of Art; Ceri Richards, John Tunnard , John Banting die
Exhibitions: Eduardo Paolozzi retrospective at Tate; Victor Pasmore retrospective at Tate; Warhol at Tate; Bridget Riley retrospective at Hayward

1972

Events: America re-elects President Nixon; North Vietnamese Spring Offensive; Miners' Strike in Britain; direct rule in Northern Ireland
John Berger TV series *Ways of Seeing*; Joseph Beuys lecture at Tate; Kasmin Gallery closes in London
Artists: Bill Woodrow leaves Chelsea School of Art
Exhibitions: *And for Today ... Nothing* at Gallery House, London; *The New Art* at Hayward; Henry Moore retrospective, Forte di Belvedere, Florence; Francis Bacon retrospective at Grand

Palais, Paris, and Kunsthalle Düsseldorf; William Scott retrospective at Tate; Patrick Heron retrospective at Whitechapel; Leon Kossoff at Whitechapel
Publications: John Berger, *Ways of Seeing*

1973
Events: OPEC provokes oil shock; Britain experiences "stagflation"; American troops withdraw from Vietnam
Garage Gallery opens in London
Artists: Tony Cragg enters Royal College of Art; Anish Kapoor enters Hornsey School of Art; Frederick Etchells dies
Exhibitions: Edward Burra retrospective at Tate, Robyn Denny retrospective at Tate; William Turnbull retrospective at Tate
Publications: first tape from *Audio Arts*

1974
Events: Miners' strike; Labour wins General Election under Harold Wilson; President Nixon resigns
Young Contemporaries changes name to New Contemporaries; Theatre of Mistakes formed
Artists: Michael Craig-Martin begins teaching at Goldsmiths' College; Richard Deacon enters Royal College of Art; David Jones dies
Exhibitions: Lucian Freud retrospective at Hayward; Ben Nicholson at Tate; *The Human Clay* at Hayward; *Art into Society/Society into Art: Seven German Artists* at ICA; *Beyond Painting and Sculpture* Arts Council tour; Joseph Beuys at ICA

1975
Events: Fall of Saigon ends Vietnam War
ACME Gallery opens; Brotherhood

of Ruralists founded; Nice Style disbands
Artists: Antony Gormley enters Goldsmiths'; Barbara Hepworth, Roger Hilton die
Exhibitions: Anthony Caro retrospective at Museum of Modern Art, New York; John Latham at Kunsthalle, Düsseldorf; Duncan Grant retrospective at Tate; *The Condition of Sculpture* at Hayward; *Nice Style High Up on a Baroque Palazzo* at Garage
Publications: David Sylvester, *Interviews With Francis Bacon*

1976
Events: America elects President Jimmy Carter; Harold Wilson succeeded as Prime Minister by James Callaghan
National Theatre opens on South Bank; Association for Business Sponsorship of the Arts founded; Controversy over purchase of Carl Andre *Equivalent VIII* by Tate; Nicholas Serota becomes director of Whitechapel
Artists: Richard Smith settles permanently in New York; Edward Burra dies
Exhibitions: *The Human Clay* at Hayward; Howard Hodgkin at Hayward; John Latham at Tate; *Video Show* at Tate; *Prostitution* at ICA; Richard Long at Venice Biennale; *Arte inglese oggi* at Palazzo Reale Milan
Publications: John Latham, *Time-Base and Determination in Events*; first issue of *Art Monthly*, first issue of *Artscribe*

1977
Events: Henry Moore Foundation inaugurated
Artists: Tony Cragg, Richard Deacon leave Royal College of Art; Antony Gormley enters Slade; Anish Kapoor enters Chelsea

School of Art; Lee Miller dies
Exhibitions: *British Painting 1952-1977* at Royal Academy; Julian Trevelyan retrospective at New Grafton Gallery, London; Michael Andrews at Anthony d'Offay Gallery, London; R. B. Kitaj at Marlborough; Theatre of Mistakes *A Waterfall* at first *Hayward Annual* contemporary art show at Hayward

1978
Artists: Tony Cragg begins teaching at Kunstakademie, Düsseldorf; Anish Kapoor leaves Chelsea School of Art; Duncan Grant dies
Exhibitions: Frank Auerbach retrospective at Hayward; Bob Law retrospective at Whitechapel; *Art for Whom* at Serpentine

1979
Events: "Winter of Discontent", Conservatives win General Election under Margaret Thatcher
Matt's Gallery opens in London
Artists: Peter Blake returns to London; Antony Gormley leaves Slade; Julian Opie enters Goldsmiths' College
Exhibitions: Allen Jones retrospective at Walker, Liverpool; John Hoyland at Serpentine; Tony Cragg at Lisson; *Un certain art anglais* at Musée d'Art Moderne, Paris
Publications: first issues of *Block* and *The London Review of Books*; Jean-Francois Lyotard, *The Post-Modern Condition*

EVERYTHING

A VIEW ON A DEVELOPING COUNTERCULTURE
IN THE MID 1960s IN LONDON

ANDREW WILSON

"MANIFESTO WORLD
Everything Everything Everything Everything
A world on the edge of destruction. [...]
The artist's entire visual field becomes the work of art
[...]."[1]
"My ultimate object is to include every thing in a single work [...]. In the end the only medium in which it will be possible to say everything will be reality. I mean that each thing, each view, each smell, each experience is material I want to work with."[2]
"The most complete change an individual can effect in his environment, short of destroying it, is to change his attitude to it [...]. To study everything we may one day isolate anything. Perhaps we may isolate everything as an object/experience/drama from which, as participant, we can extract an impulse so brilliant and strong that the environment as it is, is transformed."[3]

The mid 1960s was witness to a far-reaching attempt amongst artists and writers to search for and evolve new languages of expression and action – languages which were expressly formed by social and political identifications of engagement, and which made clear the necessity for changing social contexts within which the work was situated. In 1962, at the Edinburgh Festival, the writer and cultural activist Alexander Trocchi offered a view of what such an outlook entailed for the artist. Uncompromisingly, he declared that "Modern art begins with the destruction of the object. All vital creation is at the other side of nihilism. It begins after Nietzsche and after Dada."[4] For Trocchi, as for many artists, this new language of engagement entailed the absolute negation of any artistic or other type of categorisation. Just as the word was being questioned and destroyed by writers, so artists moved away from the object and the past to create a new space for their evolving language which asserted the urgent need for social, political and aesthetic change at the level of life. This new space beyond the object was one that Trocchi mapped in his guise as a "Cosmonaut of Inner Space", forging a new "meta-categorical"[5] grammar, claiming that "to free themselves from the conventional object and thus pass freely beyond non-categories, the twentieth century artist finally destroyed the object".[6] Trocchi opposed a polarisation of debate, and instead accepted the totality of the world – here understood in terms of a dialogue between "inner space" and "outer space"; "between the oppressions of the external world and the desire for internal liberation, between activist commitment to the continuing social struggle and dropping out of a cultural milieu that won't allow it".[7] Between 1963 and 1972 he pursued this goal through his post-situationist Project Sigma with which he aimed to spawn an engaged participatory activism – an "invisible insurrection of a million minds" – that might take over the world.

Trocchi's construction of an "interpersonal network" of like-minded people[8] that could construct this *"coup de monde"*, and the reasoning behind his strategies of refusal, provide a clear view of what was at stake in creating an active and engaged counter-culture in the 1960s. Project Sigma was born of a time in which Trocchi's reference to the destruction of the object and the necessity of creation occurring on the "other side of nihilism" was keenly felt; the threat that "the world is at the edge of extinction" from nuclear holocaust was real.[9] Trocchi's defining manifesto for Project Sigma commences with reference to Antonin Artaud's *The Theatre and its Double*, which illuminates the core of his proposal: "And if there is still one hellish, truly accursed thing in our time, it is our artistic dallying with forms, instead of being like victims burnt at the stake, signalling through the flames."[10] Trocchi, like many of his contemporaries, understood the necessity of rejecting the political, social and aesthetic structures that had put the world in danger; under the banner of *Sigma*, his cultural revolution was to be "the necessary underpinning, the passionate substructure of a new order of things".[11] The significance of the reference to Artaud was his call for a new experiential language of the theatre that was not representation, but life itself. Artaud, like Trocchi, was not contemplating a "symbol of an absent void", but, by going beyond a nihilist stance, was offering positive affirmation of a new cultural and fully socialised way of living which, in Trocchi's case, sprang from his impatience with the defining categories by which dominant culture was formed and recognised.

In going beyond the word and the object, Trocchi revealed how identity had to be subject to question, and his referencing of Artaud strikes a vital chord when examining the work of artists as different as Gustav Metzger, Mark Boyle, John Latham or David Medalla. Theatre for Artaud was concerned with the world and refused to be defined by the physical structure of a theatre or by theatrical convention. Similarly, for these artists in the mid 1960s, art entailed a direct engagement with the world and an attempt to locate meaning in a society gone mad. In Britain, as elsewhere, since the end of the 1950s artists had turned against traditional forms of art-making and moved towards the world and themselves, as material for work.[12] Traditional expressive and perceptual barriers were broken down

in this evolution of a new language of being. Another related example is provided by the Anti-Psychiatrists of the Philadelphia Foundation[13,] who were directly linked with Project Sigma. Here, this new language was realised by the curative ambience of the Foundation's Center for Treatment and Research, in mapping out fields of interaction, which recognised little distinction between analyst and analysand in the treatment of schizophrenics.

Boyle, for instance, questioned the relationship between audience and performer as much as between reality and its represented illusion. For his performance at the ICA in June 1965, *Oh What A Lovely Whore* (fig. 1), he hoped to "avoid having an audience as such".[14] In the event, he announced to the assembled audience that there was no happening and if the audience wanted one they would have to do it for themselves, whereupon the audience/participants proceeded to enact a spontaneous orgy of ritualistic destruction and creation stimulated by various objects that had been prepared earlier by Boyle, but which had, until the moment that Boyle turned the event over to the audience, remained unseen. The previous year, for their work *Street*, Boyle with Joan Hills led a party of people into a building in Notting Hill through a door marked "Theatre". They made their way down a corridor to a room in which a row of chairs faced a thick heavy curtain. After sitting down, the curtains were drawn back and the party found themselves looking though a shop window into the street outside.

(fig. 1) Titlepage of the *ICA Bulletin*, no. 150, August/September 1965; Alexander Trocchi and Allen Ginsberg during the press conference on the steps of the Albert Memorial, before the *Poetry International* at the Royal Albert Hall

Boyle's aim, "to include every thing in a single work" approached realisation with his *Dig* (fig. 2) event of 1966 and the commencement of his *Earthprobe* project in 1969.[15] *Dig*'s purpose, carried out under the

(fig. 2) Boyle Familiy DIG 6 February 1966, Happening

auspices of the Institute of Contemporary Archaeology, founded for the purpose by Boyle, was to examine – in much the same way as archaeologically discovered antiquities might be examined – artefacts that inhabit the contemporary world, much as an otherwise unknown whole society might be reconstructed from the fragmentary objects it had left behind. *Earthprobe* took this further. Mark Boyle, Joan Hills and their friends selected 1,000 sites at random by throwing darts, while blindfolded, at a map pinned to the wall;[16] as part of an on-going project, the artists then went on to record the bio-

(fig. 3) Boyle Family SON ET LUMIÈRE FOR BODILY FLUIDS AND FUNCTIONS Roundhouse 1967, Performance

logical and chemical make-up of a square surface area of each site in turn, to present this surface as a relief, and to make sound recordings of the site, for presentation along with photographs and the finished relief. By taking everything as material, the relationships of the work to its material, as much as between the material and the ways in which meanings are found, the artists developed a representational system capable of operating less in terms of metaphor but directly as a form of meton-omy.[17] However, although Mark Boyle's and Joan Hills' work aims at a form of com-plete representation[18] of a given body of material (fig. 3), it does this by underlin-ing the difficulty of presenting the whole as the sum of its parts. The global totality cannot, of course, be grasped; as David Thompson has stressed, what is being explored, questioned and tested is "not the boundless-ness of the physical world, but the limits of man's ca-pacity to see it".[19]

Work carried out by artists became models for activity; by scrutinising relationships within a total en-vironment, and one's actions within it and towards others, the course of one's actions might alter. For Trocchi, the intention of Project Sigma was to change the world, not by his own direct actions but by stimu-lating people to take full control of, and responsibility for, their lives. In this respect he explained to William Burroughs that "We arrived at the name SIGMA because it seemed semantically 'clean', being the symbol con-ventionally used in mathematics for the sum or the whole."[20] Sigma here stood for the relationship between the "whole" and the many individuals who might to-gether, spontaneously, be an active part of that new, sigmatic, "whole". At the same time that he wrote to Burroughs, Trocchi further explained that Sigma was a neutral term which indicated the necessity of begin-ning "with the fact of being alone: the one ultimate: consciousness presupposes it [...]. Now, consciously, spontaneously, to live with others: tentatively".[21] Pro-ject *Sigma* entailed the recognition of a state of alien-ation which had defined the course of Trocchi's life,

and offered a means by which alternatives to this state of being could be taken up, and society rebuilt accord-ing to a new set of socially-held values.

For Metzger, alienation was not so much the is-sue as obliteration and annihilation. With his elder broth-er, he had arrived in Britain in 1939 as a refugee from Nazi Germany when he was 12 years old; his parents subsequently perished in the Holocaust. Living under the shadow of im-minent nuclear genocide on a global scale, Metzger, in common with other artists, constructed an art and a way of living that did not so much question as present a di-rect challenge to the dominant culture which held its finger to the nuclear but-ton. Since 1958/59, Metzger's political ac-tivism – first in the Direct Action Commit-tee Against Nuclear War, later as a founder member of the Committee of 100 – was embodied within the changing fabric of his art, which had moved away from the painted object (as a former student of David Bomberg) towards what he came to describe as Auto-Destructive Art. For Metz-ger it was an "aesthetic of revulsion" which defined his art, whilst also revealing a wider condition.

(fig. 4) Gustav Metzger Poster for AUTO-DESTRUCTIVE ART. DEMONSTRATION BY GUSTAV METZGER 1961

Auto-Destructive Art developed as a process for which the concept, means of expression and actual execution of the work are treated as unified events that take place in social space (fig. 4). It was a public art in which the resources and tech-nology that would destroy the planet were harnessed as image; these would be monu-ments "to the power of man to destroy all life".[22] Just as Sigma, whether it was suc-cessful or not, intended to stimulate activ-ism, Auto-Destructive Art was meant to open up people's eyes to the horrific reali-ties of contemporary life. To these ends Metzger variously painted with acid on nylon sheets (fig. 5), which would be eaten up and destroyed by it (fig. 6); projected light through liquid crystals that at certain temperatures attain a state of perpetual struc-tural and chromatic transformation and change; pre-sented models for monoliths, either made from mild

(fig. 5) Gustav Metzger SOUTH BANK DEMONSTRATION London, 3 July 1961

(fig. 6) Gustav Metzger SOUTH BANK DEMONSTRATION London, 3 July 1961; after the performance, with St. Paul's in the background

steel that would slowly disintegrate as a result of urban pollution, or that were constructed of many elements that, over a number of years, would be ejected in a pre-programmed sequence, until nothing was left but its skeleton; or to gather together waste materials to underscore the profligacy and bankruptcy of western capitalist society. This was not iconoclastic – art is not destroyed; instead, Metzger constructed situations in which society's destructive forces can be turned in on themselves and stimulate a wider moral and actual change." "Social action",[23] as much as art, defined the intentions of Metzger's work and laid the basis of his organisation of the *Destruction In Art Symposium* (DIAS) in September 1966 (fig. 7).

(fig. 7) Poster for the *Destruction in Art Symposium* (DIAS) in September 1966, organised by Gustav Metzger

DIAS[24] reflected a wider debate, in which issues of destruction might be linked with destruction in society and science, as well as art. The remit was necessarily broad and inclusive, taking in "atmospheric pollution, creative vandalism, destruction in protest, planned obsolescence, popular media, urban sprawl/overcrowding, war, [...] biology, economics, medicine, physics, psychology, sociology, space research".[25] Providing a focus for the month-long series of events was a three-day symposium at which an eclectic (given DIAS's parameters) grouping of people discussed aspects of destruction, codifying and extending Metzger's own use of the term (fig. 8). Never an organised movement or group, DIAS nevertheless provided a marker – as did Project Sigma – for a particular moment which recognised that the concern for an objectified image was unable to engage convincingly with contemporary realities, and that the dynamics of event-structured events offered a more favourable avenue for investigation.[26] Despite the major achievement of attracting some fifty artists from ten countries to come and take part in DIAS – among which were the Viennese Institute of Direct Art (Günter Brus, Otto Muehl, Hermann Nitsch, Peter Weibel and Kurt Kren), performing outside Austria for the first time (fig. 9 and 10) – the significance of DIAS was its approach to issues of destruction from a point of view that stressed temporal and spatial dimensions, alongside a compassion for the human condition and the significance afforded to ritual, leading to catharsis, through the attempt to rediscover those experiences of reality that had been repressed by society's conventions.

(fig. 8) Ivor Davies and Gustav Metzger at the *Destruction in Art Symposium* (DIAS), London, 9 September 1966

(fig. 9) Hermann Nitsch during his lecture at the *Destruction in Art Symposium* (DIAS), London, September 1966

(fig. 10) Gustav Metzger, Wolf Vostell and Al Hansen at the *Destruction in Art Symposium* (DIAS), London, September 1966

Destruction only formed one aspect of Latham's work. The events he presented for DIAS – the burning down by incendiary devices of a number of "Skoob towers", Babel-like towers, for which books are attached to a metal armature (fig. 11), and *Film*, in which participants moved around "dressed" in "soft skoobs" – question the grammar of knowledge and known reality, showing it to constitute a dislocated and artificial set of untruths. Underpinning this is Latham's obsession with the determining metaphysics of time. He was less preoccupied with the notion of destruction than with the invalidation or dematerialisation of objects in favour of processes of cognition which were carried out in time rather than locked in space. Latham questioned and deconstructed the viewers' orthodox understanding of knowledge and its status, for which books stand as metaphorical and actual containers, in the realisation that the languages by which we live our lives evolve and function through time, even though this might often be denied in their form and appearance as a collection of words or images.

(fig. 11) John Latham Skoob Tower performance in front of the British Museum, London 1966

In this respect Latham is close to the other half of Metzger's theories of Auto-Destructive Art, which entailed an Auto-Creative Art. This aspect also connects with these artists' need to realise the world – as a set of changing entities – within their work. Metzger had codified this dialectics in both his third manifesto *Auto-Destructive Art Machine Art Auto-Creative Art*, of June 1961 and his final manifesto *On Random Activity In Material/Transforming Works Of Art*, of July 1964. This later manifesto, concerned with the transformations felt through random activity in art, as in society, was published in *Signals*, the news bulletin of the Signals Gallery directed by Paul Keeler and the artist David Medalla.[27] Medalla's own work at this time followed the idea of an Auto-Creative Art as a form of what he termed Biokinetics.

Inert material undergoes transformation into dynamic, continually changing bodies, taking its place alongside other transformations evolving in society and life in general. To these ends, Medalla harnessed water, rice, gold and silver dust, sand, powdered coal, granulated coffee beans, dried seeds, rubber, gum, ice, salt, oil and steam in a series of works of great wit and an accomplished economy of means (fig. 12). His best known works of this sort were a form of bubble machine – collectively titled *Cloud Canyons* – in which the foam which was produced followed, as Guy Brett describes, "its aleatory paths, emerging and forming according to its own energies interacting with gravity, earth currents, atmospheric pressure and the shape of the containers".[28]

(fig. 12) David Medalla CLOUD CANYONS 1961–85, soap bubble machine

For Metzger, Medalla's machines were exemplars of Material/Transforming Auto-Creative Art,[29] moving decisively away from a static, defined certitude and embracing wider, more socially concerned, forces. Work such as Medalla's *Cloud Canyons*, Latham's *Skoob Towers*, Boyle's *Earthprobe* and Metzger's acid on nylon paintings, as well as Trocchi's Project Sigma, the formation of the Philadelphia Foundation and events such as DIAS, all acted as markers, not only as bridges between the Happenings Movement and an emergent conceptualism, but also through their dissolution of barriers between activities and concern for a view of the world, typified by an emerging, interlinked mode of consciousness. In July 1967, the Philadelphia Foundation's Institute of Phenomenological Studies sponsored *The Dialectics of Liberation Conference on the Demystification of Violence* from the understanding that "The whole world is now an irreducible whole [...]. In total context culture is against us, education enslaves us, technology kills us. We must confront this. We must destroy our vested illusions as to who, what, where we are. We must combat our self-pretended ignorance as to what

goes on and our consequent non-reaction as to what we refuse to know [...]. The dialectics of liberation begin with the clarification of our present condition."[30] Although *IT*'s report of the conference focused on Stokely Carmichael's black power rally at which, instead of demystifying violence, the huge crowd cheered at every mention of it, this conference, like DIAS, drew its speakers from a broad range of disciplines and anti-disciplines (they included Allen Ginsberg, Julian Beck, Herbert Marcuse, Gregory Bateson, David Cooper, Ronald D. Laing, John Gerassi, Igor Hajek, Lucien Goldman and others), and it was Herbert Marcuse who addressed the changing conditions most inspirationally. Not calling for a revolution as such, he postulated that what was needed was an imaginative change: "If this qualitative difference today appears as utopian, as idealistic and as metaphysical, this is precisely the form in which those radical features must appear if they are really to be the definite negation of the established societies, if socialism is indeed the rupture of history, the radical break, the leap into the realm of freedom – a total rupture."[31] The hope that such a utopian rupture would release creative impulses formed the basis of the Philadelphia Foundation's next project in 1968, the Spontaneous University of the Antiuniversity. Under the calling card of "music art poetry black power madness revolution",[32] the Antiuniversity's stated emphasis was "on diversity of approach, but we shall work to unify disparate perspectives. Above all we must do away with artificial splits and divisions between disciplines and artforms and between theory and action". It is hardly surprising that Trocchi, alongside Latham and Metzger – dedicated to negotiating beyond the rupture with history and traditional thought – should be associated with the Antiuniversity, emphasising their commonly held commitment to building new cognitive frameworks for art which, in a concern for a totality of existence and experience, acknowledged no separation between subject and object.

ANDREW WILSON

NOTES

1 Gustav Metzger, "Manifesto World" (7 October 1962), reprinted in Gustav Metzger, *Damaged Nature, Auto-Destructive Art*, London 1996, pp. 62–63.

2 Mark Boyle, "Background to a Series of Events at the ICA", *ICA Bulletin*, no. 146, May 1965, p. 6.

3 Mark Boyle, untitled statement in *Control Magazine*, no. 1, 1966, n. p.

4 Alexander Trocchi, "The Destruction of the Object ..."[1962], 1 p. ms. note, Trocchi Estate. Trocchi delivered this statement as part of his presentation to the Writers Conference organised by John Calder. The audio tapes of this conference are held by the National Sound Archive, London.

5 This term underpinned much of Trocchi's work and is echoed, for instance, in a passage from his *Cain's Book*, London 1966, p. 45, in which he writes "For centuries we in the west have been dominated by the Aristotelian impulse to classify. It is no doubt because conventional classifications become a part of prevailing economic structure that all real revolt is hastily fixed like a bright butterfly on a classificatory pin [...]. Question the noun; the present participles of the verb will look after themselves."

6 Alexander Trocchi, statement at the Writers' Conference, Edinburgh Festival, 1962, Trocchi 1962 (see note 4).

7 Peter Stansill and David Zane Mairowitz, *BAMN Outlaw Manifestos and Ephemera 1965–70*, Harmondsworth 1971, p. 13.

8 One tangible demonstration of this network was the *Poets of the World/Poets of Our Time International Poetry Incarnation* at the Royal Albert Hall, London, 11 June 1965. This four-hour event was organised in part by Project Sigma in ten days and attracted an audience of over 7,000 people. Trocchi acted as the *compère*. A spontaneous invocation was composed at his flat by ten of the participants and later declaimed at a press conference at the Albert Memorial. One section of this text mapped the intersection points of an underground that was now recognised to be international, and moved freely through the fields of literature, drugs, theatre, art, pornography, and social agitation: "World declaration hot peace shower! [...]. Illumination, Now! Sigmatic New Departures Residu of Better Books & Moving Times in obscenely New Directions! Soul revolution City Lights Olympian lamb-blast! Castalia centrum new consciousness hungry generation Movement roundhouse 42 beat apocalypse energy triumph! You are not alone!", *Wholly Communion*, London, 1965, p. 9. A film of the event was directed by Peter Whitehead, with Metzger's assistance amongst others.

9 Alexander Trocchi, "Invisible Insurrection of a Million Minds", *Sigma Portfolio* item 2, 1964, p. 1. As will be seen, this was the same for Metzger and informs the activities of Jeff Nuttall who published the mimeographed magazine *My Own Mag* between 1963/64 and 1966. Nuttall's account of this period and milieu is characteristically titled *Bomb Culture*, London 1968. He was close to Trocchi and Project Sigma and in 1965, with Latham and others, created the *Stigma* environment in the basement of BetterBooks, an

oppressive labyrinth with a violent iconography of war atrocities, pornography, bodily abjection and mechanised totemic sexualised depravity.

10 Trocchi 1964 (see note 9).

11 Ibid.

12 For discussion of this see Paul Schimmel (ed.), *Out of Actions, between Performance and the Object, 1949–1979*, London 1998.

13 In June 1964, Trocchi announced that he had made contact with Aaron Esterson, Ronald D. Laing and David Cooper, who had recently founded the Philadelphia Foundation. By October 1964 he was also in correspondence with Joe Berke in New York. Berke would arrive in London the following year and worked alongside the Philadelphia Foundation, but not before founding, with Allen Krebs, the Free University of New York under the influence of Trocchi's Project Sigma ideal of a "Spontaneous University". On arrival in London late in 1965, Berke's first act was an attempt to found a Free School in Notting Hill Gate with John Hopkins.

14 Boyle 1965 (see note 2).

15 Although begun in 1968, the project was not launched in public until his ICA exhibition *Journey to the Surface of the Earth* in 1969.

16 Subsequently another dart is thrown in the same way at a large scale map of the area selected by the first dart, and then on site a right angle is thrown down onto the ground, forming the first co-ordinates of a square of predetermined size.

17 For a persuasive elaboration of this see Kristine Stiles, *The Destruction In Art Symposium (DIAS): The Radical Cultural Project of Event-Structured Live Art*, Ph. D. diss., Berkeley 1987; also her essay in Schimmel (ed.) 1998 (see note 12), pp. 272–282.

18 Echoed in other ways in works such as the *Son et Lumière for Bodily Fluids and Functions* series of performances from 1966, which link a collection of bodily fluids with the manner, action and sound of their production with an audio-visual presentation to the audience.

19 David Thompson, "Afterword", *Beyond Image: Boyle Family*, London 1986, p. 53.

20 Alexander Trocchi, draft of typewritten letter to William S. Burroughs, 12 October 1963, Trocchi Estate, London.

21 Alexander Trocchi, *The Decadence of a Tradition*, unpublished typewritten note, c. 1964, Trocchi Estate, London.

22 Gustav Metzger, untitled statement in *Art & Artists*, August 1966, p. 22. For Pat Arrowsmith, Field Secretary of the DAC, Auto-Destructive Art symbolically demonstrated the current state of society: a society whose basic ingredients are such that it seems all too likely to end up destroying itself. Pat Arrowsmith, "Auto-Destructive Art", *Peace News*, July 22, 1960, p. 11.

23 Gustav Metzger, "Auto-Destructive Art", London, June 1965, published in *Art and Artists*, August 1966, p. 1. Metzger states that Auto-Destructive Art

does not limit itself "to theory of art and the production of art works. It includes social action".

24 For a full discussion of DIAS see Stiles 1987 (see note 17) and her essay in Schimmel (ed.) 1998 (see note 12), pp. 272–282. DIAS was organised by a committee, the make-up of which reinforced the wide nature of its aims. This committee included John Sharkey, poet, filmmaker and gallery manager of the ICA; Dom Sylvester Houedard, a Benedictine monk and one of the leading figures of the concrete poetry movement in Britain; Bob Cobbing, a major concrete and phonic poet, publisher under the imprint Writers' Forum and manager of BetterBooks in Charing Cross Road; Mario Amaya, editor of *Art & Artists*, whose August 1966 issue was given over to the theme "Destruction In Art"; Ivor Davies, art historian, painter and creator of explosive happenings; the German happenings artist Wolf Vostell; Jim Haynes, who ran the Traverse Theatre Club at the Jeanetta Cochrane Theatre, was on the editorial board of *IT* and later was to create the Arts Lab in Drury Lane; and Barry Miles, who ran the bookshop of the Indica Gallery and was also on the editorial board of *IT*. Taking a less active role on the committee were Roy Ascott, cybernetic artist and organiser of the Ealing Ground Course; Enrico Baj, member of the artists' Gruppo Nucleare in Milan; and the critic Frank Popper.

25 Gustav Metzger, "Excerpts from selected papers presented at the 1966 *Destruction In Art Symposium*", *Studio International*, December 1966, p. 282.

26 Also significant here is the place accorded to concrete poetry in the development of this new aesthetic. The 1965 ICA exhibition *Between Poetry and Painting* emphasised the ways in which these artists broke down the barriers between activities – not just poetry or painting or sculpture – and engaged in investigating a new set of languages, processes and means to effect a more fully engaged representation of the world. For instance in the symposium on *Creation, Destruction and Chemical Change* at Ravensbourne College of Art in May 1966, a dry run for DIAS, Dom Sylvester Houedard made the link between Metzger's declaration that in his acid-nylon technique "it certainly isn't the strips of nylon left that are important, it is the non-nylon", and white space in the concrete poem being more important than the black areas it surrounds, energises and gives meaning to.

27 In 1963 Metzger, with the kinetic artist Marcello Salvadori, had announced the founding of the Centre for Advanced Creative Studies in Hampstead. Its handbill declared that it was "based on the belief that the accelerating interaction of society, science and technology; the recurrent explosions of technological 'progress'; the changing concepts of matter, space, time; force the artist to change his intellectual, physical and sensuous grasp of the environment. The artist is not a passive instrument of social change. He can be a determining factor in the development of society, science and technology". In 1964 Medalla, with Keeler and Guy Brett, joined Salvadori at the Centre for Advanced Creative Study. Later that year, Keeler and Medalla opened their flat as a "Showroom for the Avant Garde" (Salvadori later returned to Hampstead, with the idea of a centre linking art to science and industry). The following year this showroom moved to premises in Wigmore Street as Signals.

28 Guy Brett, *Exploding Galaxies*, London 1995, p. 53.

29 See Gustav Metzger, "David Medalla: *Cloud Canyons: Bubble Mobiles* 1964", *Signals*, no. 2, September 1964, p. 8.

30 Flyer for the *The Dialectics of Liberation Conference on the Demythification of Violence*, July 1967.

31 Herbert Marcuse, "Liberation from the Affluent Society", David Cooper, ed., *The Dialectics of Liberation*, Harmondsworth 1968, p. 177.

32 Flyer announcing the opening for the Antiuniversity of London, 12 February 1968.

ANDREW WILSON

A CRISIS OF MODERNISM

CHARLES HARRISON

This will necessarily be a somewhat personal account. I do not wish to claim an art-historical objectivity that my commitment to the project of Art & Language will inevitably be seen to impugn. I mean to argue, however, that that commitment was made in response to circumstances that have some art-historical vividness. I therefore hope that the testimony I offer may represent a retrospect on the moment in question that is better than merely personal.

The circumstances are those that bore down in different ways on all concerned with the development of art under the theoretical and practical penumbra of modernism as conceived in the later 1960s and early 1970s. It is by now an established convention of the history of art to associate that moment with crisis – perhaps a terminal crisis – in modernism itself, whether what is understood by modernism is a certain period in the broad culture of the nineteenth and twentieth centuries, a specific tendency in the art of that period, a more-or-less coherent body of theory and criticism for which the writing of Clement Greenberg is taken as representative, or some amalgam of all of these. The last formulation is perhaps the most useful to pursue. Thus we might think of modernism as a critical value, identified in an influential body of theory – rightly or wrongly, or rather rightly *and* wrongly – as the common property in those works from the nineteenth and twentieth centuries that happen to be most deserving of attention on aesthetic grounds.

The reason for preferring this formulation of modernism is that it then encourages us to ask appropri-ate questions about what sort of crisis a crisis of modernism might be. Are we referring to a failure in the authority of the theory in question, to a significant change in the properties common to those works of art that seem most deserving of attention on aesthetic grounds, to a loss of confidence in the "aesthetic grounds" themselves – in the very idea, perhaps, that "the aesthetic" is a ground at all – or to some amalgam of all three? Again, the last formulation seems the most plausible, and the most useful in explaining the sheer untidiness that characterises art- historical controversy, where the "new art" of the later 1960s and early 1970s is concerned – an untidiness carried over into art-critical practice regarding the supposedly postmodernist or post- or neo-conceptual or neo-New Art of the 1980s and 1990s.

I am seeking a means to represent the confusions of that moment of crisis where the culture of English art is concerned, but without simply replaying those confusions in another form. As had happened before, in the early 1930s, a would-be avant-garde was seeking to come to terms with the critical power and coherence of an international development, just when that power was effectively broken and the coherence lost. In the earlier instance, the development at issue was the abstractionist tendency of the European Modern Movement, its theoretical ambitions by then reduced to the pursuit of a merely formal autonomy. In the mid 1960s the first step to the overcoming of provincialism was to acquaint oneself with the professional culture of modernism in its American form, a culture composed not simply of a body of art produced principally in New York since the 1940s, but also of an accompanying critical representation of that art which itself rested on a revised and discriminating account of the entire modern tradition. To put the matter baldly, if modernism was the issue, then British Art was not. The problem was that though this account still served to make local offerings seem small-town and uninteresting, by the later 1960s both its conceptual apparatus and its art-historical narrative were already under attack and failing. As before, the aesthetic claims upon which the account largely rested seemed reduced to talk about colour and shape.

By way of illustration, I offer an English reader's experience of the American journal *Artforum*, which first became readily available in the UK following transfer of its editorial offices to New York in 1965. Though *Artforum* surveyed a heterogeneous field of production, what seemed most noticeable about the early issues was the serious attention paid to the Abstract Expressionists and to the establishment of a Modernist line of succession in painting and sculpture. By the summer issue of 1967, though, it was clear from the defensive character of Michael Fried's "Art and Objecthood" that the succession was not so much contested as already in other hands. The same issue featured Robert Smithson on an imaginary air terminal site, Sol LeWitt's *Paragraphs on Conceptual Art*, and the third of Robert Morris' *Notes on Sculpture*, which was not so much about sculpture as about the exhaustion of painting ("the mode has become antique") and the vitality of what Don Judd had called "three-dimensional work".

One point seems clear, in hindsight. However we might explain the "crisis of Modernism" in cultural or politico-economic terms, so far as the practice of art was concerned it was marked by the running down of the great twentieth-century adventure of abstraction in painting and subsequently in sculpture. In the 1960s abstract art certainly still seemed possible and interesting – more so than the local version of Pop Art and certainly more so than what remained of the native figurative tradition. But by the time English artists responded to the second historical wave of abstract art, with the kinds of painting represented in the *Situation* exhibitions and with the sculpture of Anthony Caro and his followers in the *New Generation*, the best of abstract art – Mark Rothko's, Jackson Pollock's, Barnett Newman's – was already in the past. Frank Stella kept the flame flickering

by adopting an insouciant "Queen's Regulations" attitude to Modernist painting, while Carl Andre found means to circumvent the issue of abstract composition in sculpture, by resorting to repetition of like units. But each in his way seemed to underscore the impossibility of proceeding further without a radical transformation in the understanding of artistic genres. We needed to understand the power of transatlantic Modernism in order to see what could no longer plausibly be done in the name of a substantial art, but by the time the full effects of transatlantic modernism had actually reached the shores of England, it was already a virtually exhausted resource.

In the native artistic culture of the time, significant moments of controversy and change tended to be identified with specific art schools. The majority of artists survived economically through part-time teaching, while employment practices remained sufficiently unregulated to allow the gathering of small communities of people with interests in common. At the same time, the recommendations of the Coldstream report into art education had created opportunities for anyone with a degree in art history to get part-time work in art schools. In the later 1960s, I divided my time between teaching under these conditions and working at *Studio International*, which Peter Townsend's editorship had made a receptive outlet for a broad range of artistic concerns. The journal's offices in Museum Street were a short walk from St. Martin's School of Art, which of all the London colleges seemed then the most clearly subject to the crisis of modernism and the most responsive to its effects. It was a consequence of Caro's association with the vocational sculpture course that St. Martin's was the nearest England had to an open channel for the reception of transatlantic Modernism in the early 1960s. But by virtue of other factors – among them the part-time presence of John Latham in 1966–67, and the proximity of the avant-garde venue BetterBooks – an interest in the "mainstream" concerns of abstract painting and sculpture came rapidly to coincide at the school with exploration of such divergent concerns and traditions as the very idea of a mainstream had tended to obscure. In my personal memory of the years 1966–69, a microcosmic representation of the larger crisis of modernism is played out in the small area of West Central London, from Museum Street to Charing Cross Road.

CHARLES HARRISON

In 1967, while I was teaching occasionally at St. Martin's, two stories were doing the rounds. In the first the head of the sculpture department would stick his head out of his office door at regular intervals and shout, "Very good! Make another one!". In the second, Caro refused to assess an arrangement of twigs by Richard Long, displayed in the central exhibition hall, on the grounds that its companion piece was unavailable to view, being installed on top of a mountain in Scotland. Both stories are no doubt apocryphal, but their coincidence is symptomatic. The most practised critical instruments available for the analysis of contemporary art had been forged in the encounter with hermetic arrangements of colour and form. But those instruments seemed increasingly irrelevant, and the categories of production they presumed increasingly inappropriate, in face of the new work that young artists were doing. Meanwhile those predicates by which the proscriptions of modernist theory had been conveyed – "environmental", "theatrical", "installational", "dadaist" – seemed suddenly to have been invested with the promise of liberation. Besides Long, the young artists then associated with St. Martins in one role or another included Barry Flanagan (who had worked briefly on Caro's vocational sculpture course and had subsequently shared an exhibition with Latham), Gilbert and George (then a more entertaining and more modestly picaresque double-act than they were subsequently to become), Bruce McLean, Roelof Louw and the Dutch artist Jan Dibbets. It was friendship with Flanagan during the years 1967–69 that largely led me to acquaintance with other artists of the same generation.

In 1969, Long, Flanagan, McLean, Louw and Dibbets were all included in two large surveys of a new international avant-garde, either by work actually installed, or by inclusion of material in the respective catalogues. 'Op Losse Schroeven' opened at the Stedelijk Museum, Amsterdam, in March. When Attitudes become Form: Works-Concepts-Processes-Situations-Information – Live in Your Head, opened at the Kunsthalle, Berne, in the same month before travelling to the Institute of Contemporary Arts, London, in late September, where Victor Burgin was included among the exhibitors at my instigation, and where Louw and McLean both made new work especially for this showing. With the benefit of hindsight, we might think of these as manifestations of a kind of artistic "Post-Modernism", if only by virtue of the stylistic eclecticism of the works included. The Attitudes show embraced late-minimalist, anti-form and Conceptual tendencies from America, Arte Povera from Italy and work by Joseph Beuys and his followers from Germany, besides many less easily categorised tendencies from those countries and elsewhere. John Latham was a notable omission from both shows. It remains the case that the difficult originality of his work awaits adequate acknowledgement.

As has customarily been the case with large avant-garde developments, the initially powerful sense of community and compatibility dissipated rapidly once critical distinctions emerged between divergent factions. By late 1969 it was already apparent not only that the term "Conceptual Art" stood for a distinct tendency within the larger grouping, but that there were significant disparities even among those artists to whose work the label seemed most securely to apply. The first issue of the journal Art-Language had appeared in May 1969. It was published in Coventry, where an out-of-London art college provided a teaching base for three of the four original editors, and where the implications of American minimalism were better understood than anywhere else. I first met two of the four, Terry Atkinson and Harold Hurrell, when they visited the Studio offices early in 1969. Together with David Bainbridge and Michael Baldwin, they had adopted the name Art & Language in the previous year. None of these was included either in 'Op Losse Schroeven' or Attitudes. In 1970 I organised an exhibition under the title Idea Structures at the Camden Arts Centre, bringing Art & Language together with the Joseph Kosuth, by then designated as "American editor" of Art-Language, alongside the independent English artists Victor Burgin and Keith Arnatt, in what I naïvely envisaged as a representation of the hard-line in Conceptual Art. By the end of the following year, I had made the decision to resign both from Studio and from my various part-time teaching posts, had vowed never to curate another exhibition (this, after the experience of taking a British Avant-Garde show to the New York Cultural Center) and had become editor of Art-Language. Mel Ramsden and Ian Burn had already merged their separate New-York-based collaboration with Art & Language.

Many of the reasons behind my decisions are incidental to this account, but two factors are of general relevance. The first is that it had come to seem not simply uncomfortable but unjustifiable under the circumstances of the time to dissociate the practice of criticism – and *a fortiori* the role of entrepreneur – from the self-critical practices of art. The clearest symptom of this was that the language of appreciative commentary, whether applied to the attenuations of modernist painting and sculpture or to their avant-garde would-be successors, seemed suddenly to have been drained of meaning and plausibility. The second was that, under these circumstances, the practice of Art & Language, dedicated as it was to conceptual and critical inquiry pursued as a discursive practice of art, appeared to promise an exemplary if not a possibly sufficient place of work, even if the "work" in question could not all be "art". In 1972 that promise was fulfilled with the exhibition of Art & Language's *Index 01* at *documenta 5*.

I have had no cause to revise this view, or the judgments on which it was based. Indeed both viewpoint and judgments have been continuously strengthened since 1977, when the artistic work of Art & Language was left in the hands of Michael Baldwin and Mel Ramsden alone. However hard it may have proved to accommodate the continuing work and history of Art & Language to a congenial account of the successes of British Art as kinds of public spectacle, that work is indispensable to any critically adequate thought about the international development of art over the past thirty-five years.

CHARLES HARRISON

166 | John Latham SEEIN'S BELIEVIN' 1961

169 | Keith Arnatt HOLE THAT MAKES ITSELF A AND B (DETAIL A) 1967–68

170 | Ian Hamilton Finlay Drift 1968

171 | Barry Flanagan Pile I 67/8 1968

172 | Michael Craig-Martin An Oak Tree 1973

173 | Barry Flanagan Light on Light on Sacks 1969

174 | Gilbert & George The Major's Port 1972

IS NOT ART THE ONLY HOPE FOR THE MAKING WAY FOR THE MODERN WORLD
TO ENJOY THE SOPHISTICATION OF DECADENT LIVING EXPRESSION.

175 | Gilbert & George Is Not Art the Only Hope for the Making Way for the Modern World to Enjoy the Sophistication of Decadent Living Expression 1972

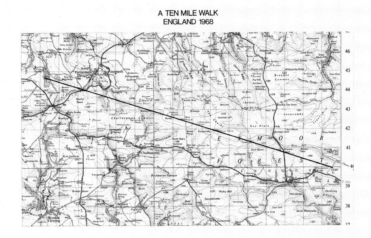

A TEN MILE WALK
ENGLAND 1968

Sensation

ContraDiction

Logic

Create a little sensation
Feel the difference that everyone can see
Something you can touch
Property
There's nothing to touch it

You've got it
You want to keep it
Naturally. That's conservation
It conserves those who can't have it
They don't want to be conserved
Logically, that's contradiction

Everything you buy says something about you
Some things you buy say more than you realise
One thing you buy says everything
Property
Either you have it or you don't

178 | Victor Burgin SENSATION 1975

179 | Mark Boyle UNTITLED 1964

180 | Howard Hodgkin FOY NISSEN'S BOMBAY 1975–77

181 | Richard Long STONE CIRCLE 1972

182 | Gilbert & George GORDON'S MAKES US DRUNK 1972

183 | Boyle Family DIG 1966

184 | Barry Flanagan HEAP 4 1967

185 | Michael Craig-Martin ON THE TABLE 1970

186 | Stephen Willats PERSON A 1974

187 | Stephen Willats THE LUNCH TRIANGLE, PILOT WORK B. CODES AND PARAMETERS 1974

189 | Leon Kossoff CHILDREN'S SWIMMING POOL 1972

190 | Leon Kossoff FIDELMA No. 1 1978

191 | Howard Hodgkin Still Life in a Restaurant 1976–77

ARTISTS' FILM IN BRITAIN

SIX MOMENTS

DAVID CURTIS

Filmmaking by artists in Britain arrives in waves. A blast of activity in the 1920s and 1930s is sustained into the War period, but followed by a post-war lull. Another explosion happens in the late 1960s, with subsequent developments forming a series of aftershocks; action followed by reaction. The catalyst to this sudden activity is often a mixture of technical and social developments. In the 1960s, a time of both relative affluence and passionate political protest, an expanding art school population found its voice through new tools – cheap Super 8 cameras, better film stocks for 16 mm, and the arrival a wholly new medium, domestic video. Film also appears to seize the imagination of artists at times when its commercial base is in crisis. Symptomatically, in the late 1990s, with British television dumbing down and the feature film industry yet again insolvent, the Turner Prize was won in three out of four successive years by filmmaking artists – Douglas Gordon (fig. 1), Gillian Wearing and Steve McQueen.[1] So it was in the late 1920s.

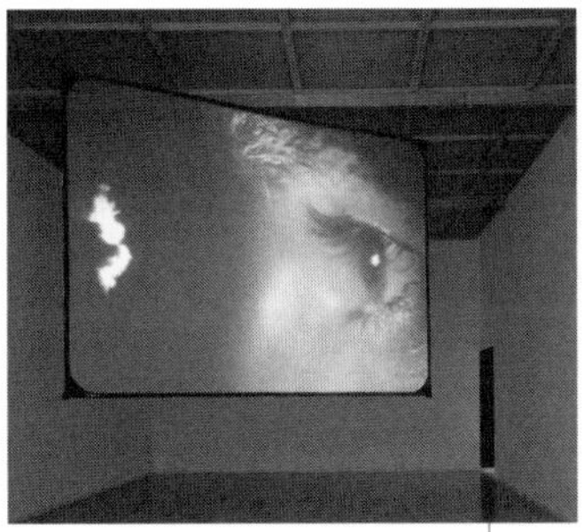

(fig. 1) Douglas Gordon
24 Hour Psycho 1993,
video installation, 5.2 x 14 x 7 m,
video, 24 h., Kunstmuseum Wolfsburg

1 1996, 1997 and 1999.

"CLOSE UP", JOHN GRIERSON, AND THE SPONSORED FILM – THE 1930s

The arrival of colour film and, particularly, of synchronised sound at the end of the 1920s threatened European cinema markets with further domination by American technology and marketing skills, and eroded contemporary certainties about cinema. Silent film's aspiration to be an international *visual* language was questioned, as was, more prosaically, its dependence on mime. Artists throughout Europe responded by getting involved. In London since the mid 1920s , intellectual debate about film had centred on The Film Society (1925–35), which each month showed new and uncensored films to its members. At its screenings a film by Sergei Eisenstein (introduced by the author) might be seen in the same programme as a science documentary, a technical demonstration or an artist's "experiment". In the audience artists sat alongside writers, scientists, industry professionals and enthusiastic amateurs. Perceiving "a shadow shaped like a tadpole (just a speck of dust wriggling in the projector gate) at a screening of *The Cabinet of Dr. Caligari*, Virginia Wolf was prompted to imagine a visual cinema in which "thought could be conveyed by shape more effectively than by words".[2] Paul Nash saw in the colour films of Len Lye "a new form of enjoyment quite independent of literary reference; the simple, direct visual-aural contact of sound and colour through ear and eye".[3] (fig. 2)

Initially, actual film experiment was sporadic. Artist filmmakers had either to find work at the industry's margins or to fund-raise for their own films. Len Lye's first forcefully primitive animation *Tusalava* (1929) was sponsored by Robert Graves and The Film Society; Norman McLaren's *7 Till 5* (1933) was made while he was still a student at the Glasgow School of Art; Oswell Blakeston wrote regularly for the critical magazine *Close Up* (1927–33) and had access to

industry resources which he employed on *Light Rhythms* of 1930 (fig. 3), made with the American-born photographer Francis Bruguiere, which was the most ambitious abstract film of its time. *Close Up* – almost the house journal of The Film Society – was funded by the private fortune of one its editors, the novelist Winifred Bryher; and her money also supported the making of *Borderline* (1930), an extraordinarily ambitious silent feature – a study in expressive gesture and body-language – directed by her partner and co-editor Kenneth McPherson, starring another regular *Close Up* writer, the poet H. D. (Helga Doorn) and the rising American star, Paul Robeson.

This scatter-shot pattern of production gave way to a period of sustained engagement between film and the visual arts when John Grierson, a visionary Scot, became head of the Empire Marketing Board (1929–33), then the General Post Office Film Unit (1933–39), where, in his search for talent, he was open to employing film-interested artists. Len Lye and Humphrey Jennings, arguably two of Britain's greatest film-artists, are known primarily by work which was sponsored or made (in Lye's case) as commercial advertising. Lye, a New Zealander who exhibited paintings and sculpture with the Seven and Five Society, drew, painted and collaged images directly onto the film-strip, making some

of the most visually inventive films of the period. Jennings and William Coldstream were painters drawn to film at a time of social crisis, precisely because it offered a more direct line of communication with a wider public, and while Coldstream returned to painting (partly at W. H. Auden's urging), Jennings made film his primary medium, and perfected a new poetic essay-form in the process. Auden himself contributed the text for *Coalface* (1935), and Benjamin Britten the music. Jennings died in an accident shortly after the end of the Second World War, having completed twenty-six short films and just one full-length film *Fires Were Started* (1943). Grierson and many of his protégés left for North America before or during the War.

"FREE CINEMA" AND FREE RADICALS – THE 1950s AND 1960s

The 1950s and early 1960s are associated with heroic solitary figures and a movement that proved a false start. Free Cinema promised new subjects and a fresh (16 mm hand-held) approach – "no film can be too personal [...] perfection is not an aim"[4] – but revealed its very British literary dependency, as the group members' aspirations moved towards feature films. Lindsay Anderson's *Oh Dreamland* (1953) shares the Independent Group's fascination with the artefacts of popular culture, but with a dissimilar aloofness from its subject. Lorenza Mazetti's more heart-felt *Together* (1956) – in which her Slade alumnus, the painter Michael Andrews, and the sculptor Edouardo Paolozzi appear as deaf-mutes at large in an uncaring city – is really a work of Italian neo-realism displaced to London. The heroic individuals include Margaret Tait, who trained with Italian Neo-Realists, then from the early 1950s spent a lifetime making "film poem" portraits of places and individuals, from her base on the island of Orkney; Paolozzi, who found collaborators able to turn his drawings and collections of graphic imagery into animations; and John Latham, who began making films, initially, as a record of his evolving and sometimes ephemeral book-reliefs,

2 "The Cinema" first published in *Arts*, June 1926; reprinted in Michael O'Pray (ed.), *The British Avant-Garde Film*, Luton 1996.

3 Paul Nash, "The Colour Film", in Charles Davy (ed.), *Footnote to the Film*, London 1938.

(fig. 2) Len Lye TRADE TATTOO 1937, 35 mm film, 7 mins. (see p. 243)

(fig. 3) Oswell Blakeston und Francis Bruguiere LIGHT RHYTHMS 1930, 35 mm film, 5 mins.

4 Collective statement of Free Cinema, distributed at their first screening at the National Film Theatre in 1956.

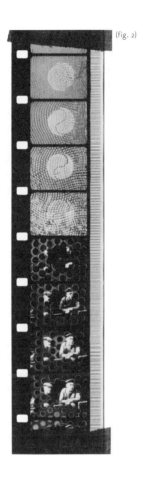

(fig. 2)

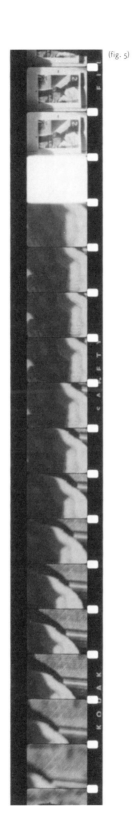

(fig. 5)

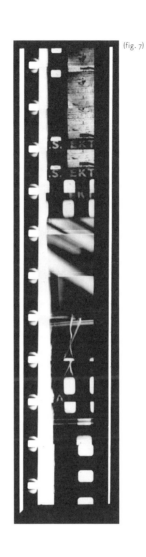

(fig. 7)

(fig. 8)

then made the blazing animation, *Speak* (1962). William Burroughs, working with the film producer and cinema owner Anthony Balch, made films for private amusement, and as experimental extensions of his cut-up writing method. Jeff Keen was one of several native surrealists who mined the world of "B" movies for their potent imagery, often working in the "amateur" gauge of Super 8.

"STRUCTURAL CINEMA", LANDSCAPE AND SYSTEMS FILMS – THE 1960s AND 1970s

Interest in experimental film regained momentum in the mid 1960s, benefiting from the proliferation of non-traditional art media of the period, and spreading in popularity in the fertile environment of the art school. A conceptual strain of film and video-making was encouraged by the presence in London of Yoko Ono, with her New York Fluxus film connections, and by Gerry Schum's commissioning of works by Barry Flanagan, Richard Long (fig. 4), Gilbert and George and Keith Arnatt (tutor and students, respectively, at St. Martin's School of Art) for his *Land Art* and *Identifications* shows. Steve Dwoskin, another recent arrival in London, provided a direct link with the New York filmmaking of Andy Warhol and Jack Smith. But the dominant group of the period were the "structuralists", also connected to St. Martin's but with another tutor, Malcolm LeGrice. Structural film in Britain had many facets. Its high theorist and most austere practitioner, Peter Gidal (another New Yorker), developed the theory of "structural materialism" which refuted cinema's dependence on systems of representation and identification and used repetition, extreme duration of shots and radical camera strategies (use of zoom, pan and focus-pulls) to force the spectator into a more active participation in the viewing process (fig. 5).

(fig. 4) Richard Long WALKING A STRAIGHT 10 MILES FORWARD AND BACK SHOOTING EVERY HALF MILE Dartmoor, England, January 1969 video, black and white, 6 mins. 3 sec., contribution to Gerry Schum's, *Land Art*

(fig. 5) Peter Gidal FILM PRINT 1974, 16 mm film, 40 mins. (see p. 243)

LeGrice and his closest colleagues (many of them ex-students) were perhaps Britain's first group of true film modernists. Fascinated by film's material substance (light, lenses, celluloid and its skin of photosensitive emulsion, etc.) and drawn to abstraction, they studiously investigated the many stages of film's "meaning-making": pre-production, the shoot with its separate collection of image and sound, and the projection event (fig. 6). LeGrice was central to the Filmaktion Group that included William Raban, Annabel Nicolson (fig. 7), Gill Eatherley, David Crosswaite and Mike Dunford, who "performed" film in multi-screen projections and live interventions, to draw attention to these constituent parts. Crucially, this generation of filmmakers built their own film workshop at the London Filmmakers' Co-operative, which reduced costs and made it possible to control every aspect of film production. Spatial exploration through cubist-like multiple viewpoints is often a characteristic of this work, as in William Raban's *Angles of Incidence* of 1973 (fig. 8). Some loosely described "structuralists" applied systems ideas to the exploration of landscape. Chris Welsby's *Seven Days* (1974) employed a camera on an astronomical mount systematically to track the position of sun-shadow and clouds from dawn to dusk on a stormy Welsh hillside for a week, becoming in effect the document of a sustained physical performance. In John Ducane's *Zoomlapse* (1975), a complex pattern of in-camera superimpositions and zoom-movements was the means to accumulate a dense temporal light-sculpture.

(fig. 6) Malcolm LeGrice BERLIN HORSE 1970, 16 mm film, 9 mins., projection on one or two screens possible

(fig. 7) Annabel Nicolson SLIDES 1971, 16 mm film, (see p. 243)

(fig. 8) William Raban ANGLES OF INCIDENCE 1973, 16 mm film, 10 mins., projection on one or two screens possible (see p. 243)

VIDEO AS VIDEO, FILM AS FILM – THE 1970s AND 1980s

Video began simply, with uncut single-take records and live relays. It was capable of little else, but its rigour suited conceptualists such as Gilbert and George (fig. 9). The sculptor David Hall began the search for an ontology of video with an elegant piece of deconstruction,

This is a TV Monitor (1974), closely followed by Steve Partridge, *Monitor 1* (1975), and others. Tamara Krikorian was among many drawn to video's willingness to be "a mirror to life", and its potential for introspection; her *Vanitas* (1977) was often shown as an

installation, duration adding to this quality (fig. 10). The technical developments in non-broadcast video which came rapidly in the late 1970s and early 1980s – colour, in-line editing, chroma-key (which made possible a form of collage) – added to the language available to artists, and to the popularity of the medium. Video's relative cheapness and its immediacy (its feed-back to the artist was as instant as in painting) were other attractions. Video also lent itself to installations – often combinations of monitors and

(fig. 9) Gilbert and George GORDON'S MAKES US DRUNK 1972, video, black and white, 12 mins.

(fig. 10) Tamara Krikorian VANITAS 1977, video, 10 mins.

other objects – and important works were made at this time by Hall, Tina Keane, Stuart Marshall, Roger Barnard, Susan Hiller, Mineo Aayamaguchi, and others.

In film, the teachings of Gidal at the Royal College of Art and his example as a polemicist in print were reflected in the political attitudes, writings and camera aesthetics of the generation who followed him, particularly Michael Mazière, Nina Danino, Nicky Hamlyn and Rob Gawthrop. Some had been his students, others succeeded him as workers at the Filmmakers' Co-op, and became contributors to the Co-op's new magazine *Undercut* (1980–90). They shared Gidal's love of shot and sequence repetition and ambiguity in the image – the title *Guesswork* (1979), by Hamlyn, is indicative – but were prepared to allow, and some even to enjoy, the representation of the human figure in

(fig. 11) Guy Sherwin PORTRAIT WITH PARENTS 1976, 16 mm film, 3 mins.

their work. Taking a different route, Tony Hill came to film from architecture and performance – and in *Waterwork* (1987), made for television, combined these interests in a disorientating underwater ballet. A formal structure, sometimes akin to the rules of a game, is important in the films of John Smith, which over 30 years have reflected the changing face of East London, the working-class area where he, like many artists, lives. Irony and visual wit undercut the secure parameters of the "documentary" in his work. Guy Sherwin is the supreme image-maker of his genera-

tion, working with Lumière-like devotion to the photographic recording of apparently simple subjects (fig. 11); his camera and film-printing strategies reveal hidden aspects of the interrelationship of time and movement.

SCRATCH VIDEO, DEREK JARMAN AND DAVID LARCHER – THE 1980s

By the mid 1980s and in the eyes of young artists, the energetic 1960s generation had become the establishment; they were now the committee members, the professors, the authors of the standard theoretical texts, the regular recipients of public funding. The artists associated with Scratch Video made work on domestic video systems, and were proudly un-funded – and free of the theorising and ideological self-flagellation of the older generation. "Scratching is so simple. Just playing with the TV remote-control [...] quickly switching stations at random, is a basic scratch."[5] The quick-switching of visual channels (artful, not random) and staccato repetitions were George Barber's particular stock in trade; *Yes Frank No Smoke* (1985) was made for club-viewing and VHS home video sales. But Scratch could be also political – as in *The Commander in Chief* (1984) by Gorilla Tapes (Gavin Hodge, Tim Morrison and Jon Dovey), with its acerbic cut-up of Ronald Reagan's speech on Dunkirk Beach. The Duvet Brothers, Sandra Goldbacher and John Scarlett Davis were other Scratch stars.

Equally out of sympathy with the structuralists was Derek Jarman. Of the same generation as LeGrice and David Hockney, he was deterred by "the strong official line" at the Filmmakers' Co-op,[6] and as a gay artist saw in Hockney a better role model. His filmmaking began with Super 8 home movies, shown to friends on a variable-speed projector which could operate at three frames per-second (instead of the usual twenty-four). This radical slowing down and aestheticising of fragments of intimate scenes remained a favourite strategy throughout his filmmaking life. Like another contemporary, Peter Greenaway, Jarman had a great love of Britain's literature, music and art; both looked for a modern way to

5 Andy Lipman, *Time Out*, no. 157, October 1984.

6 Derek Jarman, *Dancing Ledge*, London 1984, p. 128.

reflect this heritage, and Jarman in particular expressed his despair about the "uncultured" times in which he lived. Bitterness underscores Jarman's *Imagining October* (1984), a work in which a visit to Eisenstein's preserved study in Moscow leads to a meditation on the role of a (gay) artist in Soviet Russia, drawing parallels with life in Thatcher's Britain. Jarman encouraged and supported many emerging artists; *The Dream Machine* (1984), a multi-part work inspired by William Burroughs and Brion Gysin, has sections contributed by Jarman, Cerith Wyn-Evans, John Maybury and Michael Costiff.

In the 1960s and early 1970s, David Larcher worked alone, making visually complex and often elaborately optically-printed 16 mm films, based on his daily life and epic travels. By the 1990s, he had become a master of video and the digital image, with access to the most advanced technology in Europe. *EETC* (1987) marks the midway point in this transition. In a dazzling technical performance, which takes domestic material shot on film in the 1970s as its starting point, it spins off into video experiment and philosophical speculations about "image" and "trace", and his place in the cosmos.

TALES FOR THE 1980s

The 1980s also saw artists re-engaging with narrative and performance, and the themes of racial, sexual and gender difference. An early and influential female voice was that of Lis Rhodes, who confronted male silence and formalism with her *Light Reading* (1978); "she refused to be framed; she raised her hand; stopped the action; she began to read; she began to read; aloud".[7] Her teaching at the Slade and Goldsmiths' colleges encouraged many who followed her. In Tina Keane's *Shadow of a Journey* (1980), the unseen narrator's voice recalls the forced clearance of peasants from the Scottish islands in the nineteenth century, passing an oral history from one generation to another. The trauma in Mona Hatoum's *Measures of Distance* of 1988 (fig. 12) is in the present – we hear letters exchanged between the artist in London and her

7 Lis Rhodes, from the soundtrack of *Light Reading*, 1978.

(fig. 12) Mona Hatoum MEASURES OF DISTANCE 1977, video, 15 mins.

mother in war-torn Beirut, giving voice to personal and national struggles of identity. For Jayne Parker, the performing body – often her own – is the most eloquent narrator. *K* (1989) works at two levels – as metaphor, and through the direct speech of body-language. Metaphorically, she brings out into the open "things I have taken in that are not mine",[8] and we watch her in close-up as she confronts real physical fear. Gesture is central to Alia Syed's *The Watershed* (1994), where hands rubbing a woman's back speak of abuse and displacement in an immigrant community. Metaphor is also central to the work of Tacita Dean, including her early work *Eternal Womanly* (1987).

Ian Bourn is overtly a story-teller, who often gives his work the semblance of autobiography; the monologue delivered in a pub, *The End of the World* (1982), made with Helen Chadwick, constructs a telling moment of inertia and non-communication between two imaginary Londoners; more often he describes an individual's quiet failure. The process of identifying significant images through photography leads Patrick Keiller to his film narratives. He first assembles still pictures, then writes the words that loosely connect them, to be spoken by his unseen protagonist – his real subject being the layers of history and social changes that have shaped suburban Britain. Chris Newby also explores landscapes, building portraits of exotic places, such as *Stromboli* (1991), through a montage of details and sounds, often with a subtly homoerotic undercurrent, in which his camera assumes the role of a voyeuristic protagonist.

8 From an artist's statement on the film in *Beyond Imagination and Reality*, exh. cat. ICA Biennial, London 1990, p. 20.

POSTSCRIPT

Film was curiously absent from the *Freeze* show. The Young British Artists associated with film (the future Turner Prize winners) came to prominence in the mid 1990s, their arrival coinciding with the appearance of the compact portable video projector, and DVD players. Reliable exhibition technology assisted the emergence of a commercial art market for the moving image, for the first time. These YBAs were almost invariably students of film and video artists of the 1970s and

1980s. The connections between these artists across the decades are well established, but the related links between the late 1990s film and video installation and its 1970s roots, are rarely acknowledged. It is a history to be traced in the records of artist-run organisations such as the Filmmakers' Co-op and London Electronic Arts, and exhibition spaces in London such as the ACME Gallery, the Air Gallery, B2 Butler's Wharf, the ICA and Serpentine Galleries, in touring organisations such as FACT and the Film & Video Umbrella, and in regional galleries such as the Arnolfini in Bristol, the Ikon in Birmingham and the Bluecoat in Liverpool. It is also part of the complicated story of public funding in Britain, and its relation to the art market.

BRITISH PERFORMANCE

AN INCORRECT VIEW

ANTHONY HOWELL

Patrician in its origins, performance art in Britain might be said to have its roots in hoaxes and practical jokes. Take the pranks of William Cole, who was certainly the inspiration for the television series *Candid Camera*. With Virginia Woolf, Duncan Grant and others, in 1910, Cole posed as the Emperor of Abyssinia and his entourage and was given a formal reception on board the British warship, the H. M. S. Dreadnought. The "Bunga-Bunga" affair – a reference to the invented dialect used by the hoaxers – caused outrage in the establishment.

Art got into the act at the 1936 *International Surrealist Exhibition*, which attracted over 10,000 visitors, largely because of the brouhaha generated by performances such as that given by Sheila Legge, a young artist, who "covered her entire head and face in roses and was photographed as Dalí's *La Femme à la tête des roses*, wandering blindly around Trafalgar Square, tripping over reporters, onlookers and pigeons as she went. Salvador Dalí himself went one better, giving a lecture [...] whilst bolted into a diving suit and helmet – intended, as he put it, 'to show that I was plunging down deeply into the human mind'" (fig. 1).

(fig. 1) Sheila Legge as a Surrealistic Phantom at Trafalgar Square during the *International Surrealist Exhibition*, 1936

Inevitably, though, by the 1960s, it was America which proved the dominant influence. By the mid-sixties, London had grown accustomed to seeing the Martha Graham and the Merce Cunningham dance companies. The company which should have had the most impact was that of Alvin Nicolais, who "abstracted" his dancers, attached kites to their wrists and to their ankles, and dressed them as stacks of cubes or coils of wobbling spheres.

Meanwhile, in New York, the happenings had started to happen – pioneered in the late 1950s by Red Grooms and Allan Kaprow – and in the 1960s an English poet called Jef Nuttall built a messy installation in a basement in the Charing Cross Road. The Living Theatre performed *Paradise Now* at the Roundhouse. Yoko Ono's pretty Japanese assistants brought round her minimalist instructions to the poetry bookshop where I worked. In response, I began writing recipe poems – and later these turned into performance art "exercises". David Medalla had us all dress in yellow underpants and dance to *Mellow Yellow* in a liquid light show, down in a nightclub basement. For a while the scene was a volatile mixture of art, poetry and performance.

A home-grown influence was BBC radio's *Goon Show* – with Spike Milligan as its presiding genius. Milligan, with his brand of madcap Surrealism, was a key figure for the first generation consciously to consider themselves "performance artists". Ian Hinchliffe was one of these and still creates witty, rather sad performances out of battered instruments, bits of old tat, newspapers and the occasional fish.

On a visit to New York in 1972, I watched Robert Wilson's troupe perform *Homage to Joseph Stalin* at the Brooklyn Academy of Music. The performance began at 7 p.m. and ended at 7 a.m. Its elaborate slow motion tableaux amounted to a panoramic dream. Each act lasted three hours, and little changed within the act. You fell asleep, while a *corps-de-ballet* with flaming parasols were gyrating within a pyramid at three o'clock in the morning. When you drifted out of sleep an hour later they were still there, spinning slowly before your eyes …

Wilson was an influence on my own performances and on those who joined me in The Theatre of Mistakes. Wilson looked like "high art" still, but back at home, an earthier spirit was emerging. The Kipper Kids, stripped to their jock-straps, with rubber bands around their heads to squash their noses flat, were boxing themselves rather than each other at the Institute of Contemporary Arts. Perhaps there was a political subtext – a denigration of the bellicose nature of the male. The fringes of the British pop scene were getting involved as well. When not featuring in their punk band Throbbing Gristle, Genesis P. Orridge and Cosey Fanni Tutti (working as Coum Transmissions) were creating violently satirical performance-installations (such as *Prostitution* at the Institute of Contemporary Arts, in 1976). Many of these involved discordant collages of atrocities, beaver shots and slogans. They might be crawled into via tunnels of plastic sheeting, and feature filth, drugs and nudity. With her interest in sado-masochism, in porn photo-shoots, stripping and the sex-trade in general, Cosey's work was a precursor of fetishist body art and the work of Annie Sprinkle.

Carolee Schneemann was living and working in London then. More plastic sheeting – the naked artist raised by a leg from the floor by a rope as she swivelled around, writing feminist messages. Most of the performances one attended were loosely constructed, vaguely conceptual,

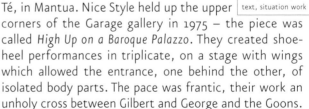

(fig. 2) Gilbert and George Under-neath the Arches London 1969

low impact affairs. The patricians had been routed – except for Gilbert and George, who made their advent in 1969 with *Underneath the Arches* (fig. 2). However, they never used the word "performance". In fact they have performed rarely, and have always referred to themselves as "living sculpture" or "singing sculpture". Despite their influence on some of us, and their success in the gallery world, they were not seminal to the time. Erroneously, these masters of ceremonial symmetry were dubbed "fascists" – because their work implied a sexual "objectification" of young men – standing, vulnerable and naked und the gaze of their suited figures – effigies as heraldic as the lion and the unicorn, or Gog and Magog – artists by appointment to Her Majesty the Queen. Their hoax succeeded too completely for London's Bohemia. Its satire was lost on most live artists, for this was a drop-out culture. Performance was an alternative practice. You didn't exhibit in galleries. You never kept anything but a scrap-book, because, man, this was about the demate-rialisation of art. And you didn't work at it. It was supposed to free you from work. What mattered was your message (and that your message was Marxist).

Paddling furiously against this current, Bruce McLean was producing work with Nice Style, his "boy band" of performers. Nice Style projected a refreshingly decadent image – tuxedos and patent-leather shoes. Very Michael Andrews. Their upper-class twit, party people projection was underpinned by a sculptural sensibility and a conceptual grounding. Like Gilbert and George, Bruce and his team were sculptors first, performers second. He was inspired by plinths – his "heavy metal" tutors at college had poured scorn on plinths and on performances. Bruce created plinth sculptures with his own body – the images are now in the Tate collection (fig. 3). He admired the giants who held up the corners of the Palazzo del Té, in Mantua. Nice Style held up the upper

(fig. 3) Bruce McLean Pose Work for Plinths I 1971, photo-documentation work of a thirty minutes piece in a gallery context, situation work

corners of the Garage gallery in 1975 – the piece was called *High Up on a Baroque Palazzo*. They created shoe-heel performances in triplicate, on a stage with wings which allowed the entrance, one behind the other, of isolated body parts. The pace was frantic, their work an unholy cross between Gilbert and George and the Goons.

In 1977 The Theatre of Mistakes created *A Waterfall* at the Hayward Gallery. This forty-eight day performance culminated in a structure of tables and chairs on which twelve performers sat, one above the other. Water was poured from cup to cup from a bucket at the bottom to one at the top, the arm movements for the pouring synchronised by timing chants derived from the Shipping Forecast. When all the water had accumulated in the top bucket, the performer at the top stood on the top chair and poured all the water in his bucket back into the bottom bucket. This was a spectacular, systemic event. Meanwhile, on another terrace of the Hayward during the same exhibition, Stuart Brisley was working through a more expressionist and actionist process which culminated in his assistant pouring bucketfuls of paint over his naked body, while he dangled by his heels from a sort of scaffold.

A low-impact build-up to a violent finale was a hallmark of Brisley's work in those days. In *10 Days, an English Lie, Hunger Makes Free*, a performance in Berlin in 1973, he had dived naked onto a table and clawed his way through the rotting food which had accumulated since the beginning of the performance ten days previously. Brisley had vomited the remains of his meal on that initial day and subsequently eaten nothing but vitamins, fruit juice and dextrose tabs, though the plate of food he would have consumed was laid on the table daily — becoming ever less appealing, as the performance wore on. His regular action was to sweep the floor. I admired the courage of this piece, and the artist's resolute deprivation of sustenance; however, my sensibilities were offended by the title, which seemed to patronise the Berlin audience and spell out the piece's "meaning" too emphatically. A later piece by Brisley, which I preferred, involved him digging a hole with his assistant, at the same *Documenta* as Walter de Maria's brass rod, which was sunk one kilometre into the earth. Brisley's simple digging — till he struck water and could go no further — seemed a resonant comment on the high technology that enabled the successful installation of the American's contribution.

(fig. 4) A Performer with Station House Opera achieves two aims with one action

By the late 1970s, several of the core-performers in The Theatre of Mistakes, myself included, felt the need to create performances in their own right. Julian Maynard Smith and Miranda Payne left the company to form one of their own. This was Station House Opera — which continues to create spectacular pieces (fig. 4). Their performances often resemble flying dreams. Whole rooms get inverted, so the audience's view is that of a fly on the ceiling. In a solo, at the ACME Gallery in 1979, Maynard Smith made his entrance in the manner of Scaramouche, swinging in from an upper storey window. Like Leonardo da Vinci, he is partly an inventor, partly an engineer. He has devised elaborate pulley systems for hoisting performers aloft, where they may dine at suspended tables. On one occasion, the company suspended huge sieves from which flour is shaken down onto a black floor, turning it into an enormous *tabula rasa*. They have built constantly evolving and mutating buildings out of breeze-blocks. They have created their own limelight, with the aid of quick-lime, to illuminate suspended scenes with performers in eighteenth-century finery, in a manner that magically evokes both the subject-matter and the vision of the painter, Joseph Wright of Derby.

The interest — for such patrician performers — is in creating "another sort of stuff". An influence on many of us has been the work of the late Stuart Sherman. The precise but elusive manipulations of objects which made up his small "spectacles" were simply like nothing one had seen before, and this was their justification. Frank Auerbach has spoken of "bringing a work of art to life". Perhaps this notion — of giving birth — exerts a pull on male artists, because it defies biological possibility. And perhaps it is largely feminism which has shifted so much of the current art-world back to a proletarian concern with the message, since the women's movement has constantly maintained that women have been gagged in the past.

(fig. 5) André Stitt during his performance *The Geek Shop*, The Woodworks Show, Vauxhall, London 1993

Whatever the cause, the battle-lines are drawn. And they are drawn on two fronts. Firstly there is an aesthetic divide. For Sylvia Ziranek, who often performed with McLean and then went on to create her own solos, notably at the Tate in 1985, rehearsal is anathema. Each performance should be unique — a view shared by artists such as Richard Layzell and André Stitt (fig. 5). Some would even prefer the work to go undocumented. It has also to feature the artist — as in the case of Orlan or Stelarc — and cannot be performed by someone else. Now The Theatre of Mistakes believed in being, not acting, and thus devised strategies for copying each other's actions, reversing each other's actions, etcetera. However, we also felt that a performance both came to life and became a made thing – and we perceived no conflict in these notions. As a made thing brought to life, and scrupulously mapped out, it could be performed by others.

Stitt, and his precursors, Stuart Brisley and Alastair MacLennon, might also maintain that the object of art is to make the world a better place. The performance is meant to teach us something, about Buddhism, or injustice, or our waste-matter. This is an "agit-prop" view, yet one actively favoured by governments, which find it easier for them to create an arts residency in a hospital than to build a new wing. We have moved a long way from the scandal provoked in the establishment by the "Bunga-Bunga" affair, except that the patrician artists still provoke scandal in the new establishment – that axis of feminism and theorising which now dominates academia and influences most curatorial initiatives, because their work fails to address any relevant issue.

I prefer a performance which is perfectly clear – although I have no idea what it is about – to a performance which is clearly about this or that, although as a set of actions it is nothing but a confused miscellany. Happily, in the best work by MacLennon and Stitt, this is not the case. It is often not particularly clear what MacLennon is on about, but the performances are delivered with impeccable timing, the pace often slow, the duration considerable, the matter only gradually evolving and the environment going through some barely perceptible transitions. The work of his that I witnessed in 1985, during the second *British Art Show*, was essentially meditative. On the other hand, Stitt's work is as percussive and explosive, physically speaking, as was the work of Steven Cripps in the early 1970s at the ACME Gallery. Cripps was an explosives artist and often had us running for cover as smoke belched from the upper windows; meanwhile, Brisley had bricked himself into the basement and could only be witnessed through a surveillance video, as he went through his ablutions or excretions.

Stitt evokes the image of the shaman. There is a degree of auto-abuse. He may tar and feather himself, becoming society's expiation. Sometimes effect undermines authenticity – dildoes being dangled more often than genuine genitals. Ulster-born, he disapproves of

the psychoanalytic approach. He is not interested in rehearsal. A performance cannot be repeated. It should respond to the seismic tremor of its time. Even so, dominant themes may be developed from piece to piece; undergoing several changes in the process. Of course, no performance is ever an exact replica of a predecessor: a rehearsed piece taken on tour is different every night. Many of Sylvia Ziranek's bright pink serendipitous performances bore a similarity to each other, even if they were all supposed to be different. The advantage of a long gestation to the creation of a rehearsed work is that the result may be very different from a previous piece which underwent the same process. Still, there is likely to be some connection – perhaps a refinement of a previous preoccupation. Without a style and an identity to the work, there is no possibility of recognition. Extreme theorists might argue that a recognisable style is already indicative of some complicity with consumerism.

A performance artist with a distinct style of his own is Gary Stevens. Stevens worked for a while with Station House Opera, but then began creating his own solos and duets (with Caroline Wilkinson) in the early 1980s. Stevens was preoccupied then by facial expression, creating performance art from the neck upwards. By the 1980s, I had turned my back on language, making pieces which were itineraries of unaccompanied action – turning arrangements of furniture through 90 degrees, then either hiding behind them as I continued to move them, or moving them while walking on them, never touching the ground (*The Table Moves*, Sydney Biennale 1982) (fig. 6). Stevens retained language in his performances, giving it a conceptual base rather than a narrative role. In *If the Cap Fits*, performed at the Institute of Contemporary Arts in 1986, he and his co-performer put on one item of clothing after another, becoming inflated Rabelaisian characters in the process (fig. 7).

(fig. 6) The Theatre of Mistakes: Anthony Howell and Peter Strickland perform *Table Move Duet* at the Künstlerhaus Bethanien, Berlin 1980

(fig. 7) Caroline Wilkinson and Gary Stevens during the performance of *If the Cap Fits*, Institute of Contemporary Arts, London 1986

Another issue which came to the fore in the late 1980s was that of audience participation: artists felt the need to question the definition of the audience as a unified body. Fiona Templeton, a founder member of The Theatre of Mistakes, moved to New York after the company's demise. In 1990, she created *You: The City* there. It was subsequently seen in London and in several large cities in Europe, each time being adapted to suit its new environment (fig. 8).

In this piece, performers took members of their audience one at a time through a city, passing each member of the audience on to a new performer at the end of their passage in the piece. Thus the London performance began by you being interviewed in an office by a woman who talked all the time, then ushered you out

(fig. 8) Fiona Templeton
YOU: THE CITY   Mickery,
Amsterdam 1990

by a different door into the street, where you were picked up by a drunken young lady who talked gushingly to you, as she walked you to the corner where a taxi door was standing open. The taxi driver proved as garrulous as the two previous interlocutors.

The ambivalence felt by many performance artists about repetition and about documentation, combined with the primitive materials available for video-taping performances in the 1960s, means that little survives of this rich era of activity in Britain. However, it is interesting to note that *You: The City* has recently been recreated, as has *The Waterfall* — to the consternation of the theoretical proletariat.

ANTHONY HOWELL

1980–90
Painting, Objects and Installations

1980

Events: America elects President Ronald Reagan
Alan Bowness becomes Director of Tate; Chisenhale Studios founded
Station House Opera formed
Artists: Graham Sutherland dies
Exhibitions: Victor Pasmore retrospective at Hayward; David Hockney at Tate
Publications: First issue of **Undercut**; Peter Fuller, **Seeing Berger**

1981

Events: Art market begins to boom
Artists: Reg Butler dies
Exhibitions: Stuart Brisley at ICA; Patrick Caulfield retrospective at Tate; Philip King retrospective at Hayward; **A New Spirit in Painting** at Royal Academy; **British Sculpture in the Twentieth Century** Part I at Whitechapel; **Objects and Sculpture** at Arnolfini, Bristol and ICA; Robert Rauschenberg at Tate

Publications: John Latham, **Event Structure**; Salman Rushdie, **Midnight's Children**

1982

Events: Falklands War
Tate establishes Patrons of New Art
Artists: Julian Opie leaves Goldsmiths' College; Ben Nicholson dies
Exhibitions: **British Sculpture in the Twentieth Century** Part II at Whitechapel; Anish Kapoor at Lisson; Stuart Brisley at Tate; Julian Schnabel at Tate
Publications: Richard Hamilton, **Collected Words**

1983

Events: Margaret Thatcher increases Conservative majority at General Election
Public Art Development Trust founded
Artists: Bill Brandt dies
Exhibitions: Henry Moore retrospective at Metropolitan, New York; Peter Blake retrospective at Tate; **New Art** at Tate; **The Sculpture Show** at Hayward and Serpentine; **Scenes and Conventions – Artists' Architecture** at ICA; Julian Opie at Lisson
Publications: Mary Kelly, **Post-Partum Document**; Jean Baudrillard, **Simulations**

1984

Events: Miners' Strike ends in defeat
Tate launches Turner Prize; Book Works founded; Interim Art opens
Artists: Roland Penrose dies
Exhibitions: Anthony Caro at Hayward; Howard Hodgkin at Whitechapel; Hans Haacke at Tate, Richard Wentworth at Tate; **American Art: Minimal Expression** at Tate; **The Hard-Won Image: Traditional Method and Subject in Recent British Art** at Tate
Publications: Frederic Jameson, "Postmodernism, or The Cultural Logic of

Late Capitalism", **New Left Review**; Martin Amis, **Money**

1985
Events: Mikhail Gorbachev President of USSR
Saatchi Gallery opens in London; Artangel founded
Artists: Howard Hodgkin wins Turner Prize; Rachel Whiteread enters Slade; Anya Gallaccio, Michael Landy enter Goldsmiths' College; Nigel Henderson dies
Exhibitions: Francis Bacon retrospective at Tate; Patrick Heron retrospective at Barbican Art Gallery, London; Josef Beuys at Anthony d'Offay; Eduardo Paolozzi Lost Magic Kingdoms at Museum of Mankind; **British Film and Video 1980–85** at Tate; Bruce McLean at Tate

1986
Events: Camberwell, Central St Martin's and Chelsea Schools of Art merge as The London Institute; Unit 7 Gallery opens in London; Paragon Press founded
Artists: Gilbert and George win Turner Prize; Damien Hirst enters Goldsmiths' College; Henry Moore dies;
Exhibitions: Frank Auerbach at Venice Biennale, awarded Golden Lion; David Mach at Riverside Studios; **Falls the Shadow** at Hayward; **Forty Years of Modern Art 1945–85** at Tate
Publications: Victor Burgin, **The End of Art Theory**

1987
Events: Washington summit "ends" Cold War; Conservatives under Margaret Thatcher retain power at General Election; Stock Market crash
Karsten Schubert Gallery opens in London
Artists: Richard Deacon wins Turner Prize; Rachel Whiteread leaves Slade
Exhibitions: Tony Cragg at Hayward; Gilbert and George at Hayward; **British Art in the 20th Century: The Modern Movement** at Royal Academy; **New York Art Now** Part 1 at Saatchi; Bruce Nauman at Whitechapel

1988
Events: Controversy over Salman Rushdie's **The Satanic Verses**
Tate Gallery Liverpool opens; Nicholas Serota becomes director of Tate; Henry Moore Sculpture Trust founded; City Racing opens; Jay Jopling becomes dealer
Artists: Tony Cragg wins Turner Prize; Michael Craig-Martin stops teaching at Goldsmiths' College; Anya Gallaccio, Michael Landy leave Goldsmiths' College, Ithell Colquhoun dies
Exhibitions: Tony Cragg at Venice Biennale; Lucian Freud retrospective at Hayward; David Hockney retrospective at Tate; **New York Art Now** Part 2 at Saatchi; **Freeze** at Port of London Authority building; **Edge 88** at Air Gallery, London; Michael Landy at Karsten Schubert

Publications: Peter Fuller, **Theoria: Art and the Absence of Grace**; first issue of **Modern Painters**

1989
Events: Fall of Berlin Wall
Art market in recession; Space Explorations founded
Artists: Richard Long wins Turner Prize; Damien Hirst leaves Goldsmiths' College; William Scott dies
Exhibitions: Tony Cragg at Tate; Michael Craig-Martin retrospective at Whitechapel; F. E. McWilliam retrospective at Tate; Michael Landy at Karsten Schubert

1990
Events: Margaret Thatcher resigns, succeeded by John Major
Artists: Charles Saatchi buys Damien Hirst's **A Thousand Years**
Exhibitions: Anish Kapoor at Venice Biennale; **The British Art Show** at Hayward; Richard Long at Tate; **Seven Obsessions: New Installation Work** at Whitechapel; **Broken English** at Serpentine; Rachel Whiteread at Chisenhale Gallery, London; **Modern Medicine, Gambler**, and Michael Landy **Market** at Building One, London; Anya Gallaccio **East Country Yard Show** at Surrey Docks in London;
Publications: last issue of **Encounter**; last issue of **Undercut**; last issue of **Artscribe**

THE PERSISTENCE OF PAINTING

CONTEXTS FOR BRITISH FIGURATIVE PAINTING, 1975–90

JAMES HYMAN

A SCHOOL OF LONDON: NATIONAL CONTEXTS FOR BRITISH FIGURATIVE PAINTING

Two men face us. Side-by-side they stand, both virtually naked: one wears just his round-rimmed glasses and the other just a t-shirt, socks and sneakers. Despite their nakedness, the effect is relaxed. There is something jovial rather than aggressive about this confrontation. There they stand arm in arm, barely containing their smirks. Behind them there is a large blank canvas, which they fill, to one side is a ladder and to the other side are some canvases. We are in an artist's studio and there to greet us are David Hockney and R. B. Kitaj (fig. 1).

    Behind the bonhomie, far removed from the macho posturing that Julian Schnabel and Georg Baselitz soon made famous, there was a serious message. This convivial photograph was a come-on. The cover illustration for the January/February 1977 issue of the political and cultural journal, *The New Review*, memorably encapsulated the two artists' advocacy of "depictions of people" that was at the centre of the conversation between them published within the journal.[1] Reactionary in tone, this conversation revealed a deep mistrust of the notion of progress, a questioning of modernism and an advocacy of rigorous life drawing.

    This photograph graphically illustrates a trend in British art to be found not only in manifesto essays and exhibitions but also major paintings from the late 1970s onwards, in which a range of British artists sought to champion figurative drawing and painting. Indeed a major painting that Kitaj began at this time, entitled *The Neo-Cubist* (1976–87), has as its roots in the cover photograph from the *New Review* and encapsulates these ambitions (fig. 2). A naked David Hockney stands facing us, shown frontally and side on, articulately demonstrating Kitaj's abilities as a meticulous draftsman, striking colourist and expressive painter.

(fig. 2) R. B. Kitaj THE NEO-CUBIST 1976–87, oil on canvas, 177.8 x 132.1 cm, private collection

    Paradoxically, it was Kitaj, an American who had come to England at the end of the 1950s, who was the most vociferous proselytiser for British figurative painting, but he was not alone in Britain, or internationally, in his ambitions for figurative painting, nor in the way his painting seemed to gain a new vigour in the early 1980s. Significantly, the gestation period of *The Neo-Cubist* was also the time in which several figurative artists working in Britain, who already had long established reputations, took their work to new heights – prominent among them, Lucian Freud, Frank Auerbach, Leon Kossoff, Howard Hodgkin and Patrick Caulfield (pls. 190, 191, 192, 194 and 205).

The exhibitions and purchases of the Arts Council of Great Britain during the later 1970s did much to encourage this engagement with drawing, painting and figuration. Monographic exhibitions staged by the Arts Council at the Hayward Gallery in London, where Catherine Lampert had a crucial role, included first retrospectives for Lucian Freud in 1974, Frank Auerbach in 1978 and Michael Andrews in 1980. Group shows had a serious polemical function, not least those devoted to drawing. In 1975 the Arts Council invited the figurative painter, Patrick George, to buy work for their collection, which he presented in an intimate exhibition called *Drawings of People*, and the following year the theme of this show was reinforced by the purchases of R. B. Kitaj, which were showcased in the complementary exhibition *The Human Clay*.[2] Such promotion gave especial prominence to art school teaching and to the fundamental importance of life drawing.[3] Frequently the suggestion of continuity, through the presentation of such "traditions" as an essential characteristic of the best British art, was used as a riposte to the supposed decadence to be found elsewhere, particularly in America.[4]

The Human Clay mainly comprised drawings and was accompanied by a highly personalised catalogue essay, inspired in large part by Kitaj's recent return to life drawing and by his belief in the importance of this practice for both figuration and abstraction. In it, Kitaj briefly wrote of a School of London, using the term loosely, as he later explained: "I meant that a School had arisen, like School of Paris and School of N. Y., where a number of world class painters and a larger number of good painters had appeared in London maybe for the first time [...]. Like N. Y. and Paris, the London School will continue until its best painters die."[5] "10 years after the Human Clay, The School of London has no peer abroad [...] the artists are just plain gifted beyond the resources of other schools. For the moment, N. Y. seems played out and Paris doesn't count."[6]

JAMES HYMAN

In *The Human Clay* Kitaj did include those artists now considered to constitute the "core" of the School of London – namely Michael Andrews, Francis Bacon, Lucian Freud (fig. 3), Frank Auerbach and Leon Kossoff – but he also deliberately blurred distinctions between abstract and figurative artists and to this end selected over 40 other artists.[7]

(fig. 3) Lucian Freud
LARGE INTERIOR W. 11
(AFTER WATTEAU) 1981–83,
oil on canvas, 186 x 198 cm,
private collection

Arts Council records show that the exhibition attracted over 10,000 visitors, but it appears to have had little immediate impact. Critical priorities were elsewhere and Kitaj's reference to a School of London passed unnoticed. Indeed when in 1981 it was proposed once again, this time by the painter, teacher and art historian Lawrence Gowing, he had apparently forgotten Kitaj's earlier reference and claimed authorship of the idea.[8]

In the years after Kitaj' and Gowing's references to a School of London, their broad conception of a School became honed down to an almost fixed core of six or seven painters. This School of London, including Andrews, Auerbach, Bacon, Freud and Kossoff as well as Kitaj, swiftly gained powerful promotion.[9] The label "School of London", despite the often-used prefix "so-called", soon became the dominant framework for the presentation of post-war British figurative painting, despite the reservations of the artists themselves. Nonetheless the idea has been greeted with little enthusiasm either by the chief beneficiaries or those to whom it might be extended.[10]

The presentation of a small core of artists owes most to Michael Peppiatt and much to the British Council exhibition which he curated, *A School of London: Six Figurative Painters* (1987).[11] Presenting Andrews, Auerbach, Bacon, Freud, Kitaj and Kossoff, this powerful exhibition provided a template for future presentations of a School of London such as *From London* (1995).[12] Despite differences, both exhibitions sought to characterise these very different artists in a way that suggested a commonality of interests. Above all, this was a group of artists for whom the Second World War and its aftermath provided a formative milieu and who, with the radicalism of Alberto Giacometti in Paris and Willem de Kooning in New York, created a radical contemporary vision of urban man attuned to a new existentialist sensibility. The same line was also pursued in other

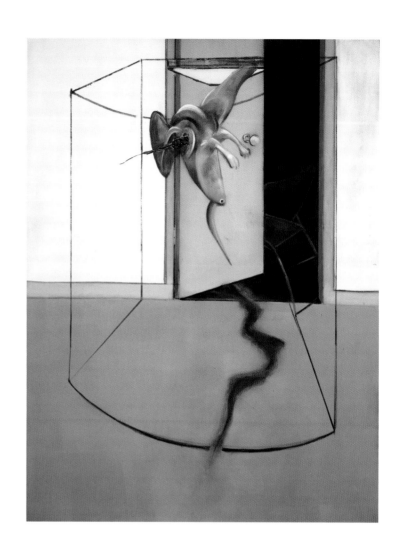

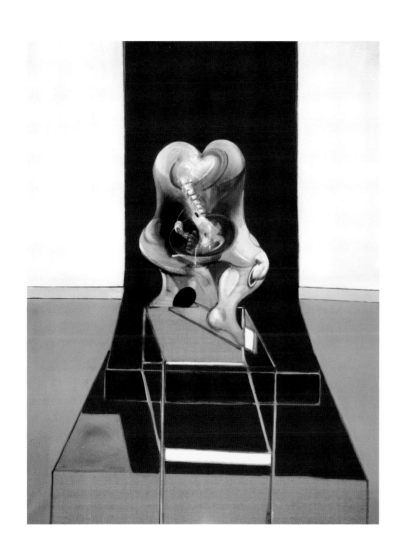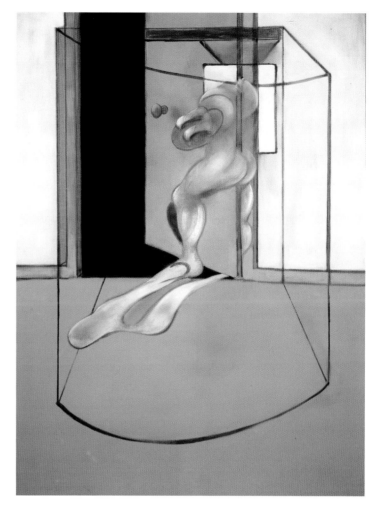

194 | Frank Auerbach Head of JYM 1983

195 | Michael Andrews THE CATHEDRAL, THE SOUTHERN FACES/ULURU (AYERS ROCK) 1987

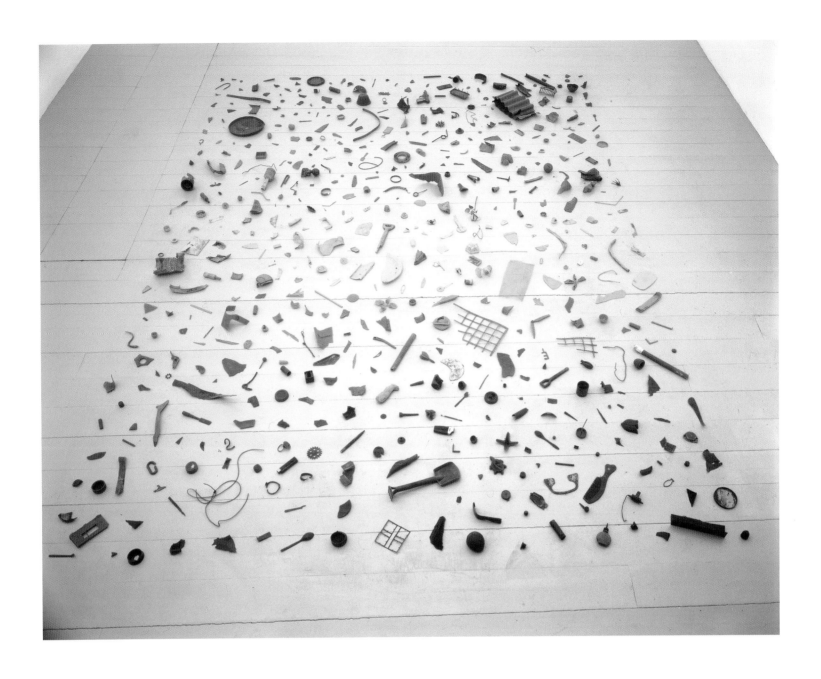

Richard Deacon Boys and Girls (Come Out to Play) 1982

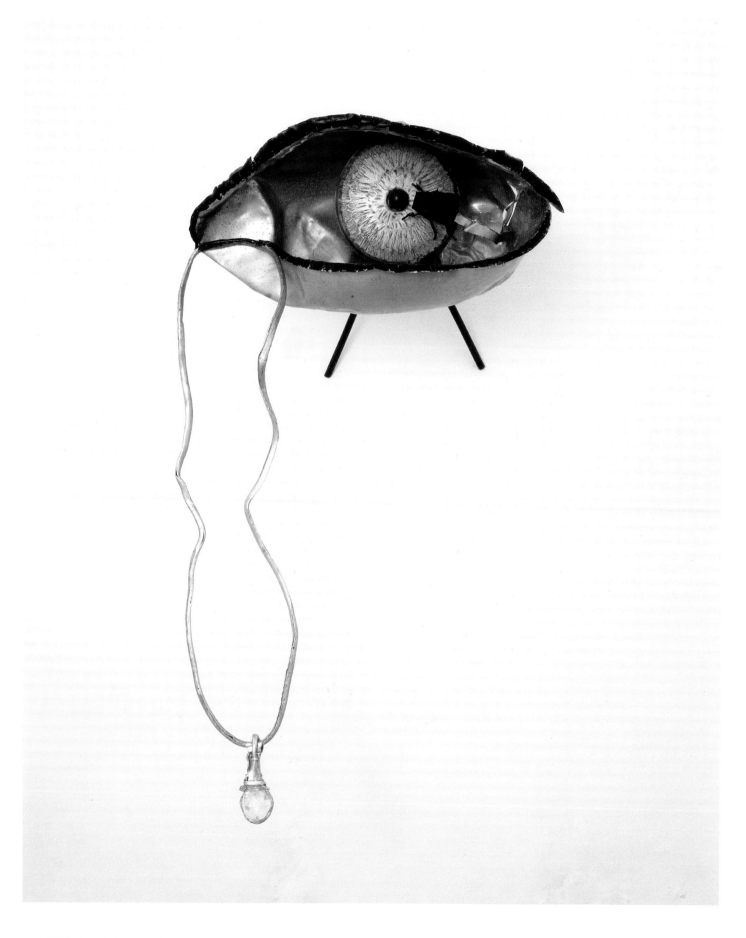

201 | Anish Kapoor WHITE SAND, RED MILLET, MANY FLOWERS 1982

203 | Antony Gormley MOTHER'S PRIDE 1980–81

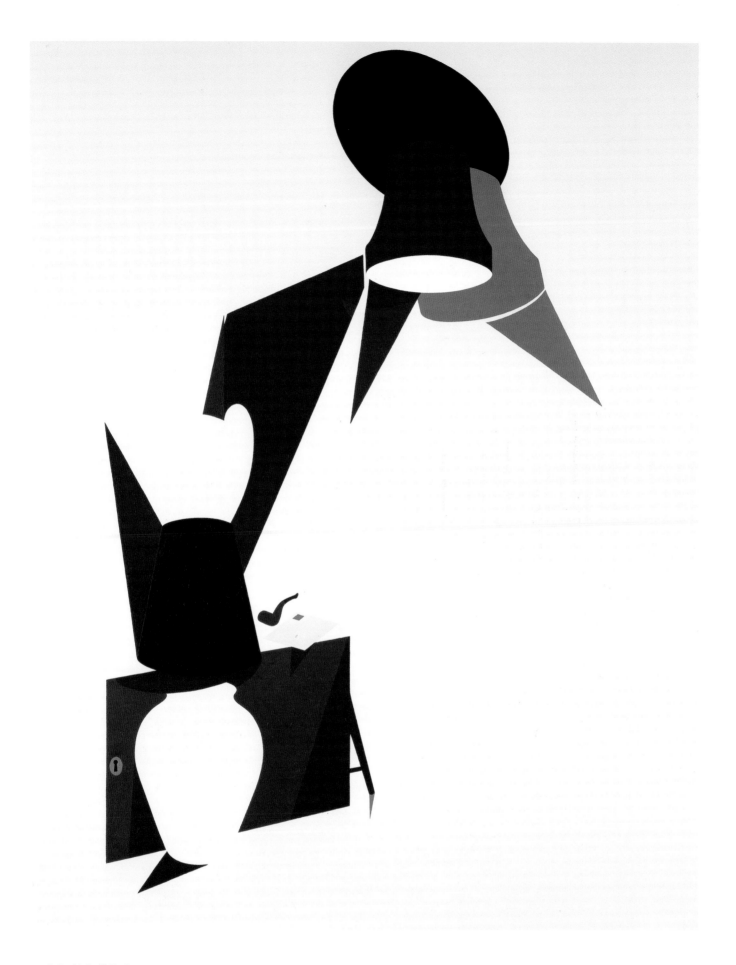

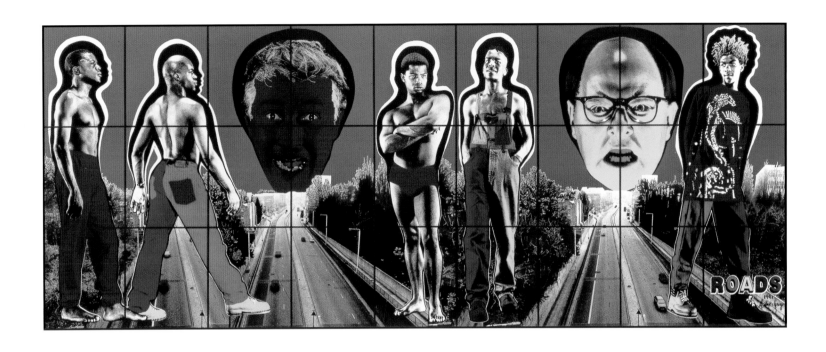

207 | Gilbert & George ROADS 1991

209 | Art & Language Index: Incident in a Museum (Francesco Sabaté) 1986

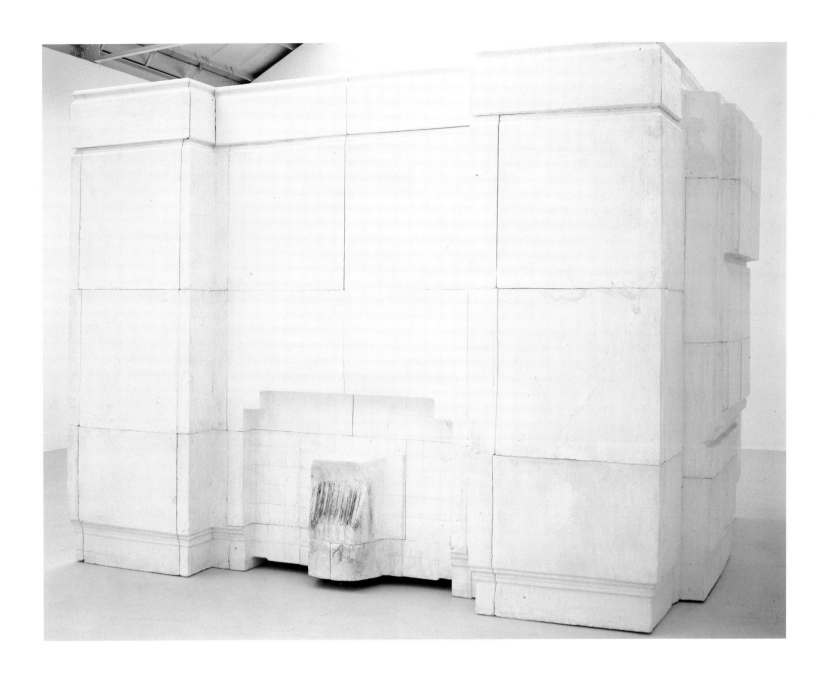

212 | Michael Landy APPROPRIATION (Video still) 1990

exhibitions that stressed the distinctive qualities of the immediate post-war period and its resonance for the painters of the School.[13] Prominent among these were *The Hard Won Image* (1984),[14] *The Forgotten Fifties* (1984)[15] and *The Transformation of Appearance* (1991).[16]

An apotheosis was reached in 1987, when the core artists of the School of London held centre stage at the most significant precursor to the present exhibition, the Royal Academy's controversial survey *British Art of the Twentieth Century: The Modern Movement*. This gave Andrews, Auerbach, Bacon, Freud and Kossoff the main gallery of the exhibition.[17] It thereby placed figurative painters of diverse ethnic backgrounds, physically and symbolically, at the heart of a national tradition.[18]

The effect of such exhibitions was to stress national continuity and specifically to secure the perception that contemporary figurative practice was embedded within a national "tradition" of art school teaching. The creation of international contexts for British figurative painting would add an entirely new dimension, reasserting the radicalism and contemporary resonance of these artists.

A NEW SPIRIT IN PAINTING: INTERNATIONAL CONTEXTS FOR BRITISH FIGURATIVE PAINTING

One cannot underestimate the impact on the reputations of established artists and the aspirations of younger painters of the Royal Academy exhibition, *A New Spirit in Painting*, in 1981. This controversial event proved to be one of the key exhibitions of the decade. Its catalogue declared that "in 1980 painting changed", and its walls displayed an array of international artists, foregrounded painting, and gave prominence to figuration and expressionism. It included a number of British artists of different generations within a context that was both international and contemporary, rather than national and historical. Its effect was thus heightened by the avoidance of narrow parochialism.

Painting and, above all, forms of figuration were once more on the international critical agenda, to be championed as a vanguard rather than as a conservative phenomenon. Placing side by side the painting of younger as well as older men, the exhibition did much to suggest to younger British artists that to paint the figure need not indicate merely the continuation of English art school teaching or the legacy of a "tradition", from Walter Sickert to David Bomberg (fig. 4), to Auerbach, Kossoff and their students. This new realignment allowed their work to assume a radical international stature.[19]

(fig. 4) David Bomberg TAJO AND ROCKS, RONDA 1956, oil on canvas, 71 x 91.5 cm, The St. John Wilson Trust

The title, *A New Spirit in Painting*, however, exposed a paradox at the heart of the exhibition. As critics at the time recognised, this was no new direction for painting, as was especially apparent from the British artists selected: Auerbach, Bacon (pl. 199), Alan Charlton (pl. 165), Freud, Hockney, Hodgkin, Kitaj, Bruce McLean. Rather, it revealed a reorientation of critical and curatorial attention towards forms of artistic practice that had become marginalised. However, such criticism, although valid, hid the fact that in significant ways the painting of even such long-established artists was changing. There was, indeed, a new spirit in painting.

The work of several of the most significant figurative painters leapt to new heights in the 1980s through a loosening up in the handling of paint, which was often married to a generous widening of these artists' palette. Certainly, the panache of Hodgkin and Auerbach, Hockney and Caulfield provided a vigorous riposte to all those who had characterised British art as drab and depressing. Auerbach's magnificent paintings of Mornington Crescent showed that behind his preoccupation with drawing there lay a dazzling colourist (pl. 194). Hockney heightened his colour, loosened his brushstrokes and shifted scale and viewpoint with new freedom. In the expansive *Mullholland Drive* of 1980 (fig. 5), one of the most ambitious of these large-scale works, the almost fauvist handling of colour showed how far Hockney had removed from the

(fig. 5) David Hockney MULLHOLLAND DRIVE. THE ROAD TO THE STUDIO 1980, acrylic on canvas, 218 x 617 cm, Los Angeles County Museum of Art

high finish of his works of a decade earlier. Even Hodgkin, for whom colour had always been fundamental, found a new range of expression, layering form and colour to add a new sensuality, luxuriance and wholeness. Such decorative complexity also came to the fore in the paintings of Patrick Caulfield. Having explored the theme of the interior in paintings of the early 1970s, he addressed still life motifs, enjoying the clash of ever more lurid wallpaper and tablecloth patterns. But by the mid 1980s Caulfield had come to refine these ever busier paintings by adopting grounds of a single intense colour, isolating still life elements and beginning to replace the previously inexpressive paint with a new textural richness.

Even tonal painters, for whom colour remained subordinate to drawing, produced work of a new-found confidence and expansiveness, matching increased mastery of the medium with more ambitious challenges, as in the case of Freud and Kossoff. Lucian Freud's paintings of his mother of the later 1970s introduced a new tenderness, emotional intensity and beauty. The harshness of the late 1960s gave way to softness, with-

(fig. 6) Leon Kossoff CHRISTCHURCH SPITALFIELDS. MORNING 1990, oil on wood, 198 x 188.5 cm, Tate , London

out diminution of intensity, and led to a series of sophisticated multi-figure portraits, initially showing two figures, as in *Naked Man and His Friend* (1979–80), and culminated in one of Freud's most ambitions composition to date, *Large Interior W. 11 (after Watteau)* of 1981–83 (fig. 3). Meanwhile, Kossoff continued his pursuit of intimately known subjects. His paintings of a new life model, Fidelma – an ongoing series begun in the late 1970s – were a moving attempt to suspend for a moment the moving presence of the model (pl. 190). At the same time, Kossoff also painted some of the most powerful landscapes of his career, showing the booking hall and exterior of Kilburn Underground station and the massive form of Christchurch, Spitalfields (fig. 6).

Nonetheless, it soon became apparent that, in the promotion of British figurative painting, it was not the new heights reached by these artists, nor their radical pursuit of the real, that was at the forefront of the claims made for them. Instead, all too often, their work was appropriated and presented as an antidote to the excesses perceived in international vanguard culture. In Britain the critic, Peter Fuller, had an undeniable

importance through his pioneering essays of the 1970s and 1980s, championing critically neglected artists such as Bomberg, Auerbach and Kossoff, but all too frequently, his acute insights into these artists were blunted by the role he assigned to them as a riposte to all that he deplored in contemporary, especially American, culture. Similarly, in America, Robert Hughes used the pages of *Time* to deride the art he saw around him in New York and to praise the supposedly antithetical values represented by Freud and Auerbach.

In the wake of *A New Spirit in Painting*, exhibitions gave a new prominence to British figurative painters. The British Council exhibition *The Proper Study* (1984), demonstrated directly the legacy of *A New Spirit in Painting*,[20] whilst its moralising title exemplified the "high seriousness" that became associated with the British artists' contribution to this international concern, against which many of the "Young British Artists" of the 1990s would react. Special issues of art journals also emphasised the position of the School of London at the heart of this perceived revival – most notably, special issues of *Art International* in 1987 and of *Art and Design* in 1988. The former focused on the "core" artists of the School[21] and the latter, although entitled "British Art Now", was entirely devoted to English and Scottish figurative painters of different generations, with the exception of an interview with the sculptor Tony Cragg. [22] (pl. 198)

Narrative painting also enjoyed a higher degree of promotion. In England it was articulately championed by Timothy Hyman, and in Scotland it dominated exhibitions of young Scottish artists, most notably, in the exhibition *The Vigorous Imagination. New Scottish Art* (1987).[23] Unlike elders such as Bacon, Freud, Kossoff, Auerbach and Euan Uglow, who all sought to deny narrative and to concentrate on the single figure, young Scottish artists developed a bold, colourful, large-scale narrative painting, most often frequented by powerful young men. Ken Currie's workers

(fig. 7) Adrian Wiszniewski CULTURE VULTURING CITY SLIPPERS 1986, pastel on paper, 207.5 x 150 cm, The British Council

had a political edge, Steven Campbell's stories were at once fantastic and prosaic, Adrian Wiszniewski's languid young men (fig. 7) were the artist's *alter ego* and Stephen Conroy's scenes suggested the honeyed nostalgia for a bygone age.

Meanwhile, in London, a preoccupation with the expressive power of paint led several young artists to work in the borders between abstraction and figuration, and incorporation of landscape elements (fig. 8) allowed critics such as Keith Patrick to champion a new romantic sensibility, shared by artists such as Christopher Le Brun, Thérèse Oulton and Hughie O'Donoghue. Le Brun's powerful large-scale paintings suggested an elusive, half-glimpsed subject, the whispered remains of a past civilisation. Oulton's intricate paintings were at once suggestive of the late landscapes of William Turner and the delicacy of Rembrandt's painting of ruffs; they suggested both a world coming in and out of view and a reverence for the traces of the past. O'Donoghue, meanwhile, created a powerful elemental realm of tempestuous seas and skies and an earthy land filled with peat bog men. Somewhat to one side was Tony Bevan, whose one-person show at the Institute of Contemporary Arts in 1987 revealed an artist who combined powerful handling of form with a moving social concern that was the legacy of a strong vein of political and social engagement, that ran through much British art of the 1970s and early 1980s. Painted with sensitivity and compassion, Bevan's pictures were a tender chronicle of those around him.

(fig. 8) Steven Campbell ENGLISH LANDSCAPE WITH A DISRUPTIVE GENE 1987, pastel on paper, 250 x 221 cm, Fundação Calouste Gulbenkian/CAMJAP, Lisbon

However, whilst the paintings of such younger artists suggested an awe of their elders, whether they were the great artists of the past or, more immediately, those of the School of London, such parameters would be profoundly challenged in the spring of 1985, when Charles and Doris Saatchi opened their magnificent gallery in Boundary Road, in North London, to show works from their collection.

The opening of the Saatchi Collection was a revelation. Its unsurpassed inaugural exhibitions gave British artists unprecedented exposure to the most important contemporary artists in the world. The experience was overwhelming. The minimal beauty of the warehouse building, the massive scale of its spaces, the in-depth presentation of each artist, and the immense power of its first exhibition of Donald Judd, Brice Marden, Cy Twombly and Andy Warhol immediately established London as one of the most significant places to see contemporary art in the whole world. This, and the gal-

lery's third exhibition of Anselm Kiefer and Richard Serra (1986–87), were undoubtedly two of the outstanding shows of the decade. The impact on the priorities of young artists was profound.

In a powerful statement of his belief in the international stature of British art, Saatchi also began to amass substantial holdings of Andrews, Auerbach, Caulfield, Freud, Hodgkin, Kitaj, Kossoff, Lisa Milroy (fig. 9), Malcolm Morley, John Murphy, Avis Newman, Paula Rego, Sean Scully, Carel Weight and Victor Willing. This culminated in exhibitions of Kossoff, Auerbach and Freud at the decade's end. It also led to the publication of New British Art in the Saatchi Collection (1989), which even included a section entitled School of London, and was compiled by Alistair Hicks, whose book The School of London: the Resurgence of Contemporary Painting appeared in the same year.[24] In each case the approach spanned generations, with Saatchi's inclusion of the venerable Carel Weight and the younger artists, Lisa Milroy and Avis Newman, anticipating the more commercial considerations, which informed Hicks' book.[25] This use of the elders of the School to help market the achievements of later generations would also be evident a decade later, with the travelling exhibition L'École de Londres: de Bacon à Bevan in 1998.[26]

(fig. 9) Lisa Milroy STAMPS 1986, oil on canvas, 189.2 x 198.1 cm, The British Council

Saatchi's presentations of contemporary art were complemented by those of the Whitechapel Art Gallery which, under the directorship of Nicholas Serota (1976–88), held major exhibitions of ambitious, expressive, twentieth-century figurative painting. These included Phillip Guston's late figurative work, Max Beckmann's triptychs, and Kiefer's meditations on German history, as well as shows foregrounding radical sculptures, from the survey exhibition British Sculpture of the 20th Century to the work of Eva Hesse and Janis Kounellis. Alongside this went the growing internationalism of the Anthony d'Offay Gallery. Initially a specialist in early twentieth century British art, including Camden Town and Bloomsbury Group artists, d'Offay transformed his gallery into London's pre-eminent venue for contemporary international art, introducing a new glamour to the London art world.[27]

By the end of the 1980s, everything was changing. In the midst of this new internationalism came a new wave of art school graduates, who unsurprisingly brought with them a new attitude. At the forefront were the students of Goldsmiths' College, who were presented, initially at least, as the antithesis of the School of London. Whilst the School of London was essentially male, there was now a gender balance. Whilst the School had been polemically championed for its continuation of "traditional" methods and media, young artists now took a pragmatic, rather than ideological approach to the use of any media to hand. Furthermore, whereas the School of London, despite its

immigrant composition, was presented at the heart of a British tradition, younger artists now allied themselves to international trends. And most crucially, whilst subjectivity, empiricism and hermeticisim had been defining characteristics, now younger artists were more detached, less referential and more ironic.

As the decade came to an end, the high seriousness of the School of London and the lofty claims made for British figurative painting were challenged by new priorities. Critical attention was about to shift again.

NOTES

1 "David Hockney in Conversation with R. B. Kitaj", *The New Review*, January/February 1977, vol. 3, no. 34–35, pp. 75–77.

2 Prior to 1975 each year the Arts Council invited two members of its Art Panel to buy work for the collection. However, from 1975 they asked a single artist to make a selection. Financial constraints necessitated a focus on drawing, but this also suited the didactic intentions of Patrick George and Kitaj. George's thoughtful catalogue essay considered the properties and functions of drawing, and his selection included works by, amongst others, Craigie Aitchison, Frank Auerbach, Jeffery Camp, Anthony Eyton, Lucian Freud, Patrick George, David Hockney, R. B. Kitaj, Leon Kossoff and Claude Rogers. *Drawings of People*, exh. cat. Arts Council, London 1975.

3 This debate was fuelled by deep anxiety about the future of art schools and, specifically, the threats to life-drawing classes posed by changes to the teaching curriculum. The editorials and letter pages of the journal *Art Monthly* give a particularly good insight into this.

4 See especially the essays collected in Peter Fuller, *Beyond the Crisis in Art*, London 1980, and his early editorials in the journal he founded, *Modern Painters*.

5 R. B. Kitaj, letter to the author, (undated, May 1989).

6 R. B. Kitaj, letter to the author, (undated, November 1987).

7 For example, Kitaj included early figurative work by Stephen Buckley, Anthony Caro, John Golding, Howard Hodgkin and William Scott.

8 Gowing believed that he coined the description School of London in the early summer of 1981 in an article for the *Sunday Times*. Here, he used it to cover "the heterogeneous group of figurative painters working in London", including William Coldstream, George, Euan Uglow and Peter Blake. Gowing also quoted an essay by Andrew Forge in *Eight Figurative Painters* (p. 8), in which he wrote that Gowing was "not only a spokesman but a substantial

contributor to what he has called the School of London. Gowing recalled that he was admonished by a number of these painters for including Peter Blake. Gowing saw this as an acknowledgement of "the Puritanism of the current devotion to the figurative principle". Lawrence Gowing, letter to the author, (undated, May 1989).

9 For a discussion of the institutional use of the term, see James Hyman, "A School of London in Little England", *Art Monthly*, October 1991, no. 150, pp. 21–23. For analysis of the origins of the idea, its use by Kitaj and its reappearance in the 1980s, see James Hyman, "The Wondering Jew [sic]: London and Diaspora", unpublished lecture for *British Art in Its Cultural Context 1956–1990*, Tate Gallery, London 8 June 1991.

10 Over 1988–89 I corresponded very extensively with many of the artists associated with the proposed School of London. With the exception of letters from Kitaj, elaborating on his conception of the School and from Gowing claiming authorship, responses to the term and its connotations were typically negative. Characteristic of these replies were those from Leon Kossoff, Howard Hodgkin and Carel Weight. Kossoff wrote that "of course I am encouraged by being grouped with people whose work I respect but I am also very uneasy since I've always tried to resist grouping and generalised categories of any sort, but the idea and its promotion, whom is included and so on, has never been discussed with me". Leon Kossoff, letter to the author, 17 December 1989. Hodgkin rejected the idea of a School of London in either the broad sense proposed by Kitaj or its subsequent narrower formulation: "with the exception of Auerbach and Kossoff, whose work is clearly, to some extent, inter-related, the others seem to have nothing in common, other than very disparate quantities of figuration […]. I wish I could feel that my work had something in common with other

artists that I admire, but even if it had this would hardly mean that togeth-er we constituted a School", Howard Hodgkin, letter to the author, 15 May 1989. Carel Weight asserted that "I do not believe that a School of London actually exists. Of course the great city is a stimulant and that is why so many artists live in it but I believe that there should be more reason for the creation of an art movement. There should be a close-knit idea like the Pre-Raphaelites, School of Bomberg, or Pop Art. The idea of a School of London seems to me to be too nebulous [...]. For the most part, however, I think that English artists are at their best as eccentric individuals from William Blake to Stanley Spencer and today P. Blake, Collins, Bellany, Rooney to mention just a few." Carel Weight, letter to the author, 23 May 1989.

11 *A School of London: Six Figurative Painters*, British Council, 1987–88. The exhi-bition travelled to Oslo, Humlebaek, Venice and Düsseldorf. Although con-ceived prior to the Royal Academy's *British Art of the Twentieth Century*, the fact that the exhibition came in its wake consolidated the impression that these artists were producing the most significant British art. As Peppiatt concluded in his catalogue essay: "from time to time, painters catch their period with such unusual insight and accuracy that their record goes down in history with the authority of fact [...]. It may well be that this is the face that our period will present to posterity", p. 13 ; see also Michael Pep piatt, "Six New Masters: Why stodgy London is now the art capital of the world", *Connoisseur*, September 1987, pp. 79–85; and the coverage of British art in *Art International*, which is discussed below.

12 *From London* (1995) included (in order of birth) Bacon, Freud, Kossoff, Andrews, Auerbach and Kitaj. A British Council exhibition, it travelled to the Scottish National Gallery of Modern Art in Edinburgh and to museums in Luxembourg, Lausanne and Barcelona.

13 For a far more detailed analysis than is here possible, see my own study, *The Battle for Realism. Figurative Art in Britain during the Cold War 1945–60*, New Haven and London 2001.

14 Organised by Richard Morphet, *The Hard Won Image* (1984) was subtitled *Tra-ditional Method and Subject in British Art*. Morphet's exhibition had a historical bias and was emphatically about the British rather than international status of these artists. Richard Morphet subsequently defined the School of Lon-don artists as sharing some common preoccupations: "intense interest in human subject matter, in the representational act and in great art of the past, the determination of the artist to develop his own work, irrespective of the degree of its acceptance by the art community at large, at whatever time [and] most of the artists also attach high importance to drawing. These characteristics transcend stylistic affinities and dissimilarities between the artists. There are also many links of friendship and mutual respect between them". Richard Morphet, letter to the author, 5 June 1989.

15 *The Forgotten Fifties* drew attention to a wide range of neglected British realist artists of the 1950s, including the "Kitchen Sink" painters – John Bratby, Derrick Greaves, Edward Middleditch and Jack Smith.

16 A Tate Gallery exhibition organised for the Sainsbury Centre, East Anglia, *The Transformation of Appearance*, included just Andrews, Auerbach, Bacon, Freud and Kossoff, in the belief that the omission of Kitaj brought greater historical validity to this grouping.

17 Curiously, this same gallery also presented sculpture by Anthony Caro. Shortly afterwards he wrote that he had had nothing to do with the pres-entation of his work in the exhibition and observed that "I don't see the other artists who were shown there as constituting a school. Nor do I think there is such a thing at the moment as a School of London [...] of course, there are certain artists who naturally form a group, for example Cubists, Impressionists, Futurists etc. But when the thing is somebody's invention, it's something unnatural and then it's not right." Anthony Caro, letter to the author, 12 May 1989.

18 Kitaj would also overlay the nationalism of his School of London with an increased stress on its immigrant composition. His *First Diasporist Manifesto*, published in 1989, represented his most elaborate attempt at postulating a theory of a diasporist School of London. As he explained "one reading of both *The Human Clay* and my manifesto [...] can illuminate a concept (my particular concept?) of School of London [...]. Cosmopolitanism can be shown, beyond doubt, to have been an emphatic force in determining the particular art resonance of these three cities – Paris, N. Y. and now Lon-don. One only dares to use the inaccurate terms Schools of N. Y. and School of London in the same breath with School of Paris because, in all three cases, extraordinary artists (Paris being out of sight in this) set an unusually high standard of world class and in each of these milieu [sic] half the artists had been born elsewhere [...]. All these places – Paris, N. Y., London, Weimar were safe havens where the rootless might play for a while and even pretend a sense of place [...] Kafka, Benjamin and Joyce are great exemplars of this mode [...] as well as Pound, Eliot and a host of other expatriates (or Jews)". R. B. Kitaj, letter to the author, undated (May 1991). Similarly, in discussing the constituency of the School of London in its 1980s reincarnation, David Sylvester, himself a Jew, proposed that "Jews have probably been more prominent in 20th Century Art here [in Britain] than in any other country, even America." David Sylvester, letter to the author, 12 May 1989. The conception of a School of London as a school of immigrants was also the starting point for a British Council exhibition, *British Figurative Painting of the Twentieth Century*, which I curated in 1992 for the Israel Museum in Jerusalem. This gave the School prominence and was initially proposed by the museum as a showcase for Anglo-Jewish artists, and as an opportunity to exhibit work from Anglo-Jewish private collec-tions, as well as the usual public collections.

19 Indeed, as Robert Rosenblum observed at the time, from a New York per-spective Bacon was pre-eminent, followed by Howard Hodgkin. Malcolm Morley, who had moved to the United States, and Christopher Le Brun, who was showing there, both had higher profiles even than Lucian Freud, Frank Auerbach, Leon Kossoff, Michael Andrews and Kitaj. Robert Rosen-blum, letter to the author, 22 May 1989.

20 Norbert Lynton's introduction begins with critique of the *A New Spirit in Painting* exhibition: "if anything had changed direction, it was the

critics/organisers who staged the show". Norbert Lynton, "Reflections on the Painting Revolution of Our Time", in *The Proper Study*, London 1984. The exhibition travelled to Delhi and Bombay and included Craigie Aitchison, Michael Andrews, Frank Auerbach, Francis Bacon, Jeffery Camp, Patrick Caulfield, Graham Crowley, Lucian Freud, Anthony Green, David Hockney, Howard Hodgkin, Ken Kiff, Peter Kinley, R. B. Kitaj, Leon Kossoff, Helen Lessore and Euan Uglow.

21 *Art International*, autumn 1987. In addition to an essay by the editor, Michael Peppiatt, and contributions from Timothy Hyman, Avigdor Arikha and Thomas West, this issue also contains interviews with Bacon, Auerbach and Kitaj.

22 "British Art Now", *Art and Design*, November 1988. This included an essay on the School of London as well as an interview with Auerbach, texts by Kitaj and an essay on Lucian Freud. It also contained essays on younger British figurative painters.

23 *The Vigorous Imagination. New Scottish Art*, Edinburgh, Scottish National Gallery of Modern Art, 1987. The exhibition included Sam Ainsley, Philip Braham, Steven Campbell, Calum Colvin, Stephen Conroy, Ken Currie, Gwen Hardie, Peter Howson, Robert Hughes, David Mach, Keith McIntyre, Hugh O'Donnell, Ron Redfern, Mario Rossi, Joseph Urie, Kate Whiteford and Adri-

an Wiszniewski. The exhibition did much to stimulate the fertile Scottish art scene of the 1990s.

24 Alistair Hicks, *New British Art in the Saatchi Collection*, London 1989.

25 Alongside their elders, Hicks' School allowed a place for a middle generation that included Maurice Cockrill, John Bellany, Andrej Jackowski, Robert Mason, Terry Setch, Ken Kiff and Paula Rego, and a younger generation comprising Christopher Le Brun, Thérèse Oulton, Hughie O'Donoghue, Arturo Di Stefano, Adam Lowe, William MacIlraith and Celia Paul. See also *School of London Drawings*, exh. cat. Odette Gilbert Gallery, London 1989.

26 In *L'Ecole de Londres: de Bacon à Bevan* at the Fondation Dina Vierny/Musée Maillol in Paris (1998) (and tour) Peppiatt broadened the scope of the School. The exhibition was almost exclusively devoted to Marlborough Gallery artists, past and present. In addition to Bacon, Freud, Kossoff, Andrews, Auerbach and Kitaj, the School was extended to include other Marlborough Gallery artists, specifically, Robert Mason, Paula Rego, Bill Jacklin, Stephen Conroy and Celia Paul. The only exception to this was the addition of Tony Bevan.

27 Artists shown by Anthony d'Offay included Georg Baselitz, Francesco Clemente, Anselm Kiefer, Janis Kounellis, Leon Kossoff, Gilbert and George, Jasper Johns, Richard Long, Brice Marden, Bruce Nauman and Andy Warhol.

JAMES HYMAN

THE NEW BRITISH SCULPTURE OF THE 1980s

ANDREW CAUSEY

The artists involved in the "New British Sculpture" of the early 1980s were not a group. There was no common approach or single direction. There was, however, confidence again, after conceptual art, in sculpture as a three dimensional object. And there was one place, the Lisson Gallery, where most of the artists grouped here exhibited. Between 1979 and 1984 Edward Allington, Tony Cragg, Richard Deacon, Anish Kapoor, Julian Opie, Richard Wentworth and Bill Woodrow, had first shows at the Lisson and have continued to exhibit there.

This exhibition demonstrates the strength of twentieth century British sculpture from Jacob Epstein, Henry Moore and Barbara Hepworth onwards. At the start of the 1980s, it was in sculpture once again that the strength of British art lay. Britain's distinctive contribution across the century was marked in 1981 by the first major retrospective of twentieth-century British sculpture initiated by Nicholas Serota at the Whitechapel Art Gallery, of which he was then director. The section devoted to new artists included Cragg, Antony Gormley, Kapoor and Woodrow. The aim was not to connect these young artists with any particular tradition of British sculpture. It was to show that a context for sculptural excellence already existed in Britain.

The beginning of the "'New British Sculpture" is generally dated to 1981, the occasion of *Objects and Sculpture*, two parallel exhibitions held at the Institute of Contemporary Arts (ICA) in London and the Arnolfini Gallery, Bristol. Allington, Deacon, Gormley, Kapoor and Woodrow were all shown there. At that point Cragg (not included in *Objects and Sculpture* because he had been shown at Arnolfini the previous year) was the most widely known. He had had a first show at the Lisson in 1979, and one at the Whitechapel in 1981. Gormley, too, had had an exhibition at the Whitechapel in 1981, and Woodrow was to show there in 1982. Under Serota's directorship since the mid 1970s, the Whitechapel had become a focus for the display of new art and the context provided both by the Lisson and the Whitechapel was international. This was not just as a new kind of British art. The new sculpture was disseminated quickly. The older artists here (those born up to 1951), Allington, Cragg, Deacon, Gormley, Wentworth and Woodrow, had had long periods as students (in Gormley's case at university as well as at art school) and were more than ready to show their art as soon as a favourable climate followed the mainly rather academic atmosphere surrounding British art in the late 1970s.

The rapid success of the new sculpture owed something, also, to the high quality of the institutional network supporting innovative art. While the moment, after two worldwide oil crises in the 1970s, was not auspicious in terms of sales, there existed for the first time a network of publicly supported exhibiting galleries around Britain, without collections of their own and comparable with German Kunstvereins. They were directed mainly by curators who had been trained in

London either at the Arts Council, with its responsibility for disseminating British culture nationally, or the British Council, with the same responsibilities abroad. The results can be seen by looking at the non-commercial galleries where these artists were first seen: in London, the Whitechapel and the ICA, elsewhere the Arnolfini in Bristol, the Fruitmarket in Edinburgh, the Museum of Modern Art, Oxford, the John Hansard Gallery, Southampton. These institutions did not have large audiences or promote sales. But they had high standards of display, published catalogues, attracted critics, and engendered debate.

In 1983 the prestige of British sculpture had risen far enough for the Arts Council to put on *The Sculpture Show* at two London venues, the Serpentine and Hayward Galleries. Though covering a much wider field than the Lisson sculptors alone, this exhibition demonstrated that there was a sense now of a growing national confidence in British sculpture. This was reflected also in exhibitions abroad like *Transformations*, the British constribution to the 1983 São Paulo Bienal, which included most of the sculptors here. The increasingly focused policy directed from London towards the support of sculpture can be traced back to the support given to Henry Moore after 1945 and the "Geometry of Fear" sculptors at the 1952 Venice Biennale. But there was now a much stronger sculptural base on which to build. A new collective energy, extending to dealers, art administrators, curators and critics, was apparent.

The new sculpture differed from much recent work in being unconcerned with the kind of space it occupied, neither site specific nor involved with critique of institutional space. It was not a sculpture of closed volumes (Gormley is an exception). It was not involved with modern or technically forward-looking materials of the kinds some earlier sculptors had adopted to register modernity or optimism. In general, materials were mixed and adopted according to the needs of the moment rather than dogma or principle. Similarly, the making of sculpture was pragmatic, with a tendency towards assembling, placing elements alongside one another, or simple and unobtrusive kinds of joining – rather than the more elaborate welding and bolting of Anthony Caro (Deacon is an exception).

Much 1960s sculpture had signalled confidence in the future. The 1970s dealt blows to the post-war consensus in the fields of economics, politics, failed mili-

tary adventures, and challenges to traditional hegemonies. A loss of confidence in humanism was to be expected. The search for ideal solutions which had driven some earlier twentieth-century sculpture was no longer possible, and a characteristic of the new sculpture was its tolerant, stoical, and sometimes critical, humour. This humour took different forms, from the creative transformations of Woodrow (pl. 200), the visual punning of Opie (pl. 204) and Allington's superabundant but empty cornucopias, to the unruly behaviour of common objects in Wentworth's work (pl. 202). It is mainly a subversive wit that recognises the contingency of man in the world and at times falls into melancholy. But generalisations of this kind are dangerous. While scepticism and a sense of emptiness and loss were common, there remained in Deacon's work a strain of the idealism of early twentieth-century Constructivism (pl. 199).

(fig. 1) Antony Gormley As Above, So Below 1988, lead, fibreglass, plaster, air, 188 x 181 x 35 cm, Louisiana Museum of Modern Art, Humlebæk, Denmark

Kapoor's sculpture shows faith in spiritual goals (pl. 201). Gormley appears closest to the classical tradition in his belief that the integral human figure can be a subject for sculpture (fig. 1).

The choice of sculpture in this section of the exhibition focuses on work of the early 1980s, to highlight the concentration of newly discovered talent and the speed with which it found a discerning – if at first quite small – public. It needs to be emphasised that the subsequent professional development of these artists has taken them in new directions. Much of their work has been larger in size, in some cases has become more aware of site, especially when work has been shown out of doors, and there are artists here who have gone on to consider issues of public sculpture that are not necessarily implicit in the works in this exhibition.

If there is one thing that connects most of the sculptors in this group it is their interest in everyday objects, however encountered and whatever is made from them. Tony Cragg's floor- and wall-pieces, made from fragments of coloured plastic, were a taking-off point for the new sculpture. Assembled from bits and pieces of urban detritus, a work like *New Stones, Newton's Tones* of 1978 (pl. 197) speaks for the consumption and throwaway culture of the modern city. Plastics, which in 1960s' sculpture had signified new materials and processes, point here to the careless disposal of the cheaply produced. There is a relationship with 1970s sculpture, especially Richard Long, whose geometrically organised sculptures of wood and stone lay similarly flat on the ground (pl. 181). But Long and other British sculptors in the 1970s saw nature as originary and inspirational, while Cragg's "new stones", ironically titled, are not stones at all. They are highly coloured and man-made, and anchor Cragg firmly within an urban discourse.

1 This work was bought in 1972 and its acquisition caused a storm in the press, on the publication of the Tate Gallery's *1972–74 Biennial Report and Illustrated Catalogue of Acquisitions in 1975*. See Carl Andre, "The Bricks Abstract", *Art Monthly*, no. 1, October 1976, p. 17.

2 *Carl Andre, Sculpture 1959–78*, exh. cat. Whitechapel Art Gallery, London 1978.

For Cragg, as for other sculptors in the group, minimalism remains a significant force for its unequivocal emphasis on the singularity of the sculptural object. Carl Andre was much admired. One of Andre's austere geometrical assemblages of bricks, *Equivalent VIII* of 1966/69 (fig. 2), had caused a furore when purchased for the Tate[1] and the artist was given a retrospective at the Whitechapel some years later.[2] But while Andre's work is understood, because its parts are undifferentiated, as presence, Cragg's work is seen simultaneously as presence and representation. The fragments give it a pictorial character setting up a tension between parts and whole. This tension increased as Cragg moved from geometrical formats to the creation of contours round the works – drawing with fragments – in wall pieces like *Palette* of 1982 (pl. 198).

(fig. 2) Carl Andre EQUIVALENT VIII NEW YORK 1966, 1966–69, brick, each element 6.6 x 9.4 x 20 cm, overall 13.8 x 97 x 120.5 cm, Tate, London

Bill Woodrow also deals with the discards of an urban culture. His concern is with transformation, the process through which one things become another (pl. 200). The force of his work is in the relationship between two things that are generally physically connected and made from the same material, and raise questions about the extent to which they share identity and meaning. An undercurrent of violence is common. It is registered in *Crow and Carrion* of 1981 (fig. 3), which is made from two umbrellas, in the hand that holds the broken umbrella, represented as flat, like a stain on the road, and vulnerable to the pecking of the bird. Woodrow's work, like others here, is marked by the shock of sudden change, the de-familiarisation of

(fig. 3) Bill Woodrow CROW AND CARRION 1981, umbrellas, 36 x 133 x 70 cm, Arts Council Collection

the familiar which Sigmund Freud associated with the uncanny. Though Cragg and Woodrow, like other sculptors here, include everyday objects in their work, their handling is distinct from earlier usages in Pop and *Nouveau Réalisme*. Theirs is not a celebration of consumer culture, and it is anti-monumental. Unlike César in France or John Chamberlain in America, these artists are not elevating urban junk by putting it on a pedestal.

Edward Allington's contribution to *Objects and Sculpture* was austere. He showed "ideal standard forms" in white plaster, arranged on a minimalist-type grid. By contrast, the colourful, representational and abundant cornucopias which followed seem life-enhancing and at odds with the entropy and fragmentation of Cragg's and Woodrow's work. But this may not be so. Allington's work is about surfaces and the images of things and not necessarily the original objects themselves (fig. 4). Cornucopias, in any case, though they seem to reflect nature at its most lavish, are associated with the artifice of the baroque, and the tensions established are between nature and artifice, the plenitude of the natural and the emptiness of elaborate and enticing surfaces that have nothing behind them and are no more than empty shells. Allington's work here, and Opie's also, read as surfaces as much as they do as solid forms, and it is this, alongside their colours, that

(fig. 4) Edward Allington IDEAL STANDARD FORMS 1980, plaster, 47.5 x 300 x 228 cm, Tate, London

gives them not only a pictorial character but one that is theatrical as well. "Sculpture" is not a word that can be used, as in modernism, to define a practice wholly distinguishable from other art practices. Sculpture here is an impure art that overlaps freely and unapologetically with other arts.

Richard Wentworth is also concerned with common objects. His currency – a bucket, a broom or some lightbulbs – is not things that in themselves hold our attention. They are the casual, classless objects of Jasper Johns, things Marcel Duchamp might have used as readymades. But those objects were at rest while Wentworth's are generally precarious, in states of tension and transition. Buckets tip and threaten to spill their contents, ladders would collapse on us if climbed. There is an apparent simplicity to this work, the sculptures are not over large and there is absence of rhetoric. The seamlessness of a work like *Toy* of 1983 (pl. 202) adds to the enigma. There is not the same display of process as there is with Woodrow, which accounts for the cool finality of Wentworth's sculptures.

Julian Opie, born in 1958, is the youngest of the Lisson artists and had his first exhibition there in 1983, the year after he left art college. A major preoccupation for younger artists has been appropriation, repetition and the second-handness of imagery, which Opie has explored, using video as well as three dimensional art and examining the relationship between sculpture, manufactured objects and architectural models. In early works like *A Pile of Old Masters* of 1983, welded sheets of cut steel are the ground for painted images that include artworks, food, office equipment and luggage. There is a tension, as with Cragg, between the presence of the sculpture as a whole and the representational function of objects individually. It *is* a sculpture because it is one thing, made from one material. The individuality of canonical masters from Rembrandt to the present day is suppressed, as the canvases are regularised in terms of size (as if they were reproductions in a book), while, paradoxically, being presented in a painting style that emphasises brushwork and plays on ideas of handling and authenticity.

All the sculptors looked at so far have been concerned in one way or another with everyday objects. Anish Kapoor is different. Kapoor's solutions may have something in common with others in the group. Like Cragg, for example, he made highly coloured works on floor and walls. But the parallel ends there. Kapoor's coloured forms, symbolising domes and mountains, flowers, ladders and enclosures, constitute a landscape of symbolic shapes that realise in physical form a cosmology related to space, landscape and plant symbolism, and stresses the correspondence of outer and inner worlds, temporal reality and the imagination. The idea of conveying non-material values through strong colours recalls Yves Klein, and Kapoor's art, like Klein's, rejects the idea that working with the symbolic imagery of traditional cultures is not permissible in contemporary art. The juxtaposition of raw stone and blood red paint in *Wound* of 1988 (fig. 5) is appropriate to the identity of the work, even if the mixture of media in this way transgresses established sculptural practice. Kapoor's use of stone in *Wound* is, like that of Joseph Beuys or

(fig. 5) Anish Kapoor WOUND 1988, limestone and pigment, 308 x 432 x 331 cm, private collection Zürich

Richard Long, unmediated, relating directly to the originary status of stone as natural and part of the earth's crust.

Like Kapoor, Richard Deacon stands somewhat apart from other artists in this group. His starting point is not in everyday objects, he does not share Kapoor's search for a spiritual cosmology, and technically his work is distinct because of its relatively complex construction. His forms are abstract, but for Deacon abstraction means, rather than resisting readings that relate his work to things in the world, encouraging multiple readings by means of metaphor. While there are references to parts of the body – ears, mouths, vaginas – Deacon's sculpture is less about body parts as such than openings, where inside and outside join and communication is enabled. In that sense Deacon's sculpture is about the experience of being in a peopled world, without the need for recourse to solid, embodied forms. His sculptures have extraordinary presence, but not on account of volume or weight. They are rarely made up of closed forms and they are positioned in relation to the ground so as to deny gravity. Diverse metaphorical readings are possible, some can be read as emerging from the ground, like an opening flower, and in general the feeling of controlled energy is suggestive not so much of motion as of passage, the possibility of change from one state to another. The interlocked, curving shapes of many Deacon sculptures suggests a throwback to modernism and the sculptural compositions of Caro and his circle. But this would be to misunderstand the unity of the individual works, which is what gives them presence and connects them with minimalism. Deacon, together with Gormley, is the artist here who seems most at ease with the longer tradition of sculpture, but Deacon has rigorously examined how that tradition needs to be re-examined, with minimalism in mind.

Though Deacon is aware of the body as sentient and able to communicate, he is not concerned, like Gormley, with the human figure as such. Gormley is different in a number of ways from the other artists here and is not connected with the Lisson Gallery. In taking on the subject of the integral figure Gormley goes against the grain of sculpture, since the demise of the classical tradition through its misuse in the sculpture of the 1930s dictators. Starting with *Mould, Hole and Passage* in 1981, Gormley has made figure sculptures from

ANDREW CAUSEY

casts of his own body, first having himself covered in plaster and then having sheets of lead moulded from the plaster (fig. 1). These are non-heroic works, and though they are literally of himself, there is no element of personal expression or gesture in the finished sculpture. The sculptures are passive and object-like, and though the almost ritualistic process of being "buried" in plaster and then making a coffin-like enclosure of lead is important to him, it is not the sense of being momentarily buried alive which matters so much as the contrast between enclosure inside the mould and wider ambient spaces. Gormley is the only sculptor in this group whose work inherits the 1970s concern with site specificity.

An artist who bears comparison with Gormley is the considerably younger Rachel Whiteread. Whiteread also uses the casting process, though in her case the cast is the sculpture, while Gormley converts the cast back into the positive form of the body. Both start from an event or place involving themselves, and while the work of both has strong human resonances, in each case the work involves absence, in the sense that what remains is the shell or container that once surrounded the body. As Gormley's works recall traditional death effigies, so Whiteread's *Ghost* of 1990 (pl. 211) reminds one of a cenotaph. *Ghost* is the cast of a room she once lived in. Her sculptures, made from casts of such things as baths, mattresses and the underside of chairs, are the things closest to the body in everyday life and associated with it, metonymically (fig. 6). A difference between the two is the absence in Whiteread of a sense of the transcendent body and a concern instead with the social – the things ordinary people use – the places ordinary people live in.

(fig. 6) Rachel Whiteread TABLE AND CHAIR (GREEN) 1994, rubber and polystyrol, 68 x 83 x 122 cm, Luhring Augustine Gallery, New York

FREEZE AND ITS AFTERMATH

RICHARD SHONE

Earlier this year there was an exhibition in London (at the Barbican Art Gallery) that surveyed art in London in the 1950s. It was remarkable for the jostle of works by well-known artists and by comparatively obscure or forgotten ones. Of course, there is nothing new about this: decade shows, if thoroughly selected, with one eye on lasting achievement, the other on historical record, inevitably bring about surprising juxtapositions. They melt down our tidy sense of period and upset our categorising prejudices. Such shows are often outside our own personal experience of the chosen time-span. We have to pit our knowledge of history and of particular works against the aims and researches of the selector (in the case of the Barbican exhibition, for example, photography played a prominent role, whereas in the decade itself there was little or no public or gallery support for the medium, in spite of its influence on many artists in the show).

In the present exhibition, however, looking at the list of works chosen to represent British art in the immediate post-*Freeze* years, it is gratifying to find that they chime with my own memories of having found them exciting and exceptional when they were first exhibited in the early 1990s. To be sure, there were other artists at work who produced memorable shows and images, chief among them Fiona Rae, Ian Davenport, Angus Fairhust, Mat Collishaw and Abigail Lane. There are others still who, of the same generation, did not hit their stride until a little later, in particular

Sarah Lucas and Richard Patterson. But this section of the exhibition (as elsewhere) aims to distil, as succinctly as possible, through outstanding works, the complexion and complexities of the few years under review. It was a time of considerable change in aesthetic sensibility and in the way art was shown and marketed; it saw a great expansion of the London art world and a quickly attained international attention for the newly emerging generation of British artists.

The pre-eminent position at that time of Goldsmiths' College in London is by now well known and documented. With the exception of Rachel Whiteread, all the artists represented in this section studied at the College. Several factors determined this high profile (on a level with the centrality of the Slade School of Art before the First World War or the Royal College of Art in the 1960s): freedom of choice, the abolition of departmental categories (sculpture, painting, printmaking, etc.), a variety of artist-teachers holding a range of viewpoints (e.g. Jon Thompson, Michael Craig-Martin, Richard Wentworth), intellectual stimulation and an emphasis on the preparation for being a professional artist, out in the world. This last aspect soon manifested itself in the famous *Freeze* exhibition, organised by Damien Hirst and others in 1988, which took advantage of the prevailing climate of slick entrepreneurship that was current in British business life. For *Freeze* and similar, subsequent group shows, corporate sponsors were pursued, proper catalogues were produced and critics and collectors were buttonholed. A slightly older generation of Goldsmiths' graduates, including Julian Opie, Lisa Milroy, Simon Linke and Mark Wallinger, had already begun to exhibit in prominent commercial galleries and group exhibitions abroad. This bred an air of confidence and expectation in their juniors.

The attention generated by *Freeze* and its follow-on shows such as *Modern Medicine* and *Gambler* (both 1990) worked – and with rapid results. Three *Freeze* exhibitors – Michael Landy, Ian Davenport and Gary

(fig. 1) Michael Landy installation view of MARKET, exhibition at Building One, 1990

Hume – showed together in a new central London gallery, Karsten Schubert Ltd., at the end of 1989. Charles Saatchi acquired from *Gambler* Damien Hirst's *A Thousand Years* (pl. 214), a great early purchase by the leading collector of new British art, and the first of Hirst's remarkable sequence of works from the early 1990s: its mixed media became notorious – "steel, glass, flies, maggots, MDF, insect-o-cutor, cow's head, sugar, water". Also in 1990 Landy displayed *Market* (fig. 1), the first of a series of spectacular works which came to a head a decade later with *Break Down*, (2001), in which the artist systematically inventoried and destroyed all his possessions. In the same year Davenport had a prestigious, sell-out show of paintings at Leslie Waddington's gallery, and in the following year Karsten Schubert gave solo exhibitions to Rachel Whiteread (who had studied at the Slade School of Art) and Anya Gallaccio, also a *Freeze* exhibitor (fig. 2).

(fig. 2) Anya Gallaccio PRESERVE (BEAUTY) 1991, three panes of 6 mm glass, 800 gerberas, 195.8 x 354 x 3.8 cm, Karsten Schubert Gallery, London

What were the connections between these artists, beyond their age and, for the most part, their student years at Goldsmiths'? With a perspective on British art immediately preceding them, I think we can say that none was motivated by didactic, socio-political issues; all took for granted the lessons of conceptual and minimal art; none was (at the time) a legibly figurative artist; and many introduced autobiographical and personal elements into their work. Materials used were invariably demotic, drawn from their immediate environment – household paints, bread-crates, fruit and flowers, discarded furniture and mattresses (in this respect, they were materially in tune with artists such as Richard Wentworth and Bill Woodrow). Most difficult of all to characterise is perhaps a shared

directness and confidence in their imagery, whether dealing in grand, universal themes or in more particular observations from contemporary life. Much has been made of a sometimes sharp humour informing their work, a confrontational stance that admits of the comic as well as the bleak. Humour was certainly to the fore in the zippy, appropriating paintings of Fiona Rae and the subversive double entendres of Sarah Lucas's early sculptures such as *Two Fried Eggs and a Kebab* of 1992 (fig. 3). But as time has passed, it is perhaps a pervasive melancholy that has risen more strongly to the surface. It is a melancholy of urban disaffection and of social despoilment: the work must be seen within the broader context of a long-serving conservative government, increasing inequality of wealth, the juxtaposition of gleaming new office blocks and substandard housing, power-dressed yuppies on night-time city pavements where the homeless begged in every doorway. As the immediacy of this context recedes (though the bitter fruits of such alienation remain), the outstanding works of the period maintain an aesthetic momentum beyond the local.

(fig. 3) Sarah Lucas TWO FRIED EGGS AND A KEBAB 1992, photograph, fried eggs, kebab, table, 76.2 x 152.4 x 89 cm, courtesy Saatchi Collection, London

Landy's video *Appropriation* (pl. 212), though related in theme, can barely hint at the power of *Market*: the curious exhilaration and full oppressive sadness of that installation had to be experienced at first hand. Gary Hume's door paintings, (pl. 210) with their high-gloss surfaces and institutional connotations, reflect the viewer in images that combine entrance with exit, immediate realism with apprehensive future. Photographs of Rachel Whiteread's *House* (fig. 4), no longer extant, convey something of the work's sculptural presence but not the intensity of time arrested or the resonant details of the looming concrete cast itself. Fortunately such works as *Room* and *Ghost* (pl. 211) exist to remind us of the elegance of her abstract sculptural procedures and their haunting disclosures. A year before *House* drew national and international attention to Whiteread and generally raised the public perception of the new art, Anya Gallaccio made one of her finest installations for the Institute of Contempo-

(fig. 4) Rachel Whiteread HOUSE 1993–94, concrete and plaster, height 10 m, destroyed

rary Arts in London, *red on green* of 1992 (pl. 213). Its formal arrangement was simple – ten thousand red roses densely massed in a large flat rectangle on the gallery floor – but its metaphorical charge, as the roses withered and died to become brittle ghosts of their former selves, was deeply unsettling.

The work of Damien Hirst epitomises the general change in sensibility of this time, at its most extreme. Again, simple powerful presentation, derived from aspects of minimalist art, was the framework for subject matter of a highly charged and, for some, shocking

(fig. 5) Damien Hirst WITH DEAD HEAD 1991, black-and-white photograph on aluminium, 55.2 x 75.3 cm, courtesy Jay Jopling

(fig. 6) Damien Hirst THE PHYSICAL IMPOSSIBILITY OF DEATH IN THE MIND OF SOMEONE LIVING 1991, tiger shark, glass, steel, formaldehyde solution, 213 x 518 x 213 cm, Saatchi Gallery, London

content. He tackled head-on the eternal themes of life, death and regeneration, freedom and liberty, beauty and ugliness, with a youthful romanticism checked by a sharp sense of everyday design and objects (fig. 5). These included basic office furniture, showcases, ashtrays, billboard colour, the accoutrements of operating theatres and pharmacist shops. *A Thousand Years* (1990) is the earliest of a series of works that branded themselves on those who saw them, from the great tiger shark in a tank (fig. 6) to the divided cows in twelve glass cases to the lamb in formaldehyde of *Away From the Flock*. Where several of Hirst's contemporaries remained resolutely urban in their imagery, continuing a trend from Pop Art of the 1960s to the "new sculptors" of the 1980s, Hirst was engaged with the animal world and its natural cycles, as seen in *A Thousand Years* and in his astonishing *In and Out of Love*, of the following year. This multi-media installation was the *mise-en-scène* for the hatching from pupae of innumerable exotic Malaysian butterflies and their terminal flutter among potted plants.

Hirst remains the best known among this group of artists, massively profiled in the press, his work grabbing the headlines in which initial derision and notoriety have given way in recent years to an amused tolerance. He is probably the only current artist to have his name and works mentioned in T. V. soap operas and on quiz shows. While the actual works were perhaps too personal to have a direct impact on his fellow practitioners, they had a generally liberating influence, a generosity of permission, that made the 1990s the de-

cade of the young British artist, in Britain and abroad. Public acceptance or, at least, public awareness of this generation has been fuelled by intense media interest and the punctuation marks provided by certain "scandalous" works – from Hirst's shark and Marcus Harvey's *Myra* (a "portrait" of an infamous child murderer shown at *Sensation* at the Royal Academy in London, and elsewhere, in 1997–98), to the phallus-nosed mannequins of Jake and Dinos Chapman (fig. 7) and Tracey Emin's installation of her unmade bed, in all its squalid reality, shown as part of the exhibition of work by artists shortlisted for the Turner Prize in 1999. This annual event at the Tate Gallery (as it was then called) provided a feeding frenzy for the press and outraged media comment. Whereas the

(fig. 7) Jake and Dinos Chapman HAPPY KISSMYARSE 1996, view of installation of *Full House*, Kunstmuseum Wolfsburg (detail)

prize in the 1980s had been awarded to older, more established British artists (Malcolm Morley, Richard Deacon, Howard Hodgkin) with few murmurs of dissent, the 1990s saw younger, much more controversial recipients such as Whiteread and Hirst (in 1993 and 1995, respectively). At the same time, it became obvious that these and other artists complicitly communicated to their own generation, even if at quite superficial levels, a sense of urgency and fitness for the times in a way that had not been experienced, perhaps, since David Hockney, Peter Blake, Allen Jones and others had expressed the youth culture and social changes of the 1960s.

International attention was captured, and with it came a critical assessment of the *Freeze* artists and their contemporaries not always in tune with their home-grown fame. Commercial galleries in Europe and the United States eagerly took on the "Brits", a rush that culminated in more official survey shows such as *General Release* at the Venice Biennale in 1995 and *Brilliant! New Art From London* (at Minneapolis and Houston in 1995–96). What had sometimes appeared novel and *outré* in Britain was seen as timid and amateurish, when installed elsewhere. The emphasis on the artists' Britishness was not always helpful. The catalogue cover of *Brilliant!*, for example, showed a photograph of the devastating results of an IRA bomb in the heart of London's financial district but the media presentation of the show relied on nostalgic stereotypes. Neither image was appropriate to the content of the exhibition. The raw political reportage of the photograph has little affinity with the works produced and nostalgia for an earlier Britain of friendly policemen, corner-shops and a dull settled society living on fish-and-chips is a long-buried cliché.

It is almost inevitable that this loosely connected group of artists will continue to be herded together in subsequent accounts of British art. They conveniently fit the desire for a neat characterisation of the *fin-de-siècle*, with its historic roots entwined around the beacon of a new century. Indeed, this exhibition is the first to survey the modern movement in Britain during the whole of the twentieth century, and in spite of tremendous stylistic differences and concerns, the *Freeze* generation of artists brings the history to a startling finale. The movement that began in 1910–12 with an influx of foreign art that galvanised receptive young artists in Britain, ended with a burst of confidence that successfully grafted post-modern practice onto the long British tradition of poetic realism.

BRITISH ART SCHOOLS

AND THE INFLUENCE OF ART EDUCATION IN THE TWENTIETH CENTURY

NICK DE VILLE

"The exhibition is in part an examination and acknowledgment of the success of art schools, their presence and effects on recent art and its milieu. [...] There is a very long tradition of decrying the failure of art schools, because they are behind the times or too swayed by them, because their graduates are ill prepared and useless. [...] In contrast, what is decried in recent writing is not the art school's failure but its success, the numbers of artists and careers it can now produce."[1]

1 Howard Singerman, in *Public Offerings*, ed. Howard Singerman, exh. cat., Museum of Contemporary Art, Los Angeles, New York 2001, p. 284.

"It is the exclusive institutional concentration in recent years upon the narrowest sector of activity – video; performance; conceptual installation, none of it necessarily unworthy in itself – that, with all the talk in justification of 'innovation' and 'cutting edge', has created the new academicism. Again it is no accident that all such work – which celebrates the primacy of idea over practice and the appropriation of the material world into the work of art – should derive from the remarkable rehabilitation of the works and principles of Marcel Duchamp. This was begun by Richard Hamilton in the 1960s (neither he nor Duchamp could draw very well), and their subsequent universal diffusion through that remarkable apostle, Joseph Beuys..."[2]

2 William Packer, *Financial Times*, 18/19 December 1999.

Art schools are blamed for changes in art for which they are not responsible. On the whole, art schools reflect cultural changes they have done little, consciously, to set in train. If anything they are, as cultural institutions, representations of what was. What they display most eloquently is the persistence of ideas about the art (and craft) of being an artist, often far beyond the relevance of those ideas to anyone but a few nostalgics. In the twentieth century, the Beaux-Arts tradition of drawing, painting and modelling, founded on the discipline of direct observation, was given a very British character by the devotion of the Euston Road School of art educators – William Coldstream, Lawrence Gowing, Claude Rogers, Patrick George, Euan Uglow – to Paul Cézanne's project. For a time it could be argued credibly that their scrupulous "measure and mark" observational painting was a modernisation of the Beaux-Arts tradition, not least because its visual parsing of the subject provided a natural science-like underpinning to the curriculum. The values of the Euston Road School were a continuing influence on the curriculum at The Slade, The Royal College of Art (fig. 1), Camberwell School of Art and their numerous provincial satellites well into the latter half of the century.

(fig. 1) Rodrigo Moynihan THE TEACHING STAFF OF THE PAINTING SCHOOL Royal College of Art 1949–50, oil on canvas, 213.4 x 334.6 cm, Tate, London

Set against the persistence of this tradition were uncertain forces for change. Some were never likely to fit easily into institutional frameworks of timetable, curriculum and class teaching. However, I hope here to describe some telling episodes in the slow move away from the Beaux-Arts curriculum. As I have already indicated, this was largely a story of reaction and assimilation in response to changes that were, for the most part, already afoot in the wider world.

In Britain at the opening of the century, the Beaux-Arts education was very much alive, even if overlaid with a veneer of Victorian artistic fashion, most notably of the Pre-Raphaelite school and its second coming, the Arts and Crafts movement. The progressive response to this established curriculum was the on-going importation of new artistic ideas, pre-eminently from France. The artists' group most closely allied with this importation was the New English Art Club, which was itself closely linked to The Slade School of Fine Art, then the most progressive of London's art schools. In time, a group of younger members, led by Walter Sickert, Spencer Gore and Lucien Pissarro, came to align itself with the emerging generation of Post-Impressionists. It began to meet at 19 Fitzroy Street, not far from the Slade. These meetings eventually became formalised as the Camden Town Group, which counted amongst its number Henry Lamb, Harold Gilman, Augustus John and Percy Wyndham Lewis.

Organisations such as these were a distinctive feature of British art of the early decades of the century. They were also characteristic of the somewhat patrician Bohemia located at that time in upper Bloomsbury. As a rule, such groups were formed by younger artists intent on distinguishing themselves from previous generations, often through their attachment to new influences from abroad, and with a strong affiliation to a particular art school. They reflected both the beleaguered state of progressive art in Britain, and the recognition that organisations for its promotion had to be set up on a self-help basis, outside existing institutions. Art schools only begrudgingly acknowledged the implications of such groups, and their curricula reflected the conservatism of most British art. In the aftermath of the First World War, some advocated a return to Primitivism. Naturally, they were disinclined to find much benefit in study or intellectual reflection. Despite such persistent undercurrents of insularity, there were those amongst the rising generation with a more expansive outlook, such as Henry Moore and Barbara Hepworth, both of whom benefited from the newly-established scholarships offered by the Royal College of Art. The College was enlightened enough to offer Moore a teaching post on the completion of his studies, although the nature of the milieu in which he began to teach can be judged from the accusations of immorality and extreme leftist leanings – attributes considered undesirable in a teacher at the College – which were provoked by exhibitions of his work. In 1932, before these murmurings could come to a head, he moved to Chelsea School of Art to help set up their new Sculpture Department.

If progressive art movements offered mere pin pricks to the Beaux-Arts model of art education, there were, in the latter half of the inter-war period, intimations of a more fundamental opposition. In 1933 Walter Gropius, director of the Bauhaus from 1919 to 1928, addressed a meeting of the Design & Industry Association on the subject of art education. In his paper, Gropius described the relationship the Bauhaus had sought to forge between the artist and the larger world:

"Our object was [...] to liberate the creative artist from his other-worldliness and reintegrate him into the workaday world of realities; and at the same time to broaden and humanise the rigid, almost exclusively material mind of the business man. Our governing conception of the basic unity of all design in its relation to life, which informed all our work, was therefore in diametrical opposition to that of 'art for art's sake', and the even more dangerous philosophy it sprang from: business as an end in itself."[3]

3 Walter Gropius. The address was published in *The Journal of the Royal Institute of British Architects*, May 1934.

Unlike previous forces for change which had challenged the Beaux-Arts model, the Bauhaus was more than a new art movement, it was a new – technocratic – institutional model, and it undertook to change the relationship between the artist and "the workaday world of realities". The implications for art education were fundamental, although it would not be until the 1950s that Bauhaus-inspired experiments would appear in Britain.

The pioneers of the 1950s included Olive Sutton at Manchester School of Art and William Johnstone at the Central School of Art. The Central's educational experiments were built on its tradition of radicality. During the 1930s, members of the British section of Artists' International Association, many of whom were designers and illustrators, had been involved in the school and used its facilities to produce pamphlets, handbills and posters. Now Johnstone brought in artists such as Eduardo Paolozzi, Victor Pasmore, Richard Hamilton, William Turnbull and Alan Davie to impart new ideas in the teaching of the school's design courses. In the north the Yorkshire Education Authority organised a number of summer schools, which were influential in recasting the curriculum at Leeds College of Art and King's College of the University of Durham (soon to become the University of Newcastle-upon-Tyne).

The Institute of Contemporary Arts was later to celebrate these developments in an exhibition entitled *A Continuing Process. The New Creativity in British Art Education 1955–65*.[4] The exhibition identified Pasmore, Hamilton, Harry Thubron and Tom Hudson as key figures in the new art education. In the 1960s their ideas were to be disseminated widely through their influence with the membership of the three government committees charged with drawing up reports on the development of the art education system.[5]

Both Pasmore and Hamilton taught in the Fine Art Department at the University of Newcastle-upon-Tyne, although their influence was confined to the first, foundation, year course. Hamilton taught with Pasmore, taking over leadership of the course after Pasmore's departure. Hamilton's views on art education reflected his involvement with The Independent Group, and a visit in 1958 to the Hochschule für Gestaltung at Ulm, a new German art school where Bauhaus pedagogic principles were being extensively reconsidered and reformulated. The rationality of Hamilton's approach can be judged from his own words: "The tasks I set my first year students are designed to allow only a reasoned result. Rarely is a problem presented in terms which permit free expression or even an aesthetic decision. The student is prompted to think of his work as diagrams of thought processes – equipment which will enable him to derive further conclusions. Artistic personality or manipulative charm is coincidental to the result."[6]

Under Hamilton, the curriculum was predominantly a series of projects designed to foreground the experiential uncovering of the principles of visual language and perception. The projects were concerned to foster an inquiry attitude both to ideas and phenomena; they gave much value to a scientific and technological outlook and were concerned to explore visual language in a way which was, effectively, an empirical experience of what, elsewhere, was being theorised as the principles of semiotic analysis. Equally important, the traditional master/apprentice tutorial system of teaching was superseded by team teaching. The seminar discussion was designed to foster the notion of the "informed audience" which displaced the sovereign authority of the "master".

Hamilton also brought to his teaching a veneration for Duchamp. In 1934 Duchamp had published a collection of 94 items including facsimile notes, drawings and photographs for the *Large Glass* (fig. 2) under the title *Boîte verte (Green Box)*. Hamilton had first come across the *Green Box* when he was a student at the Slade (1948–49). American art historian George Heard Hamilton subsequently made an English translation of the notes and Richard Hamilton began a correspondence with Duchamp which resulted in a typographical version, published in 1960. Their friendship led to Hamilton being asked to organise the Duchamp retrospective at the Tate in 1966. As the centre-piece of the exhibition, the *Large Glass*, was too fragile to be moved from Philadelphia, Hamilton set about fabricating a replica in his studio in Newcastle (fig. 3). Hamilton's commentary on his recon-struction included remarks on Duchamp's approach to art-making which are remarkably consonant with his approach to teaching: "Duchamp's attitude to painting after 1912 moves progressively to a point where the act of creation can be no more than the nomination of a mass-produced object to the status of art. This seemingly perverse proposition is the logical extension of a point of view which caused Duchamp to divorce the sensual and manipulative aspects of painting from his purely conceptual interests of that time. The techniques of the *Glass* – the craftsmanship and even the planning method – are devised to isolate the artist from any emotional relationship with his medium.

(fig. 2) Marcel Duchamp La Mariée mise à nu par ses célibataires, même (Le Grand Verre) Stockholm 1991–92, replica of the original (New York 1915) made by Ulf Linde, 208 x 189 cm, Moderna Museet, Stockholm

(fig. 3) Richard Hamilton reconstructing the *Large Glass* of Marcel Duchamp, London 1965

4 The exhibition was organised by David Thistlewood and Sandy Nairne in 1981.

5 The reports were produced by the Coldstream (1960 and 1970) and Summerson (1964) Committees.

6 Richard Hamilton, *Collected Words 1953–1982*, London 1985, p. 169.

Drawing is mainly draughtsmanship of a geometric kind. Paint is applied in flat areas contained by boundaries of lead wire. There are no passages where the Duchamp hand cannot be followed quite faithfully without the least consciousness of forgery."[7]

7 Richard Hamilton, *The Bride Stripped Bare By Her Bachelors Even Again*, exh. cat. The Hatton Gallery, Newcastle-upon-Tyne 1966.

Apart from the new foundation courses such as that pioneered by Pasmore and Hamilton at Newcastle, art school teaching in the early 1960s was still largely cast in its pre-war mould. Its conservatism has been spectacularly mythologised through the dissidence of students (David Hockney's spat with the Royal College of Art) and academic staff (the dismissals of John Latham from St. Martin's School of Art, for his chewing of Clement Greenberg's *Art and Culture* and Art & Language members from Coventry Polytechnic, for setting up an art theory course). In 1968 widespread student dissatisfaction led to a wave of organised unrest in universities and polytechnics. These events, in which art students attracted a disproportionate amount of attention in the media, echoed the more widespread and revolutionary student unrest experienced in France. The Government set up a Select Committee to report on the causes of the unrest. Four art colleges were investigated by the Committee: three – Hornsey, Guildford and Brighton – where there had been serious breakdowns in staff/student relations leading to sit-ins, strikes and demonstrations; and one – Manchester – which had remained free of unrest. The Select Committee concluded that at Hornsey – site of the most celebrated student actions – there was dissatisfaction with both the national education system and with the administrators of the college. For their part, the senior administrators saw the actions of both teaching staff and students as "an attempt to remove the authority of the senior staff and impose a state of anarchy".

This turmoil illustrates the way in which the 1960s was a tale of two parts, in which institutional resistance to change was still strong. However, the student protests of 1968 and the rapid recruitment of younger artists into an expanding higher education system meant that ideas adapted from the Bauhaus model continued to gain currency. A key initiative was the "A" course of the sculpture department at St. Martin's School of Art, which was set up as an alternative to the St. Martin's tradition which had formed around the Advanced Sculpture course, launched by Frank Martin

in the late 1950s and much celebrated for Anthony Caro's teaching and the success of the "New Generation" sculptors of the mid 1960s (fig. 4).

(fig. 4) Graduation picture of the members of the Many Deed Group, who worked together at St. Martin's School of Art, London

The staff on the "A" course included Peter Kardia, William Tucker, Garth Evans and Gareth Jones. The course sought to widen the prevailing discourse of sculpture, by opening up the debate about the nature of contemporary art to influences as diverse as linguistics, phenomenology, cybernetics, psychology and cultural theory. Although its approach to these fields was less than systematic, engagement with them expanded the horizons of art's possible subject matter. The course was a canny response to the student ferment gripping the country (and notably reflected in the work of St. Martin's students Gilbert and George and Bruce McLean). Richard Deacon is but one student who saw the "A" course as a crucible (fig. 5) within which he

(fig. 5) Richard Deacon and Gilbert and George, St. Martin's School of Art, London 1972

could test the feeling that – as Richard Long put it – "the language and ambition of art were due for renewal".

The pedagogic ideas tested out on the St. Martin's "A" course were most comprehensively applied to undergraduate Fine Art education by Jon Thompson, who arrived at Goldsmiths' College in 1970 with a remit to reorganise the course. This encouraged media to be reconsidered with the broadest frames of reference, students were organised in open group structures, seminars became the principle fori, additional forms of intellectual inquiry were added to art history courses. There was an insistence on the cultural situatedness of the individual practitioner, in place of the valorisation of the autonomous and self-willed artist. Course structure and teaching methods were adaptable and changed often. These ideas reflected Thompson's keen appreciation of the implications of a key passage in the second Coldstream Report of 1970: "we do not believe that studies in fine art can be adequately defined in terms of chief studies related to media. We believe that studies in fine art derive from an attitude which may be expressed in many ways".[8]

8 "The Structure of Art and Design Education in the Further Education Sector", paragraph 26. *The Joint Report of the National Advisory Council on Art Education and the National Council for Diplomas in Art and Design*, London 1970.

Thompson has offered his own ruminations on the consequences of the academic model he brought into being at Goldsmiths' in the catalogue of the exhibition *Public Offerings*, whose British participants were mainly ex-Goldsmiths' students:[9] "Most critical commentators on the Goldsmiths' artists describe the work as a collision between Duchamp and Minimalism. Naive though this description is, it is not entirely erroneous. Two of the earliest shows (of conceptual art) at the Saatchi Gallery [...] were of great importance to successive years of Goldsmiths' students graduating between 1986 and 1990 [fig. 6]. Indeed, they exemplify two of the main concerns shaping attitudes at Goldsmiths' at that time: the desire to be formally lucid and materially direct, and the intention to deal with the emerging complexities of contemporary life in an open-handed way. [...] Beneath the smart outward show and assumed rhetorical ease, this so-called Goldsmiths' style, which by now has come to represent a much broader strand of British contemporary art, is focused in reality on the question of 'values'. This is its Duchampian aspect. Sceptical towards both the market and the institutions of cultural attribution, at its toughest – and here it is appropriate to cite the work of artists like Tracey Emin, Sarah Lucas, Bob and Roberta Smith, Mark Wallinger and Gillian Wearing – it is steeped in the spiritual ennui that attends all radical forms of doubt."[10]

The final note of equivocation that Thompson strikes in his reflection suggests some scepticism about both the institutional development of the Bauhaus-inspired model in British art education, and the academisation of the relationship between minimalism and Duchamp. Inevitably his remarks take us back to Hamilton and what William Packer terms his "rehabilitation of the works and principles of Marcel Duchamp". Around the time of his reconstruction of the *Large Glass*, Hamilton was also involved in two other considerable "rehabilitations". One was his catalogue for Francis Picabia's first British retrospective, the other the restoration of Kurt Schwitters' *Merzbau*, which was rescued from its barn in the Lake District. In these projects, Hamilton was foregrounding a very different immediate past to the one proposed by the then academic fashion for Pablo Picasso, Henri Matisse and Pierre Bonnard.

9 Of the artists in *Public Offerings*, Thomas Demand, Damien Hirst, Gary Hume, Sarah Lucas, Steve McQueen, Jane and Louise Wilson studied at Goldsmiths' College on either the undergraduate or postgraduate programme.

(fig. 6) The artists at the opening of *Freeze* in August 1988: Ian Davenport, Damien Hirst, Angela Bulloch, Fiona Rae, Stephen Park, Anya Gallaccio, Sarah Lucas, Gary Hume

10 Jon Thompson, in Singerman (see note 1), p. 219–208.

Duchamp, Schwitters and Picabia evoke Dada and Surrealism – the foregrounding of the dream state, the unconscious, the mechanics of poetics. The *Large Glass'* long title, *La Mariée mise à nu par ses célibataires, même (Grand Verre)* (*The Bride Stripped Bare By Her Bachelors, Even [Large Glass]*), indicated the mechanistic/mystic sexual cycles which determine its structure – proposing what Rosalind Krauss subsequently called "The Optical Unconscious". It is not surprising that such unruly ideas thrived better outside the academic framework. If there was to be a sea-change in British art schools, a more appropriate model was the cool rationality offered by American Minimalism. The collision of Minimalism and Duchamp was precisely that: a collision. In this light we can see Hamilton's "rehabilitations" of the mid 1960s to be overshadowed by one of the great dialectical confrontations of late twentieth century art. In *The Optical Unconscious*, Krauss adopts an image for this confrontation from the writings of Theodor Adorno. She portrays him musing about Surrealism, and as he does so, an image begins to take form. "Its ground is a series of white geometric planes, the stark streamlined architecture of Bauhaus rationalism. [...] And gleaming and new, this architecture will admit of no crime, no deviation. It will be a machine stripped down for work, a machine to live in. But there, suddenly, on the stretch of one of its concrete flanks, a protuberance begins to sprout. Something bulges outward, pushing against the house's skin. Out it pops in all its nineteenth century ugliness and absurdity, a bay window with its scrollwork cornices, its latticed windows. It is the house's tumour, Adorno thinks. It is the underbelly of the pre-war technorationalism, the unconscious of the modernist *Sachlichkeit*. It is surrealism, connecting us, through the irrational, with the other side of progress, with its flotsam, its discards, its rejects. Progress as obsolescence."[11]

11 Rosalind E. Krauss, *The Optical Unconscious*, Cambridge, Mass., 1993, pp. 33–34.

Through Hamilton's activities in the mid 1960s, we can trace an artist/teacher with a teacher's predilection for the pedagogic principles of the Bauhaus (and its artistic consequences), but – for a moment – balanced by Modernism's "tumour": Schwitters, Picabia, Duchamp. In this he personifies the best ambitions of British art education over these last several decades, although, on the whole, that balance has proved elusive, and its value for the future is even more uncertain.

STRANGE PATRONAGE

PROMOTING TWENTIETH CENTURY BRITISH ART

MARGARET GARLAKE

Art, so the fiction runs, emerges from the studio as the unmediated product of individual creativity. It may then be purchased, exhibited and subjected to curatorial interpretation, which will determine how it is seen and understood; it may be promoted as the characteristic product of a group, a region, a city or a nation. Thus an aesthetic impulse merges into a process of constant mediation between individuals and institutions.

Certain questions run insistently through the diverse terrain of patronage: How was modernity defined and renewed through patrons? What conflicts did modernity engender? What is the relationship between politics and patronage and between institutional patronage, the avant-garde and commercial patrons? And in the complexity of these constructions, where, irreducibly, is the artist?

Since the end of the eighteenth century, London has been considered an art world centre, yet paradoxically modernity is problematic. David Solkin has argued that the primacy given to literature has handicapped the visual arts, as have the focus on commercialism at the expense of state support and the notion of the artist as an amateur. Consequently, "radically modern art" has been marginalised[1] and, when it emerges, art institutions evolve efficient systems to neutralise it. A similar point has been made about the mid 1930s: "whenever the discourse of British art has refused the equation of modernism with internationalism and of both with artistic merit, it has tended inexorably to pick out the aesthetically reassuring and the parochially modern – which is to say the second-rate".[2]

Here I am concerned with the ways in which various kinds of patronage moulded perceptions of British art in the twentieth century. Since the subject is immense, I have focused on exemplary moments that demarcate changes in the ways that art is produced and functions in society. Because these moments derive from individuals rather than committees, I have also emphasised the contributions of a small number of people to creative, interpretative and structural developments. In the first half of the century, shifts in patronage were initiated by wealthy individuals; even when they worked through institutions, they retained the model of private patronage.

In concentrating on state institutions rather than private patrons, I am acutely aware of having bypassed figures who were fundamental to the patronage system. They include such creative mavericks as John Quinn, the American lawyer, collector on a heroic scale and enthusiast for English art, who arranged the first

1 David Solkin, "The British and the modern", Brian Allen (ed.), *Towards a Modern Art World. Studies in British Art 1*, New Haven/London 1995, pp. 1–6.

2 Charles Harrison, "England's climate", Allen 1995 (see note 1), p. 220.

Vorticist exhibition in New York in 1917 and wished to acquire every important work by Henri Gaudier-Brzeska;[3] Eric Gregory, founder of the Gregory Fellowships at Leeds University; Colin Anderson, stalwart of the Contemporary Art Society and chair of the Orient Line who filled his ships with contemporary art, or E. J. Power, whose collection of mid-century French and American art was bought virtually off the easel and almost immediately exhibited both by the Arts Council and the Institute of Contemporary Arts (ICA) (fig. 1).

And a full account should acknowledge the collections of the Tate (despite its notorious conservatism until John Rothenstein retired in 1967), the Scottish National Gallery of Modern Art (especially for British Surrealism), Southampton City Art Gallery or Leicestershire Education Authority, for which Stewart Mason bought cutting-edge contemporary art after the Second World War with the *élan* of a private collector (fig. 2), to name a few at random. We should also note the metamorphosis of the Royal Academy from a club for artists of sometimes astonishing conservatism to the purveyor of popular scholarly exhibitions. Associated with it are the lesser-known academic exhibiting societies which sustain, for instance, portraiture and the unpublicised sculptors of public monuments. Finally, the Henry Moore Foundation has operated since 1977 as a private patron on a scale unprecedented in the twentieth century, to extend the informed reception of sculpture through research and exhibitions.

Fry – "the animator and advocator of the younger British painters"[4] – was a prime mover in establishing the Contemporary Art Society (CAS) in 1910. It was founded to encourage "young living British artists by purchasing their recent work"[5] and to buy recent art for presentation to museums. The CAS demonstrates the persistent dichotomy within art patronage between support for artists, and reception, oriented towards the viewer. Though the organisation suffered a

crisis in the early 1970s, it astutely developed a collaboration with the corporate sector,[6] providing high-quality, albeit "safe", contemporary art for offices.

Though the CAS has contributed a wide range of art to regional galleries, complaints of metropolitan bias run through the century: a survey in 1946 proclaimed: "The provinces are very badly served".[7] An exception was Leeds, a rich northern city where, in 1902, Alfred Orage had founded the Leeds Arts Club as a left-wing, pro-feminist intellectual locus for an emergent middle class. The young Herbert Read was to become one of its members (fig. 3).[8] Michael Sadler and Frank Rutter, Curator of the City Art Gallery (1912–17) injected a modernist strand into the Club and Leeds in general, assisted by Sadler's collection, which included works by Wassily Kandinsky. Many years later, the Gregory Fellowships were also considered powerful encouragements to decentralisation.[9]

Read's precursor in the formation of an institutional art world was Maynard Keynes, best known as a radical economist. Yet artists were his familiars; he habitually wrote at Charleston, home of Vanessa Bell and country locus of the Bloomsbury group. In 1925 he organised the London Artists' Association, a cooperative intended to ensure Bloomsbury artists a guaranteed annual income. The guarantors included Keynes himself and Samuel Courtauld, benefactor and collector of Impressionism. The Association – wound up in 1933[10] – demonstrated the need for a national support system for artists and established the networking and cross-membership between organisations that were to be the power base of the art world after 1945.

During the 1920s reception was given a high priority, as government and the business community became conscious of the need to support commercial initiatives with civilising cultural activities. Understanding that high culture conveyed prestige and influence, the Treasury gave a small grant in 1930 for "cultural propa-

3 Judith Zilczer, *"The Noble Buyer": John Quinn, Patron of the Avant-garde*, Washington D. C. 1978.

4 Clive Bell, *Old Friends*, London 1956, p. 83, quoted in Judy Collins, "Roger Fry's Social Vision of Art", Christopher Green (ed.), *Art Made Modern. Roger Fry's Vision of Art*, exh. cat. Courtauld Gallery, London 1999, p. 73.

5 Collins in Green (ed.) 1999 (see note 4), p. 73.

6 See Alan Bowness, "Introduction", Alan Bowness et al., *British Contemporary Art 1910–1990. Eighty Years of Collecting By the Contemporary Art Society*, London 1991, pp. 13 ff.

7 *The Visual Arts. A Report Sponsored By the Dartington Hall Trustees*, London et al. 1946, p. 23.

8 See Michael Paraskos, "Herbert Read and Leeds", Benedict Read and David Thistlewood (eds.), *Herbert Read. A British Vision of World Art*, exh. cat. Leeds City Art Galleries with the Henry Moore Foundation, London 1993, pp. 25–33.

9 Marian Williams, "A Measure of Leaven: The Early Gregory Fellowships at the University of Leeds", Margaret Garlake (ed.), *Artists and Patrons in Post-war Britain (Courtauld Research Papers, no. 2)*, Aldershot 2001, pp. 55–93.

10 Robert Skidelsky, *John Maynard Keynes. The Economist as Saviour, 1920–1937*, vol. II, London 1992, pp. 243, 527.

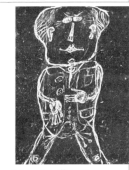

(fig. 1) Jean Dubuffet MONSIEUR PLUME PLIS AU PANTALON (PORTRAIT OF HENRI MICHAUX) 1947, oil on canvas, 130 x 97 cm, Tate, formerly E. J. Power Collection, London

(fig. 2) Lynn Chadwick THE WATCHERS 1960, bronze, height 235 cm, Loughborough University of Technology, Leicestershire

(fig. 3) Gisèle Freund HERBERT READ and PEGGY GUGGENHEIM London 1939, Solomon R. Guggenheim Foundation, courtesy Ziva Kraus and Ikona Gallery

ganda".[11] In 1936 the British Council was established, its aims described as "political and commercial",[12] though through suspicion or parsimony, it was at first funded by W. E. Rootes, a leading car manufacturer. However, it proved too valuable an asset to international relations to be left in private hands; thus it stood on the cusp between private and state patronage.

Like other organisations, the British Council was absorbed into the state machinery during the Second World War. The War Artists' Advisory Committee (WAAC), devised by Kenneth Clark (fig. 4), then Director of the National Gallery, was formed late in 1939 within the Ministry of Information. Though Clark was concerned simply to keep artists working,[13] the WAAC was expected to provide an optimistic record of conflict, just as during the Great War artists had been employed to produce "pictorial propaganda".[14] War art proved extremely popular, helping to establish an enduring taste for modern narrative painting.

Clark was also a member of the Committee for the Encouragement of Music and the Arts (CEMA), which in 1945 evolved into the Arts Council, with Keynes as its first Chairman-designate, though he died before he could take office.[15] State patronage came into existence as a direct result of the war and post-war politics; while the Arts Council was a by-product of the Attlee government's emphasis on planning, which established it as the cultural arm of the Welfare State, the British Council, its counterpart abroad, was answerable to the Foreign Office and charged with promoting British culture as a bulwark against communism. The sophistication with which it played out its Cold War role is evident from a comparison with the CIA's blundering attempts to conduct a parallel programme.[16]

Keynes announced the Arts Council in a broadcast in July 1945. The published transcript – perhaps presciently – announced: "Strange patronage of the arts has crept in", though Keynes surely said "state".[17] He was almost apologetic for his creation: "It

has happened in a very English, informal, unostentatious way – half-baked if you like". He apparently envisaged resistance, though the Council was welcomed for its promise to fulfil a real need: one commentator noted that while state patronage had previously been preoccupied with "preserving the art of the past", now it was "essential [...] that Government patronage of living art in all its forms should be continued and extended".[18] Yet it was attacked in the right-wing press as a potential purveyor of a standardised "state art"; the attacks were absurd but they contributed to a paralysing timidity among the Council's professional staff.

The bulk of the Arts Council's resources went to opera, acting out an agenda of power and class-based priorities, of metropolitan privilege and regional deprivation, of reception privileged over creators. The small, cash-starved Art Department was run by a former librarian, Philip James, a man of admirable populist intentions who was seldom able to put them into practice. Consequently, he was delighted when the Council became the principal source of revenue for the ICA in the early 1950s: "They arrange their own exhibitions, many of which relieve the Arts Council of a certain responsibility, especially in the field of avant-garde art."[19]

James' taste for contemporary art rarely emerged, though he determinedly sought out younger artists when he organised the exhibition-competition 60 Paintings for '51 for the Festival of Britain in 1951 (fig. 5). This popular event evoked an embarrassing display of anti-modernism, when Members of Parliament protested about the £500 purchase prize awarded to William Gear for his Autumn Landscape, a painting considered outrageously abstract (fig. 6).[20] Though the furore was beneficial both to Gear and the Council, which was seen to be able to cope with modernity, the exhibitions that it toured around the country drawn from its own collection remained relentlessly centrist until well into the 1950s, following an assumed normative taste rather than stimulating it. No negotiation with the public took place,

(fig. 4) Graham Sutherland KENNETH CLARK 1964, oil on canvas, 54.6 x 45.7 cm, National Portrait Gallery, London

(fig. 5) Cover for the catalogue of the exhibition-competition 60 Paintings for '51 for the Festival of Britain, London 1951

(fig. 6) William Gear AUTUMN LANDSCAPE 1950, oil on canvas, 183.2 x 127 cm, Laing Art Gallery, Tyne and Wear Museums, Newcastle-upon-Tyne

11 The phrase was used by Rex Leeper, quoted in Frances Donaldson, The British Council. The First Fifty Years, London 1984, pp. 19ff.

12 Memo, [1934], PRO/BW 82/6.

13 The War Artists, exh. cat. Imperial War Museum and Tate Gallery, London 1983, p. 157.

14 Ibid., p. 7.

15 For the CEMA-Arts Council transition, see Robert Skidelsky, John Maynard Keynes. Fighting for Britain, 1937–46, vol. III, London 2000, pp. 286–99.

16 See Frances Stonor Saunders, Who Paid the Piper? The CIA and the Cultural Cold War, London 1999.

17 Lord Keynes, "The Arts Council: Its Policy and Hopes", The Listener, vol. XXXIV, no. 861, 12 July 1945.

18 The Visual Arts (see note 7), p. 12.

19 "The ICA", Arts Council Paper no. 298, 19 February 1951, quoted in Margaret Garlake, New Art New World. British Art in Post-War Society, New Haven and London 1998, p. 21.

20 Ibid., pp. 170 ff.

and, in the docile society of the late 1940s, none was expected. Democratisation has not been a prominent feature of arts provision; it only flourished in the counter-cultural activities of the 1960s.

The Council's only aesthetic criterion was "quality", which was unable to compete with sport, betting and American films, though it fuelled an attitude in the London headquarters that was little short of imperialist. Contrary to government advice to make "the Arts more accessible [...] if necessary, with less ambitious standards",[21] the regions were tightly controlled from London until 1956, when the Council's hegemony was successfully challenged by the South-West Arts Association, which became the first Regional Arts Association (RAA). Inadequately funded – by local authorities, industry and other sources – the RAAs suffered from ill-defined roles which oscillated between a putative "folk" element and sophisticated theatre. Their replacement in the 1980s by Regional Arts Boards, under the rhetoric of devolution, again increased the Council's centralisation.

In the late 1960s, when Jennie Lee was appointed the first Minister for the Arts, it seemed that adequate state support for the arts had been accepted as a corollary of civilised government. The White Paper, A Policy for the Arts (1965), promised help for individual artists for the first time and "a fully comprehensive policy for the arts", acknowledging arts funding as a social service.[22] The heights of the mid 1960s, when an efflorescence of new art forms, from performative media to concrete poetry, shattered perceptions of the nature of art, were not to be repeated; after the demise of the Wilson government in 1970, arts patronage became steadily less politically compelling.

The Arts Council's most satisfactory role was its discreet support for smaller institutions, especially the Institute of Contemporary Arts (ICA), which was established in 1948, in perhaps the most creative act of patronage in British twentieth-century art, by Read and a group of friends who included Roland Penrose. All had roots in Surrealism and close links with France or North America, which were impressively demonstrated when Penrose persuaded his friend, Alfred Barr, Director of the Museum of Modern Art, New York to lend Pablo Picasso's Les Demoiselles d'Avignon to the Institute's exhibition 40,000 Years of Modern Art in December 1948.

21 "Nineteenth Report of the Select Committee on Estimates, Session 1948–9", The Arts Council, no. 315, paragraph 39, quoted in Robert Hutchison, The Politics of the Arts Council, London 1982, p. 119.

22 HMSO, A Policy for the Arts: the First Steps, Cmnd. no. 2601, 1965.

Until its move to Carlton House Terrace in 1968, the ICA was like a private club for artists and art enthusiasts – little known, but of inestimable value for those who frequented it. Its international attitude led it constantly to bring new art to London, in defiance of the inturned chauvinism that threatened to stifle English culture until the 1960s. Thus African and Oceanic art jostled works from the European "canon"; Jackson Pollock's huge One: Number 31, 1950 graced the tiny gallery in 1953; Jean Dubuffet, Wols and Henri Michaux held their first solo exhibitions in London there, while enterprises like Growth and Form (1951) and Place (1959) changed the very concept of an exhibition.[23] Psychoanalysis, science and anthropology were the early ICA's intellectual planks, fundamentally changing perceptions of art's status and social roles.

The Institute's most controversial moment was the international competition for a monument to the Unknown Political Prisoner, in 1953. Almost certainly underwritten by the CIA, this undesired entry into Cold War politics left the Institute unblemished, guilty only of naïvety.[24] However, it was a public relations disaster: the maquettes were widely considered incomprehensible; indeed the event probably impeded, rather than encouraged, enthusiasm for sculpture.

As principal advisor to the London County Council's art programme, the Arts Council was, unusually, obliged to intervene and lead. In 1948 the LCC, the civic authority for London, initiated a populist project to show sculpture in parks. Sculpture in the Open Air attracted nearly 150,000 visitors to Battersea Park, where guide-lecturers explained "difficult" works by such leading modernists as Henry Moore, Jacques Lipchitz and Ossip Zadkine to willing audiences (fig. 7). The exhibitions continued for many years, though none matched the success of the first, which was copied across Western Europe. Nowhere were the tensions of universalising patronage so apparent as in the LCC's projects – an early public art programme – which began in 1956, to commission works of art for its schools and housing estates. The Arts Council patiently

23 For Place see Toby Treves, Place, Garlake 2001 (see note 9), pp. 154–82.

24 On this event see Robert Burstow, "The limits of modernist art as a 'Weapon of the Cold War': reassessing the unknown patron of the Monument to the Unknown Political Prisoner", Oxford Art Journal, vol. XX, no. 2, 1997, pp. 68–80.

(fig. 7) Henry Moore THREE STANDING FIGURES 1948, height 218 cm, Darley Dale Stone, Battersea Park, London

negotiated the production of art that was neither *retar-dataire* nor outrageously modern. Well-received — much of it is still in place — its themes, forms and materials (often concrete) can be identified as "Welfare State sculpture" (fig. 8).

(fig. 8) Siegfried Charoux THE NEIGHBOURS 1959, cement, height 150 cm, Quadrant Estate, London

(fig. 9) David Annesley LOQUAT 1965, painted steel, 106.7 x 228.6 x 91.4 cm, Waddington Galleries, London

If the ICA balanced the needs of artists and viewers, the Arts Council and the LCC were oriented firmly towards reception. Unsurprisingly, artists took matters into their own hands. The Artist Placement Group (APG), devised by Barbara Steveni and John Latham, was a provocative residency scheme set up in 1966 to explore relationships between artists and industry, in situations where the purpose was to demonstrate alternatives to commercial practices rather than to produce (art) commodities. It is no coincidence that the APG and corporate patronage emerged more or less simultaneously.

The latter briefly coincided with fashionable art-and-high-society at the Whitechapel Art Gallery in the mid 1960s. The exhibition programme devised by Bryan Robertson, the Director of the Gallery (1952–68), had provided (as the Tate had not) an international, particularly an American, context for British art — and had gained an international reputation.[25] The *New Generation* exhibitions that Robertson organised for the Peter Stuyvesant Foundation were among the initiatives that kick-started corporate patronage and indirectly contributed considerably to the Tate when in 1973, Alistair McAlpine donated fifty-nine New Generation sculptures from his own collection (fig. 9).[26]

The difficulty of producing such large-scale sculpture prompted the establishment of SPACE (Space Provision Artistic, Cultural and Educational Ltd.) — by Bridget Riley, Peter Sedgley and Peter Townsend who, as editor of *Studio International* (1966–76), was one of the most powerful voices in support of artists' initiatives. SPACE did more to facilitate art production than any institution; its remit was to provide affordable studio space, capable of accommodating contemporary work. The Greater London Council made an unused warehouse available;

25 On Robertson and the Whitechapel Art Gallery see Mary Yule, "A place for living art: the Whitechapel Art Gallery 1952–1968", Garlake 2001 (see note 9), pp. 94–124.

26 Frances Spalding, *The Tate, a History*, London 1998, p. 174. See also *The Alistair McAlpine Gift*, exh. cat. Tate Gallery, London 1971.

the Arts Council paid for its conversion and, by 1985, SPACE was running ten studio complexes in London.

While the Council supported APG and SPACE, the rigidity of its structure prevented it from responding to the threat posed by the Community Arts Movement. Politically committed to inclusivity and rejection of the amateur-professional divide, Community Arts' favoured media included festivals, murals, puppetry, popular music and folk arts, crucially ignoring the Council's bedrock criterion of "quality". When, in the late 1960s, the Council hesitantly developed a structure to investigate new art forms, it did so in panic, rather than as a coherent policy, but the structure made it possible to carry out that function of state funding bodies that has been described as diminishing "the risk of experimental or avant-garde activities":[27] through skilful manipulation of the funding process, the Council managed to absorb, fragment and neutralise Community Arts.[28]

Throughout this time, private commercial galleries like Gimpel Fils, the Redfern, Erica Brausen's Hanover Gallery and Helen Lessore's Beaux-Arts (devoted to realism) supported artists and, especially from the late 1950s, encouraged them to show in continental Europe and the United States. While the prelude to commercial acceptance abroad was often participation in a British Council exhibition, the crucial part played by supportive dealers in the process of internationalisation should not be under-rated. The British Council's role in the same process was political, long-term and extremely sensitive, at a time when national status was measured by high culture.

Under Lilian Somerville (1948–70), the Council's Fine Art Department organised exhibitions that were admired by museum directors world-wide. Concerned primarily with reception, they were directed towards targeted opinion makers. Somerville left her own mark in the Council's emphasis on sculpture, an impact first apparent at the 1952 Venice Biennale, with the exhibition famously identified by Read's phrase "the geometry of fear".[29] It signalled a new aesthetic of linearity and voids and a new sculptural technology, aligned with an existential mindset. Four years later, the concentration on sculpture

27 Milton C. Cummings Jr. and Richard S. Katz, *The Patron State. Government and the Arts in Europe, North America & Japan*, New York and Oxford 1987, p. 11.

28 See Owen Kelly, *Community Art and the State. Storming the Citadel*, London 1984. See also Hutchison 1982 (see note 21), pp. 52 ff. For information on the Arts Council's response, I am indebted to Paul Shackleton's unpublished M.A. thesis, *New activists, New Art and the Arts Council 1968–74*, London 1993.

29 Herbert Read, "New Aspects of British Sculpture", exh. cat. XXVI Venice Biennale, 1952.

was vindicated when Lynn Chadwick won the Grand Prize for Sculpture in Venice, echoing Moore's triumph of 1948 (fig. 2).

After the war, the international response to Henry Moore's work was unparalleled, especially in Germany, where the Council was invited to tour Moore exhibitions in 1949/50 and again in 1953/54. His work seems to have represented both contemporary culture and a means of catharsis, for, if the return of Germany to full democracy and nationhood was the diplomatic priority, the German people faced the huge burden of reconciliation with the recent past. German critics found Moore's sculpture resonant with the psychological needs of their society, writing of its "natural" references as counters to the dehumanising nature of a mechanised world; "The work of Henry Moore [...] represents all of us in our western impotence against mass and the machine."[30] (fig. 10)

During the 1950s, the Venice Biennale was the arbiter of European contemporary aesthetics. Somerville showed successively Moore, Barbara Hepworth, Graham Sutherland and Ben Nicholson, international "modern masters", yet artists whose most innovatory work had been done in the 1930s. Reception in most European centres was respectful rather than enthusiastic. Until New York became dominant in the mid 1950s, the crucial judgements came from Paris, where the issue was whether new British art posed a threat to French hegemony or "was tagging along behind Paris".[31]

The São Paulo Bienal, established in 1951, offered opportunities to show a wider range of artists, being distant from the scrutiny of European critics. Somerville succumbed to diplomatic pressure to participate: "We have to go on making a name in São Paulo, commercially and industrially, artistically and culturally"[32] and — irresistibly — "France and Italy, to name no others, will make every effort to be more than adequately represented."[33] The flexible approach culminated in a group exhibition of experimental photography in 1971, produced as a response to problems caused by the political situation in Brazil (fig. 11). Though the radicalism of Roadshow — which contained work by Keith Arnott, Victor Burgin and Keith Milow, among others — was largely overlooked, it was highly praised by two respected Brazilian critics.[34] Today it is a poignant reminder that the Council's exhibitions more often favoured work grounded in mainstream modernity.

Clearly, large institutions cannot risk unqualified support for experimental art, while the process of testing and acceptance removes it from the category of the truly experimental. Such limitations are illustrated by two events in the mid 1970s, a moment of political and social radicalism. In May 1976 the British Council mounted Arte inglese oggi 1960–76 [English Art Today], in Milan. It included a performance art section[35] with Genesis P-Orridge and Cosey Fanni Tutti whose work was concerned with bondage, mutilation and pornography. Though their performance, Towards Thee Crystal Bowl, was well received by a large audience, it had been amended and rendered less radical for the occasion. In October 1976 the same artists organised Prostitution at the ICA, an incontrovertibly avant-garde exhibition in that its pornographic imagery (stored in boxes only opened on request) generated a "moral panic", with immense press coverage and questions in Parliament. Roy Shaw, Secretary-General of the Arts Council, commented: "The ICA was an example of the risks involved in supporting the experimental arts"; the Institute, in turn, was punished by the Council's insistence that it immediately plan for strenuous cost-cutting.[36]

By the late 1970s, a very wide range of options — often non-commercial — existed for showing and seeing cutting-edge contemporary art. The pioneering Victor Musgrave opened Gallery One in 1954; establishing a model of well-judged eclecticism, he was the first to exhibit Yves Klein in London; Denis Bowen's New Vision Centre Gallery (1956–66), in many respects Musgrave's counterpart, steadfastly promoted young, foreign, exclusively abstract artists. The modish Robert Fraser Gallery was famously devoted to Pop Art; the short-lived Signals Gallery to kinetic art; both had an enduring im-

30 Die Welt, 22 March 1950, in British Council report, "Henry Moore – Europe 1949/50", Henry Moore Foundation Archive, quoted in Margaret Garlake, "Henry Moore as cold warrior", Biuletyn Historii Sztuki, vol. LXI, nos. 3–4, 1999, p. 349.

31 British Council, Fine Art Advisory Committee Minutes, 26 May 1948, quoted in Garlake 1998 (see note 19), p. 19.

32 Consul General, São Paulo to Sir Nevile Butler, 7 August 1950, British Council BRA/641/57, 7 August 1950, quoted in Margaret Garlake, "The British Council and the São Paulo Bienal", The British Council, Britain and the São Paulo Bienal, London 1991, no. 60, p. 44.

33 Sir Nevile Butler to the Secretary of State, British Council BRA/641/57, 4 September 1950, Garlake 1991 (see note 32).

34 Ibid., p. 90.

35 Arte inglese oggi 1960–76, exh. cat. British Council, 2 vols., Milan 1976.

36 For a full account of Prostitution see Simon Ford, Wreckers of Civilisation. The Story of COUM Transmissions and Throbbing Gristle, London 1999, pp. 6.2–33.

(fig. 11) Genesis P. Orridge and Cosey Fanni Tutti Towards Thee Crystal Bowl Paris Bienniale 1975

(fig. 10) Henry Moore Family Group 1948–49, bronze, height 152 cm, edition of 4, Barclay Secondary School, Stevenage

pact on English artists. By the 1970s, a strong "alternative" support structure had developed in which gallery directors were intimately involved with artists' work. Robin Klassnik, originator of Matt's Gallery, told James Hall: "I've done and shown what I've enjoyed, what I would have loved to make. Artists are the tools through which I operate."[37] At the ACME Gallery in 1978, Stuart Brisley conducted a ten-day long performance that involved him crawling naked through the rotting remains of food cooked daily and left untouched. However, such gestures of aesthetic excess were not applauded by a government intent on "good management" and art that paid for itself.

The savage funding cuts of the 1980s forced a recognition that the post-war art support system was no more. State patronage either became relativised (the British Council) or struggled to find a new identity (the Arts Council), while the commercial sector became steadily less adventurous. *Freeze* – which appropriated many corporate promotional techniques[38] – was a presentational triumph for artists who have since slipped into the mainstream. The chronicle of what has been called "High Art Lite" demonstrates that avant-gardes and counter-cultures are incompatible with formal support systems, while the diverse forms of twentieth century patronage suggest that the most successful promoters of contemporary art were idiosyncratic enthusiasts, unacquainted with business plans or targets. Fortunately, though there are never enough of them, they continue to emerge and will no doubt continue to support the artists of the twenty-first century.

37 James Hall, "Full of East End promise", *The Independent*, January 1991.

38 Julian Stallabrass, *High Art Lite. British Art in the 1990s*, London and New York 1999, pp. 52 f.

MARGARET GARLAKE

THE ROLE OF
THE CRITIC

NORBERT LYNTON

Max Nordau's *Degeneracy [Entartung]* was a bestseller in Britain, too.[1] Three years after the German original, an English version was published in 1895 and needed reprinting seven times before the year was out. Nordau's vilification of anything progressive in the arts was welcomed: reviewers claimed to have had their own doubts about many of his targets. George Bernard Shaw produced an effective counterblast, *The Sanity of Art*, using Nordau's own rhetoric against him and asserting the necessity of creative work.[2] James Whistler's court case of 1878 against John Ruskin was still a vivid memory. Having won his suit and been awarded token damages of one farthing, the smallest amount possible, Whistler emerged, bankrupt but famous, to publish his witty version of the drama. Ruskin's words about a "coxcomb [...] flinging a pot of paint in the public's face" remain available to anyone wanting to re-use them, safe in the knowledge that no other artist is likely to risk a libel action in Britain to defend his professional honour.

Much has changed in British art since then, yet the attitudes revealed in those late-Victorian exchanges live on. Those who enjoy drawing attention to artistic innovation by denouncing it often echo Nordau's language. English responses to visual art (Scotland and Wales are evidently more liberal, but London remains the inevitable centre and powerhouse) lack the confidence bred by a tradition of engagement. The English term for being decently educated is to be "well-read"; contrast that with *Bildung* and *gebildet*. Oscar Schmitz's essays on the English, *Das Land ohne Musik* (1920), enlarged for London publication in 1925, say little about music or the other arts.[3] Schmitz sketches the morals, manners and politics of "the broad middle class" of England, as compared with its equivalent in Germany and, sometimes, France. In England common sense rules, in the place of French sensuousness and German intellectual enquiry. English education "is always based on facts" and has never approached Germany's *allgemeine Bildung* (which, he admits, can lead to arrogance and dogmatism). The French have their aesthetic education and sexual maturity. The English, serious about sport and politics-as-sport while distracting themselves with their empire, avoid philosophy and aesthetics, and value the arts only as decoration and amusement. In Germany philosophy is part of education. In England it is left to specialists. Even in 1900, the media exercised tremendous power in forming "public opinion". Today, with the added power of radio and television, we might say that their hold is even stronger and public interest in anything is as transient as theirs. Our art critics rarely swim against this stream and risk being swept

1 Max Nordau (1849–1923), *nom de plume* of Simon Maximilian Südfeld, a rabbi's son, was trained in medicine and became eager to extend into the cultural field Cesare Lombroso's teaching, that criminality was a pathological condition requiring eradication.

2 An anonymous, book-length rebuttal of Nordau, *Regeneration*, appeared in 1895, but seems to have made no impact. George Bernard Shaw's counterattack, the same year, was first published as a long open letter to the American journal *Liberty*. In 1908 an amended version of this was published as a book.

3 Schmitz used as the book's motto Friedrich Nietzsche's words from *Beyond Good and Evil* about the Englishman's "lack of music": "he has no rhythm, no dance, in the movements of his soul and of his body; nay, he even lacks a desire for rhythm and dance; in other words – for music".

aside by it when they try to. Art commentaries should probably appear in the sports section of our newspapers, unlike the contributions of literary and film critics, which can assume some interest and intelligence in the reader.

The key texts in aesthetics, from Alexander Baumgarten via Immanuel Kant, Georg Wilhelm Hegel and Friedrich Schlegel (one of Nordau's "imbeciles") to Martin Heidegger and Theodor Adorno, were German, until French critical theory erupted in the second half of the twentieth century. This has altered the tone of cultural discourse in Britain, too, but is understood only at the academic level. The media refer to postmodernism (good and now) and something remote called modernism (bad and dead). We no longer speak of avant-gardes, but the media lust after the latest and most outrageous innovations, in the hope that something still more shocking will emerge. Art history entered the conservative British academic system only in the 1930s and was accepted as a normal element in universities and art schools after 1960. A sense of history should help to stabilise the situation, but there is a view that fiddling with theoretical structures makes attention to art itself look naff.

British art criticism was and remains the work of artists – not necessarily the best and never the most successful – and of writers looking for a role as cultural commentators at various levels of commitment. Art historians have joined in, and often stand closer to artists than the *ad hoc* writers who frequently represent traditional prejudices. Artist/writers tend to fight for their own corners. In 1900 the best newspapers and literary journals, such as *The Atheneum*, employed specialist critics to report on art exhibitions. A range of art journals supplied artists and non-artists with information and opinions: *Artist*, *Magazine of Art*, *Art Journal*, etc. From 1892 on, *The Studio* reported on art and the crafts in words and plentiful illustrations and quickly achieved international status, but its presentation of contemporary art remained tentative, even amateurish, until its rebirth as *Studio International* in 1964. Other journals, serving the art trade and collectors, would include some accounts of

the art scenes of Paris and of London but were dedicated to antiques and old masters.

In the 1890s, when Edward Burne-Jones was lauded abroad as the great English symbolist, and Sir Frederic Leighton, essentially a classicist, was President of the Royal Academy,[4] Impressionism divided critics and their public. The general suspicion of paintings not relying on exact drawing and a fine finish was sharpened by the conviction that anything valuable in Impressionism had already been achieved by John Constable and by William Turner. The new art from Paris met with some response but, as in Germany, nationalism powered resistance to imports. Radicalism was everywhere associated with anarchism and assassinations. In this context R. A. M. Stephenson's much-praised book *The Art of Velasquez* (1895) persuasively designated Diego Velázquez the father of Impressionism, tying the new art to a wider tradition.[5] Nonetheless, Impressionism was still generally derided as artless and mindless. Claude Monet and Alfred Sisley were singled out as particular offenders against "beauty".

Walter Sickert, a disciple of Whistler and of Edgar Degas, persuaded other artists to join him in an informal group of London Impressionists. His own paintings were mostly urban and often dour in motif and manner, asserting character as much through formal means as through subject-matter. Likewise, his forthright critical writings.[6] His effort to dissociate meaning in art from detailed naturalism and literary content link him to Roger Fry and to Clive Bell, who worked, from 1910 on, to promote what Fry named Post-Impressionism and presented in two London exhibitions of 1910 and 1912. The first of these exhibitions occasioned a famous public outcry. Dominated by the work of Paul Cézanne, Paul Gauguin and Vincent van Gogh, it was denounced as anarchical and degenerate[7]. The second met with more genuine interest. It combined mostly later work from Paris – Henri Matisse (including *La Danse I*), Pablo Picasso, André Derain etc. – with more or less comparable English and Russian art.[8] Together, Fry's exhibitions had something of the effect of the New York *Armory Show* of 1913: it was no longer possible to ignore modern art, as a problem only for foreigners.

4 Elected President of the Royal Academy and knighted in 1878, Frederic Leighton was honoured with a peerage, shortly before his death in 1896 – to this day, the only artist to be made a "Lord".

5 Robert Stephenson (1847–1900), a painter and prominent teacher of art, wrote art criticism regularly in the 1880s and 1890s.

6 Born in Munich, of Danish-Irish descent, Walter Sickert (1860–1942) lived in London and, at times, Dieppe, from 1868 on and was a frequent visitor to Paris. His first ambition had been to be an actor. His talk and writing, and sometimes his painting, reflected his self-image as a performer.

7 See J. B. Bullen (ed.), *Post-Impressionists in England – The Critical Reaction*, London and New York 1988. Some of the fiercest condemnations came from established artists. One of these, Wake Cook, had previously published *Anarchism in Art*, clearly following Nordau. Nordau's language is echoed in many reviews of the 1910 exhibition.

8 In 1911 the Russian Ballet performed at Covent Garden and, though its "savages prancing about" in *Prince Igor* shocked some ladies, the performances were warmly and often intelligently received, even as "a serious form of art". See Richard Buckle, *Diaghilev*, London 1979, pp. 202–209.

Roger Fry[9] is now rightly seen as the major British art critic of the early twentieth century, and wrongly blamed for promoting the vice called formalism. A serious painter and esteemed art historian, Fry associated Post-Impressionism with an attention to expressive design and colour, generally abandoned in western art since Byzantium and the *quattrocento*. He had come to terms with Cézanne's problematic example, influenced both by Maurice Denis' account of the painter as a new classicist and by Julius Meier-Graefe's presentation of him as Edouard Manet's great successor, purveying intense experiences of nature through concentration, without denying nature's richness.[10]

Fry's assertion that art's value resides not in subject-matter but in its artistic transformation countermanded the English habit of looking through art at motifs and stories and responding only to these. He prioritised what Eugène Delacroix called "the musical element in painting", and thus he could admire, after Cézanne, also Gauguin, van Gogh and the younger artists of Paris. An apparently more dogmatic insistence on "Significant Form" came from his friend, Clive Bell, who is accused of narrowness, though he stated that his concept was hypothetical as well as, inevitably, rooted in individual responses. These, as Fry pointed out, had a democratic base: one's maid might have easier access to the new art than the "well-read".

His successor as champion of modern art was a man with different priorities. Herbert Read[11] was primarily a poet and a literary critic. As a young man in Leeds, he encountered anarchism and progressive ideas at the Leeds Arts Club – an adventurous centre offering lectures, debates and exhibitions, and easy contact with like-minded individuals. In the collection of Michael Sadler, Vice-Chancellor of Leeds University, he also saw van Goghs, Kandinskys and Klees, for the first time and himself drew some abstract designs. But it was as a poet and writer that he first made his mark on the new London literary scene of Ezra Pound, T. S. Eliot and the Sitwells, from 1918 onwards. Read only

began to write about art after making an intensive study of German aesthetic theory, whilst engaged in editing the philosophical studies of T. E. Hulme, a friend of the Vorticists, who had been killed in the War. Through his multifarious activities as writer and lecturer on art, literary figure and educationalist, it might be said that Read brought German thought back into English awareness and rebuilt the bridge that had existed in the age of Samuel Coleridge.[12] Returning to London in 1933, after a spell in Edinburgh, he quickly became a key figure in the Hampstead circle of artists and writers that embraced Henry Moore, Ben Nicholson, Barbara Hepworth and Paul Nash, soon also émigré artists such as László Moholy-Nagy, Naum Gabo and Piet Mondrian. His first catalogue text presented Hepworth's sculpture and was followed by his influential *Art Now: an Introduction to the Theory of Modern Painting and Sculpture* (1933) and a slim volume on Moore, in 1934.[13]

Fry's death in 1934 left a vacancy. Read's mission was more universal and addressed a wider world. He gladly championed new artists, but individual works of art were rarely Read's public concern; perhaps they never touched him as poems did. His sympathies were too broad for him to be seen as any tendency's permanent ally. Closely associated with England's constructive art of the 1930s, he suddenly endorsed its enemy, promoting London's historic *International Surrealist Exhibition* of 1936 as a protest against "the rottenness of our civilization", and linking it to the English tradition of poetic irrationality (Lawrence Sterne, William Blake, Lewis Carroll, etc.). Later on, he became identified with a new generation of British sculptors (Kenneth Armitage, Reg Butler and others), whose work he presented at the 1952 Venice Biennale, and, by the time he was knighted, in 1953 ("for services to literature"), he had become a leading international figure. Yet he questioned the enduring value of Abstract Expressionism, and the rise of Pop Art, during his last

9 Roger Fry (1866–1934) was one of the founders of *The Burlington Magazine*, in 1930. In 1906, appointed curator of painting at the Metropolitan Museum, New York, he also received an invitation to direct the National Gallery in London. In 1911 he turned down an offer to become the Director of the Tate Gallery. Fry's essays on subjects ranging from "Negro Sculpture" and Mexican art to El Greco and Cézanne, reprinted in *Vision and Design* (1920), profoundly influenced Henry Moore and his generation. See Frances Spalding, *Roger Fry, Art and Life*, London 1980; Christopher Reed (ed.), *A Roger Fry Reader*, Chicago and London 1996; and Christopher Green (ed.), *Art Made Modern – Roger Fry's Vision of Art*, London 1999.

10 Meier-Graefe's *Entwicklungsgeschichte der modernen Kunst* (1904) was published in England as *Modern Art* in 1908. Fry's Omega Workshops (1913–19) probably owed something to Meier-Graefe and to the Wiener Werkstätten, as well as the British Arts and Crafts movement, born in the 1860s.

11 Among other activities for which Sir Herbert Read (1893–1968) was noted was his role, with Roland (later, Sir Roland) Penrose, in founding the Institute of Contemporary Arts in London, as a centre for an interested public, as well as for artists and critics, presenting exhibitions, lectures and debates. See the exhibition catalogue edited by Benedict Read and David Thistlewood, *Herbert Read: A British Vision of World Art*, Leeds City Art Galleries, Leeds 1993.

12 Through Hulme, Read discovered the writings of Wilhelm Worringer, whose *Form in Gothic* (1910) he translated and edited in 1927. Later, he dedicated his widely read collection of essays, *The Philosophy of Modern Art* (1952) to Worringer, as "my esteemed master in the philosophy of art". Read also supported the exhibition, *20th Century German Art*, at the New Burlington Galleries in London in 1938 a retort to the *Degenerate Art Exhibition* launched in Munich the previous year, at the opening of which Max Beckmann delivered his celebrated speech, "On the Theory of My Painting" ("Meine Theorie der Malerei").

13 Also: *Art and Industry, the Principles of Industrial Design* (1934), *Art and Society* (1937) and *Education through Art* (1943), all reprinted several times.

years, made him doubt art's faculty for self-renewal. For all this, the arts remained, for Read, the essential voice of freedom, challenging all established systems. Anarchism was still his base, after 1918, the anarchism of a pacifist. He believed in what he called "positive criticism", knowing that "the pragmatical Englishman" enjoys his "hearty scorn of a phenomenon so disturbing to his complacency as modern art".[14] Thus he was not only the first English writer to argue the historical importance of such artists as Pablo Picasso, Georges Braque and Henri Matisse: he "gave modern art its scientific credentials", as Patrick Heron wrote, in 1952.[15]

Heron never set out to be a critic but was persuaded to be one from 1945 on, mostly for London's prestigious political and cultural journal, *The New Statesman and Nation*, and for New York journal, *Arts*, until 1958. Then he ceased, though he subsequently went on to produce occasional texts about individual artists and polemical lectures and essays on the demolition of art education in England, and on America's art chauvinism. Heron was a painter who wrote eloquently about particular artists, mostly of Paris, and with keen insight also about his artist friends in London and St. Ives, notably Ben Nicholson and Roger Hilton. Like Read, he valued positive criticism, hoping to draw readers closer to art. His language was clear and personal, conveying unconventional reflections with an insistence some found rebarbative. His editor at *The New Statesman* complained that readers tired of his endless talk of colour, line and space. The readers of *Arts* expected art talk and enjoyed Heron's prompt praise of the new American painting, though Heron himself changed his mind about this only ten years later, when he decided it was limited and lacking in dynamics. He charged America with cultural imperialism, and English critics with bowing obsequiously before the Americans while showing only lukewarm interest in their own country's art. Since the latter had generally been dismissive of Abstract Expressionism at first sight, and had then only gradually learned to be more courageous, this seemed an ungenerous response, yet it is true that British art (Heron included) was generally under-regarded by our critics, who were dazzled by grandiose presentations of Jackson Pollock, Mark Rothko, Morris Louis, and their peers. As

14 Quoted from the preface to *Art Now* (1933), where Read goes on to speak of the fate of new art in Germany, so highly esteemed at home and supported by official institutions, and now suddenly denounced as "Kultur-bolschewismus".

15 In *The New Statesman and Nation*, 29 March 1952.

with Fry, the art of Paris gave Heron the yardsticks by which painting still had to be judged – notably the work of Georges Braque, Paul Klee and Pierre Bonnard (the last-named grossly undervalued at his death in 1947, when Heron first wrote about him) – but his analyses were both more intense and more principled than Fry's.

An exhibition of paintings by Matisse and Picasso at the Victoria and Albert Museum in 1945–46, intended as a refreshing import after years of blockade, launched a critical and media hubbub. Matisse looked serious and good because the Picassos, all wartime and mostly of monstrous women with mad hats, looked so appalling. The general press mocked. Serious art critics tried to acknowledge Picasso's fierceness as timely, but could not cope with it. This was the response of some artists, too; others, such as Victor Pasmore, saw in it a final line drawn under centuries of figurative art and were thrilled by the sense of new horizons opening up. In only the second of his critical essays, Heron wrote about the exhibition calmly. He showed fundamental differences between Picasso and Cézanne, by commenting on the superhuman size of Picasso's women and the indivisibility of "the poetic and the purely pictorial".[16]

During the 1950s, two other English critics became influential, principally through the columns of *The Listener* and *The New Statesman*: John Berger and David Sylvester. John Berger was a Marxist painter, who turned to art criticism for a while, before embarking on an alternative career as a novelist and writer.[17] He sought a phalanx of artists working to a programme not unlike Leo Tolstoy's: art must communicate with everyone and therefore be naturalistic in idiom, and it must convey moral (for Tolstoy religious, for Berger socially progressive) messages. Influenced by Marxist art historians, he looked for living equivalents of such social critics as William Hogarth and Fernand Léger, found a few among British artists, but discovered the most potent contemporary art in the work of Renato Guttuso and other Italian realists: these, he announced in 1956, were Europe's vanguard.[18] David Sylvester came into art via a

16 See *Painter As Critic, Patrick Heron: Selected Writings*, Mel Gooding (ed.), London 1998, pp. 4–7.

17 John Berger (born 1926) largely abandoned art criticism in 1961 and soon after left Britain to live on the Continent and write novels and books on various subjects and only occasional articles on art. *Permanent Red*, a selection of his art writings published in 1960, had less impact than his BBC television series *Ways of Seeing*, published as a little paperback 1972 and often reprinted. Its often simplistic assertions are still encountered among the young.

18 John Berger, preface to *Realist Painters of "La Colonna"*, exh. cat. Leicester Galleries, London 1956, cited in James Hyman, *The Battle for Realism. Figurative Art in Britain During the Cold War 1945–1960*, London and New Haven 2001, p. 228, note 66.

brief experience of painting and an intense engagement with individual artists and with existentialist thought in London and Paris.[19] Already in 1948 he promoted a selection of realistic London painters as an "Ecole de Londres".[20] Soon he concluded that Francis Bacon and Alberto Giacometti were the true avant-garde, and he wrote about them again and again, engaging his passion as well as his intelligence and exceptional verbal skills to promote an ever-deeper understanding of their art. Matisse and Picasso, and in some respects Klee, were his lodestars from the first. René Magritte was his long-term research project but was never central to his thinking.

Whereas Berger started from socio-political convictions, Sylvester discovered his sense of greatness through individuals; he listened to them, strove to fathom their unspoken motivation, and promoted them energetically. The realism he sought had to relate to the modernist heritage and be guided by the imagination, not precepts. He believed in genius, and focused on it with a persistence hitherto exclusive to English literary criticism. Berger wanted art to address society and to change it. Sylvester hoped to persuade the widest possible public of art's potency, but his immediate mission was to the educated, the "opinion makers", whose fears of innovation and powerful expression he hoped to still.

Both Berger and Sylvester saw abstract art as the enemy, and thus reinforced a general British prejudice. Growing interest in Klee, from the late 1940s on, and the rise to prominence of major new artists working in the borderlands of abstraction and figuration – notably Nicolas de Staël and Jean Dubuffet – taught Sylvester the significance of process. America's new abstract painting, energetically promoted in Europe from the mid 1950s on and first sampled and then surveyed at the Tate Gallery in 1956 and 1959, convinced neither Berger nor Sylvester. Berger's comment on a Pollock retrospective in 1958 was that his art proved "the disintegration of our culture". Sylvester, seeking human immediacy, could not find it in those large, rather repetitive abstracts until he accepted the offer of a visit to America in 1960 and met the artists of the New York School. On his return, he echoed the American (and German?) judgment on English art, that it never achieved true greatness because of England's traditional virtues of moderation and tact.[21]

This judgment was used, in the early 1960s, against the artists of St. Ives, in Cornwall, including Ben Nicholson, Barbara Hepworth, Roger Hilton, Patrick Heron and Peter Lanyon, who are generally said to have infused landscape sensations into art that often looked abstract. These painters had been seen as the British avant-garde in the 1950s, and honoured and collected abroad while English critics generally still resisted abstraction. The art historian and critic, Sir Alan Bowness, wrote repeatedly about their work in newspaper reviews, catalogues and books, often addressing an international readership. His intimacy with most of the artists he wrote about, as well as his art-historical base, made him a convincing champion, a calm but firm voice among the many timid and often ill-informed art writers of the time, who seemed content to echo existing prejudices.[22]

The prejudice against abstraction worked against the constructivist movement which developed from Pasmore's sudden turn, in 1948, from fine, selective representational painting to making abstract compositions, followed by geometrical constructions. The group that formed around him included Kenneth and Mary Martin and Anthony Hill, and the 1960s saw the growth of a wider Constructivist movement with international connections. All this was largely ignored and occasionally mocked by English critics. Naum Gabo, who lived in London and Cornwall from 1935 to 1946 and frequently returned to London, had some standing here, though no work entered the Tate's collection until two constructions were accepted as gifts in 1958. Younger Continental Constructivists, such as Max Bill and Paul Lohse, though shown occasionally, were never recognised here. For some critics, straight lines and geometrical forms signalled intellectualism and, therefore, not art.[23] Even today, English constructivism is actively written out of history. Telling instances of this are two London exhibi-

19 David Sylvester (1924–2001) was a tireless writer, interviewer, broadcaster, organiser and installer of exhibitions.
20 See David Sylvester, "The Problems of Painting", *L'Age Nouveau*, nos. 31–33, 1947, cited in Hyman 2001 (see note 18), p. 24, note 76. In his book, Hyman examines Berger's and Sylvester's critical activity in the 1950s in some detail.

21 The view that English art was prevented from true greatness by the national habit of tolerance and fair play was voiced by the German art historian Nikolaus Pevsner, the renowned teacher and *animateur*, in his Reith Lecture series on "The Englishness of English Art", broadcast by the BBC in 1955 and printed as a bestseller in and after 1956; it was prefigured in Dagobert Frey, *Englisches Wesen im Spiegel seiner Kunst*, Berlin and Stuttgart 1942.
22 Sir Alan Bowness (born 1928) worked as a critic and taught art history at the Courtauld Institute of Art, London University, until 1980–88, when he was Director of the Tate Gallery. At the Tate, he did much to strengthen the collection of modern art, including the representation of contemporary works. His major innovations included the development of regional outposts, at St.Ives and Liverpool, and the founding of the Patrons of New Art and the still controversial Turner Prize. See Frances Spalding, *The Tate. A History*, London 1998.

tions presenting *The Sixties Art Scene in London* (1993) and *Transition. The London Art Scene in the Fifties* (2001). To ignore Victor Pasmore and his circle is especially shocking in the case of the latter: they were then the "cutting edge" feared by the cultural establishment. This negation was prepared already by the Royal Academy's large *British Art in the 20th Century* exhibition of 1987 – curated and catalogued by art historians and critics – in which the whole of constructivism was represented by one Pasmore relief.

A full account of the role of art critics would have to explore systematically their function as exhibition curators as well as writers and broadcasters. It should assess their influence on the inner and outer art publics, and on the establishment controlling national and regional expenditure on the arts, often operating through "independent" organisations whose existence depends on official favour. It should also ask how much any of this affects the character and production of art. A short and incomplete answer is that, at any point in the story, some art is favoured by the mature and solid public, and some art is favoured by "the young" and is promoted in order to oust the other sort. The media are increasingly likely to focus on one or two stars of both kinds, one as "great and good", the other as "naughty but nice". Both sorts are served by ambitious curator/critics, eager to shine among their international competitors. The situation breeds a self-consciousness that inhibits honest assessment. Little writing now suggests personal enthusiasm. Media notice, and thus visitor numbers, measures success. Reviews in the press now favour the big shows and largely ignore the galleries.

Lawrence Alloway[24] was the first critic to record and celebrate the changeover from Paris to New York, as the principal focus for the limited public who were interested in contemporary art. He firmly welcomed Abstract Expressionism in Britain and dealt fiercely with British critics' general denial and then slow acceptance of it, followed, as Heron complained, by uncritical enthusiasm. Many artists responded with immediate interest, often with admiration. Alloway's support was the more remarkable for the fact that, during 1952–55, while Assistant Director at the Institute of Contemporary Arts, he had been a key member of the Independent Group, who were associated with it, yet united in their opposition to Read's high-minded focus. Alloway insisted that the mass media were part of culture, not culture's enemy, and mocked 1930s abstraction for its Platonic idealism.

This makes it surprising that he was so ardent a champion of the New York School, with its pursuit of sublimity. Alloway coined the term, "Pop Art", for mass-media imagery, on an analogy with "Pop Music" and was not altogether pleased, when it became associated with paintings he judged lightweight. (American critics, too, took a disdainful view of their own "Pop Art", which they saw as undermining modern art's hard-won, exalted status). The American critic Clement Greenberg had long ago distinguished sharply between serious modernist art and any tendency to popularisation; his reputation stood high in London in the early 1960s, particularly among the *Situation* artists.[25] In New York, Alloway championed American Pop Art, but among his last acts in London was organising the *Situation* exhibition of 1960, featuring large-scale abstract paintings, mostly hard-edge and flat, but some gestural, by a slightly older circle of painters, including Harold and Bernard Cohen, Robyn Denny, William Turnbull, John Hoyland, Gillian Ayres and Richard Smith. *Situation* asserted a professionalism impatient of the semi-amateur status sometimes claimed by British artists and sometimes wished for them, and disdained the poetic semi-abstraction associated with the St. Ives painters. It received little attention from the critics. The sudden enthusiasm for Pop Art switched attention away from *Situation*, but almost all the individual painters in the shows – and Anthony Caro, whose new abstract constructed metal sculpture was represented in a second *Situation* show, in 1961 – went on to prove their importance. But abstraction was still feared, whereas Pop Art was fun, and easier to write and read about.[26] As a part-time critic in the 1960s, I championed abstraction in the face of this prejudice. Marvellous things were happening, that owed some impetus to *Situation*: most obviously

23 My own work as a critic, mostly in the 1960s and for some years regularly, as London correspondent of *Art International* and art critic of *The Guardian*, initially reflected my interest in the St. Ives artists and included a positive response to Abstract Expressionism, to the bold abstract painting launched as *Situation* in 1960, to aspects of Pop Art, and to contemporary constructivism.

24 Lawrence Alloway (1926–90) had little formal education. He wrote for many publications, including *Art News and Review* (founded 1949) and *Art International*, as its London correspondent. In 1961 he went to visit New York and stayed there, working as art critic of *The Nation* and, for some years, as a curator at the Guggenheim Museum.

25 So high that the artist John Latham and his friends in 1966 chewed up a copy of Greenberg's ubiquitous collection, *Art and Culture*, and turned it into a phial of distilled spit. The resulting artwork was subsequently acquired by the Museum of Modern Art, in New York and is deemed too fragile to travel to Europe for the present exhibition.

26 Richard Hamilton, a major artist whose standing in Britain has vacillated while his fame abroad rose early and remains high, is an outstanding instance of an artist writing vividly and entertainingly about his own work. See his *Collected Words 1953–1982*, London 1982.

the emergence of new sculptors, William Tucker and Phillip King among them, and a whole range of confident abstract painters, including Bridget Riley, Paul Huxley and John Walker.[27]

For critics and an enthusiastic public, Pop Art was a holiday from seriousness and from the problem of abstraction. Nobody cared to notice the socio-political content of some of it, nor its deft use of modernist and English traditions. The 1960s' liberal spirit should have relaxed old aversions. Its innate pluralism should have led to easier acceptance of contemporary art, but the plot was thickened by the arrival of conceptual art, in little shows in tiny galleries, and then also at the Institute of Contemporary Arts in an international exhibition. *When Attitudes Become Form. Live in Your Head* (1969) included only three British artists and produced more crossness than discussion among our critics. Their aversion still held in 1972, when the Arts Council presented at the Hayward Gallery a survey of British Conceptual Art in *The New Art*, curated by Anne Seymour, a young art historian. Critics generally disdained this gathering of works in diverse media by Gilbert and George, Richard Long, Barry Flanagan, Victor Burgin, John Stezaker and others, plus a roomful of texts by Art & Language, and an important catalogue.[28] On the other hand, the exhibition helped a new generation of critics to emerge, eager to engage with something not already supported by the establishment. Among them was Richard Cork, recently down from Cambridge, fiercely "cutting edge" in his first writings, but subsequently the benign art critic of *The Times* (until 2002). In 1974 an exhibition of conceptual art, bought by him for the Arts Council, toured Britain as *Beyond Painting and Sculpture*.

Some of the conceptual artists made literary art works, or works combining photographic images and words. Generally, they were highly articulate and ready to promote their work through their own writings, published in *Studio International* and a few other art journals such as *Art Monthly*, founded in 1976. The emphasis placed on

liberal studies in English art schools since the early 1960s, combined with the tense self-awareness occasioned by the art-school uprisings of 1968, bred a new taste for power through articulate action. Moreover, the swell of talented and marketable young artists during the 1960s made it necessary for younger artists to find ways of bypassing the replete commercial system. Their work employs unconventional means: performance art, videos, photographic art, installations, and so on. Several of these artists produced saleable versions of non-gallery work, including fine photographs of Land Art. The national and then also regional galleries have learned to accommodate conceptual art in its many forms, and now stand accused of having lost interest in everything else. It is uncertain where the old enemy, the controlling establishment, now stands.

With many artists writing about their own or their friends' art, as well as organising and promoting their own exhibitions,[29] critics have tended to become more vociferous, to make themselves heard above a hubbub further intensified by endless PR releases. Reason and sensibility cut little ice now: attitude counts above attention and language alters to fit. David Sylvester's death deprived us of the critic most devoted to following instinct and intelligence, to penetrate work worthy of his focus. A shallower passion has been shown by writers preaching loudly against all or most of the art made public in recent years. Peter Fuller was the first outstanding instance.[30] In his positive comments he appeared to be promoting traditionalism and nationalism. From his first master, Berger, he soon turned to Lord Clark of *Civilisation*, the 1969 TV series and bestselling book (which Fuller had earlier designated "rubbish"), without adopting Clark's subtle language and positive tone.[31] Like Ruskin, but without his attendant enthusiasms, he was eager to tell art what it should be doing.

There is no need to end on negatives. British art is multifarious and often excellent, most of it ignored

27 Bryan Robertson, then Director of the Whitechapel Art Gallery, had the wit and wisdom to show figurative and abstract painters together in the first *New Generation* show, in 1964. In 1965 his *New Generation* show of sculptors was, and probably had to be, all abstract.

28 An otherwise unknown critic, Peter Spence, reviewed the exhibition at some length in a journal not much seen in the art world, *The New Humanist* (November 1972). The then Director of the Tate, (Sir) Norman Reid, sent a photocopy of it to me at the Arts Council, suggesting I might copy it to my staff, as he had done to his. He thought it exceptionally interesting. I recall that it offered a positive response, combined with some questioning of individual contributions.

29 *Freeze*, organised by Damien Hirst in 1988, was an important historical moment. There is a long tradition of exhibitions presented by artists' groups, inside and outside the commercial sites, but Hirst was still a student at the time, and the moment was ripe.

30 Peter Fuller (1947–1990) began as a follower of Berger, but by 1980 had turned against him. Marxist priorities were replaced by aesthetic ones, partly in emulation of Ruskin, whose socialism he ignored while adopting his often missionary tone. In long articles and printed lectures he issued anathemas against whole swathes of modern art, occasionally in terms equivalent to Nordau's – in 1980 he called Richard Hamilton "a whore of an artist" – arguing now from grounds of sensibility to press home judgments that sounded moral. He had a great success with this, attracting the media and a wide public. In 1988 he launched *Modern Painters* (echoing the title of Ruskin's great work), which continues to credit him as founder but has adopted a wide-ranging programme he could not have countenanced. His caustic *Seeing Berger* (1980) was republished in *Seeing Through Berger* (1988). He produced several other books, some of them collections of his writings; yet others have been assembled posthumously.

by the media. Some honestly thoughtful critics — artist/writers, as well as writers — undertake their essential role, as before.[32] This one, and then that, attracts the limelight — just now, Matthew Collings, whose anything-goes manner, enjoyed by many, screens his commitment. It is dangerous to imply that nothing matters, when addressing people attached to a "hearty scorn" for your subject. Yet this distinguishes him from a few admired critics who specialise in denunciation. Collings is fun to read and to watch on the box, apparently an innocent wandering in artland. The disparagers present themselves as voices crying in the wilderness, while profiting from the gathering crowds. Others are more direct: Richard Dorment, Marco Livingstone, Stuart Morgan, Adrian Searle, Mel Gooding, Sacha Craddock, William Packer, and others want art to thrive and people to know it. Very few of them have regular media slots. Bryan Robertson, the wisest and deftest among us, writes very rarely. What was certainly a *fin de siècle* period, with "Young British Art" repeating symbolism's dance of death to the media's piping, is ending in boredom. Symbolism provided seeds of renewal; Young British Artists' widening output must contain some, too, to flourish — perhaps through less peripatetic forms and methods. Some cry "The centre cannot hold; / Mere anarchy is loosed upon the world",[33] but centres don't yield that easily. Art lives, adds, moves on. We must learn to ignore the piper or teach him better tunes.

31 *Civilization* was never rubbish; neither was it the great cultural reconnaissance many still think it. Claiming to present a "personal view", but devoted to eloquent praise of the canonical greats of, mostly, European art and culture, it averted its gaze from modern art: "I believe that order is better than chaos, creation better than destruction. I prefer gentleness to violence, forgiveness to vendetta," etcetera. By implication, modern art was devoted to the negative term in each pair.

32 *Art Monthly* now uses as many artist-writers as critics.

33 From W. B. Yeats, "The Second Coming", a response to another *fin de siècle*.

NORBERT LYNTON

CATALOGUE OF WORKS IN THE EXHIBITION

EILEEN AGAR

THE ANGEL OF MERCY
1934   plaster, gouache and
collage, height: 44 cm
Dr. Jeffrey and Ruth Sherwin
Pl. 51

EDWARD ALLINGTON

THE SILENT SONG
OF THE SHELL
1983   painted plaster,
Polystyrene, steel, plastic
grapes, mussels and lemons,
140 x 100 x 100 cm
The Artist, courtesy Lisson
Gallery, London

MICHAEL ANDREWS

THE COLONY ROOM
1962   oil on board,
120 x 182.2 cm
The St. John Wilson Trust
Pl. 142

MELANIE AND ME SWIMMING
1978–79   acrylic on canvas,
182.9 x 182.9 cm
Tate, London

THE CATHEDRAL, THE SOUTHERN
FACES/ULURU (AYERS ROCK)
1987   acrylic on canvas,
243.8 x 388.6 cm
Trustees of the Derek Williams
Collection, Loan to
The National Museums &
Galleries of Wales
Pl. 195

DAVID ANNESLEY

SWING LOW
1964   painted steel,
126 x 180 x 36 cm
Fundação Calouste Gulbenkian/

CAMJAP, Lisbon
Pl. 160

KENNETH ARMITAGE

FIGURE LYING ON ITS SIDE
(NO. 5)
1957   bronze, width: 82.5 cm
The British Council
Pl. 110

JOHN ARMSTRONG

UNIT ONE COMPOSITION
1933   oil on canvas,
74 x 61 cm
Dr. Jeffrey and Ruth Sherwin
Pl. 63

KEITH ARNATT

HOLE THAT MAKES ITSELF
A AND B
1967–68   colour photo-
graphs, each 50.8 x 50.8 cm
The British Council
Pl. 169

LIVERPOOL BEACH BURIAL
1968   colour photograph,
50.8 x 40.6 cm
The British Council
Pl. 176

PORTRAIT OF THE ARTIST AS A
SHADOW OF HIS FORMER SELF
1969–72   colour photograph,
121.6 x 121.6 cm
Artist's collection

ART & LANGUAGE

UNTITLED PAINTING
1965   mirror mounted
on canvas,
25.4 x 184.7 x 15 cm
Piessens Collection, Belgium

PAINTING – SCULPTURE
1966–67   silk screen on
canvas, two parts,
each 68.5x 61.5 cm
Mulier Mulier Collection,
Knokke-Zoute, Belgium

ABSTRACT ART NO. 8
1967   silk screen on canvas,
60.9 x 38.1 cm
Mulier Mulier Collection,
Knokke-Zoute, Belgium

100% ABSTRACT
1967   acrylic on canvas,
85 x 62 cm
Private collection, Herentals,
Belgium

MAP OF A THIRTY-SIX SQUARE
MILE SURFACE AREA
OF THE PACIFIC OCEAN WEST
OF OAHU
1967   linotype on paper,
60.5 x 51.5 cm
Mulier Mulier Collection,
Knokke-Zoute, Belgium

SECRET PAINTING
1967–68   acrylic on
canvas, 152.5 x 152.5 cm
Mulier Mulier Collection,
Knokke-Zoute, Belgium

A PORTRAIT OF V. I. LENIN
IN THE STYLE OF
JACKSON POLLOCK
1980   oil and enamel
on canvas,
239 x 210 cm
Mulier Mulier Collection,
Knokke-Zoute, Belgium

INDEX: INCIDENT IN
A MUSEUM X
1986   oil on canvas,
174 x 271 cm
Mulier Mulier Collection,
Knokke-Zoute, Belgium

HOSTAGE VIII
1986   oil and canvas on
plywood, with acrylic on
canvas on plywood inserts,
190 x 183 cm
Mulier Mulier Collection,
Knokke-Zoute, Belgium

INDEX: INCIDENT IN A
MUSEUM (FRANCESCO SABATÉ)
1986   acrylic on canvas,
175 x 275 cm
Les Abattoirs, Toulouse
Pl. 204

INDEX XIV (NOW THEY ARE)
1991   oil on canvas,
191.7 x 163.5 cm
Mulier Mulier Collection,
Knokke-Zoute, Belgium

LAWRENCE ATKINSON

VORTICIST COMPOSITION
c. 1914–15   oil on canvas,
106.5 x 85 cm
Dr. Jeffrey and Ruth Sherwin
Pl. 8

ABSTRACT COMPOSITION NO. 1
1914–15   paper and
water-colour on paper,
26.3 x 17.9 cm
Leeds Museums and
Galleries

ABSTRACT
c. 1915–20   oil on wood,
129.5 x 50.8 cm
Arts Council Collection,
Hayward Gallery, London

FRANK AUERBACH

STUDY AFTER 'DEPOSITION'
BY REMBRANDT II
1961   oil on board,
180.3 x 121.9 cm
Private collection, courtesy
Anne Faggionato, London
Pl. 143

HEAD OF JYM
1983   oil on canvas,
52 x 62.5 cm
James Hyman, London
Pl. 194

FRANCIS BACON

FIGURE STUDY I
1945–46   oil on canvas,
123 x 105.5 cm
Scottish National Gallery
of Modern Art, Edinburgh.
Accepted by Her Majesty's
Government in lieu of
inheritance tax on the
estate of Gabrielle Keiller
(1908–95) and allocated
to the Scottish National
Gallery of Modern Art,
1998
Pl. 94

FIGURE STUDY II
1945–46   oil on canvas,
164 x 150 cm
Kirklees Cultural Services,
Huddersfield Art Gallery
Pl. 81

MAN KNEELING IN GRASS
1952   oil on canvas,
198 x 137 cm
Private collection,
courtesy Massimo Martino
Fine Arts & Projects,
Mendrisio

TRIPTYCH INSPIRED BY THE
ORESTEIA OF AESCHYLUS
1981   oil on canvas, three
panels, each 198 x 147.5 cm
Astrup Fearnley Collection,
Oslo, Norway
Pl. 193

JOHN BANTING

THE COUPLE
c. 1933   oil on board,
29 x 39 cm
Dr. Jeffrey and Ruth Sherwin
Pl. 54

ARIES
1935   oil on canvas,
43 x 53.5 cm
Dr. Jeffrey and Ruth Sherwin
Pl. 62

VANESSA BELL

ABSTRACT PAINTING
c. 1914   oil on canvas,
44.1 x 38.7 cm
Tate, London
Pl. 9

ABSTRACT COMPOSITION
1914   oil on canvas,
92.7 x 62.2 cm
Ivor Braka Ltd., London

DESIGN FOR LADY
IAN HAMILTON'S RUG
1914   bodypaint and graphite
on paper, 40.2 x 62.2 cm
The Courtauld Institute
Gallery, London

PORTRAIT OF DAVID GARNETT
1915   oil on board,
76.4 x 52.6 cm
National Portrait Gallery,
London

VANESSA BELL OR
DUNCAN GRANT

PAMELA
1914   Omega printed linen,
60 x 79 cm
The Gallery of Costume,
Manchester City Galleries
Pl. 12

PETER BLAKE

CHILDREN READING COMICS
1954   oil on hardboard,
36.7 x 47.1 cm
Tullie House Museum
& Art Gallery, Carlisle
Pl. 125

THE LOVE WALL
1961 collage construction,
125 x 237 x 23 cm
Fundação Calouste Gulbenkian/
CAMJAP, Lisbon
Pl. 129

THE BEATLES
1963–68 acrylic on
hardboard,
121.9 x 91 cm
The St. John Wilson Trust
Pl. 133

DAVID BOMBERG

STUDY FOR
'VISION OF EZEKIEL'
c. 1912 black chalk and
pencil on paper,
56.5 x 68.6 cm
Tate, London, donation by
estate administration of Mrs.
Helen Bentwich, 1972

THE DANCER
1913–14 watercolour
and charcoal on paper,
37.7 x 27.5 cm
Trustees of the Cecil Higgins
Art Gallery, Bedford
Pl. 5

STUDY FOR MUD BATH II
(FRONT)
COMPANY, HILL 60, ST. ELOI
(BACK)
1914 gouache, 45 x 68 cm
Ivor Braka Ltd., London
Pl. 10B, A

DEREK BOSHIER

ENGLAND'S GLORY
1962 oil on canvas,
126 x 101 cm
Museum Sztuki, Lódz
Pl. 127

DRINKA PINTA MILKA
1962 oil on canvas,
155 x 124.5 cm
Royal College of Art
Collection, London
Pl. 137

MAN VERSES LOOK
VERSES LIFE VERSES TIME
VERSES MAN ABOUT
1962 oil on canvas,
183 x 183 cm
Private collection
Pl. 144

PAULINE BOTY

MY COLOURING BOOK
1963 oil on canvas,
122 x 152 cm
Museum Sztuki, Lódz
Pl. 139

MARK BOYLE

UNTITLED
1964 metal and wood
on black painted wooden
background,
85 x 81 cm
Arts Council Collection,
Hayward Gallery, London
Pl. 179

MARK BOYLE AND JOAN
HILLS

OLAF STREET STUDY
1966 brick, stone, glass and
earth in resin on board,
213.4 x 218.4 cm
Arts Council Collection,
Hayward Gallery, London
Pl. 168

BOYLE FAMILY

VIDEO compilation
of early films (DIG;
EARTH, AIR, FIRE, WATER;
INSECTS, REPTILES
AND WATER CREATURES)
1966, compiled 2002
DVD, running time:
c. 15 minutes
Boyle Family
Pl. 184

BILL BRANDT

PARK STREET CRESCENT
IN BLACKOUT
1939 gelatine silver print,
32.5 x 39 cm
Arts Council Collection,
Hayward Gallery, London

AIR-RAID SHELTER IN
LIVERPOOL STREET
TUBE TUNNEL
1940 gelatine silver print,
32.5 x 38.4 cm
Arts Council Collection,
Hayward Gallery, London

OLD LADY IN PIMLICO
AIR-RAID SHELTER
1940 gelatine silver print,
33 x 40 cm
Arts Council Collection,
Hayward Gallery, London

VICTOR BURGIN

SENSATION
1975 triptych, photographic
prints, three panels,
each 119.4 x 83.8 cm
Arts Council Collection,
Hayward Gallery, London
Pl. 178

EDWARD BURRA

NEWS OF THE WORLD
1933–34 gouache,
78.6 x 54.6 cm
Bury Art Gallery
Pl. 57

THE BAND
1934 watercolour,
55.5 x 76 cm
The British Council

THE TORTURERS
1935 watercolour,
75.5 x 54.5 cm
Ivor Braka Ltd., London
Pl. 58

THE THREE FATES
c. 1937 watercolour,
132.1 x 111.8 cm
Ivor Braka Ltd., London
Pl. 40

REG BUTLER

ARCHAIC HEAD
1952 lead bronze,
width: 26.5 cm
Collection Ken Powell

WORKING MODEL FOR
MONUMENT TO 'THE UNKNOWN
POLITICAL PRISONER'
1955–56 forged and painted
steel, bronze and plaster,
223.8 x 87.9 x 85.4 cm
Tate, London, donation by
Cortina and Creon Butler
Pl. 106

ANTHONY CARO

BABY WITH A BALL
1955 bronze, unique cast
76 x 48 x 52 cm
Private collection, courtesy
Annely Juda Fine Art, London

SCULPTURE SEVEN
1961 steel, painted green,
blue and brown,
178 x 537 x 105.5 cm
Private collection, courtesy
Annely Juda Fine Art, London
Pl. 145

POMPADOUR
1963 steel, painted pink,
300 x 490 x 271 cm
Kröller-Müller Museum,
Otterlo, The Netherlands
Pl. 155

PATRICK CAULFIELD

VIEW OF THE ROOFTOPS
(VIEW OF THE CHIMNEYS)
1965 oil on canvas,
122 x 244 cm
Private collection

FOYER
1973 acrylic on canvas,
213.4 x 213.4 cm
David Bowie, courtesy
Chertavian Fine Arts

THE BLUE POSTS
1989 acrylic on canvas,
289.5 x 205.7 cm
The British Council
Pl. 205

DESK
1991 acrylic on canvas,
274.3 x 213.4 cm
Musée National d'Histoire
et d'Art, Luxembourg
Pl. 206

LYNN CHADWICK

TWO FIGURES
(DANCING FIGURES)
1956 bronze, height: 184 cm
Artist's collection
Pl. 105

ALAN CHARLTON

DOUBLE CHANNEL PAINTING
1972 acrylic on canvas,
244 x 335 cm
The Berardo Collection –
Sintra Museum of Modern Art
Pl. 165

CECIL COLLINS

OBSEQUIES OF TIME
1933 charcoal, pen, brush,
black ink, gum on paper,
38 x 55.8 cm
Dr. Jeffrey and Ruth Sherwin

ITHELL COLQUHOUN

TREE ANATOMY
1942 oil on wood panel,
57 x 29 cm
Dr. Jeffrey and Ruth Sherwin

THE DANCE OF THE NINE OPALS
1942 oil on canvas,
54.5 x 68.5 cm
Dr. Jeffrey and Ruth Sherwin
Pl. 88

TONY CRAGG

NEW STONES – NEWTON'S
TONES
1978 found plastic objects,
366 x 244 cm
Arts Council Collection,
Hayward Gallery, London
Pl. 197

PALETTE
1982 painted wood, plastic,
carpet, laminated wood,
record and paper,
236 x 310 cm
Kunstmuseum Wolfsburg
Pl. 198

GEORGE AND THE DRAGON
1984 plastic, wood and
aluminium,
110 x 400 x 120 cm
Arts Council Collection,
Hayward Gallery, London
Pl. 196

INSTINCTIVE REACTIONS
1987 cast steel,
240 x 350 x 450 cm
Kunstmuseum Wolfsburg

MICHAEL CRAIG-MARTIN

ON THE TABLE
1970 objects and water,
122 x 122 cm, height variable
Collection Jessica Craig-Martin
Pl. 185

AN OAK TREE
1973 glass of water, glass
shelf, chrome brackets, printed
text, 14.6 x 46.5 x 13.8 cm
(objects), 30.4 x 30.4 cm (text)
Courtesy National Gallery of
Australia, Canberra
Pl. 172

ALAN DAVIE

ALTAR FOR THE BLUE DIAMOND
1950 oil on hardboard,
180 x 241 cm
Private collection
Pl. 103

IMAGE OF THE FISH GOD
1956 oil on hardboard,
122 x 152.5 cm
The British Council
Pl. 104

IMP OF CLUBS
1957 oil on canvas,
213 x 172.7 cm
Ulster Museum Collection,
by kind permission
of the Trustees of the
National Museums and
Galleries of
Northern Ireland

THE ALCHEMIST
1958 oil on canvas,
225 x 300 cm
Private collection
Pl. 114

RICHARD DEACON

BOYS AND GIRLS
(COME OUT TO PLAY)
1982 lino and plywood,
91.5 x 183 x 152.2 cm
The British Council
Pl. 199

MIRROR, MIRROR
1983–84 mixed media,
198.5 x 152.4 x 30.5 cm
Southampton City Art Gallery

ROBYN DENNY

TED BENTLEY
1961 oil on canvas,
210 x 180 cm
Private collection
Pl. 153

SLOT
1961 acrylic on canvas,
213 x 168 cm
Fundação Calouste Gulbenkian/
CAMJAP, Lisbon
Pl. 145

JACOB EPSTEIN

CROUCHING SUN GODDESS
c. 1910 limestone,
37.5 x 10.8 x 13.3 cm
Nottingham City Museums &
Galleries, The Castle Museum
and Art Gallery

ONE OF THE HUNDRED PILLARS
OF THE SECRET TEMPLE
c. 1910 pencil on paper,
42 x 25.4 cm
Claire and James Hyman,
London
Pl. 11

STUDY FOR 'ROCK DRILL'
1913 black crayon on paper,
53.3 x 64.1 cm
Ivor Braka Ltd., London
Pl. 18

SKETCH OF DOVES
1913 Black chalk
and watercolour,
57 x 44.5 cm
The New Art Gallery, Walsall

THE ROCK DRILL
1913–15 /reconstruction 1976
polyester resin (figure), metal
(drill), wood (drill bit),
205 x 141.5 cm
Birmingham Museums &
Art Gallery, presented by
Ken Cook and Ann Christopher
(Friends of the Museum
and Art Gallery)
Pl. 17

DOVES
1914–15 marble,
64.8 x 78.7 x 34.3 cm
Tate, London
Pl. 4

FREDERICK ETCHELLS

STILTS
c. 1914–15 gouache
and pencil, 32 x 20 cm
The British Council
Pl. 22

PROGRESSION
1914–15 pen and inks on
paper, 14.3 x 22.3 cm
Trustees of the Cecil Higgins
Art Gallery, Bedford

MERLYN EVANS

TYRANNOPOLIS
(THE PROTESTERS)
1939 oil on canvas,
76 x 91.5 cm
Dr. Jeffrey and Ruth Sherwin
Pl. 66

IAN HAMILTON FINLAY
WITH JIM NICHOLSON

SUMMER POEM
1967 silk screen,
58.5 x 45 cm
Victoria Miro Gallery, London

IAN HAMILTON FINLAY

DRIFT
1968 construction,
painted wood and fish net,
33.5 x 141 x 5 cm
Towner Art Gallery & Local
Museum, Eastbourne
Pl. 170

SEAMS
1969 silk screen,
43.5 x 56.3 cm
Victoria Miro Gallery, London

IAN HAMILTON FINLAY
WITH RICHARD DEMARCO

A ROCK ROSE
1971 silk screen,
44.5 x 61 cm
Victoria Miro Gallery, London

IAN HAMILTON FINLAY
WITH JIM NICHOLSON

HOMAGE TO MODERN ART
1972 silk screen, 76 x 54 cm
Victoria Miro Gallery, London

SAIL WHOLEMEAL
1972 silk screen, 76 x 54 cm
Victoria Miro Gallery, London

IAN HAMILTON FINLAY
WITH RICHARD ENGLAND

HMS ILLUSTRIOUS
1972 silk screen,
49.6 x 76 cm
Victoria Miro Gallery, London

IAN HAMILTON FINLAY
WITH JUD FINE

LUFTWAFFE – AFTER
MONDRIAN
1976 lithograph,
41.5 x 53 cm
Victoria Miro Gallery, London

BARRY FLANAGAN

SAND/MUSLIN
1966 sand and muslin,
15.5 x 104.5 x 75 cm
Arts Council Collection,
Hayward Gallery, London

HEAP 4
1967 hessian filled with
sand, 15 pieces,
60 x 131 x 100 cm
Arts Council Collection,
Hayward Gallery, London
Pl. 184

PILE I 67/8
1968 hessian, 28 x 48 x 45 cm
Artist's collection, courtesy
Waddington Galleries
Pl. 171

LIGHT ON LIGHT ON SACKS
1969 40 bales of rags,
reflector, 200 x 530 x 240 cm

S.M.A.K. Collection
(Stedelijk Museum voor
Actuele Kunst), Ghent
Pl. 173

LUCIAN FREUD

HEAD OF A BOY WITH A BOOK
1944 Conté crayon and
coloured chalk on paper,
48 x 30.5 cm
Scottish National Gallery
of Modern Art, Edinburgh.
Bequeathed by
Gabrielle Keiller 1995

GIRL WITH FIG LEAF
1947 etching, no. 1 of an
edition of 10, 29.8 x 23.8 cm
Courtesy Swindon Museum
and Art Gallery, Swindon,
Borough Council, UK
Pl. 80

DEAD COCK'S HEAD
1951 oil on canvas,
20.3 x 12.7 cm
Arts Council Collection,
Hayward Gallery, London

OWL
1952 Conté and coloured
pencil on grey paper,
21.5 x 21.5 cm
Private collection, courtesy
Faggionato Fine Arts, London
Pl. 107

KINGCUPS – SOUVENIR OF
GLEN ARTNEY
1967 oil on canvas,
24 x 19 cm
The New Art Gallery, Walsall

PORTRAIT OF FRANCIS BACON
(UNFINISHED)
c. 1970 oil on linen,
36 x 36 cm
Private collection

NAKED GIRL WITH EGG
1980–81 oil on canvas,
75 x 60.5 cm
The British Council
Pl. 192

THE PAINTER'S MOTHER
1984 oil on canvas,
87.6 x 70 cm
Private collection

TWO MEN
1987–88 oil on canvas,
106.7 x 75 cm
Scottish National Gallery
of Modern Art, Edinburgh

ROGER FRY OR
FREDERICK ETCHELLS

MECHTILDE
1913 Omega printed linen,
55 x 79 cm
The Gallery of Costume,
Manchester City Galleries

NAUM GABO

COLUMN
1938 Perspex, 20 x 30 cm
S. Martin Mason
Pl. 35

ANYA GALLACCIO

RED ON GREEN
1992 10,000 red roses
on stalks, dimensions
variable
Claire and James Hyman,
London
Pl. 213

HENRI GAUDIER-BRZESKA

DUCK
c. 1914 marble,
6.5 x 12 x 4 cm
Kettle's Yard, University
of Cambridge

LE MARTYR DE ST. SÉBASTIEN
1914 ink on paper,
25.5 x 36.8 cm
Imperial War Museum, London

STUDY FOR BIRD SWALLOWING
A FISH
1914 pen and ink on paper,
30.5 x 37 cm
Kettle's Yard, University
of Cambridge
Pl. 19

BIRD SWALLOWING A FISH
1914 bronze, 31 x 60 x 29 cm
Kunsthalle Bielefeld
Pl. 20

THE WRESTLERS
1914 herculite cast,
76 x 97 cm
Dr. Jeffrey and Ruth Sherwin,
Leeds

WILLIAM GEAR

AUTUMN LANDSCAPE
1950 oil on canvas,
44 x 41 cm
Tyne and Wear Museums,
Newcastle-upon-Tyne

GILBERT AND GEORGE

IS NOT ART THE ONLY HOPE
FOR THE MAKING WAY
FOR THE MODERN WORLD TO
ENJOY THE SOPHISTICATION
OF DECADENT LIVING
EXPRESSION
1971 charcoal and paint on
paper, 280 x 450 cm
Private collection, courtesy
Massimo Martino Fine Arts &
Projects, Mendrisio

GORDON'S MAKES US DRUNK
1972 DVD and
framed certificate,
running time: 9 minutes
Arts Council Collection,
Hayward Gallery, London
Pl. 182

IN THE BUSH
1972 DVD and
framed certificate,
running time: 16 minutes
Arts Council Collection,
Hayward Gallery, London

THE MAJOR'S PORT
1972 35 black-and-white
photographs, 140 x 208 cm
Kunstmuseum Wolfsburg
Pl. 174

FUCK
1977 photopiece, 16 panels,
241 x 201 cm
Kunstmuseum Wolfsburg
Pl. 188

ROADS
1991 photopiece, 27 panels,
253 x 639 cm
Kunstmuseum Wolfsburg
Pl. 207

ANTONY GORMLEY

MOTHER'S PRIDE
1982 slices of bread and
wax, 305 x 190 x 0.8 cm
Modern Collections,
London
Pl. 203

RISE
1983–84 lead, fibreglass,
plaster and air,
30 x 58 x 190 cm
Artist's collection

TREE
1984 lead, fibreglass, plaster
and air, 472 x 60 x 30 cm
Artist's collection

DUNCAN GRANT

TENNIS PLAYER
1913 pencil, watercolour and
oil on canvas, 24.8 x 15.9 cm
The Courtauld Institute
Gallery, London

MALE DANCER (SKETCH FOR
A PAINTED SCREEN)
1913–14 oil on paper,
31.7 x 23.7 cm
The Courtauld Institute
Gallery, London

FEMALE DANCER (SKETCH
FOR A PAINTED SCREEN)
1913–14 oil on paper,
34.8 x 22.9 cm
The Courtauld Institute
Gallery, London
Pl. 6

PORTRAIT OF IRIS TREE
1915 oil on board,
63 x 76 cm
Reading Museum Service,
Reading Borough Council,
purchased with assistance
from the Victoria and Albert
Purchase Grant Scheme
Pl. 7

RICHARD HAMILTON
AND OTHERS

FUN HOUSE
1956 wood, metal and other
materials, 427.5 x 186.8 cm
IVAM, Instituto Valenciano
de Arte Moderno, Generalitat
Valenciana, Gift of Richard
Hamilton, Great Britain
Pl. 126

RICHARD HAMILTON

THIS IS TOMORROW. POSTER
1956 silk screen on paper,
76.5 x 50.7 cm
Collection Rita Donagh

THIS IS TOMORROW. COLLAGE
OF THE SENSES
1956 collage, 21 x 22.1 cm
Museum Ludwig, Cologne

WHITLEY BAY
1965 oil on photograph on
panel, 81.3 x 121.9 cm
Birmingham Museums & Art
Gallery
Pl. 140

SWINGEING LONDON 67 II
1968–69 oil on canvas and
silk screen, 67 x 85 cm
Museum Ludwig, Cologne

TREATMENT ROOM
1984 mixed media,
548 x 548 x 304 cm
Arts Council Collection,
Hayward Gallery, London
Pl. 196

EPIPHANY
1964 (1989) cellulose on
aluminium fabric, Ø 112 cm
IVAM, Instituto Valenciano
de Arte Moderno,
Generalitat Valenciana
Pl. 141

NINA HAMNETT

VIEW OF OMEGA INTERIOR
1917 oil and graphite on
paper, 46.9 x 30.7 cm
The Courtauld Institute
Gallery, London
Pl. 13

ADRIAN HEATH

CLIMBING COMPOSITION
GREEN AND BLUE
1950 oil on canvas,
81.5 x 50.6 cm
Collection Ken Powell
Pl. 96

NIGEL HENDERSON

PHOTOGRAM WITH STRAINER
1949 photogram,
35.6 x 47.7 cm
The Henderson Estate

HEADS SEEN THROUGH PUB
WINDOW
1949–53 photograph,
20.3 x 25.4 cm
The Henderson Estate

SHOP FRONT, BETHNAL
GREEN (S. LAVNER)
1949–53 photograph,
20.3 x 25.4 cm
The Henderson Estate

SHOP ENTRANCE
(GIRL AND BEAD CURTAIN)
1949–53 photograph,
20.3 x 25.4 cm
The Henderson Estate

PETTICOAT LANE MARKET
1952 photograph,
20.3 x 25.4 cm
The Henderson Estate

VERTICAL STATUE
1952 stressed photographic
print mounted on board,
50.9 x 23.5 cm

Arts Council Collection,
Hayward Gallery, London
Pl. 111

NIGEL HENDERSON AND
EDUARDO PAOLOZZI

STUDY FOR PARALLEL OF
LIFE AND ART
1952 photographs,
ink and pencil on board,
35.5 x 77.5 cm
The Henderson Estate
Pl. 124

NIGEL HENDERSON,
EDUARDO PAOLOZZI AND
PETER AND ALISON
SMITHSON

PARALLEL OF LIFE AND ART.
RECONSTRUCTION
1953 / reconstruction 2002
80 panels: 15 panels,
each 95 x 60 cm; 35 panels,
each 40 x 50 cm and
30 panels, each 25 x 35 cm
The Henderson Estate

NIGEL HENDERSON

HEAD OF A MAN
1956–61 oil and
photographic processes on
card, 152.4 x 121.9 cm
Arts Council Collection,
Hayward Gallery, London
Pl. 120

BARBARA HEPWORTH

LARGE AND SMALL FORM
1934 white alabaster,
25 x 45 x 24 cm
The Pier Gallery, Stromness,
Orkney
Pl. 32

TWO FORMS
1934–35 grey alabaster,
20.4 x 43.5 x 18.3 cm
Private collection
Pl. 41

TWO FORMS
1934–35 white alabaster,
14.3 x 29.4 x 15.3 cm
Private collection
Pl. 42

FORM OPUS 82
1934–36 marble,
height: 29 cm
Gimpel Fils, London

CONOID, SPHERE AND
HOLLOW II
1937 white marble,
32 x 35.5 x 30.5 cm
UK Government Art Collection

HELICOID IN SPHERE
1938 wood,
26 x 25 x 22.5 x 30.5 cm
S. Martin Mason
Pl. 34

CONICOID
1939 teak, height: 20.4 cm
Leeds Museums and Galleries
Pl. 37

PATRICK HERON

RED VERTICALS
1957 oil on canvas,
86 x 112 cm
Scott Collection
Pl. 100

BLUE PAINTING (SQUARES
AND DISC)
1958–59 oil on canvas,
152.4 x 121.5 cm
Collection Ken Powell

BIG GREY – WITH DISC:
JUNE – SEPTEMBER 1959
1959 oil on canvas,
213.4 x 152.4 cm
The Artist's Family, courtesy
Waddington Galleries
Pl. 101

ANTHONY HILL

UNTITLED
1950 oil on canvas
with collage,
52.7 x 36.4 cm
Collection Ken Powell
Pl. 98

RELIEF CONSTRUCTION
1955–56 aluminium
and Perspex, 61 x 61 x 6.5 cm
The British Council
Pl. 112

RELIEF CONSTRUCTION
1960–61 vinyl and alumini-
um, 91.5 x 91.5 x 8.5 cm
Fundação Calouste Gulbenkian/
CAMJAP, Lisbon
Pl. 118

ROGER HILTON

JUNE TO SEPTEMBER 1953
1953 oil on canvas,
33 x 44 cm
Dr. Jeffrey and Ruth Sherwin

OCTOBER '56 (BROWN,
BLACK & WHITE)
1956 oil on canvas,
140 x 127 cm
The British Council
Pl. 113

DANCING WOMAN
1963 oil and black chalk
on canvas, 152.5 x 127 cm
Scottish National Gallery of
Modern Art, Edinburgh
Pl. 136

DAMIEN HIRST

A HUNDRED YEARS
1990 glass, steel, MDF
board, flies, fly zapper and
bowls of sugar water,
213 x 426 x 213 cm
Kunstmuseum Wolfsburg
Pl. 214

DAVID HOCKNEY

GOING TO BE A QUEEN
FOR TONIGHT
1960 oil on card,
122 x 91.4 cm
Collection of the Royal
College of Art, London
Pl. 128

I'M IN THE MOOD FOR LOVE
1962 oil on canvas on board,
127 x 101.6 cm
Collection of the Royal
College of Art, London
Pl. 130

SUNBATHER
1966 acrylic on canvas,
183 x 183 cm
Museum Ludwig, Cologne

HOWARD HODGKIN

ANTHONY HILL AND
GILLIAN WISE
1963–66 oil on canvas,
107 x 127 cm
Private collection
Pl. 135

FOY NISSEN'S BOMBAY
1975–77 oil on wood,
71.1 x 91.6
Arts Council Collection,
Hayward Gallery, London
Pl. 180

STILL LIFE IN A RESTAURANT
1976–77 oil on wood,
92.7 x 118.1 cm
The British Council
Pl. 189

IT CAN'T BE TRUE
1982 oil on wood,
76.5 x 71 cm
Blackburn Associates Ltd.

JOHN HOYLAND

FEB. 12/62. NO. 21
1966 oil on canvas,
213.4 x 243.8 cm
Private collection
Pl. 162

GARY HUME

FOUR DOORS I
1989–90 gloss paint
on four canvases,
239 x 594 cm
The Saatchi Gallery,
London
Pl. 205

PAUL HUXLEY

UNTITLED NO. 36
1964 oil on canvas,
173 x 173 cm
Fundação Calouste Gulbenkian/
CAMJAP, Lisbon
Pl. 159

HUMPHREY JENNINGS

COMMODE WITH SWISS ROLL
1936 photograph with
collage,
21.5 x 25.5 cm
Dr. Jeffrey and Ruth Sherwin
Pl. 59

ALLEN JONES

9TH BUS,
YELLOW OCHRE LADY
1962 oil on canvas/
rhomboid, 62.2 x 62.2 cm
Private collection
Pl. 148

HERMAPHRODITE
1963 oil on canvas,
213.4 x 121.9 cm
Lent by the Board of Trustees
of the National Museums and
Galleries on Merseyside (the
Walker, Liverpool)

DAVID JONES

LLYS CEIMIAD: LA BAISSÉE
FRONT, 1916
1937 watercolour,
38.7 x 32.3 cm

The National Library of Wales,
Aberystwyth
Pl. 50

ILLUSTRATION TO THE
ARTHURIAN LEGEND:
GUENEVER
1938–40 watercolour on
paper, 62.2 x 49.5 cm
Tate, London

APHRODITE IN AULIS
1940–41 pencil, ink
and watercolour on paper,
61 x 79 cm
Tate, London
Pl. 78

PETER JOSEPH

CREAM COLOUR WITH
BLACK BORDER
1970 acrylic on canvas,
300 x 147.5 cm
Courtesy Lisson Gallery,
London
Pl. 164

ANISH KAPOOR

1000 NAMES
(NOS. 10 AND 11)
1979–80 mixed media,
pigment,
left side: 29 x 91.5 x 91.5 cm,
right side: 18 x 91.5 x 91.5 cm
Artist's collection, courtesy
Lisson Gallery, London

WHITE SAND, RED MILLET,
MANY FLOWERS
1982 wood, cement
and pigment,
101 x 241.5 x 217.4 cm
Arts Council Collection,
Hayward Gallery, London
Pl. 201

PHILLIP KING

ROSEBUD
1962 plastic,
152.5 x 183 x 183 cm
artist copy, artist's collection
Pl. 157

RIPPLE
1963 plastic,
188 x 89 x 77 cm
Fundação Calouste Gulbenkian/
CAMJAP, Lisbon
Pl. 146

R. B. KITAJ

HOMAGE TO
HERMAN MELVILLE
1960 oil on canvas,
152.4 x 152.4 cm
Collection of the Royal
College of Art, London

REFLECTIONS ON VIOLENCE
1962 oil and collage
on canvas, 152.4 x 152.4 cm
Hamburger Kunsthalle
Pl. 131

LEON KOSSOFF

BUILDING SITE,
VICTORIA STREET
1961 oil on board,
122.5 x 184.8
Arts Council Collection,
Hayward Gallery, London

CHILDREN'S SWIMMING POOL
1972 oil on board,
182.9 x 213.4 cm
Arts Council Collection,
Hayward Gallery, London
Pl. 189

FIDELMA NO. 1
1978 oil on board,
92 x 61 cm
James Hyman, London
Pl. 190

HENRY LAMB

IRISH TROOPS IN THE JUDEAN
HILLS SURPRISED BY A
TURKISH BOMBARDMENT
1919 oil on canvas,
182.8 x 218.4 cm
Imperial War Museum,
London

MICHAEL LANDY

APPROPRIATION
1990 3 DVDs
Simmons & Simmons
Pl. 212

PETER LANYON

ST. JUST
1953 oil on canvas,
243.8 x 121.9 cm
Private collection

WHEAL OWLES
1957–58 oil on Masonite,
120.5 x 181.5 cm
Private collection
Pl. 99

DARK MINE COAST
1964 gouache on paper,
76.4 x 57.8 cm
UK Government Art Collection

JOHN LATHAM

FULL STOP
1961 ink on canvas,
301 x 249 cm
Courtesy Lisson Gallery,
London
Pl. 167

SEEIN'S BELIEVIN'
1961 books on board,
canvas bond, 122 x 91 x 20 cm
Courtesy Lisson Gallery,
London
Pl. 166

BOB LAW

BLACK PAINTING # 48
1966 oil on canvas,
175 x 168 cm
Private collection
Pl. 163

PERCY WYNDHAM LEWIS

DRAWING FOR
TIMON OF ATHENS
1912 ink, gouache and
watercolour on paper,
38 x 28.5 cm
Private collection

THE VORTICIST
1912 watercolour on paper,
61.5 x 48 x 3 cm
Southampton City Art Gallery
Pl. 1

THE COURTESAN
1912 pen, pastels on paper,
57.5 x 42.3 x 2.3 cm
Victoria and Albert Museum,
London
Pl. 2

ABSTRACT DESIGN
1912 ink, watercolour
and collage, 24.3 x 39 cm
The British Council
Pl. 15

THE CROWD (REVOLUTION)
1915 oil and pencil
on canvas, 200.7 x 153.7 cm
Tate, London. Gift of
the Friends of the
Tate Gallery, 1964
Pl. 23

DRAWING OF THE GREAT WAR
No. 1 (THE MENIN ROAD)
c. 1918 watercolour
on paper, 54.2 x 72 x 2.1 cm
Southampton City Art Gallery
Pl. 26

DRAWING OF GREAT WAR
No. 2
c. 1918 watercolour on
paper, 54.2 x 72 x 2.1 cm
Southampton City Art Gallery
Pl. 27

BATTERY POSITION
IN A WOOD
1918 ink and
watercolour on paper,
31.7 x 46.9 cm
Imperial War Museum, London
Pl. 14

RICHARD LONG

LINE MADE BY WALKING,
ENGLAND
1967 black-and-white
photograph,
30 x 37 cm
Private collection, Düsseldorf,
courtesy Konrad Fischer
Galerie

A TEN MILE WALK, ENGLAND
1968 map fragment,
68.5 x 63.6 cm
Private collection, courtesy
Konrad Fischer Galerie
Pl. 177

STONE CIRCLE
1972 stones,
14 x 426.7 x 426.7 cm
Arts Council Collection,
Hayward Gallery, London
Pl. 181

AN 84 MILE CANOE JOURNEY
DOWN THE RIVER SEVERN.
A JOURNEY OF THE SAME
LENGTH AS RIVER AVON
1977 two frames,
each 84.5 x 120 cm,
one frame: black-and-white
photograph, 40 x 58 cm,
one frame:
pencil and ink on paper,
84.5 x 120 cm
Private collection, Krefeld

F. E. MCWILLIAM

THE LONG ARM (FIST RAISED
IN A REPUBLICAN SALUTE)
1939 lime wood and paint,
188 x 17 x 17 cm
Dr. Jeffrey and Ruth Sherwin
Pl. 44

CONROY MADDOX

THE LESSON
1938 oil on canvas,
81 x 71 cm
Dr. Jeffrey and Ruth Sherwin

ONANISTIC TYPEWRITER
1940 typewriter,
23 x 40 x 40 cm
Conroy Maddox Surrealist

KENNETH MARTIN

WORKING DRAWING FOR
SCREW MOBILE
1955 pencil and coloured
crayon on graph paper,
76.2 x 55.9 cm
The Estate of Kenneth Martin,
courtesy Annely Juda
Fine Art, London

SCREW MOBILE
1956 copper,
height: 16 cm, Ø 42 cm
The Family of Adrian Heath

MARY MARTIN

COLUMBARIUM
1951 plaster,
21.5 x 21.5 x 2.5 cm
The Estate of Mary Martin,
courtesy Annely Juda
Fine Art, London
Pl. 115

SPIRAL MOVEMENT
1954 painted wood,
61 x 61 x 7.6 cm
Arts Council Collection,
Hayward Gallery, London

WHITE FACED RELIEF
1959 construction,
painted wood on wood,
61 x 91.5 x 18.5 cm
Fundação Calouste Gulbenkian/
CAMJAP, Lisbon
Pl. 119

WHITE DIAGONAL
1963 stainless steel, Formica
and wood, 85 x 85 x 11.5 cm
The Estate of Mary Martin,
courtesy Annely Juda Fine Art,
London
Pl. 147

BERNARD MEADOWS

THE BLACK CRAB
1953 bronze, height: 42 cm
Dr. Jeffrey and Ruth Sherwin
Pl. 108

REUBEN MEDNIKOFF

ARBOREAL BLISS
1935 oil on canvas,
60 x 49.5 cm
Dr. Jeffrey and Ruth Sherwin
Pl. 52

LEE MILLER

PORTRAIT OF SPACE,
NR. SIWA, EGYPT
1937 silver gelatine
modern print,
27.8 x 30.2 cm
Photograph by Lee Miller,
© Lee Miller Archives,
Chiddingly, England
Pl. 47

COCK ROCK OR THE NATIVE,
NR. SIWA, EGYPT
1939 silver gelatine
modern print,
27.8 x 27.8 cm
Photograph by Lee Miller,
© Lee Miller Archives,
Chiddingly, England

HENRY MOORE SKETCHING IN
HOLBORN UNDERGROUND
STATION (SCENE FROM THE
FILM OUT OF CHAOS)
1943 silver gelatine
modern print,
25.3 x 25.5 cm
Photograph by Lee Miller,
© Lee Miller Archives,
Chiddingly, England

JEREMY MOON

CONCORD
1964 acrylic on canvas,
127.5 x 373 cm
Fundação Calouste Gulbenkian/
CAMJAP, Lisbon
Pl. 152

HENRY MOORE

DOG
1922 marble,
height: 17.8 cm
The Henry Moore Foundation,
donated by the artist 1977

THE SNAKE
1927 marble
Private collection

GIRL WITH CLASPED HANDS
1930 Cumberland
alabaster,
height: 38.1 cm
The British Council
Pl. 31

HEAD AND BALL
1934 Cumberland alabaster,
width: 51 cm
The Henry Moore Foundation
Pl. 43

HOLE AND LUMP
1934 elmwood,
height: 68.6 cm
The Henry Moore Foundation,
donated by the artist 1979

MOTHER AND CHILD
1936 Ancaster stone,
height: 30.8 cm
The British Council
Pl. 33

TWO FORMS
1936 brown Hornton stone,
width: 64 cm
The Henry Moore Foundation,
donated by Irina Moore 1979

STRINGED RELIEF
1937 bronze and nylon,
(edition of 2 + 1 ap),
width: 49.5 cm
The Henry Moore Foundation,
donated by the artist 1977

MOTHER AND CHILD
1938 bronze and red string,
(edition of 9 + 1 ap),
height: 9.5 cm
The Henry Moore Foundation

STRINGED FIGURE
1938 bronze and string,
20.3 x 35.6 x 25.4 cm
Arts Council Collection,
Hayward Gallery, London
Pl. 36

FIGURE
1939 bronze and string,
width: 25.3 cm
Leeds Museums and Galleries

HEAD
1939 bronze and string,
(edition of 6 + 1 ap),
height: 13.7 cm
The Henry Moore Foundation

MOTHER AND CHILD
1939 bronze and string
(edition of 9 + 1 ap),
width: 19 cm
The Henry Moore Foundation,
donated by Irina Moore 1977

STRINGED FIGURE
1939 lead and violet string,
width: 25.4 cm
The Henry Moore Foundation,
donated by Irina Moore 1977

THREE POINTS
1939–40 cast iron, unique,

width: 20 cm
The Henry Moore Foundation,
donated by Irina Moore 1977

EIGHTEEN IDEAS
FOR WAR DRAWINGS
1940 pencil, wax crayon,
coloured crayon, watercolour
wash, pen and ink on
cream medium-weight weave,
27.4 x 37.6 cm
The Henry Moore Foundation,
donated by the artist 1977
Pl. 73

SECOND SHELTER
SKETCHBOOK
1940–41 pencil,
wax crayon, coloured cray-
on, watercolour, wash,
pen and ink, gouache,
each 20.4 x 16.5 cm
Tube Shelter Scenes,
p. 4
Study for Shelterers in
the Tube, p. 5
Women and Children
With Bundles, p. 6
Three Figures Sleeping:
Study for Shelter Drawing, p. 7
Study for Shelter Drawing,
p. 12
Study for Tilbury Shelter
Scene, p. 13
Study for Group of Shelterers
During an Air Raid, p. 17
Study for Brown Sleepers
in a Shelter, p. 18
Study for Mother and Child
Among Underground
Sleepers, p. 20
Figure Studies: People Sharing
Blankets, p. 22
Study for Tube Shelter
Perspective: The Liverpool
Street Extension, p. 24
Study for Shelter Scene:
Three Groups of Sleeping
Figures, p. 27
Sleeping Figures, p. 28
Tube Shelter Perspective,
p. 29
Sleeping Figures, p. 30
Study for Row of Sleepers,
S. 32
Study for Shelter Scene:
Bunks and Sleepers, p. 33
Sleeping Positions, p. 39
Sleeping Figures, p. 43
Group of Shelterers, p. 48
Studies for Tube Shelter
Scene and Figure in a
Shelter, p. 51
Groups of Shelterers, p. 55
Sleeping Figures, p. 57
Sea of Sleepers, p. 62
Study for Two Women
Wrapped in Blankets, p. 66
Sleeping Shelterer, p. 69
Bunks and Sleepers, p. 73

Bunks and Sleepers, p. 75
Shelter Mother and Child
   Studies, p. 76
Two Figures Sharing Same
   Green Blanket, p. 80
Sleeping Positions, p. 81
Study for Shelter Sleepers,
   p. 84
Dozing Shelterers, p. 85
Sleeping Shelterers, p. 88
Restless Sleepers, p. 91
Four Shelter Scenes, p.93
The Henry Moore Foundation,
Gift of Irina Moore 1977
Pl. 74–77, 82

LARGE SHELTER SKETCHBOOK
1941   sketchbook with 16
drawings, 29.2 x 24.2 cm
The Henry Moore Foundation

MOTHER AND CHILD
AMONG UNDERGROUND
SLEEPERS
1941   pencil, wax crayon,
watercolour, wash,
pen and ink, gouache on
cream medium-weight move,
48.5 x 43.9 cm
The Henry Moore Foundation

TUBE SHELTER PERSPECTIVE
1941   pencil, wax crayon,
coloured crayon, watercolour,
wash, gouache on
off-white lightweight wove,
29.2 x 24.2 cm
The Henry Moore Foundation,
donated by the artist 1977

FALLING WARRIOR
1956–57   bronze,
194 x 96 x 88 cm
Board of Trustees of the
National Museums and
Galleries on Merseyside
(The Walker, Liverpool)

CASE FULL OF OBJECTS FROM
MAQUETTES STUDIO
Plaster maquettes by Henry
Moore and found objects from
his studio, from the Henry
Moore Foundation
The Henry Moore Foundation

PAUL NASH

THE MENIN ROAD
1919   oil on canvas,
182.8 x 317.5 cm
Imperial War Museum,
London
Pl. 29

THE SHORE
1923   oil on canvas,
62.2 x 94 cm
Leeds Museums and Galleries

NORTHERN ADVENTURE
1929   oil on canvas,
91.5 x 71.2 cm
Aberdeen Art Gallery
and Museums
Pl. 39

LANDSCAPE OF THE
MEGALITHS
1934   oil on canvas,
49.5 x 73 cm
The British Council
Pl. 38

BATTLE OF GERMANY
1944   oil on canvas,
121.9 x 181.8 cm
Imperial War Museum,
London
Pl. 92

ECLIPSE OF THE SUNFLOWER
1945   oil on canvas,
71.1 x 91.4 cm
The British Council
Pl. 91

CHRISTOPHER NEVINSON

THE FIRST SEARCHLIGHTS
AT CHARING CROSS
1914   oil on canvas,
60.9 x 40.6 cm
Leeds Museums and Galleries

COLUMN ON THE MARCH
1915   oil on canvas,
63.8 x 76.6 cm
Birmingham Museums &
Art Gallery, presented by
Sir Adrian Cadbury in
memory of Laurence and
Joyce Cadbury
Pl. 25

THE HARVEST OF BATTLE
1919   oil on canvas,
182.8 x 317.5 cm
Imperial War Museum,
London
Pl. 30

BEN NICHOLSON

STILL LIFE -19 GREEK
LANDSCAPE
1931–36   oil and
pencil on canvas,
68.5 x 77.5 cm
The British Council

1934 (WHITE RELIEF)
1934   oil on board,
15.2 x 20.3 cm
Dr. & Mrs. W. T. Mason

PROJECT FOR DROP
CURTAIN FOR MASSINE'S
BEETHOVEN 7TH SYMPHONY
BALLET
1934   oil on board,
25.5 x 22 cm
Dr. & Mrs. W. T. Mason

1942 (TWO FORMS)
1942   oil on canvas,
96 x 97.2 x 7 cm
Southampton City Art Gallery
Pl. 71

1944 (RELIEF)
1944   oil on board,
25.5 x 22 cm
Dr. & Mrs. W. T. Mason

NOVEMBER 11–47
(MOUSEHOLE)
1947   oil on canvas,
mounted on wood,
46.5 x 58.5 cm
The British Council
Pl. 90

JULIAN OPIE

FIVE OLD MASTERS
1984   oil on steel,
150 x 120 x 70 cm
Courtesy Lisson Gallery,
London
Pl. 204

GRACE PAILTHORPE

OCTOBER 3 AND 4 (WIND)
1935   watercolour on paper,
28.5 x 39 cm
Private collection,
Saffron Walden
Pl. 45

COMPOSITION
(APRIL 22, 1940)
1940   oil on board,
58.5 x 40.5 cm
Dr. Jeffrey and Ruth Sherwin
Pl. 69

EDUARDO PAOLOZZI

UNTITLED (MATERNITY)
1946   collage on board,
19.5 x 13.8 cm
Scottish National Gallery
of Modern Art, Edinburgh.
Bequeathed by Gabrielle
Keiller, 1995

COLLAGE
1948   collage on board,
91.4 x 152.4 cm
Private collection
Pl. 38

COLLAGE
1950   collage on paper,
38.1 x 24.9 cm
Collection Ken Powell
Pl. 97

THE CAGE
1951   bronze,
148 x 75.6 x 75 cm
Arts Council Collection,
Hayward Gallery, London
Pl. 116

THE PHILOSOPHER
1957   bronze,
height: 188 cm
The British Council
Pl. 121

DIANA AS AN ENGINE
1963–66   welded and
painted aluminium,
height: 162.6 cm
The British Council
Pl. 132

VICTOR PASMORE

POSTER FOR
THE LONDON GROUP
1948   lithograph,
15.8 x 49.2 cm
Collection Ken Powell
Pl. 86

RECTANGULAR MOTIF IN
BLACK AND WHITE
1949   collage,
110.5 x 83.2 cm
The Family of Adrian Heath
Pl. 97

RELIEF IN WHITE, BLACK,
BROWN AND LILAC
1957   painted wood
on board,
95.3 x 102.9 cm
The British Council
Pl. 109

ROLAND PENROSE

UNTITLED (COLLAGE)
1937   collage,
80.5 x 55.4 cm
Scottish National Gallery
of Modern Art, Edinburgh.
Bequeathed by Gabrielle
Keiller, 1995
Pl. 61

OCTAVIA
1939   oil on canvas,
77.5 x 63.5 cm
Ferens Art Gallery, Hull City
Museums & Art Gallery
Pl. 53

PETER PHILLIPS

GRAVY FOR THE NAVY
1963   oil on canvas
and hardboard,
240 x 159 x 5 cm
Gallery Oldham
Pl. 134

CERI RICHARDS

DRAWING FOR A RELIEF
1936   black ink,
wash on paper,
43 x 51.5 cm
Dr. Jeffrey and Ruth Sherwin
Pl. 46

BRIDGET RILEY

MOVEMENT IN SQUARES
1962   tempera on board,
123.2 x 121.3 cm
Arts Council Collection,
Hayward Gallery, London
Pl. 151

CREST
1964   emulsion on board,
166 x 166 cm
The British Council
Pl. 149

CATARACT 3
1967   emulsion on board,
221.9 x 222.9 cm
The British Council
Pl. 150

APRÈS-MIDI
1981   oil on linen,
231 x 197 cm
Private collection,
courtesy Karsten Schubert,
London

BALI
1983   oil on linen,
237 x 195 cm
Private collection, courtesy
Karsten Schubert, London

BLUE RETURN
1983   oil on linen,
177 x 152.5 cm
Private collection,
courtesy Karsten Schubert,
London

WILLIAM ROBERTS

THE RETURN OF ULYSSES
1913   chalk and
watercolour on paper,
30.5 x 46 cm
Tate, London
Pl. 3

THE RETURN OF ULYSSES
1913   oil on canvas,
30.5 x 45.7 cm
Nottingham City Museums
& Galleries, The Castle Museum and Art Gallery

TOMMIES FILLING THEIR
WATER BOTTLES
WITH RAIN FROM A SHELL,
AUGUST 18, 1918
1918   ink, pencil, chalk,
watercolour on paper,
50.8 x 38.1 cm
Imperial War Museum, London
Pl. 28

BURYING THE DEAD AFTER
A BATTLE
1919   black crayon,
50.2 x 45.7 cm
Imperial War Museum, London

HELEN SAUNDERS

VORTICIST DESIGN
(MAN AND DOG)
c. 1915   gouache on paper,
38 x 30 cm
Private collection
Pl. 24

VORTICIST COMPOSITION IN
BLUE AND GREEN
1915   ink and watercolour
on paper, 25 x 19.5 cm
Private collection
Pl. 16

KURT SCHWITTERS

MR. CHURCHILL IS 71
1945–47 collage and gouache,
19.5 x 16 cm
Dr. Jeffrey and Ruth Sherwin

TIM SCOTT

ROUND MIDNIGHT
1961   glass and emulsion
paint on wood,
121.9 x 198.1 x 121.9 cm
Arts Council Collection,
Hayward Gallery, London

WILLIAM SCOTT

TABLE STILL LIFE
1951   oil on canvas,
142 x 183 cm
The British Council
Pl. 102

SEATED FIGURE
1953 oil on canvas, 153 x 76 cm
Scott Collection

ORANGE STILL LIFE
1956–57 oil on canvas,
122 x 152.5 cm
Scott Collection

RICHARD SMITH

PACKAGE
1962 oil on canvas,
152.5 x 213.5 cm
Fundação Calouste Gulbenkian/
CAMJAP, Lisbon

FLAP TOP
1962 oil on canvas,
172.7 x 177 cm
Private collection
Pl. 158

STANLEY SPENCER

NUDE, PORTRAIT OF
PATRICIA PREECE
c. 1935 oil on canvas,
76.2 x 50.8 cm
Ferens Art Gallery, Hull City
Museums & Art Library
Pl. 49

SELF-PORTRAIT
1936 oil on canvas,
61.5 x 46 cm
Stedelijk Museum, Amsterdam

GARDENS IN THE POUND,
COOKHAM
1936 oil on canvas,
91.5 x 76.2 cm
Leeds Museums and Galleries
Pl. 48

SELF-PORTRAIT NUDE
1938–39   pencil on
wallpaper, 213.4 x 53.4 cm
Private collection, courtesy
Massimo Martino Fine Arts
& Projects, Mendrisio

THE SISTERS
1940 oil on canvas,
121.9 x 76.2 cm
Leeds Museums and Galleries
Pl. 72

SHIPBUILDERS ON THE CLYDE:
BURNERS
1940 oil on canvas,
triptych, centre panel
106.7 x 153.4 cm,
wings each 50.8 x 203.2 cm
Imperial War Museum, London
Pl. 70

SHIPBUILDERS ON THE CLYDE:
WELDERS
1941 oil on canvas, triptych,
centre panel c. 106 x 153 cm,

wings each c. 51 x 205 cm
Imperial War Museum, London

GRAHAM SUTHERLAND

RED TREE
1936 oil on canvas,
56.4 x 92.1 cm
Collection B.P., London

GORSE ON SEA WALL
1939 oil on canvas,
62.2 x 48.3 cm
Ulster Museum Collection,
by kind permission of the
Trustees of the National
Museums and Galleries of
Northern Ireland
Pl. 67

BLACK LANDSCAPE
1939–40   oil and sand
on canvas, 81 x 132.1 cm
Tate, London
Pl. 68

FOUR STUDIES OF
BOMB DAMAGE
1941   chalk, ink, wash
and pencil on paper,
25 x 19.2 cm
Arts Council Collection,
Hayward Gallery, London
Pl. 83

SLAG LADLES
1942   gouache on paper,
51.4 x 37.7 cm
Imperial War Museum, London
Pl. 84

TIN MINE - A DECLIVITY
1942   watercolour, gouache,
pen and black ink and wash,
coloured chalks, wax crayons
and pencil,
47.5 x 94.5 cm
Ivor Braka Ltd., London
Pl. 79

TIN MINE: EMERGING MINER
1942   gouache on paper,
116.8 x 73 cm
Leeds Museums and Galleries

TIN MINE - A DECLIVITY
1942   gouache on paper,
mounted on cardboard,
117 x 73 cm
Leeds Museums and Galleries

RED LANDSCAPE
1942   oil on canvas,
94.5 x 127 x 7 cm
Southampton City Art Gallery
Pl. 89

OPENCAST COAL PRODUCTION:
DRAGLINE DEPOSITING
EXCAVATED EARTH
1943   gouache on paper
on board, 69.3 x 66.1 cm
Leeds Museums and Galleries
Pl. 85

THORN TREE
1945–46   oil on canvas,
127 x 101.5 cm
The British Council
Pl. 99

JOE TILSON

FOR JOS, JANUARY 1, 1963
1962–63 oil on wood,
182 x 244 cm
Private collection
Pl. 138

JULIAN TREVELYAN

CAPTIVE IN EDEN
1936   slate and paint,
40.5 x 30.5 cm
Dr. Jeffrey and Ruth Sherwin
Pl. 60

WILLIAM TUCKER

FLORIDA
1962   fibreglass and steel,
119.2 x 96.5 x 49.5 cm
Arts Council Collection,
Hayward Gallery, London
Pl. 156

MEMPHIS
1965–66   plywood and
fibreglass (1 edition of 3),
76.2 x 142.3 x 165.1 cm
The British Council

JOHN TUNNARD

DIABOLO ON THE QUAY
1936   oil on canvas,
43 x 61 cm
Dr. Jeffrey and Ruth Sherwin
Pl. 65

WILLIAM TURNBULL

HEAD
1955   bronze,
22.9 x 22.9 x 61 cm
Arts Council Collection,
Hayward Gallery, London
Pl. 117

HEAD 2
1955   bronze,
14 x 12.7 x 20.3 cm

Artist's collection, courtesy
Waddington Galleries

APHRODITE
1958   bronze,
190.5 x 50.2 x 73.7 cm
Artist's collection, courtesy
Waddington Galleries
Pl. 122

25–1959
1959   oil on canvas,
254 x 190.5 cm
Artist's collection, courtesy
Waddington Galleries
Pl. 161

EDWARD WADSWORTH

ABSTRACT COMPOSITION
1915   gouache, pen
and pencil on paper,
41.9 x 34.3 cm
Tate, London
Pl. 109

CAMOUFLAGE, DRYDOCKED
FOR SCALING AND PAINTING
1918   woodcut,
33 x 26.3 cm
Imperial War Museum, London

AIRY NOTHINGS
1937   tempera,
53.4 x 38.1 cm
Private collection, courtesy
Crane Kalman Gallery, London

CLUSTER
1937   tempera,
54.4 x 38.1 cm
Private collection, courtesy
Crane Kalman Gallery, London

ALFRED WALLIS

TRAWLER
c. 1925   oil on board,
31.8 x 48.9 cm
Arts Council Collection,
Hayward Gallery, London

HARBOUR WITH
TWO LIGHTHOUSES
AND MOTOR VESSEL
c. 1932   oil on cardboard,
51 x 64 cm
Kettle's Yard, University
of Cambridge
Pl. 55

WHITE HOUSES
c. 1932   oil on board,
20 x 17 cm
S. Martin Mason

ST. IVES HARBOUR AND
GODREVY YACHT,
PINK AND GREEN
c. 1934–38   oil on
cardboard, 32 x 46.5 cm
The Pier Gallery,
Stromness, Orkney
Pl. 56

WHITE SAILING SHIP -19
THREE MASTS
c. 1934–38   oil on paper,
23 x 35.5 cm
The Pier Gallery, Stromness,
Orkney

RICHARD WENTWORTH

TOY
1983   galvanised and
tin-plated steel,
31 x 41 x 62.5 cm
Arts Council Collection,
Hayward Gallery, London
Pl. 202

SAVING DAYLIGHT
1983   steel with lightbulbs,
120 x 8 cm
Artist's collection, courtesy
Lisson Gallery, London

RACHEL WHITEREAD

GHOST
1990   plaster on steel frame,
269 x 356 x 318 cm
The Saatchi Gallery, London
Pl. 211

STEPHEN WILLATS

PERSON A
1974   photographic prints,
Letraset text, typed text,
ink on card, 18 panel work,
six panels each 76 x 51 cm,
twelve panels
each 38 x 25.5 cm
Collection Martin Rewcastle
Pl. 186

A STATE OF AGREEMENT
(GERMAN VERSION)
1974   photographic prints,
gouache, Letraset text
on card, four panels,
each 55 x 70 cm
Artist's collection, courtesy
Galerie Thomas Schulte, Berlin

THE LUNCH TRIANGLE
PILOT WORK B. CODES
AND PARAMETERS
1974 photographic prints,
gouache, Letraset text,
typed text, ink, paper on
card, three panels,
each 76.2 x 50.8 cm
Artist's collection, courtesy
Galerie Thomas Schulte, Berlin
Pl. 187

A MOMENT OF ACTION
PILOT WORK A. CODES
AND PARAMETERS
1974   photographic prints,
gouache, ink, typed text,
Letraset text on card,
six panels,
each 40,6 x 63,5 cm
Artist's collection, courtesy
Galerie Thomas Schulte, Berlin

BILL WOODROW

LA LACRIMA
1983   industrial gas light
reflector, glass stopper,
enamel and acrylic paint,
75 x 55 x 45 cm
Artist's collection
Pl. 200

CROW AND CARRION
1981   umbrellas,
37 x 100 x 55 cm
Arts Council Collection,
Hayward Gallery, London

BOEING
1981   car doors, clothes and
suitcase,
180 x 320 x 180 cm
Saatchi & Saatchi London

ARTISTS' BIOGRAPHIES

compiled by Jenny Horstmann and Annelie Lütgens
with Thomas Köhler, Lisa Köpper, Jule Schäfer and
Christin Schrader

EILEEN AGAR
(born in Buenos Aires, 1899, died 1991)

Eileen Agar came to London with her family, after her Scottish father retired from business, and attended school there from the age of twelve. From 1921 to 1924, she studied part-time at the Slade School of Art and from 1927 to 1930 continued her studies in Paris, where she met Louis Marcoussis and visited Brancusi's studio. Agar first saw an exhibition of Surrealist art at a commercial gallery in Paris in 1929 and made the acquaintance of the movement's leaders, including André Breton and Paul Éluard. Back in London, Agar joined the London Group in 1933, at the suggestion of Henry Moore, and contributed to the *International Surrealist Exhibition* in 1936. Between 1935 and 1944 she maintained close personal relations with the painter Paul Nash. In the paintings, collages and objects that she made during this period, she experimented with new, unusual materials and techniques of automatic painting. Agar is a typical representative of English Surrealism, which reveals unexpected combinations of forms and objects, but rarely draws on political or psychological themes. The Second World War interrupted her artistic activity, though she resumed it in 1946 and took part in the Surrealist exhibition at the Galerie Maeght in Paris in 1947. By the time of her death in 1991, she had produced a large body of work in a variety of techniques. Agar was elected to the Royal Academy in 1990.

Eileen Agar, exh. cat. National Galleries of Scotland, Edinburgh 1999.

EDWARD ALLINGTON
(born in Troutbeck Bridge, Westmoreland, 1951)

Edward Allington studied at Lancaster College of Art from 1968 to 1971 and the Central School of Art and Design from 1971 to 1974. Along with Tony Cragg, Richard Deacon, Antony Gormley, Anish Kapoor, Alison Wilding and Bill Woodrow, he is one of a group of artists who contributed to the flowering of British sculpture in the 1980s that became known as the "New British Sculpture". The rich variety of his floor sculptures and sculptural installations includes architectural fragments and organic forms, everyday objects and artificial flowers and light. Allington always seems to be in pursuit of an ideal of beauty, and his works amount to a series of Post-Modernist proposals for what that ideal might resemble. In 1977 he had his first solo exhibition at 1B Kensington Church Walk, London, and a second exhibition followed at the Spacex Gallery in Exeter in 1982. In 1989 he won a prize at the *John Moores Exhibition* in Liverpool. In 1993 Allington was the Gregory Fellow in Sculpture at the University of Leeds. His works have been included in numerous international exhibitions on British sculpture.

Edward Allington, exh. cat. Galerie Adrien Maeght, Paris 1986.
Edward Allington, exh. cat. Bonner Kunstverein, et al. Bonn 1992.

MICHAEL ANDREWS
(born in Norwich, 1928, died 1995)

The painter Michael Andrews was publicity-shy and rarely exhibited. He came to be seen as an outsider by his contemporaries and peers on the British art scene. Andrews' reputation for being a slow worker was based on the relatively small number of paintings he ever completed. He never ceased painting the human figure and, indeed, his paintings of the 1960s, in particular, include a number of complex group compositions. Paintings such as *The Colony Room* (1962) mostly show friends and relatives in everyday situations and casual postures. Nonetheless, the portrayal of urban society and its attendant anxieties is a central theme in his work. Instead of working from sketches, Andrews preferred to use photographs as drafts and to transfer these directly onto the canvas.

Michael Andrews. "The Delectable Mountain": The Ayers Rock Series and Other Landscape Paintings, exh. cat. Whitechapel Art Gallery, London 1991.
Michael Andrews, exh. cat. Tate Gallery, London 2001.

KENNETH ARMITAGE
(born in Leeds, 1916, died 2002)

The textured bronzes of Kenneth Armitage show fragile figures engaged in everyday pursuits, such as going for a walk or listening to music. Towards the end of the 1950s, his works became steadily more monumental, and the torsi of his figures, with their protruding limbs, flatter. Armitage's work of the 1950s is often associated with the term "The Geometry of Fear" (Herbert Read) and he exhibited alongside the artists associated with this tendency at the Venice Biennale in 1952 and 1958 and *Documenta* 1, 2 and 3. However, his view of humanity was less bleak than that of, say, Reg Butler and Lynn Chadwick, and he was more interested than they in the relationship of the individual to the family or social grouping. In the 1960s, Armitage experimented with new materials such as wax, resin and aluminium, whilst in his later works he turned again to his favourite material, bronze.

Norbert Lynton, *Kenneth Armitage*, London 1962.
Kenneth Armitage and Tamsyn Woollcombe (eds.), *Kenneth Armitage. Life and Work*, Much Hadham 1997.

JOHN ARMSTRONG
(born in Hastings, Sussex, 1893, died 1973)

John Armstrong studied at the St. John's Wood School of Art before and after the First World War, but was largely self-taught and developed a style of painting which was influenced by Giorgio de Chirico and Pierre Roy. The Leicester Gallery gave him his first solo exhibition in 1928. In 1933, he became a member of Unit One. In the 1930s Armstrong worked increasingly for stage and film, while still painting. For example, he designed the costumes and sets for the ballet *Façade* (1931) and sets for films by Alexander Korda, including *Henry VIII*, *The Scarlet Pimpernel* and *Rembrandt*. From 1932 to 1952 Armstrong produced posters for the company Shell-Mex. In 1933 he completed eight murals on themes relating to transport and travel for the dining hall of the Shell-Mex House in London. During the Second World War, Armstrong worked as an Official War Artist. In 1951 he made some murals for the Festival of Britain, but he returned mainly to easel painting in the years that followed. Armstrong's themes are usually mythological, religious or political, and show a strong sense of decorative design.

John Armstrong. A Retrospective Exhibition, exh. cat. Royal Academy of Arts, London, London 1975.
Ewan Mundy, *John Armstrong, 1893–1973*, London 1989.

KEITH ARNATT
(born in London, 1930)

In the 1960s, Keith Arnatt was one of the first artists in Britain to be associated with the new developments in performance and conceptual art. After completing his studies at Oxford School of Art and the Royal College of Art in London, in 1958 Arnatt became interested in incorporating his body into his work and in working in the media of video and photography. Among his best-known performances was his *Self-Burial-TV Interference Project* (1969). This photo series showed Arnatt burying himself in a hole in the ground. For a whole week, it was screened for split seconds at a time, at arbitrary intervals in the normal scheduled programme of one of the public television networks in Germany. Although Arnatt may be seen as a representative of conceptual art on account of the numerous actions he performed, photography has always ranked high on his list of priorities. The series *Pictures from a Rubbish Tip* (1989) and *One Foot Has Not Yet Reached the Street*, exhibited in London in 1997, show large-format photographs of household objects, toys, disposable articles and scraps of clothes Arnatt had found on rubbish heaps. These pictures, with their uncompromising subject-matter, bear witness to a highly individual approach to questions of colour and composition and offer prospects of a new-found landscape.

Keith Arnatt, *Rubbish and Recollections*, Llandudno 1989.

ART & LANGUAGE

This group of artists, which at times numbered up to thirty members, came into being with the foundation of the Art & Language Press in 1968 and the publication of the first issue of the journal *Art-Language* (1969). Among the central figures of the group were Terry Atkinson, Michael Baldwin, David Bainbridge, Ian Burn, Joseph Kosuth, Harold Hurrell, Mel Ramsden and the art historian Charles Harrison, although the membership swiftly diminished from 1976 onwards, to the point where the group now only comprises Baldwin, Ramsden and Harrison. In their mainly conceptual works, the members of Art & Language referred to Marxist theories and to the concept that art is mentally dependent on language. The group's intention was to question the tradition of the avant-garde and related concepts, such as individualism and innovation. While the early works consist mainly of printed texts, the later studio painting tackled the artistic canon in an ironical way – hence the series, *Painted by Mouth*, of 1981 to 1982, whose title was to be taken literally, and a series of pictures "painted in the manner of Jackson Pollock". In 1986 Michael Baldwin and Mel Ramsden were nominated for the Turner Prize for their series *Incidents in a Museum*.

Charles Harrison, *Essays on Art & Language*, London 2001.
Too Dark to Read. Motifs rétrospectifs 2000–1965, exh. cat. Musée d'Art Moderne, Villeneuve d'Ascq 2002.

LAWRENCE ATKINSON
(born in Manchester, 1873, died 1931)

After completing his studies in music and singing in Berlin and Paris, Atkinson went on to earn a living as a singing teacher in London, and there came into contact with the local literary and artistic scene. His early works were strongly influenced by Fauvism, but Atkinson met the Vorticist Percy Wyndham Lewis shortly afterwards and joined the Rebel Art Centre in 1914. From then on, Atkinson painted abstract, geometricised pictures that were characterised by asymmetrical composition and strong diagonals. Atkinson also made sculpture and wrote poetry up to the time of his death.

Lawrence Atkinson. Abstract Sculpture and Painting, exh. cat. Eldar Gallery, London 1920.

FRANK AUERBACH
(born in Berlin, 1931)

As an eight-year-old boy, Frank Auerbach was sent to spend the war years in Great Britain. He never again saw his parents, who had stayed on in Germany. In 1947 he took British citizenship. In his paintings, Auerbach restricts himself to a few motifs taken from his immediate environment, such as parks, buildings or people he feels close to. From the start, his paintings were distinguished by his use of a thick impasto, applied with the aid of brushes, knives and his bare hands, and heavily reworked, over a period of time. Whilst, during the 1950s, Auerbach worked predominantly with earthy colours and with black and white, his later works have acquired a more intense, expressionistic coloration. In 1986, he represented Great Britain at the Venice Biennale.

Robert Hughes, *Frank Auerbach*, London 1990.
Frank Auerbach. Paintings and Drawings 1954–2001, exh. cat. Royal Academy of Arts, London 2001.

FRANCIS BACON
(born in Dublin, 1909, died 1992)

"The visitors [...] were shocked by paintings which were so mercilessly horrible that their mind boggled at the sight of them." These were the words used by the critic John Russell to describe the effect of Francis Bacon's paintings on the public in 1945. As early as 1931, this autodidact had decided to give up his work as a window-dresser and dedicate himself wholly to painting. His central theme was the representation of man, his loneliness, his fears and his vulnerability. The violence of his imagery was reflected in his manner of working: He applied colour over a large area, smeared and, at times, hurled it onto the canvas. The motifs of the scream and the crucifixion were repeated over and over again in his work and, by the artist's own admission, were to be interpreted as symbols of man's innate cruelty. From 1970 onwards, Bacon's painting was characterised by its radiant colours and open spatial composition. Bacon is held to be one of the most important British painters of the 20th century and was honoured with countless retrospectives in Europe and North America, including two at the Tate Gallery, London (1962 and 1985), one at the Grand Palais, Paris and the Kunsthalle Düsseldorf (1971–72), and another at the Centre Georges Pompidou, Paris, and the Haus der Kunst, Munich (1996–97).

David Sylvester et al., *Looking Back at Francis Bacon*, London 1990.
Francis Bacon, ed. Francis Bacon and Bernhart Schwenk, exh. cat. Centre National d'Art et de Culture Georges Pompidou, Paris, and Haus der Kunst, Munich, Ostfildern-Ruit 1996.
Michael Peppiatt, *Francis Bacon. Anatomy of an Enigma*, London 1996.

JOHN BANTING
(born in London, 1902, died 1972)

Banting studied in London in the early 1920s and then was employed in a bank. In 1922 he met Peggy Guggenheim, Nina Hamnett, Constantin Brancusi and Man Ray in Paris. Later, he would be close to Louis Aragon and other artists close to the Surrealists. Under their influence, he abandoned his own painting in the style of *Neue Sachlichkeit* (New Objectivity) and turned to Surrealism. He joined the London Group in 1927 and took part in the *International Surrealist Exhibition* in London in 1936. His paintings of the 1930s betray the influence of Max Ernst. During the Second World War, Banting was an air-raid warden in London and made documentary films for the Ministry of Information. At the same time, he was a member of the Marxist group People's Convention and edited the journal *Our Time*, in which he published numerous articles and satirical drawings. Banting designed several exemplary book jackets for the Hogarth Press.

Julian Trevelyan. "John Banting: An English Surrealist", in *Painter and Sculptor*, nos. 1/2, Summer 1958, pp. 6–9.

VANESSA BELL
(born in London, 1879, died 1961)

The painter and designer Vanessa Bell and her younger sister, the writer Virginia Woolf, were central figures in the literary and artistic Bloomsbury Group, whose initial meetings were held in the house of their brother, Thoby. Bell's paintings, which were influenced by the works of Paul Cézanne and Henri Matisse, were characterised by her use of strong contours, simplified areas and clear colours. In 1907 she married the critic Clive Bell, whose book *Art* (1914) was an attack on English philistinism, and developed the theory of "significant form". In 1914 she undertook the first of a number of experiments in the field of abstract painting. At the same time, Bell worked as a commissioned designer. For example, she designed book titles for Virginia Woolf, created textile patterns and stage sets and decorated town and country houses. Since collaboration with other artists was very important to her, she realised a great number of artistic projects together with Duncan Grant and Robert Fry at the Omega Workshops, from 1913 to 1919. After 1920 Bell concentrated on traditional modes of figurative painting, showing a predilection for landscapes, figures in interiors and still lifes.

Frances Spalding, *Vanessa Bell*, London 1983.

Regina Mahler, *The Selected Letters of Vanessa Bell*, London 1993.

PETER BLAKE
(born in Dartford, Kent, 1932)

Peter Blake was a central figure in British Pop Art, for whom the gaudy insignia of popular culture have always provided a rich source of inspiration. His early works may be divided into two categories: on the one hand, the more naturalistic paintings, showing boys and girls reading comics or displaying the symbols of their youth culture and, on the other, the fantastic representations of the circus world and its protagonists. Blake's later works are full of photos of famous pop stars and screen actors, as well as record covers and pin-ups, reflecting the pop and fan culture of the 1960s. The most celebrated example of this was the record cover which he and his wife, Jann Howarth, designed for the Beatles' record *Sergeant Pepper's Lonely Hearts Club Band* (1967). In 1969 Blake moved to the West of England, where he stayed for ten years and co-founded the short-lived Brotherhood of Muralists (1975). Over the years, elements of the fantastic have played an increasingly important role in Blake's work and prompted allusions to literary works such as *Alice in Wonderland* and the dark fairies of Shakespeare. In 1983 there was a major retrospective of Blake's work at the Tate Gallery, London and the Kestner Gesellschaft, Hanover. Peter Blake was awarded a knighthood in 2002.

Peter Blake, ed. Michael Compton, exh. cat. Tate Gallery, London 1983.

Marina Vaizey, *Peter Blake*, London 1986.

DAVID BOMBERG
(born in Birmingham, 1890, died 1957)

After completing his studies at the Slade School of Art in 1913, David Bomberg started to exhibit widely and, in the company of his artist colleague Jacob Epstein, made a journey to Paris where he made the acquaintance of Pablo Picasso, André Derain, Max Jacob, Moïse Kisling and Amedeo Modigliani. His paintings from that time were characterised by a geometricisation which invited comparison with the Vorticists. However, although Bomberg took part in a Vorticist exhibition in 1915, he refused throughout his life to be officially tied to this group of artists. His paintings from the 1920s, in which he reworked impressions from his travels in the Middle East, already anticipated his later Expressionistic, impastoed paintings of landscapes, flowers and the human figure. Through his work as a teacher from 1947 to 1953, Bomberg acquired numerous followers, who become known by the names of the Borough Group and Borough Bottega. Frank Auerbach, Leon Kossoff and Gustav Metzger were among his students at this time.

William Lipke, *David Bomberg. A Critical Study of His Life and Work*, London 1967.

Richard Cork, *David Bomberg*, New Haven 1987.

DEREK BOSHIER
(born in Portsmouth, 1937)

Derek Boshier attended the Royal College of Art at the same time as David Hockney, Allen Jones and R. B. Kitaj, and quickly became identified as one of the leading figures of the British Pop Art scene. At the beginning of the 1960s, Boshier concentrated on painting the icons of the American mass media and the consumer world; the themes of his large-scale, colourful pictures included the heroes of space travel, magazine covers, flags, and material from cornflakes and toothpaste advertisements. There followed a period during which Boshier produced an interesting body of photo-based experimental work. Then, in the 1980s, he moved to Houston, Texas, where he lived and worked for a total of thirteen years. The paintings he produced there were more restrained in their colours – sometimes only in black and white – and concentrated on socio-political subjects. More recently, Boshier's works have been influenced by the cultural diversity and the media symbols of the metropolis of Los Angeles.

Derek Boshier. Selected Drawings 1960–1982, exh. cat. Bluecoat Gallery, Liverpool 1983.

Derek Boshier. Recent Works, London 1996.

PAULINE BOTY
(born in London, 1938, died 1966)

Pauline Boty, who became known as "the Wimbledon Bardot", is considered as one of the founders of the British Pop Art movement in the 1960s, along with Peter Blake, Allen Jones, Derek Boshier, Peter Phillips and David Hockney. She was the only woman artist to be featured in Ken Russell's celebrated film for the BBC, *Pop Goes the Easel* (1962). Her colourful canvases were inspired by the imagery of European and American cinema. These included the homages she painted to Jean Paul Belmondo, Marilyn Monroe and Monica Vitti. At times, her paintings resembled collages. In her later works, Boty became preoccupied with political topics. She based *Countdown to Violence* (1964) on the assassination of the American President. She dealt in a critical way with representations of the female body in advertising and pin-ups in her controversially received work *It's a Man's World* (1965), which was a critical take on representations of the female body in pin-ups and the advertising industry. Pauline Boty took part in numerous group exhibitions before her early death at the age of only twenty-eight, in 1966.

Pauline Boty (1938–1966). The Only Blonde in the World, exh. cat. Whitford Fine Art and Mayor Gallery, London 1998.

The Sixties Art Scene in London, exh. cat. Barbican Art Gallery, London 1993.

MARK BOYLE AND JOAN HILLS
(born in Glasgow and Edinburgh, in 1934 and 1936)

The lawyer, poet and self-taught painter, Mark Boyle and the painter, Joan Hills, have worked together since 1958. In 1964 they produced their first random studies of demolition sites. In 1966 they held their first joint exhibition; in 1967 they created a light environment for the pop group Soft Machine. Since the late 1960s, not only Boyle and Hills, but their two children, Sebastian and Georgia, have worked together as a family collective and are now internationally known as "Boyle Family". From the outset, Boyle Family have been concerned with questions of nature and the environment. They have tried to reproduce materials and structures as closely as possible. For their lifelong project *Journey to the Surface of the Earth*, which they began in 1968, they identified a large number of sites by throwing darts at a map of the world. Since then, they have travelled to many of these sites and taken casts of a two metre square area of the surface of the earth, as a means of recording its biological and chemical composition. They have then gone on to make sound recordings of the site, for re-presentation along with photographs and finished reliefs. In Mark Boyle's own words: "My ultimate object is to include everything. In the end the only medium in which it will be possible to say everything will be reality." In 1978 Boyle Family represented Great Britain at the Venice Biennale.

Johannes L. Locher, *Mark Boyle's Journey to the Surface of the Earth*, Stuttgart 1978.

Beyond Image. Boyle Family, exh. cat. Hayward Gallery, London 1986.

BILL BRANDT
(born in Hamburg, 1904, died 1983)

Bill Brandt's artistic career as a photographer began in Paris in 1929. It was there that he met Man Ray, became his assistant and was deeply affected by his approach to his work. Brandt's own photo-journalistic output as well as his artistic nude and portrait photographs were characterised by a marked feeling for chiaroscuro contrasts and harmonious composition. In the 1930s Brandt worked for several London newspapers, and in his documentary photographs recorded the wretched circumstances of the workers' families in the North of England. During the war, he followed the crowds of people looking for protection in the air-raid shelters of London and there documented the atmosphere of fear and defiance. In the 1950s Brandt distanced himself from photo journalism. His main subjects were now nudes, landscapes and portraits. Francis Bacon, Henry Moore and Dylan Thomas were but a few of the many artists and writers he portrayed.

Nigel Warburton (ed.), *Bill Brandt. Selected Texts and Bibliography*, Oxford 1993.

VICTOR BURGIN
(born in Sheffield, 1941)

Victor Burgin studied painting at the Royal College of Art in London from 1962 to 1965 and at Yale University from 1965 to 1967. As a student in North America, Burgin shared the widespread dissatisfaction of many artists with the strict formalism which dominated painting at the time. In the early 1970s, under the influence of semiotic theory, he began to work with photography – and to treat this as a medium which was inseparable from language. This new direction in his work was evident in his contribution to the group exhibition *The New Art* at the Hayward Gallery London in 1972. He

questioned modernist notions of the purity and uniqueness of the individual work of art (paintings in particular) and set out to demonstrate that art could be used as an instrument for social change. Burgin sees his various activities as writer, teacher, photographer and manipulator of verbal and visual texts as one and the same thing, deriving from the same pedagogical impulse to classify art as a form of political education.

Victor Burgin, *Between. Victor Burgin*, Oxford 1986.

EDWARD BURRA
(born in Rye, Sussex, 1905, died 1976)

Edward Burra studied at Chelsea Polytechnic from 1921 to 1923, then for two years at the Royal College of Art. In the late 1920s and early 1930s he made drawings and collages which were inspired by Dadaism and George Grosz, in particular. Burra lacked Grosz's political incisiveness, but was fascinated with the world of cinemas, dance halls and music halls. In 1927 Burra met Paul Nash and, like him, took an interest in avant-garde journals, especially those from Germany. Burra took part in the exhibition *Art Now* at the Mayor Gallery in 1934 and exhibited there with Unit One in the same year, as one of the few artists in the group who were close to Surrealist tendencies. In 1936, he took part in the *International Surrealist Exhibition* in London and in *Fantastic Art, Dada and Surrealism* at the Museum of Modern Art in New York. Burra reacted to the outbreak of the Spanish Civil War in 1936 with works marked by an atmosphere of violence. After 1945 he worked as a costume and stage designer and as a book illustrator. His late landscapes and still lifes communicate an atmosphere of beauty and menace. The Tate Gallery devoted a retrospective to Burra in 1973, as did the Hayward Gallery in 1985.

Andrew Causey, *Edward Burra. Complete Catalogue*, Oxford 1985.

Edward Burra, exh. cat. Hayward Gallery, London 1985.

REG[INALD] BUTLER
(born in Buntingford, Hertfordshire, 1913, died 1981)

Reginald Butler trained as an architect and taught architecture from 1937 to 1939, and then spent twelve months working as an engineer. During the war, as a conscientious objector, he went to work in a smithy in Sussex. In 1944 he began to produce works in cast and forged iron as a sideline to his new occupation, earning a living as an editor of architectural journals. In 1950 he abandoned architecture altogether in order to devote himself full time to sculpture. In 1953 he won the international

competition for a *Monument to the Unknown Political Prisoner*. This was at the height of the Cold War, and his original maquette for the project caused such a scandal when it was placed on view at the Tate Gallery that it was destroyed by one of the visitors to the exhibition. Butler took part in the Venice Biennale in 1952 and 1954 and in *documenta 1* and *documenta 2* in Kassel in 1955 and 1959, respectively. Although his work was exhibited in many prestigious exhibitions in the 1960s, he withdrew from the art world entirely in 1963 in order to make a fresh start. In the following ten years, he produced sculptures that reproduce portions the human anatomy with almost pathological precision. Only after his death did the Tate Gallery devote a comprehensive retrospective to Butler's work.

Reg Butler, exh. cat. Tate Gallery, London 1983.

Reg Butler 1913–1981, London 1986.

ANTHONY CARO
(born in New Malden, Surrey, 1924)

With his abstract, constructed and vividly painted steel sculptures, Anthony Caro revolutionised the attitudes and working methods of the traditional sculptor, at the beginning of the 1960s. Caro's early figurative bronzes were still influenced by Pablo Picasso, Willem De Kooning and Jean Dubuffet and were infused with the humanist vision of Henry Moore, with whom he had worked as an assistant in the early 1950s. Then, under the immediate impact of a visit to New York in 1959–60 and of personal encounters with Kenneth Noland, David Smith and the critic Clement Greenberg, Caro took to experimenting with new materials and spatial concerns. He was one of the first artists to use modern welding techniques to construct steel sculptures out of elementary, vertical and horizontal shapes. These flowing arrangements of flat and heavy forms, which invite comparison with abstract painting, appear to defy gravity. Caro rejected the plinth, in favour of placing his works directly on the floor. Through his teaching at St. Martin's School of Art in London, Caro had a strong influence on the succeeding generation of British sculptors: thus, Barry Flanagan, Richard Long and Gilbert and George were among his students. Since the 1960s Caro has been widely celebrated as Britain's leading sculptor, and he has enjoyed a highly successful international career, with notable retrospectives at the Museum of Modern Art, New York (1975) and in the Trajan Markets in Rome (1992). In recent years, Caro's work has reflected an increasing interest in architecture and issues of scale. He has moved effortlessly between figurative and abstract modes of expression, sometimes involving the use of mythological and narrative elements, as in the *Trojan War* series (1992) and *The Last Judgement*, at the 1993 Venice Biennale. Anthony Caro was knighted in 1987.

Anthony Caro. Skulpturen 1969–84, exh. cat.
Kunstmuseum Düsseldorf, Düsseldorf 1985.
Dieter Blume, *Anthony Caro. Catalogue Raisonné*, 5 vols.,
Cologne 1981 and 1985.
Anthony Caro. Sculpture Through Five Decades, 1955–1994,
London 1994.

PATRICK CAULFIELD
(born in London, 1936)

Patrick Caulfield attended the Royal College of Art in the early 1960s, at the same time as David Hockney, R. B. Kitaj and Allen Jones, yet he does not like to be labelled as a Pop artist. Taking his inspiration from painters such as Fernand Léger and Juan Gris, Caulfield has chosen to distance himself from the imagery of mass consumption and to take up some of the classic subjects of European painting, such as the still life and portrait, though not without "modernising" these, by concentrating on the "ordinary" imagery of picture postcards and office and restaurant interiors. Up until the 1980s, Caulfield's paintings revealed strong affinities to the work of certain abstract artists of the period, thanks to his strong emphasis on black outlines and large contrasting areas of uniform colour. Since then, the scale of many of his paintings has increased in size, the black outlines have disappeared, and the forms have been simplified. In recent years, Caulfield has made increasing use of the print medium. His work has gained widespread recognition in Britain and abroad, thanks, in part, to the success of his travelling retrospectives of 1981 and 1999.

Patrick Caulfield. Paintings, exh. cat. Tate Gallery,
London 1981.
Patrick Caulfield, exh. cat. Hayward Gallery, London 1999.

LYNN CHADWICK
(born in London, 1914)

As a trained architectural draughtsman, Lynn Chadwick first worked as a furniture and textile designer after the Second World War, before devoting himself fully to sculpture. Up to the end of the 1940s, he concentrated on the construction of sculptural mobiles made of metal, aluminium and balsa wood. His totemistic works of the 1950s are reminiscent of animal figures and archaic ritu-

als. Construction has always played an important part in Chadwick's method of working. Instead of forming material and working on it directly, he would first build a kind of metal skeleton, which he then covered with the relevant materials and turned into a solid sculpture. In his later works, geometric elements moved into the background and Chadwick began to concentrate on soft, organic forms. Lynn Chadwick's contribution to post-war art was honoured with the International Prize for Sculpture at the Venice Biennale in 1956.

Lynn Chadwick. Sculpture 1951–1991, exh. cat. Yorkshire
Sculpture Park, Wakefield 1991.
Dennis Farr and Eva Chadwick, *Lynn Chadwick. Sculptor.*
With a Complete Illustrated Catalogue, 1947–1996, Stroud 1997.

ALAN CHARLTON
(born in Sheffield, 1948)

Ever since his time at the Camberwell School of Art in London at the end of the 1960s, Alan Charlton has preferred to work with standardised wooden boards from the DIY store instead of with colour and canvas. These monochrome painted boards are the basic elements for his geometric, Minimalist compositions in brown, green, red as well as in black and white, whose spatial effect is central to the artist's intentions. For many years now, Charlton has experimented, above all, with different shades of grey.

Alan Charlton, exh. cat. Institute of Contemporary Arts,
London 1991.

CECIL COLLINS
(born in Plymouth, 1908, died 1989)

This painter of visionary and fantastic images trained initially with a motor engineering firm in the port of Plymouth from 1922 to 1923. Subsequently, he attended art school in Plymouth from 1923 to 1927 and the Royal Academy of Arts in London from 1927 to 1931, where he won the William Rothenstein Prize for drawing from nature. Collins taught from 1940 to 1943 at Dartington Hall and from 1951 to 1957 at the Central School of Arts. In 1958 he won the first prize for his painting *Christ Before the Judge* at the *John Moores* exhibition in Liverpool in 1958. His oeuvre, with its religious and spiritual themes, shows the influence of William Blake, Paul Klee, Marc Chagall, and the Surrealists. Collins was represented in the *International Surrealist Exhibition* in London in 1936 with two paintings. His book *The Vision of the Fool* was published in 1947. From the late 1930s onwards, Collins carried out a number of important commissions for reli-

gious art, including an altar for Chichester Cathedral, besides continuing with his own work in the studio and teaching commitments.

Cecil Collins, exh. cat. Tate Gallery, London 1989.
The Vision of the Fool. Early Drawings of Cecil Collins,
exh. cat. Anthony d'Offay Gallery, London 1991.

TONY CRAGG
(born in Liverpool, 1949)

As a preparation for training in the natural sciences, Tony Cragg worked as a laboratory assistant in a bio-chemical research laboratory from 1966 to 1968. He made his first drawings and rubber objects at this time. From 1969 to 1970 he attended the Foundation Course at Gloucestershire College of Art and Design in Cheltenham and then moved on to Wimbledon School of Art from 1970 to 1973, and the Royal College of Art from 1973 to 1977. In 1977 Cragg moved to Wuppertal, where he continues to live and work today. Cragg's artistic outlook was shaped by his encounter with Arte Povera, Land Art, Minimal Art and Conceptual Art, in the early 1970s. *New Stones Newton's Tones* (1978) was a floor installation consisting of pieces of plastic rubbish, arranged by colour, and his inclusion of this work in his first one-man exhibition at the Lisson Gallery in London contributed to his international breakthrough. In 1984 Cragg returned to his studio, where, in 1986, he produced his first works in glass, plaster and cast metal, based on the forms of ordinary household objects. He sees such objects as organic metaphors for living creatures, and they have been central to his formal language since 1984. In 1988 Cragg represented Britain at the Venice Biennale and was awarded the Turner Prize in London. In 1995 he was given an extensive retrospective at the Centre Georges Pompidou in Paris. Cragg has taught at the Düsseldorf Art Academy since 1978, becoming a full Professor and Pro-Rector in 1988. In 2001 he was appointed to a Professorship at the Hochschule der Künste in Berlin. Cragg was elected to the Royal Academy in London, 1994.

Tony Cragg, exh. cat. Hayward Gallery, London 1987.
Lucinda Barnes, *Tony Cragg. Sculpture 1975–1990*,
London 1991.
Germano Celant, *Tony Cragg*, London 1996.

MICHAEL CRAIG-MARTIN
(born in Dublin, 1941)

From 1961 to 1966, Michael Craig-Martin studied painting at Yale University, first as an undergraduate, then as a graduate student. During his time there, he met many of the leading East Coast

American artists and was particularly impressed with the exhibition *Primary Structures* at the Jewish Museum in New York, which included work by Robert Morris, Donald Judd, Carl Andre and Sol LeWitt. On his return to Britain, Craig-Martin turned to making objects which dealt with the physical experience of space, scale and mobility, including the "impossible" wooden boxes which featured in his first solo exhibition at the Rowan Gallery in London in 1969. In his frequently large-scale murals, sculptures and paintings, Craig-Martin creates model situations that provoke the viewer. One of his most influential works, *Oak Tree*, combined a glass of water and a shelf with a printed text, suggesting a wholly unexpected reading of these objects in their given context. In his works of 1972–73 Craig-Martin explored the interaction between the viewer and the work of art, through the use of mirrors and integration of text in multi-part presentations. His complex works only seem unambiguous at first glance. They contain hidden allusions both to modern art and to associated questions of authorship and the position of the viewer in relation to the work of art. In 1973–88 Craig-Martin taught at Goldsmiths' College in London, some of the main protagonists of Young British Art, including Damien Hirst, Gary Hume and Julian Opie, were among his students. In 1989, Craig-Martin had a retrospective at the Whitechapel Art Gallery, London. In the last twenty years he has undertaken many public art commissions, including a ceiling for the new British Embassy in Berlin, which was opened in 2000.

Michael Craig-Martin. A Retrospective: 1968–1989, exh. cat. Whitechapel Art Gallery, London 1989.

Eckhard Schneider (ed.), *Always Now. Michael Craig-Martin*, exh. cat. Kunstverein Hannover, Hanover 1998.

ALAN DAVIE
(born in Grangemouth, Scotland, 1920)

Alan Davie first encountered the work of Jackson Pollock and Robert Motherwell in the collection of Peggy Guggenheim in Venice in 1948 and was one of the first European artists to come to grips with the new language of Abstract Expressionism. As a painter who was also prolific in a variety of other media, Davie made an important contribution to the internationalisation of British art in the immediate aftermath of the Second World War. Davie's work is not only influenced by the artistic concepts of the Surrealists and the Abstract Expressionists of the United States, but directly inspired by his taste for literature and activity as a professional jazz musician. Like many other artists, in the

1950s Davie became interested in Zen Buddhism and the depth psychology of C. G. Jung. Searching for ways to express a collective unconscious, he used archetypal symbols, words and excerpts from texts in his paintings. The immediate impact of the forces of nature that he experienced in the 1960s while diving, gliding and sailing, left its mark on his later works.

Alan Bowness (ed.), *Alan Davie*, London 1967.

Douglas Hall and Michael Tucker, *Alan Davie*, London 1992.

RICHARD DEACON
(born in Bangor, Wales, 1949)

Richard Deacon, one of the best-known protagonists of the "New British Sculpture", first studied in the sculpture department at St. Martin's School of Art in London (1969–72), where he devoted most of his energy to performance. His performance work gained him admission to the Royal College of Art (1974–77), but once there he decided to focus exclusively on making objects. In the sculptures for which he became known in the 1980s, he used a variety of welding, riveting, gluing and laminating techniques to combine prefabricated sheets of plastic and wood into sizeable units. The biomorphic forms of the resulting voluminous, curved objects evoke associations of human organs, animals and plants. At the same time, they reveal the structures of the wood, metal and other materials employed. Deacon received the Turner Prize in 1987, and has since received numerous other awards, in addition to exhibiting widely in Britain and abroad.

Richard Deacon, ed. Joanna Skipworth, exh. cat. Whitechapel Art Gallery, London 1998.

Jon Thompson et al., *Richard Deacon*, London 2000.

ROBYN DENNY
(born in Abinger, Surrey, 1930)

Robyn Denny belonged to the first generation of students from the Royal College of Art to be influenced by Abstract Expressionism from the United States in the 1950s. He moved from a gestural type of painting to more strictly structured compositions. In 1960, he was a co-organiser of the first, highly influential *Situation* exhibition, in which he and seventeen other young artists, including Richard Smith, Bernard Cohen and John Hoyland, mounted an ambitious British riposte to the challenge presented by contemporary American abstraction. In the 1950s and 1960s Denny took up numerous teaching positions and worked as an art critic

for international magazines. In the 1960s he developed his characteristic hard-edge style, under the influence of the writings of Charles Biederman.

Robyn Denny, exh. cat. Tate Gallery, London 1973.

JACOB EPSTEIN
(born in New York, 1880, died 1959)

Jacob Epstein, whose early work was deeply influenced by his encounter with Brancusi in Paris in 1911, was not a member of the Rebel Art Centre, but was close to the Vorticists for a time. He contributed two drawings to the first issue of *Blast* (June 1914), and in 1915 he sent in to a group exhibition in London the first version of his *Rock Drill*. This was a threatening, robotic plaster figure mounted on a real drill of the kind used in mining. After the 1920s, when he became a public figure, Epstein concentrated on modelling portrait busts of the rich and the famous, including Albert Einstein and Jawaharlal Nehru, which attracted favourable comment on account of their remarkably empathetic feeling. However, the large stone carvings which he made in the 1920s and 1930s met with public hostility and incomprehension on account of their expressiveness, their strong connection with the geometric forms of "primitive" art and their blatant display of nudity. The thinly veiled anti-Semitism of some critics' attacks on Epstein's work bore a resemblance to the treatment meted out to "degenerate" artists in Nazi Germany.

Jacob Epstein, *Epstein. An Autobiography*, London 1963.

Jacob Epstein. Sculpture and Drawings, ed. Evelyn Silver, exh. cat. Leeds City Art Galleries, Leeds, and Whitechapel Art Gallery, London, Leeds 1987.

Richard Cork, *Jacob Epstein*, London 1999.

June Rose, *Daemons and Angels. A Life of Jacob Epstein*, London 2002.

FREDERICK ETCHELLS
(born in Newcastle-upon-Tyne, 1886; died 1973)

Frederick Etchells studied art at the Royal College of Art from circa 1908 to 1911 and afterwards rented a studio in Paris, where he met Picasso, Braque and Modigliani. In 1911 he collaborated on Roger Fry's mural scheme for the Borough Polytechnic with Duncan Grant and others and contributed to the *Second Post-Impressionist Exhibition* at the Grafton Galleries, later the same year. Etchells joined the Omega Workshops in 1913, but was one of the group of artists around Wyndham Lewis, who walked out of this a few months later, in order to set up their own, rival Rebel Art Centre. Etchells contributed to *Blast* nos. 1 and 2 and was included in the Vorticist exhibition in New York in 1917. He was also included in Wyndham Lewis' *Group X* exhibition at the Mansard Gallery in London in 1920, but soon afterwards gave up painting for a successful career as an architect. He translated some of the writings of Le Corbusier, and his office building for W. S. Crawford Ltd, in 1930, was a milestone in the history of modern English architecture, in the opinion of Nikolaus Pevsner. In later years, Etchells specialised in building and restoring churches.

Rosemary Ind, "Frederick Etchells. Plain Homebuilder Where Is Your Vortex?", in *ICSAC Cahier*, no. 8/9, 1988, pp. 145–167.

IAN HAMILTON FINLAY
(born in Nassau, Bahamas, 1925)

Ian Hamilton Finlay has created a complex oeuvre since the 1950s, as a landscape artist, poet and sculptor. Finlay, who grew up in Glasgow, became famous, from 1966 onwards, for the garden empire which he designed in the midst of the Pentland Hills in South Scotland and called *Stonypath* or *Little Sparta*. In 1961 he founded the publishing house Wild Hawthorn Press, in 1962 the literary journal *Poor. Old. Tired. Horse.*, where he published his own works, best categorised as concrete poetry. He turned to sculpture with an exhibition of constructed toys at the home of the publisher John Calder in 1963 and first successfully combined poetry with sculpture in the poems he engraved on glass, in 1964. From 1965 to 1967 Finlay investigated the poetic and metaphoric content of inscriptions under the slogan of a "New Classicism". The Axiom Gallery in London held his first solo exhibition in 1968. In the 1970s, Finlay frequently collaborated with other artists or artisans. His objects and sculptures, whose form and meaning are characterised by Classicist strictness on the one hand and irony and humour on the other, are created from the most diverse materials such as porcelain, neon, plaster and stone. He has executed numerous open-air projects since the 1980s. In 1987 Finlay participated in the *documenta 8* in Kassel.

Yves Abrioux and Stephen Bann, *Ian Hamilton Finlay. A Visual Primer*, London 1985, 2nd edition 1992.

Alec Finlay (ed.), *Wood Note Wild. Essays on the Poetry and Art of Ian Hamilton Finlay*, Edinburgh 1995.

BARRY FLANAGAN
(born in Prestatyn, North Wales, 1941)

Barry Flanagan first studied architecture and sculpture in Birmingham and took employment as a frame-maker and set designer for films, before going on to enrol in the sculpture course at St. Martin's, where he was a student of Phillip King. As an enthusiastic fan of Alfred Jarry, he published a weekly journal, *Silâns* (1964), in which he also included his own poetry. In 1966 Flanagan took part in the *Destruction in Art Symposium* in London, along with Yoko Ono and Tony Cox, and held a joint exhibition with John Latham in Bangor, Wales. The Rowan Gallery in London mounted his first solo exhibition the same year. In 1969, he was included in the London showing of the international exhibition *When Attitudes Become Form*. In the 1970s Flanagan was active in a wide variety of artistic fields, studying dance with Carolyn Carlson and working with the London dance group Strider, at the same time as experimenting with traditional sculptural materials and techniques, including bronze casting and ceramics. In 1979, he made a *Leaping Hare*, which was to become something of a trademark for his later work. In the years that followed, he created several more bronze hares rearing up on their hind legs or leaping through the air. In 1982 Flanagan represented Britain at the Venice Biennale. His work is represented in public collections all over the world.

Barry Flanagan. Sculpture, exh. cat. Venice Biennale, British Pavilion, London 1982.

Barry Flanagan. A Visual Invitation: Sculpture 1967–1987, exh. cat. Tyne and Wear Museums Service, Newcastle-upon-Tyne 1987.

LUCIAN FREUD
(born in Berlin, 1922)

Lucian Freud, who came to Britain as a child with his family in 1932, studied at art school in London and held his first one-man exhibition by the time he was twenty. His early portraits and still lifes were a sharp reaction against the Neo-Romanticism of English wartime painting and still showed the influence both of *Neue Sachlichkeit* and of international Surrealism. His first manner, which was characteristically spiky and linear, and remarkable for its penetrating psychological insight, earned him the sobriquet of "the Ingres of Existentialism" (Herbert Read). At the end of the 1950s, a change of style could be noticed: Freud now used brushes made of sable which allowed the application of a thicker coat of paint and heightened the intensity of his paintings. The central themes in Freud's later work are the nude and the portrait, by which it should be understood that the nudes could equally well be interpreted as portraits. As Freud himself put it: "I want my colour to seem like flesh. [...] I want my portraits to consist of people, not to look *like* people." Henceforth, Freud concentrated on painting his immediate circle of friends and relations, though colleagues such as Francis Bacon, Frank Auerbach and, more recently, the performance artist Leigh Bowery, continued to sit for him. A travelling retrospective of Freud's work went to Berlin, Paris and Washington in 1987–88, ending up at the Hayward Gallery in London. In 2002 a touring retrospective of Freud's works was organised by the Tate Gallery in London, to commemorate the artist's eightieth birthday.

Robert Hughes, *Lucian Freud*, London 1987.

Bruce Bernard and Derek Birdsall (eds.), *Lucian Freud*, London 1996.

Lucian Freud. Early Works, exh. cat. Scottish National Gallery of Modern Art, Edinburgh 1997.

NAUM GABO
(born in Bryansk, Russia, 1890, died 1977)

Naum Gabo (né Pevsner), who was born in Russia but became a United States citizen in 1952, was one of the most influential exponents of Constructivism. He was the younger brother of Antoine Pevsner, but called himself Gabo after 1915, to avoid being confused with the latter. Gabo studied medicine, mathematics and natural sciences in Munich and made contact with avant-garde artists in Paris, when he visited his brother there in 1913 and 1914. During the First World War, Gabo went to Oslo, where he made his first geometric constructions. In 1917, he and his brother returned to Russia, where they published their *Realist Manifesto*, which laid the theoretical basis for Constructivism. Gabo's sculptures changed from static, architectonic constructions of planes into stereometric, transparent webs of light and space. In 1922 he moved to Berlin and developed contacts with the Bauhaus and the De Stijl group. In 1930 he held his first solo show, *Konstruktive Plastik*, at the Kestner Gesellschaft in Hanover. In 1932 he moved to Paris, where he joined the association Abstraction-Création. In 1935 Gabo settled in London, where he co-edited the journal *Circle*. He became close friends with the artists Ben Nicholson and Barbara Hepworth, whose work he influenced, and with the architect Leslie Martin and the poet and critic Herbert Read. Gabo also taught the younger, St. Ives-born artist Peter Lanyon for a short period and influenced him in his move towards a more abstract, constructive style, from 1940 onwards. In 1946 Gabo settled permanently in the United States, where he created a number of large-scale, constructive, public sculptures and reliefs.

Naum Gabo. Sixty Years of Constructivism, exh. cat. Tate Gallery, London 1987.

Martin Hammer and Christina Lodder, *Constructing Modernity. The Art and Career of Naum Gabo*, New Haven 2000.

ANYA GALLACCIO
(born in Glasgow, 1963)

Anya Gallaccio was still a student at Goldsmiths' College, when she took part in Damien Hirst's legendary exhibition *Freeze*, in 1988. She quickly became known for her ephemeral objects and installations, which bore an evident relationship to Arte Povera and the paintings of Mark Rothko and Barnett Newman. Working with perishable materials such as flowers, oranges, chocolate and blocks of ice, she provokes an immediate sensory response on the part of the viewer, along the lines of: "What do 10,000 roses smell like?" (*red on green*, 1991). The sheer quantity of the materials she uses enhanced the quality of their colour. Gallaccio once pressed 8386 narcissi between two sheets of glass on the floor (*preserve* (*cheerfulness*), 1991). Gallaccio's early works were installed in large, derelict buildings, as in the case of *Prestige* (1990), which consisted of 21 whistling tea kettles, placed in the tower of a disused pumping station in Wapping. *A Time Bomb*, comprising a slow-melting, thirty-five ton block of ice, three metres high, invited comparison with Richard Serra's sculptures, but Gallaccio is concerned with flux, rather than permanence: salt trickled onto the ice, creating a hole in the block and causing it gradually to melt.

Small, Medium, Large, Lifesize, exh. cat. Centro per l'Arte Contemporanea Luigi Pecci, Prato, Madrid 1992.
Anya Gallaccio, *Chasing Rainbows*, Glasgow and Newcastle-upon-Tyne 1999.

HENRI GAUDIER-BRZESKA
(born in St. Jean-de-Bay near Orléans, 1891, died 1915)

Henri Gaudier- Brzeska grew up in France, but moved to London in 1911 with his companion Sophie Brzeska and quickly established important contacts on the literary and artistic scene. He made friends with Percy Wyndham Lewis, Ezra Pound and Jacob Epstein and from 1913 onwards began, under the influence of the last-named, to switch from smaller works in clay to sculptures made of stone, which were characterised by abstract and soft forms, in the manner of style of Cubist and "primitive" art. He became a member of the Rebel Art Centre and of the Vorticist group, taking part in their exhibition in 1915 and making a number of contributions to both issues of the Vorticist journal *Blast*. Concurrently, Gaudier also sent work to exhibitions organised by the Allied Artists' Association and the London Group. The artist was not quite 24 years old when he was killed in the First World War in 1915.

H. S. Ede, *Savage Messiah. A Life of Gaudier-Brzeska*, London 1931.
Henri Gaudier-Brzeska, 1891–1915, ed. Jeremy Lewison, exh. cat. Kettle's Yard Gallery, Cambridge 1983.

WILLIAM GEAR
(born in Methil, Fife, 1915; died 1997)

William Gear first studied painting, then art history, in Edinburgh from 1932–37. In 1937–38 he studied with Fernand Léger in Paris. After the war, in which he served with the Royal Corps of Signals in the Middle East and Italy, he worked with the Allied Control Commission in Germany in 1946–47 and held a one-man show in Celle and Hamburg. From 1947–50 he lived in Paris, as one of a small number of Scottish artists, including Eduardo Paolozzi and William Turnbull, who were among the first to renew links with the international avant-garde. Whilst there, he exhibited with the CoBrA Group in 1949. Back in Britain, Gear rose to prominence with his painting *Autumn Landscape* (1950), which won a purchase prize from the Arts Council, but caused a scandal in the right-wing press on account of its supposedly radical abstraction. In reality, this work struck a fine balance between abstraction and representation and established a secure basis for his future work. Gear continued to paint and exhibit widely, in parallel to his teaching activity as Head of the Faculty of Fine Art at Birmingham College of Fine Arts, from 1964–75.

William Gear, 75th Birthday Exhibition: Paintings, Works on Paper, CoBrA and After, exh. cat. Redfern Gallery, London 1990.

GILBERT (PROESCH) AND GEORGE (PASSMORE)
(born in the Dolomites, Italy, 1943, and in Devonshire, 1942)

"Our life is one single large sculpture" is how Gilbert and George, who have been working together for over thirty years, describe their joint collaboration. After declaring themselves to be "living sculptures" in 1969, their gestures, their mimicry, their appearance and their everyday actions, as well as their inner emotions, have become part of a total work of art, "Gilbert & George". This artistic couple has discovered in the notion of totality a key to achieving the complete fusion of art and life. Since the end of the 1970s, the indivisibility of art and life has also developed into the principal theme of their photo-collages, which give visible expression to the life of the outside world and to the life and language of the city and its streets. In the process, the various pictorial forms of Gilbert and George's works have developed from being initially loose conglomerations of photographs situated in close relation to each other to embodying large-scale symmetrical figure compositions, whose subjects extend well beyond the limits of the individual frame. For the last twenty years, Gilbert and George have increasingly chosen to dwell on themes such as homosexuality, religion, and the monarchy, in ways which have seemed calculated to challenge commonplace assumptions. Their exhibitions in Russia, China and elsewhere have served to bring their spectacular work to the attention of an unusually wide public.

Gilbert & George. The Complete Pictures, 1971–1985, London 1986.
Wolf Jahn, *The Art of Gilbert and George or An Aesthetic of Existence*, London and New York 1989.
Gilbert & George, *The Words of Gilbert & George*, London 1997.

ANTONY GORMLEY
(born in London, 1950)

Antony Gormley has become one of the most celebrated living British artists and is noted especially for his large-scale monumental works, the best-known of which are the *Fields* of some 35,000–40,000 hand-sized terracotta figurines, which have been exhibited throughout Europe and North America since their inception in 1991, and the welded iron *Angel of the North* in Gateshead, England (commissioned in 1995), which alludes to the site's historical past as an important centre for the production of steel. Gormley, who was born in London, studied art history, anthropology and archaeology at Trinity College in Cambridge, before going on to complete his artistic education at the Slade School of Art and Goldsmiths' College. Unusually for his generation, and for the circle of artists loosely associated with the New British Sculpture, he has always been preoccupied with the human figure (usually his own), its scale, and its relationship both to the viewer and the wider environment. His entire output has strong spiritual and humanist dimensions. His less well-known, but exquisitely refined, drawings show affinities to the artistic productions of the Theosophists and of Joseph Beuys. His work has been exhibited frequently in Britain and abroad. In 1994 he received the Turner Prize.

Antony Gormley, exh. cat. Tate Gallery, Liverpool 1993.
John Hutchinson et al., *Antony Gormley*, London 2000.

DUNCAN GRANT
(born in Rothiemurchus, Inverness, 1885, died 1978)

After studying art in London and Paris, Duncan Grant went on, in 1908, to join the Bloomsbury Group, which had been formed by Clive and Vanessa Bell. Grant developed a friendship with Roger Fry and quickly became a central figure in this circle of artists and writers. In 1911 he and other members of the group received a commission through Fry to collaborate on a mural painting for the Borough Polytechnic in South London. Around this time, Grant also met Pablo Picasso and Henri Matisse at the home of Gertrude Stein in Paris, and their work was later to have a decisive influence on his paintings and fabric designs. Grant, who was a pacifist, worked as a farmhand during the First World War. From 1913–19 he was also active as a co-director of the Omega Workshops, which had been established by Fry to give gainful employment to artists, in the production of furniture, ceramics and textiles. After the Omega Workshops closed in 1919, Grant continued to collaborate with Vanessa Bell on interior decoration schemes for town and country houses. He now also began to enjoy success, with his paintings of still lifes, landscapes and portraits, executed in a style which combined realism with modernist influences. Before the outbreak of the Second World War, Grant joined the committee of the pacifist Artists' International Association. In 1959 the Tate Gallery devoted a retrospective to his work. The farmhouse at Charleston, Sussex, where Duncan Grant and Vanessa Bell lived for many years, has now been opened to the public and commemorates the work of these artists and their associates from the Bloomsbury Group.

Simon Watney, *The Art of Duncan Grant*, London 1990.

Frances Spalding, *Duncan Grant*, London 1997.

RICHARD HAMILTON
(born in London, 1922)

Just What Is It That Makes Today's Homes So Different, So Appealing? This collage, composed of fragments from advertising pictures and texts, was Hamilton's pictorial contribution to the exhibition *This Is Tomorrow* at the London Whitechapel Art Gallery in 1956. Later on, it practically became a manifesto of Pop Art on account of its innovative iconography. Together with sculptors such as William Turnbull and Eduardo Paolozzi, the architects Alison and Peter Smithson and the cultural critics Reyner Banham and Lawrence Alloway, Hamilton was a core member of the Independent Group, which started out in 1952 within the context of the programme of exhibitions and discussions at the Institute for Contemporary Arts in London. The Group refused to treat popular culture as kitsch, and their activities were influenced by their wide-ranging interest in science fiction, American comics, advertising, film, jazz and even car-racing. Richard Hamilton was a close friend of his fellow artists Marcel Duchamp and Dieter Roth, and collaborated with each of these on a number of projects. He was also largely responsible for saving Kurt Schwitters' third and last (uncompleted) *Merzbau* from neglect and destruction (Hatton Gallery, Newcastle-upon-Tyne). Many of Hamilton's most powerful works, including his head-on attack on Thatcherism in *Treatment Room* (1984), reflect his deep concern with political issues. His approach to his work is characterised by a constant desire to experiment with new imagery and new possibilities for creating images with the aid of technology. Typical of this was his experiment with the artistic potential of computer technology in *Seven Rooms – Bathroom*, his contribution to *Documenta 10* in 1997, and this is one of the reasons for the enduring appeal of his work to successive generations of younger artists.

Richard Hamilton, *Collected Words, 1953–1982*, London 1982.

Richard Hamilton, exh. cat. Tate Gallery, London 1992.

Richard Hamilton, *Imaging James Joyce's Ulysses*, London 2001.

ADRIAN HEATH
(born in Maymo, Burma, 1920, died 1992)

The painter Adrian Heath received his training at the Slade School of Art from 1939 to 1940 and again 1945 to 1947. His first solo exhibition, of landscape paintings, was at the Musée des Beaux-Arts de Carcassonne in France in 1948. There followed an exhibition at the Redfern Gallery in London in 1953. Around 1950–52 Heath's studio became the focal point for the group of artists who referred to themselves as the British Constructivists (Victor Pasmore, Kenneth and Mary Martin, Anthony Hill and Heath himself) and of sympathetic colleagues, including Eduardo Paolozzi, William Scott, Roger Hilton and Terry Frost, whose collective *Broadsheet*, no. 1 (1951) amounted to a manifesto, seeking to make connections with other modernist practices. All these artists were included in Lawrence Alloway's book *Nine Abstract Artists* and an exhibition with the same title at the Redfern Gallery in London the following year. Heath's early work of 1950–58 was based on proportional divisions and sub-divisions of the format of the canvas. In his own estimation, this work was "entirely non-objective and the direct perception of nature was severely excluded". In his later work, which came to terms with Abstract Expressionism, he developed a style of painting that is sometimes reminiscent of Arshile Gorky. The Museum am Ostwall in Dortmund gave Heath his first solo exhibition in Germany in 1961. His work is represented in numerous British and international collections.

Adrian Heath. Paintings and Gouaches, exh. cat. Hanover Gallery, London 1960.

Adrian Heath. Paintings, exh. cat. Redfern Gallery, London 1990.

NIGEL HENDERSON
(born in London 1917, died 1984)

The British painter and photographer Nigel Henderson first studied biology before deciding to train as an artist at the Slade School in London, where he completed his studies in 1949. Even before the Second World War, he came into contact with the art world through his mother, who had helped Peggy Guggenheim to set up her short-lived Guggenheim Jeune Gallery in London in 1938. He kept in touch with the members of the Bloomsbury Group and worked on collages and paintings which were predominantly influenced by the French Surrealist Yves Tanguy. After the war, he spent some time in Paris, together with his fellow student Eduardo Paolozzi, and made the acquaintance of artists such as Alberto Giacometti, Georges Braque and Hans Arp. In the following years, Henderson started experimenting with the medium of photography. First, he chose subjects from his immediate environment, in the working-class district of Bethnal Green, somewhat in the spirit of the pre-war Mass Observation movement. Subsequently, he started to experiment with the artistic possibilities of photography and collage and to combine photographic images with *objets trouvés*. From 1955 to 1961 he ran a semi-commercial enterprise, Hammer Prints Ltd., with Eduardo Paolozzi. Henderson was one of the key figures of the Independent Group, whose work is only now beginning to gain the recognition it deserves.

Heads Eye Win. Nigel Henderson, exh. cat. Norwich School of Art Gallery, Norwich 1982.

Victoria Walsh, *Nigel Henderson. Parallel of Life and Art*, London 2001.

BARBARA HEPWORTH
(born in Wakefield, Yorkshire, 1903, died 1975)

Barbara Hepworth set out as a figurative sculptor after completing her training at the Royal College of Art in 1924, but took an early interest in carving. Her early works have often been compared to those of her first husband, John Skeaping, and of her friend and contemporary Henry Moore. In the

1930s, however, after Hepworth came together with her future second husband, the painter Ben Nicholson, she developed into a leading advocate of abstraction and became a member of the artists' groups Abstraction-Création and Unit One. For all that she was an abstract artist, however, Hepworth stayed close to nature, and the curved, amorphous forms which recurred in her work might be seen to reflect the rhythms and contours of natural forms. Together with Henry Moore and the critic Herbert Read, Hepworth and Nicholson were at the centre of an artistic community in the North London suburb of Hampstead, which Read once referred to as a "gentle nest of artists", and whose members included Naum Gabo and, for a while, Piet Mondrian. At the outbreak of war, Hepworth, Nicholson and Gabo moved down to the artists' colony at St. Ives in Cornwall, where they went on to influence a younger generation of abstract artists connected to the landscape. Throughout this period, Hepworth cultivated an approach to her work which was inspired by the ideal of "truth to materials" and interpreted in modernist circles as an expression of personal and artistic integrity. After the war, Hepworth worked mainly in bronze and stone, her work grew in scale and she developed a particular fondness for the monolith. Like Henry Moore she also tended increasingly to favour public over private forms of sculptural expression.

Josef Paul Hodin, *Barbara Hepworth*, London 1961.

Penelope Curtis and Alan G. Wilkinson, *Barbara Hepworth*.

A Retrospective, exh. cat. Tate Gallery, Liverpool 1994.

PATRICK HERON
(born in Leeds, 1922, died 1999)

Patrick Heron, who studied at the Slade School of Art, made a name for himself as an art critic as well as an abstract painter. Thus, in the late 1940s, he worked as an art critic for the journal *New Statesman and Nation* and, in the late 1950s, as the London correspondent of the New York newspaper *Arts*. In 1955 he published his influential book *The Changing Forms of Art*. His early representational still lifes and interiors with figures were initially inspired by Henri Matisse and Georges Braque. Under the influence of American Abstract Expressionism – an influence he defined as reciprocal – Heron turned away from representational painting in the mid 1950s to create colourful abstracts with soft, geometric forms. Heron spent long periods in St. Ives, before finally settling there in 1956 and shortly afterwards moving into the studio that had been occupied by Ben Nicholson. Throughout his later career, he was deeply influenced by the land-

scape of Cornwall, and he turned again to freer forms and figurative elements, after the period of his most intense engagement with abstraction and the "stripe paintings" of the late 1950s.

Mel Gooding, *Patrick Heron*, London 1994.

Patrick Heron, exh. cat. Tate Gallery, London 1998.

ANTHONY HILL
(born in London, 1930)

Anthony Hill studied at St. Martin's School of Art from 1947 to 1949 and at the Central School of Art and Crafts in London from 1949 to 1951. Until 1954, he worked as an abstract painter and *collagiste*. In 1954 he began to work on reliefs which he called *Orthogonal Constructions*. Around 1965 he began to produce two-sided reliefs, and these developed into three-dimensional sculptures from around 1970 onwards. The artist professes to be a "Constructivist", even though the historical period of Constructivism has long since passed. In the 1970s he studied Russian formalism, and he called a series of reliefs *Hommage à Chlebnikov*. Hill, who corresponded with Marcel Duchamp in the 1950s and met him in 1959, emphasises the need for artistic activity to be imbued with theory, in the spirit of T. S. Eliot's dictum: "Art without intellectual context is vanity."

Lawrence Alloway, *Nine Abstract Painters*, London 1954.

Anthony Hill. A Retrospective Exhibition, exh. cat. Arts Council of Great Britain, London 1983.

ROGER HILTON
(born in Northwood, Middlesex, 1911, died 1975)

Roger Hilton, who had spent over two years in Paris before the war as a student of Roger Bissière, was one of the few British artists working in an abstract style in the 1950s. Hilton's early works, which were influenced by the Paris art scene and the CoBrA group, were limited to simple forms and a range of basic colours, including black and white and a selection of earthy shades. His free abstractions and flowing contours suggested parallels between the landscape and the female form, and these metaphorical elements served to distinguish his work from that of his early friends in the British Constructivist group. Hilton drew inspiration from the periods he spent in the artists' colony of St. Ives and from the rolling countryside of Cornwall, which he visited for the first time in 1956, as the guest of Patrick Heron, and where he finally settled in 1965. In the last years of his life, when he was tied to his sick-bed, he created a large quantity of colourful, primitivist gouaches.

Roger Hilton. *Paintings and Drawings 1931–1973*, London 1974.

Roger Hilton, exh. cat. South Bank Centre, Hayward Gallery, London 1993.

DAMIEN HIRST
(born in Bristol, 1965)

Damien Hirst studied at Goldsmiths' College, London, from 1986–89. In 1988, while still a student, he curated the legendary exhibition *Freeze* in an abandoned warehouse in London's Docklands, where he exhibited his own work alongside that of his colleagues, including Angela Bulloch, Mat Collishaw, Angus Fairhurst, Gary Hume, Abigail Lane, Sarah Lucas and Anya Gallaccio. This exhibition established the nucleus of the Young British Artists or "YBAs", as they came to be known after a series of seven exhibitions held at the Saatchi Gallery, London, starting in March 1992. Hirst's works deal with issues of life and death and arouse feelings of anxiety in the spectator. Hirst became a household name almost overnight, through the publicity associated with exhibiting a giant tiger shark in a glass tank full of formaldehyde at the Saatchi Gallery in 1991. This work belonged to a spectacular series of dead and sometimes dissected animals, including a whole sheep (*Away from the Flock*) and a bisected pig (*This Little Piggy Went To Market, This Little Piggy Stayed at Home*). In *A Thousand Years*, a bloody calf's head and an insectocutor formed the main constituents of a fly hatchery and extermination trap. *Mother and Child Divided* – a cow and its calf cut lengthways and displayed in separate glass cases filled with formaldehyde – was the work which brought Hirst to international fame, when it was exhibited in the Aperto, at the 1993 Venice Biennale. Hirst constantly seeks to violate the traditional conceptions of art and of so-called good taste. He has decorated a London restaurant in the clinically cool style of a *Pharmacy*. A whole series of his sculptures deals with the themes of medicine and the human anatomy. Hirst was awarded the Turner Prize in 1995. He now lives in Devon and has increasingly diversified his activities into the fields of gastronomy, advertising, popular music, film and video.

Damien Hirst, *I Want to Spend the Rest of My Life Everywhere, With Everyone, One to One, Always, Forever, Now*, London 1997.

DAVID HOCKNEY
(born in Bradford, Yorkshire, 1937)

David Hockney won his first prize for art before even leaving the Royal College of Art in London in 1962, where he studied alongside other artists of the British Pop Art movement, such as R. B. Kitaj,

Derek Boshier and Allen Jones. Hockney's early drawings and graphic works derived formal inspiration from illustrations, pictorial satire and children's drawings. In 1962 he took part in the exhibition *Young Contemporaries*. After his move to Los Angeles in 1964, his paintings reflected his new-found enthusiasm for the light, bungalows, swimming pools and palms of California. Through the use of acrylic paints and a cool, though bright, palette, he succeeded in imbuing these two-dimensional arrangements of three-dimensional space with a sense of unreality and an almost surreal kind of radiance. The swimming-pool paintings of 1964 to 1967 are among his best-known works. In the 1970s Hockney turned to making set designs, in addition to his activities as a painter, printmaker and draughtsman. His photo-collages from this time, which were first exhibited at the Centre Georges Pompidou in Paris in 1982, betrayed his indebtedness to Cubism and his abiding love of Picasso's work. Since then, Hockney has continued to work in a number of fields and has produced large-scale, colourful landscape paintings of the American West Coast which reflect his continuing fascination with photographic and other techniques for re-presenting reality. A retrospective of Hockney's paintings was held at the Kunst- und Ausstellungshalle in Bonn in 2001.

David Hockney. A Retrospective, ed. Maurice Tuchman, exh. cat. Los Angeles County Museum of Art and tour, New York 1988.

Paul Melia (ed.), *David Hockney,* Manchester 1995.

HOWARD HODGKIN
(born in London, 1932)

Howard Hodgkin is best known, as a painter and graphic artist, for the glowing intensity of his colours. Like Patrick Caulfield, he first rose to prominence with the Pop Art generation who exhibited as *Young Contemporaries* in the early 1960s, but, as with Caulfield, his artistic intentions set him apart from his generation and his subsequent development followed an independent course. Although Hodgkin's pictures always relate to an object, or represent friends or family members in private interiors, they appear to be almost abstract on account of their flat surfaces and animated brushwork. Hodgkin prefers using wooden boards to canvas as the support material for his paintings and often paints the edges of these variously sized boards, so that the frame of the picture is fully integrated into the work itself. In the 1980s Hodgkin created *Autumn Leaves,* a series of prints on moist, handmade paper inspired by his journeys to India, which were exhibited at the Tate Gallery.

In 1984 he represented Britain at the Venice Biennale. He was awarded the Turner Prize in 1985 and received a knighthood in 1992.

Howard Hodgkin Paintings, exh. cat. The Modern Art Museum of Fort Worth, Texas, London 1995.

Andrew Graham-Dixon, *Howard Hodgkin,* London 2001.

JOHN HOYLAND
(born in Sheffield, 1934)

John Hoyland, who is one of Britain's foremost abstract painters, first came to prominence at the time of the *New Generation* exhibition at the Whitechapel Art Gallery in 1964. His Colour Field painting was heavily influenced by the artistic theories and concepts of the followers of Clement Greenberg, which had been formed at the time of Abstract Expressionism. In the course of his frequent stays in the United States, Hoyland became acquainted with Morris Louis, Kenneth Noland, Helen Frankenthaler and Robert Motherwell, and was confirmed in his expressive use of colour through studying the working methods of Hans Hofmann. As Hoyland once put it: "Paintings are there to be experienced, they are events." After the mid 1970s, Hoyland no longer simply poured or brushed colour onto the canvas but applied it in thick layers, with a spatula, thereby giving his paintings the qualities of reliefs. From the 1980s onwards, he also increased his pictorial vocabulary, by adding triangles, diagonals and circular areas to the rectangles which had previously dominated many of his compositions.

John Hoyland, exh. cat. Waddington Galleries, London 1990.

Paul Moorhouse, *John Hoyland,* exh. cat. Royal Academy of Arts, London 1999.

GARY HUME
(born in Kent, 1962)

Gary Hume studied art from 1985 to 1988 at Goldsmiths' College in London. In 1988 he joined other artists of his generation in the exhibition *Freeze,* organised by Damien Hirst, which might be considered the springboard for the Young British Artists. As a student, Hume worked primarily with installations of video and sculpture, and he only subsequently developed an ambition to open up new possibilities for painting. After leaving Goldsmiths', Hume worked on a series of monochrome *Door Paintings,* which were schematic depictions of the kind of doors to be found in hospitals. He then went on to use these images in high-gloss lacquer paintings on canvas or aluminium sheets. These

offered large surfaces in which viewers could see their own image reflected and thus become integrated into the work itself. After 1993, Hume moved away from this highly purist approach, to concentrate on creating forms from lines, female bodies, plants and animals. In 1996, Hume was nominated for the Turner Prize. In 1999, he represented Britain at the Venice Biennale. Hume lives and works in London.

Gary Hume. Paintings, exh. cat. Kunsthalle Bern, Berne 1995.

Gary Hume, ed. Clarrie Wallis, exh. cat. XLVIII Venice Biennale, British Pavilion, London 1999.

PAUL HUXLEY
(born in London, 1938)

Paul Huxley studied at Harrow School of Art from 1951 to 1956 and then at the Royal Academy Schools in London. His first solo exhibition took place at the Rowan Gallery in London in 1963, where he would regularly exhibit his works for the next twenty years. He was a prizewinner at the legendary exhibition *New Generation* at the Whitechapel Art Gallery in London in 1964, where he exhibited alongside Patrick Caulfield, David Hockney, John Hoyland and Bridget Riley. His painting – like that of many artists of his generation – is characterised by a self-imposed limitation to a few geometric forms, developed out of his individual response to Abstract Expressionism. Even within these limitations, however, he managed to introduce variations within series and a relaxation of rigid geometry to achieve livelier and lighter forms than might be expected.

Paul Huxley. Recent Paintings, exh. cat. Mayor Rowan Gallery, London 1989.

HUMPHREY JENNINGS
(born in Walberswick, Suffolk, 1907, died 1950)

Humphrey Jennings was the most important British documentary filmmaker of the 1940s. He studied theatre in Cambridge from 1926 to 1929 and graduated with honours. After a variety of other activities, he joined John Grierson's GPO Film Unit in 1934, where he worked as an actor, stage designer and director of documentary films. His films *Locomotives* and *Post Haste* appeared that year. In 1936 he was one of the co-organisers of the *First International Surrealist Exhibition,* and, a year later, he, Charles Madge and Tom Harrison founded the Mass Observation movement. The documentary films he made during the Second World War, including *Listen to Britain* (1942) and *Fires Were*

Started (1943), which documented Britain's feeling of solidarity under the German attacks, marked Jennings' breakthrough as a director. His book *Pandaemonium, 1660–1886. The Coming of the Machine as Seen by Contemporary Observers*, a historical collage of the Industrial Revolution, was published after the Second World War. Jennings died in 1950, while filming in Greece.

Humphrey Jennings, *Pandaemonium, 1660–1886.*
The Coming of the Machine as Seen By Contemporary Observers,
ed. Mary-Lou Jennings and Charles Madge,
London 1995.
Brian Winston, *Fires Were Started*, London 1999.

ALLEN JONES
(born in Southhampton, 1937)

From 1955 to 1959 Allen Jones studied painting and lithography at Hornsey College of Art in London, where the teaching mainly followed Paul Klee's *Pedagogical Sketchbook*. During that time, he travelled to Provence and to Paris, where he encountered, and was deeply impressed by, the work of Robert Delaunay. In 1959 he enrolled on a course at at the Royal College of Art, where Patrick Caulfield, David Hockney, Derek Boshier and R. B. Kitaj were among his fellow students, but was asked to leave the College at the end of his first year and returned to Hornsey – this time, as a teacher. Allen Jones' work of the early 1960s was strongly influenced by the writings of Friedrich Nietzsche, Sigmund Freud and C. G. Jung. His works were founded in a belief that creativity feeds on the unconscious and combines male and female elements. In 1963 Jones was awarded the Prix des Jeunes Artistes at the Paris Biennale. In 1964 he and his first wife moved to New York and journeyed around the USA. In New York Hockney drew his attention to the pictorial world of mass consumption and advertising and, for a while, he abandoned two dimensional painting for three-dimensional, illusionist objects with erotic subjects. His hyperrealist table sculpture, whose top was supported by a half-naked kneeling female figure, acquired instant notoriety. In the 1970s Jones designed the sets for several television films and stage plays. In 1979 the Walker Art Gallery held a comprehensive retrospective of his work which afterwards went to London, Sunderland, Baden-Baden and Bielefeld. In 1982/83 Jones was a Guest Professor at the Hochschule für bildende Künste in Hamburg, in 1986 he became a member of the Royal Academy.

Marco Livingstone, *Allen Jones. Sheer Magic*, London 1979.
Marco Livingstone, *Allen Jones Prints*, Munich 1995.

DAVID JONES
(born in Brockley, Kent, 1895, died 1974)

Like Percy Wyndham Lewis and Merlin Evans, David Jones was equally accomplished as artist and writer. During his studies at Westminster School of Art in London, he developed an enthusiasm for English landscape watercolours and the work of William Blake. In 1921 he converted to Catholicism. His search for the spiritual roots of life and art lead him to Ditchling in 1922, where he joined a guild of artist-craftsmen that had been founded by the stone carver Eric Gill. In the late 1920s Jones set out hiking through Great Britain, visiting various monasteries and throwing himself into watercolour painting. In 1931, he joined the Seven and Five Society, a group of progressive artists that also included Ben Nicholson, Christopher Wood and Ivon Hitchens. He exhibited with them at the Goupil Gallery and took part in the Venice Biennale and the World Fair in New York. In 1937 he published *In Parentheses*, which dealt with his harrowing experiences in the First World War and took as its underlying theme the continuance of the most ancient aspects of British culture in modern times.

Paul Hills (ed.), *David Jones. Artist and Poet*,
Aldershot 1997.

PETER JOSEPH
(born in London, 1929)

Peter Joseph abandoned a career in advertising in the mid 1970s, in order to devote himself exclusively to painting. His paintings from this period are dominated by geometrical forms, primary colours and optical effects. In addition, Joseph worked on outdoor projects and installations with colourful walls. In the 1970s the formats of his paintings became more intimate, and his compositions took on a more meditative character, in keeping with Joseph's growing interest in poetry, philosophy and music. In 1971 he started to develop a compositional scheme, which consisted of a monochrome square in the centre of the canvas, offset by a darker, surrounding field. Joseph's work is distinguished from that of other Minimalists by a certain romantic sensibility, akin to that of the American painter Mark Rothko.

Peter Joseph, ed. Matthew Higgs, exh. cat. Lisson Gallery,
London 1998.

ANISH KAPOOR
(born in Bombay, 1954)

Anish Kapoor has lived and worked in London since 1972, receiving his artistic training first at Hornsey College of Art and then at Chelsea School of Art. His work took a decisive turn as a result of a visit he made to India in 1979, when he was struck by the mystical qualities of the coloured pigment which he saw piled up on sale in the markets and in front of the temples. He started to use pigment on clustered geometric forms distributed in space and to incorporate the space itself and the presence of the viewer into his overall concept. Thus, his sculptures and installations, using elements as diverse as air, water, stone and pure colour, are activated in the field of tension between presence and absence, place and non-place, space and void, and body and soul. Over the past decade, Kapoor has worked on an increasingly large scale, in traditional materials such as alabaster and polished steel, as well as the humble materials with which he set out. Recent projects have included a public art commission for the Great Court of the British Museum and a vast temporary installation in the gutted shell of the Baltic Mills, which he temporarily turned into a unitary sculptural space. Anish Kapoor represented Britain at the Venice Biennale in 1990, where he was awarded the Premio 2000, and was awarded the Turner Prize in 1991. He was given a large retrospective at the Hayward Gallery in 1998 and has recently been commissioned to create a new sculptural installation in the Turbine Hall of Tate Modern.

Germano Celant, *Anish Kapoor*, London 1996.
Anish Kapoor, exh. cat. Hayward Gallery, London 1998.

PHILLIP KING
(born in Kheredine, Tunisia, 1934)

Phillip King studied modern languages at Cambridge, before training as a sculptor, first as a student of Anthony Caro at St. Martin's School of Art from 1957 to 1958 and then (on Caro's recommendation) as an assistant to Henry Moore from 1959–1960. On a visit to *documenta 2* in Kassel in 1959, King encountered the work of Constantin Brancusi at first hand and was deeply impressed with a large display of American Abstract Expressionist paintings. These experiences, coupled with a three-month stay in Greece, where his thinking was influenced by his observations of the relationship of man to nature, led him to destroy all his earlier work and make a fresh start. Colour now became an important element of his predominantly large-format sculptures, which were initially made of plastic and soon afterwards of painted aluminium and steel. In 1968 he represented Britain at the Venice Biennale, together with Bridget Riley. This helped to launch King's international career, which was further consolidated by a retrospective of his work, which toured a number of European cities in 1974–1975. King's numerous public art commissions include one for the European Patent Office in Munich in 1978. To this day, the central theme in his work remains an investigation into the relationship between sculpture, the viewer and the surrounding space. King has spent a term as an Artist Trustee of the Tate Gallery and has been active as an art school lecturer over many years, ending up as the Professor of Sculpture at the Royal College of Art. In 1999 Phillip King was elected President of the Royal Academy in London.

Phillip King. The Artist in Conversation with Victor De Circasia and John Edwards, Wakefield 1992.
Tim Hilton, *The Sculpture of Phillip King*,
London 1992.

R. B. KITAJ
(born in Cleveland, Ohio, 1932)

R. B. Kitaj came to Britain to study at the Ruskin School of Drawing in Oxford (1958–59) and the Royal College of Art in London (1959–61) and subsequently spent most of his working life in Britain. Kitaj's painting in the early 1960s was largely representational, in defiance of the current vogue for abstraction, and his example encouraged other artists such as David Hockney, Patrick Caulfield and Allen Jones to broaden the range of subject-matter in their work. Kitaj's interests and sources of inspiration extended to aspects of history, politics, sociology, psychology, iconography and literature. In the 1960s and early 1970s, Kitaj created numerous visual readymades and print collages, in collaboration with the master screen-printer Chris Prater. In the late 1970s, with his friend David Hockney, he led a much publicised campaign for a return to life class in the art schools and to the study of the human figure. The colouring and formal design of his later paintings and drawings have been strongly influenced by French nineteenth century art, especially the pastels of Edgar Degas. In recent years, Kitaj has placed strong emphasis in his work on his Jewishness and the predicaments of the Jewish Diaspora.

R. B. Kitaj. A Retrospective, ed. Richard Morphet,
exh. cat. Tate Gallery, London 1994.
Marco Livingstone, *R. B. Kitaj*,
London 1999.

LEON KOSSOFF
(born in London, 1926)

Leon Kossoff's painting may be compared to that of Frank Auerbach, for its pictorial directness and employment of thick impasto. Like Auerbach, Kossoff also concentrates on a deliberately narrow range of subjects. This may be no accident, since both artists were fellow students at David Bomberg's evening classes at the Borough Polytechnic in the early 1950s. Kossoff mainly paints people close to him, in intimate interiors, or passers-by in anonymous public places, such as underground stations or swimming baths. His dark paintings of individuals wearing a frightened expression create rather a gloomy atmosphere and convey feelings of isolation and urban *Angst*. Many of Kossoff's drawings show his interest in coming to terms with the great figures in European art, such as the French painter Nicolas Poussin (1594–1665). Kossoff, who is frequently associated with the so-called School of London, including Francis Bacon, Frank Auerbach and Lucian Freud, represented Britain at the Venice Biennale in 1995.

Leon Kossoff, exh. cat. Tate Gallery, London 1996.
Leon Kossoff, exh. cat. Annely Juda Fine Arts, London 2000.

HENRY LAMB
(born in Adelaide, Australia, 1883, died 1960)

Henry Lamb completed his studies in medicine in Manchester before deciding to study painting, first in London and then, in 1907–08, in Paris. He exhibited a portrait of the writer Lytton Strachey at the first Post-Impressionist exhibition in 1910 and became a member of the Camden Town Group in 1911–12. In 1913 he met Stanley Spencer and both men served as medical orderlies in the First World War. In 1917 Lamb took part in the campaign in Palestine, and in 1919 he attempted to assimilate these experiences in a number of large-scale works, including *Irish Troops in the Judaean Hill, Surprised by a Turkish Bombardment* (1919), whose composition reveals the clear influence of Vorticism. After the First World War, Lamb concentrated mainly on portraiture, and Stanley Spencer sat for him in 1928. Lamb was associated with the Bloomsbury Group and portrayed several of its members in a soft, Post-Impressionist style. Lamb worked as an Official War Artist in the Second World War. In the final years of his life, when he suffered from poor health, he mainly painted landscapes and still lifes.

Keith Clements, *Henry Lamb. The Artist and His Friends*,
Bristol 1985.

MICHAEL LANDY
(born in London, 1963)

Michael Landy studied at Loughborough College of Art and Goldsmiths' College in London. In his videos and drawings, he creates an artificial world which evokes the collapse of social norms and the depths to which people can sink in the inhuman working and living conditions of the modern service society. His best-known works include *Market* (1990), a large installation in an East London warehouse, which was a punning commentary on exchange mechanisms in a late capitalist economy, and *Scrapheap Services* (1996), that presented a fictitious cleaning company that offers its services to a wealthy society but also takes over the disposal of people. Other important projects have been *Michael Landy at Home, 7 Fashion Street* in London in 1999 and the travelling exhibition *Diary*, which started at Cornerhouse, Manchester in 2000. In 2001 Landy staged *Break Down*, a ritualistic classification and destruction of all his material possessions, in a recently vacated department store in Oxford Street, in central London.

Michael Landy and Julian Stallabrass, *Break Down*, London 2001.

PETER LANYON
(born in St. Ives, 1918, died 1964)

Peter Lanyon, who was born in St. Ives, studied in Penzance and, briefly in 1937, at the Euston School Road in London. Back in St. Ives, he met Barbara Hepworth, Ben Nicholson and Naum Gabo in 1939, after they had moved there from London, on the outbreak of war. The influence of Ben Nicholson and Naum Gabo profoundly altered the character of his work, and he stopped painting for a while in order to concentrate on making abstract constructions. After the war, Lanyon returned to painting landscapes with figurative connotations, which became progressively freer and more lyrical, under the early influence of American Abstract Expressionism and (from 1959) aerial perspective. As he put it, "The pictures now combine the elements of land, sea and sky – earth, air and water." In 1964 Peter Lanyon lost his life in a gliding accident.

Andrew Lanyon, *Peter Lanyon, 1918–1964*, Newlyn 1990.
Peter Lanyon, exh. cat. Tate Gallery, London 1998.

JOHN LATHAM
(born in former Rhodesia, today's Zimbabwe, 1921)

John Latham's work is impossible to categorise in a straightforward way, but has something in common with a wide variety of concepts and styles, from Tachism and assemblage to Conceptual Art,

Performance Art, Fluxus, video, film, installation and auto-destructive art. In his work, Latham deals with the position of the artist in society and the significance of art and of language, as well as with scientific theories on the origins of the cosmos, and of space and time. Latham's preoccupation with exploring the links between art and science has been a central feature of his work, ever since graduating from Chelsea School of Art in 1950. In 1964 Latham began a series of "Skoob Tower" ceremonies, which culminated in the ritual burning of sculptures made of books, to suggest that "perhaps the cultural base [of society] has been burned out". Together with Barbara Steveni and other artists, in 1966 Latham founded the Artist Placement Group (later re-established as O + I), which took a critical look at the position of the artist in social structures and the role of the "incidental person". In 1975 Latham held a solo exhibition at the Kunsthalle Düsseldorf and another at the Tate Gallery, London the following year. In 1977 he was invited to take part in *documenta 6*, in Kassel. In 1991 Latham was given a retrospective exhibition at the Staatsgalerie in Stuttgart, which then moved on to the Museum of Modern Art in Oxford. To this day, John Latham is artistically and politically active on the art scene and has gained belated recognition as one of the most radical and innovative artists of his generation.

John Latham. Kunst nach der Physik, exh. cat. Staatsgalerie Stuttgart and Museum of Modern Art, Oxford, Stuttgart 1991.

John A. Walker, *John Latham. The Incidental Person – His Art and Ideas*, Middlesex 1995.

BOB LAW
(born in Brentford, Middlesex, 1934)

Bob Law moved to St. Ives in 1957, in order to devote himself to pottery and painting and there met Ben Nicholson and other artists. Law's work became increasingly abstract under the influence of the work of Mark Rothko and Barnett Newman, which he saw at the exhibition *New American Painting* at the Tate Gallery in 1959, although he always worked to the scale of the human figure, with arms outstretched. In his "field paintings" from this period, Law not only recorded the time and place of painting the works, but the feelings he experienced in his close encounters with nature and the elements. In 1960 Law started working on his series of "Black Paintings", which were made through the application of successive layers of paint, whose original colour could only be guessed at through the top layer of black. In the late 1970s Law branched out into making small-scale, heavily

patinated, bronze sculptures, whose symbolic forms relate to the "metaphysical field paintings" of the early 1960s.

Bob Law. Drawings, *Sculpture and Paintings*, exh. cat. Newlyn Art Gallery, Newlyn, and Kettle's Yard Gallery, Cambridge 1999.

PERCY WYNDHAM LEWIS
(born on a yacht off the Canadian coast, 1882, died 1957)

Wyndham Lewis played an important part in early British avant-garde movements, as writer, poet and Vorticist painter. On completion of his studies at the Slade School of Art in 1901, he spent several years travelling in Europe, including a long spell in Paris. Back in London, he first joined the Camden Town Group before Roger Fry invited him to join the newly established Omega Workshops, in 1913. Following a quarrel with Fry, however, he withdrew from this artistic circle, founded the Rebel Art Centre in 1914 and published the short-lived journal *Blast*. Taking his lead from the sub-title of this "Review of the Great British Vortex", the poet Ezra Pound promptly proclaimed the birth of a new movement, Vorticism, of which Lewis was the self-appointed leader. Stimulated by the Futurists' use of forms, Lewis' works from that time show a mechanistic abstraction, along with a variety of geometric elements. After the Vorticists dispersed or died during the First World War, Lewis tried in vain to reassemble the British avant-garde by founding Group X in 1919. His later oil paintings are predominantly portraits (Edith Sitwell, T. S. Eliot) or depict scenes populated by fantastic creatures – motifs which are also to be found in his literary work.

Jeffrey Meyers, *The Enemy. A Biography of Wyndham Lewis*, London 1980.

Paul Edwards, *Wyndham Lewis. Painter and Writer*, New Haven 2000.

Paul O'Keefe, *Some Sort of Genius. A Life of Wyndham Lewis*, London 2000.

RICHARD LONG
(born in Bristol, 1945)

Richard Long attended the West of England College of Art from 1962–65 and St. Martin's School in London from 1966–68, where he was a contemporary of Barry Flanagan, Bruce McLean, Gilbert and George and others who share his ambition of stretching the definition of sculpture to the limit. Long's first work relating to the landscape dates back to 1964, and, from the late 1960s on, he became obsessed with the idea of working in, and

with, the landscape and with related problems of movement and time in natural space. In contrast to the traditional landscape artist, who reacts to what he sees from a fixed viewpoint, Long finds it important to communicate to the viewer the range and intensity of his own experiences in nature, with the aid of his maps, texts, photographs and spatial installations. Long's approach differs from that of the American Land Artists on account of the lightness and transitoriness of his interventions, which may be interpreted as pauses for meditation in the course of his progress through the landscape.

Richard Long. Works 1966–1977, exh. cat. Stedelijk Van Abbe Museum, Eindhoven 1979.

Richard Long. Walking. Circles, exh. cat. South Bank Centre, Hayward Gallery, London 1991.

F. E. MCWILLIAM
(born in Banbridge, Ireland, 1909, died 1992)

The sculptor Frederick Edward McWilliam studied at the Slade School in Oxford from 1928 to 1931 and then went to Paris. His first works show the influence of Constantin Brancusi, though later he joined the Surrealists. In 1939 the London Gallery presented his first solo exhibition. Like Picasso in his Surrealist paintings, McWilliam in his sculptures dissolves the organic unity of the human form to create new combinations of individual fragments, such as *Spanish Head* (1938–39) and *Long Arm: Fist Raised in a Republican Salute* (1939). Along with other British artists, McWilliam took part in activities such as "Artists Help Spain" and exhibited at the Artists' International Association (AIA) in 1937. After returning from the Second World War, McWilliam took up working again in the formal language he had developed in the late 1930s. In 1947 he created a sculpture garden for Roland Penrose's and Lee Miller's farm in Sussex. In 1951 he took part in the Festival of Britain on the South Bank of the Thames. His works were included in the exhibition *Dada and Surrealism Reviewed* in the Hayward Gallery London, in 1978.

F. E. McWilliam. Early Sculptures, 1935–1948, London 1982.

F. E. McWilliam. Sculpture, 1932–1989, ed. Mel Gooding, exh. cat. Tate Gallery, London 1999.

CONROY MADDOX
(born in Birmingham, 1912)

As in the case of many English artists of his generation, from the mid 1930s onwards, Conroy Maddox was decisively influenced by the ideas and concepts of Surrealism, although he declined an invitation to take part in the seminal *International Surrealist Exhibition* in London in 1936, on the grounds that too many artists had been included who had no claim to be called "Surrealists". Maddox's collages, paintings, gouaches, objects and texts, which are inspired by the work of Max Ernst, Giorgio de Chirico and Óscar Domínguez, focus on the images and visions of the unconscious. Going against the principles of academic art, Maddox inserted visions and fantasy figures into otherwise realistic paintings such as *The Lesson* (1938).

Conroy Maddox. Surrealism Unlimited 1968–1978, exh. cat. Camden Arts Centre, London 1978.

Silvano Levy (ed.), *Surreal Enigmas. Conroy Maddox,* Staffordshire 1995.

KENNETH MARTIN
(born in Sheffield, 1905, died 1984)

In the 1920s Kenneth Martin combined working as a graphic artist with studying art at Sheffield School of Art. In 1930 he married the painter Mary Balmford. In the 1930s Martin painted in a naturalistic style, but his enthusiasm for Russian Constructivism led him to turn his back on figurative painting from 1949 onwards. After 1951 Martin concentrated mainly on kinetic work, creating his first mobiles out of wood and sheet metal. In that year, he took part in the exhibition *British Abstract Art* at the AIA Gallery in London, and in 1955 held a joint exhibition with his wife, Mary Martin, at the Heffer Gallery in Cambridge. In the 1960s he worked mainly on his series of *Screw Mobiles* – spiral constructions of wire, whose twisting movements recall the movements of dancers. From 1969 on, Martin returned to painting and drawing, and in 1975 he created a series, *Chance and Order*, that was based on a system of parallel lines. His public art commissions included a large *Oscillation* for the Department of Engineering at Cambridge University in 1961.

Kenneth Martin, exh. cat. Waddington Galleries, London 1984.

Kenneth and Mary Martin, exh. cat. Annely Juda Fine Art, London 1987.

MARY MARTIN
(born in Folkestone, 1907, died 1969)

Mary Balmford studied from 1925 to 1932 at Goldsmiths' College and the Royal College of Art. In 1930 she married the painter Kenneth Martin, but she continued to paint landscapes and still lifes under her maiden name. Around 1950 she abandoned figurative painting and embarked on an intense engagement with abstract art. In 1951 she created her first "Constructivist" reliefs, based on variations of simple geometric elements. She shared her first solo exhibition with her husband at the Heffer Gallery in Cambridge. In 1956 she, Kenneth Martin, Victor Pasmore and other members of the "Constructivist Group", together with members of the rather differently orientated Independent Group, took part in the exhibition *This Is Tomorrow* at the Whitechapel Art Gallery in London. The Constructivists were united in their conviction that painting was not an adequate medium for abstract art. In her reliefs Mary Martin used materials as different as plaster, Plexiglas, wood, steel and, in her last years, aluminium and plastic.

Mary Martin, exh. cat. Tate Gallery, London 1984.

Kenneth and Mary Martin, exh. cat. Annely Juda Fine Art, London 1987.

BERNARD MEADOWS
(born in Norwich, 1915)

Bernard Meadows studied at the Royal College of Art and was Professor of Sculpture there from 1960 to 1980. In the 1950s, Meadows explored the formal possibilities of animal shapes, such as cocks and crabs, as vehicles for human feelings. This enabled him to get away from the excessive influence of Henry Moore, whose assistant he had been from 1936 to 1939 and from 1946 to 1948, and to find his own visual language as a sculptor. He first came to international attention in 1952, when he exhibited in the British Pavilion at the Venice Biennale, along with Robert Adams, Kenneth Armitage, Reg Butler, Lynn Chadwick, Geoffrey Clarke, Eduardo Paolozzi and William Turnbull. The phrase "geometry of fear", which Herbert Read first used in his catalogue introduction for this exhibition, seems particularly appropriate as a description of Meadows' work, since Read also alluded to "ragged claws, scuttling across the floors of silent seas". Only in the late 1970s and early 1980s did Meadows' sculpture begin to change, with the introduction of a more sensitive, erotic mood.

Alan Bowness, *Bernard Meadows. Sculpture and Drawings,* London 1995.

REUBEN MEDNIKOFF
(born in London, 1906, died 1972)

Reuben Mednikoff was of Russian Jewish origin, but rebelled against the Orthodox religion as a child. According to Grace Pailthorpe, his therapist, artistic partner and lifelong companion, many of his pictorial motifs sprang from these early experiences. Mednikoff was friends with the Surrealist poet David Gascoyne, who wrote England's first Surrealist manifesto in 1935. He himself wrote poetry, which was published in the journal *Poets' Corner*. Mednikoff and Pailthorpe first met in 1935 and began to explore the unconscious in the fields of art and psychology. In the years which followed, Mednikoff evolved his own artistic language. Paintings like *The Orgiastic Melody, September 1937* and *The Flying Pig* of 1938 depict strange, organic machines. In 1936, Mednikoff and Pailthorpe exhibited their work, including Mednikoff's *April 23 & 25, 1935 (Arboreal Bliss)* and Pailthorpe's *October 3 & 4, 1935* at the *International Surrealist Exhibition* in London. After the Second World War, both artists continued to work collaboratively and to experiment with art therapy and creative meditation, at the same time as developing their own forms of artistic expression.

Grace Pailthorpe 1883–1971, Reuben Mednikoff 1906–1975, exh. cat. Oliver Bradbury and James Birch Fine Art Gallery, London 1984.

GUSTAV METZGER
(born in Nuremberg, 1926)

As a child Gustav Metzger was forced to flee Great Britain in order to escape persecution as a Jew. His parents fell victim to the Holocaust. Metzger first earned his living as a carpenter and gardener and devoted himself to revolutionary politics before deciding in 1944 to become a professional artist (initially, a sculptor). He studied part-time with the former Vorticist David Bomberg and later became his assistant for a while, though he broke with him in 1953. His fellow pupils at Bomberg's "Borough Bottega" included Frank Auerbach and Leon Kossoff. Metzger described a visit to the Independent Group's exhibition *This is Tomorrow* (1956) as "one of the deepest art experiences of my life". As a painter, performance artist and art theorist, Gustav Metzger is seen as the father of auto-destructive art. In 1959 and 1960 he published his first two manifestos of "Auto-Destructive Art" and in 1966 organised the *Destruction in Art Symposium* (DIAS) in London. In 1974 Metzger published a call on artists to join him for three "Years without Art, 1977–1980", in protest against increasing commercialisation. Recently, Metzger has produced large-format photographs, in which he focuses critical attention on the relationship between this medium and history.

Gustav Metzger, *Damaged Nature, Auto-Destructive Art,* London, 1996.

Gustav Metzger, *Manifeste, Schriften, Konzepte,* Munich 1997.

LEE MILLER
(born in New York, 1907, died 1977)

Lee Miller made her career as a model and studied art in New York, before leaving for Europe in 1929 to continue her studies in Paris, Florence and Rome. In Paris she met Man Ray, and became his student, model and lover. Together they developed the technique of solarisation, beginning in 1929. In 1932 she separated from Man Ray and returned to New York, where she ran a photographic studio, as she had done in Paris, and concentrated mainly on portrait photographs. Back in Paris in 1937, Miller met her future husband, Roland Penrose, and became closely involved with Picasso, Eluard and the Surrealists. Miller spent the war years with Penrose in London, before returning to France as a war reporter to cover the Liberation of Paris for *Vogue*, and to Germany, where she photographed Hitler's former apartment in Munich and entered Dachau the day after its liberation by American troops. After the War, Miller continued for a while with her activities as a photo-journalist and exhibited her work from time to time, though a reassessment of her importance has only been possible in the last few years. Farley Farm, in Chiddingley, Sussex, where she and Roland Penrose had lived since 1949, was recently opened to the public.

Antony Penrose, *The Lives of Lee Miller*, London 1985.

JEREMY MOON
(born in Altrincham, Cheshire, 1934, died 1973)

Jeremy Moon trained as a lawyer, but turned to painting in the early 1960s. In 1961, he studied briefly at the Central School of Art, but his development was largely as an autodidact. He became a teacher at St. Martin's School of Art and from 1963 on exhibited regularly at the Rowan Gallery in London, as did two of his contemporaries, Bridget Riley and Phillip King. Jeremy Moon's large-format abstract paintings – incunabula of pure visuality – can be said to fall between Colour-Field painting and Op Art. His usually bright, serial compositions playfully test the extremes of logic and irrationality, calm and motion. Moon's promising career was tragically cut short by his early death.

Norbert Lynton, *Jeremy Moon. Paintings and Drawings, 1962–1973*, London 1973.

HENRY MOORE
(born in Castleford, Yorkshire, 1898, died 1986)

"I believe I was around eleven when I decided to become a sculptor." These words characterise Henry Moore's undeviating development. He studied sculpture at the Leeds School of Art and the Royal College of Art and was influenced by the ancient Egyptian and pre-Columbian sculpture, as well as the African and Polynesian art he saw in the British Museum. In 1928 Moore received his first official commission, to design a relief for the new administrative headquarters of the London Underground. His work aroused great controversy. That year, the Warren Gallery presented his first solo exhibition, for which Jacob Epstein wrote the catalogue introduction. In 1933, together with Paul Nash, he founded the group Unit One. In 1936 he took part in the *International Surrealist Exhibition* in London, and in 1938 in the *Exhibition of Abstract Art* at the Stedelijk Museum in Amsterdam. From the early 1920s to the Second World War, he worked almost exclusively in wood and stone, in keeping with the notion of "truth to materials". Although he experimented with geometric abstraction and, from 1932 on, made sculptures based on compositions with holes, his major interest remained the human figure. During the Second World War, he was named an Official War Artist and sketched people in air-raid shelters in the London Underground (*Shelter Drawings*). In 1946 a travelling retrospective of Moore's work went to the Museum of Modern Art in New York, and in 1948 he won the International Prize for Sculpture at the first postwar Venice Biennale. These two events laid the basis for Moore's growing international reputation and for the large-scale commissions for public sculptures in bronze – many of them in West Germany – which made him into a household name and led to major exhibitions in almost every country in the world. The Henry Moore Foundation, which was inaugurated at Much Hadham in Hertfordshire in 1977, has performed an invaluable service over the years, not only in promoting Moore's work, but in assisting young artists and supporting the study of sculpture of all periods.

David Sylvester (ed.), *Henry Moore. Complete Sculpture, 1921–48*, vol. 1, London 1957.

Susan Compton, *Henry Moore*, London 1988.

Henry Moore Bibliography, ed. Alexander Davis, vol. 1, 1898–1970, Much Hadham 1992.

PAUL NASH
(born in London 1889, died 1946)

Paul Nash initially trained as a draughtsman and illustrator before going on to the Slade School of Art from 1910–11, where he formed a lasting friendship with his fellow student Ben Nicholson. In 1913 Roger Fry invited him to join the recently established Omega Workshops. In 1914 Nash enlist-ed in the army and saw active service at Ypres in February 1917, where many of his fellow officers were killed. He found an outlet for his experiences in the six months during which he worked as an Official War Artist in 1918–19 and painted apocalyptic images of the war-torn landscape, including the *Menin Road* and *We Are Making a New World*. After the War, Nash diversified into creating stage sets and costumes. At the beginning of the 1930s, he experimented with Surrealist elements and concepts and participated in several Surrealist group exhibitions. His paintings of this period steer a course between Surrealism and abstraction and are notable for the novelty of their formal invention. In 1933 Nash was one of the founding members of the London artists' group Unit One. During the Second World War, he produced landscape paintings which had a metaphorical dimension, in addition to depicting the immediacy and the terror of aerial warfare.

Andrew Causey, *Paul Nash*, Oxford, 1980.

James King, *Interior Landscapes. A Life of Paul Nash*, London 1987.

CHRISTOPHER NEVINSON
(born in Hampstead, London, 1889, died 1946)

Shortly after finishing his studies at the Slade School in London in 1912, Christopher Nevinson went to live and work in Paris for some time. There, he shared a studio with Amedeo Modigliani and kept company with avant-garde artists, including the Italian Futurists, whose enthusiasm for technology he shared, and whose use of dynamic, geometricised forms influenced him strongly. Together with Percy Wyndham Lewis and Edward Wadsworth, he organised a celebrated dinner in honour of the Futurist Filippo Tommaso Marinetti in November 1913, and in June 1914 he joined Marinetti in publishing *Vital English Art: A Futurist Manifesto*. War became a central theme in Nevinson's work and his first one-man show, mainly of war paintings, in 1916, was a great success. The following year Nevinson was appointed an Official War Artist, and he was among the first artists to record his impressions of the landscape seen from the air. Urban themes, peaceful landscapes and flower paintings form the core of his later, less radical work.

C. R. W. Nevinson. Retrospective Exhibition of Paintings, Drawings and Prints, exh. cat. Kettle's Yard Gallery, Cambridge 1988.

Richard Ingleby et al., *C. R. W. Nevinson. The Twentieth Century*, exh. cat. Imperial War Museum, London 1999.

BEN NICHOLSON
(born in Denham, Buckinghamshire, 1894, died 1982)

Ben Nicholson had little formal training apart from a short spell at the Slade School in 1910–11, when he formed a close friendship with his fellow student Paul Nash. His early landscape paintings are deliberately naïve in style and strongly inspired by Pablo Picasso and Georges Braque, as well as by the simple sea paintings of the former sailor and autodidact Alfred Wallis, whom Nicholson had discovered in St. Ives in 1928. Although Ben Nicholson never completely turned his back on representational painting, his international reputation is above all based on the originality of his geometric abstractions, which were profoundly influenced by the pictorial structures of Cubism. In the 1930s Nicholson and his second wife, Barbara Hepworth, became members of the Paris group, Abstraction-Création, and of Paul Nash's artists' group, Unit One, in London. At the same time, he moved on from painterly abstraction to creating a series of geometric white reliefs, which reflected the impact made on him by his first visit to Mondrian's studio in Paris in 1934. After the Second World War, Nicholson reintroduced representational elements into many of his works and was increasingly drawn to elements of the Cornish landscape. The oil paintings that he made in St. Ives and after his move to Switzerland in 1958 gave further proof of his sensitive eye for colour and line, as did his drawings of landscape and architectural subjects.

Ben Nicholson, exh. cat. Tate Gallery, London 1993.
Norbert Lynton, *Ben Nicholson*, London 1993.
Sarah Jane Checkland, *Ben Nicholson. The Vicious Circles of His Life and Art*, London 2000.

JULIAN OPIE
(born in London, 1958)

Julian Opie, who studied at Goldsmiths' College in London from 1979 to 1982, quickly gained a reputation as one of the youngest representatives of the "New British Sculpture" with his brightly painted, two- and three-dimensional metal cutouts of images from the popular culture of everyday life. Later, he used a computer programme to simplify these models, reducing them to their essence, like pictograms, and placing them on large metal signs. These signs were positioned in public spaces, to point out what people expected to see, and what they did not. Thus, they depicted stylised sheep and cows, along with people, automobiles and buildings. The signs functioned like traffic signals, as a means of showing the way. Opie had his first solo exhibition at the Lisson Gallery in London in 1983, and has since taken part in numerous international exhibitions, including *documenta 8* in Kassel in 1987. In 1994 he held a retrospective of his work at the Hayward Gallery in London, which then moved to the Kunstverein in Hanover.

Julian Opie, exh. cat. Kölnischer Kunstverein, Cologne 1984.
Julian Opie, exh. cat. South Bank Centre, Hayward Gallery, London 1993.

GRACE PAILTHORPE
(born in Sutton, Surrey, 1883, died 1971)

Grace Pailthorpe was trained as a physician. During the First World War, he worked as a surgeon, but then she turned to psychotherapy, becoming a pioneer in the treatment of psychological ailments caused by war. Pailthorpe believed that liberating people was linked to developing their freedom of expression to the full and that artistic creativity played an important role in this connection. She shared a highly intense professional and personal partnership with the poet and painter Reuben Mednikoff, whom she met in 1935, and this relationship lasted to the end of their lives, but was at its most intense for the period up to July 1940, when the two of them departed to New York. André Breton saw, and admired, Mednikoff's and Pailthorpe's work at the *International Surrealist Exhibition* in 1936. In their research into the unconscious and attempts to use painting as a key to its innermost recesses, Pailthorpe and Mednikoff ran parallel to the English Surrealists, but they (along with Ithell Colquhoun) were formally expelled from that group in July 1940. On returning to Britain from North America with Reuben Mednikoff at the end of the Second World War, Pailthorpe continued to combine her practice as an artist with her activities as an art therapist for the remaining twenty years of her life.

Sluice Gates of the Mind, The Collaborative Work of Dr. Grace Pailthorpe and Ruben Mednikoff, eds. Nigel Walsh and Andrew Wilson, exh. cat. Leeds Museums and Galleries, Leeds 1998.

EDUARDO PAOLOZZI
(born in Leith, Edinburgh, 1924)

Eduardo Paolozzi's initial ambition was to be a commercial artist, and he was admitted to Edinburgh College of Art on that basis. During the War, he continued to study art and encountered Amédée Ozenfant's *Foundations of Modern Art*, which changed the course of his life. He also saw an exhibition of Kurt Schwitters' collages at a private gallery in London in 1944. On graduating from the Slade School of Art in 1947, Paolozzi went to live in Paris for two years, where he met many of the leading members of the artistic avant-garde, including Arp, Brancusi, Calder, and Giacometti, and was particularly impressed by Jean Dubuffet's "Art Brut". In 1952 Paolozzi was a founding member of the Independent Group at the Institute of Contemporary Arts and gave a celebrated epidiascope projection, *Bunk*, of his own collages and tearsheets, at its inaugural event. Paolozzi laid the basis for his international fame with the collages that he created at this time and with his bronze sculptures, combining mechanical and biological forms. His brightly painted aluminium sculptures of the 1960s and his screenprint series, such as *As is When* (1965), brought him close to the younger generation of Pop Artists and were widely exhibited abroad. In the 1970s Paolozzi began to take an interest in architecture and the environment and received a number of public commissions, including one to decorate the London Underground station at Tottenham Court Road in 1980. Paolozzi was Professor of Sculpture at the Academy of Fine Arts in Munich from 1981 to 1991. He was elected to the Royal Academy of Art in 1979 and knighted in 1981. In 1999 the Scottish National Gallery of Modern Art in Edinburgh inaugurated the Dean Gallery, which houses a large body of work donated by the artist.

Eduardo Paolozzi. Sculpture, Drawings, Collages and Graphics, London 1976.
Paolozzi, exh. cat. National Galleries of Scotland, Edinburgh 1999.
Robin Spencer (ed.), *Eduardo Paolozzi. Writings and Interviews*, Oxford 2000.

VICTOR PASMORE
(born Warlingham, Surrey, 1908, died 1998)

Victor Pasmore enrolled at Harrow School of Art for three year and later attended evening classes at the Central School of Art in London. In 1934 he was elected to the London Group, at a time when his work was still under the influence of Fauvism. In 1937 he joined Claude Rogers and William Coldstream in setting up a School of Drawing and Painting, which later became widely known as the Euston Road School and included other noted artists, such as Graham Bell and Vanessa Bell among the teaching staff. Pasmore's conversion to abstraction at the end of the 1940s was sudden and dramatic. It began with an intense preoccupation with collage and continued with a series of black and white reliefs. During this period, he became an central figure in the informal group of British Constructivists, including Adrian Heath and Kenneth and Mary Martin. From 1949 onwards, Pasmore was a pioneer of Bauhaus teaching methods, and in 1954 he joined forces with Richard Hamilton, to develop a "Basic Form" course for the Fine Art Department of Newcastle University, which was inspired by the Bauhaus' pedagogical principles. In 1957 the two artists collaborated on an innovative exhibition project, *an exhibit*. Pasmore exhibited at the Venice Biennale in 1960. He took part in a number of public art projects and was Consulting Director of Urban Design at Peterlee New Town from 1954 to 1977. In later years, he devoted a good deal of energy to printmaking, producing images of soft and organic, abstract forms.

Alan Bowness and Luigi Lambertini, *Victor Pasmore, with a Catalogue Raisonné of the Paintings, Constructions and Graphics, 1926–1979*, London 1980.

Norbert Lynton, *Victor Pasmore. Paintings and Graphics, 1980–92*, London 1992.

ROLAND PENROSE
(born in London, 1900, died 1984)

Roland Penrose played a key role in the small, but active, group of British Surrealists, as a writer and organiser, as much as in his capacity as an artist. Thus, he was a prime mover behind the group who met in his house in Hampstead to plan the *International Surrealist Exhibition* at the New Burlington Galleries in London in 1936. He also set up the London Gallery and launched the influential *London Bulletin*, both of which continued until 1940, in addition to playing a key role (with Herbert Read) in establishing the Institute of Contemporary Arts in 1947–48. As a close friend of Max Ernst and Pablo Picasso, Penrose brought about exhibitions of these artists in the 1930s, at the same time as assembling one of the most important collections of international Surrealism anywhere. But Penrose also made a name for himself as a writer and a collector, not least as author of the first biography of Picasso in the English language. His own slim *oeuvre* is mainly associated with the quintessentially modern technique of collage, with its propensity for surprising juxtapositions and readymade imagery. He successfully extended the compositional principle of the collage to his paintings and objects of the 1930s and employed it to good effect in the postcard cut-outs of his final years.

Roland Penrose, *Scrapbook 1900–1981*, London 1981.
The Surrealist and the Photographer. Roland Penrose, Lee Miller, exh. cat. National Galleries of Scotland, Edinburgh 2001.

PETER PHILLIPS
(born in Birmingham, 1939)

Peter Phillips studied at the Royal College of Art from 1959 to 1962, alongside R. B. Kitaj, Allen Jones, Derek Boshier, Patrick Caulfield and David Hockney. These young artists exchanged reproductions of the work of Jasper Johns and Robert Rauschenberg between themselves. In his dynamic montage paintings, Phillips reflected on the world of commercial images and the aggressive advertising style of post-war American culture. In 1963 Phillips took part in the *3ème Biennale des Jeunes* in Paris, and in 1964 his works could be seen at the *New Generation* exhibition at the Whitechapel Art Gallery, London, and in the large Pop Art exhibition that was shown in The Hague, Vienna and Berlin. Together with Allen Jones, Phillips travelled in the United States, living in New York from 1964 to 1966. In 1965 the Kornblee Gallery presented his first solo exhibition. Phillips has accepted teaching positions in a number of different countries and has travelled extensively in Africa, Australia and the Far East. The Westfälischer Kunstverein in Münster presented his first retrospective in 1972.

RetroVISION. Peter Phillips Paintings, 1960–1982, exh. cat. Walker Art Gallery, Liverpool 1982.

CERI RICHARDS
(born in Dunvant, Wales, 1903, died 1971)

Ceri Richards studied in the mid 1920s at the Royal College of Art in London, where he was drawn into the current of European Modernism. As a young artist, he was influenced by the art of Wassily Kandinsky, Pablo Picasso, Henri Matisse and Max Ernst, and in the 1930s this highly talented draftsman also turned to making reliefs and paintings that were close to the formal world of Surrealism. In the 1940s his works took on an apocalyptic character. He interpreted the experience of the Second World War as part of the natural cycle of birth and death – an experience which found its parallel in the mystical allegories of sexuality and violence in the poetry of Dylan Thomas, to which Richards was instinctively drawn. In 1962 Richards was represented in the British Pavilion at the Venice Biennale.

Ceri Richards (1903–1971), exh. cat. Tate Gallery, London 1981.
Mel Gooding, *Ceri Richards*, London 2002.

BRIDGET RILEY
(born in London, 1931)

In the mid 1960s, Bridget Riley gained international recognition as a British Op Art artist, although the over-simplistic branding of her work led to a period when, in the words of the critic Robert Hughes, "few painters have been so ruthlessly plagiarised". Her characteristic style purposefully made it difficult for the viewer to grasp the picture as a whole. The often curved horizontal and vertical lines create the illusion of movement and three-dimensionality. While, in the beginning, Riley's works, such as *Movement in Squares* (1961) and *Crest* (1964), were strictly black-and-white, warm and cold shades of grey began to appear in the mid 1960s, leading to the emergence of strong, contrasting colours in wavy, then vertical or horizontal striped bands. Her work from the latter half of the 1980s onwards marks the introduction of first diagonal, then lozenge patterns and a shift towards the use of unprecedently strong hues. In 1968 Riley represented Britain at the Venice Biennale, where she was awarded the International Prize for Painting. This was followed by numerous exhibitions of her work in Britain and abroad. At the end of the 1990s, her work was re-discovered by a young generation of painters. In 1999 she exhibited at the Kunstverein für die Rheinlande und Westfalen in Düsseldorf, and in 2001 in the Dia Center for the Arts, in New York.

Bridget Riley, *Dialogues on Art*, London 1995.
Bridget Riley, *The Eye's Mind. Collected Writings 1965–1999*, London 1999.
Raimund Strecker (ed.), *Bridget Riley. Ausgewählte Gemälde 1961–1999*, Ostfildern-Ruit 2000.

WILLIAM ROBERTS
(born in Hackney, London, 1895, died 1980)

After completing his studies at the Slade School in London in 1913, William Roberts produced figurative paintings on religious and mythological themes. For a brief period, he worked with the artists of the Omega Workshops before Percy Wyndham Lewis persuaded him to join the Rebel Art Centre and the Vorticists. From then on, Roberts' work consisted of abstract paintings that were distinguished by Cubist and mechanistic forms. In 1914, Roberts signed the Vorticist Manifesto; in 1915, he took part in their exhibition and contributed to the journal *Blast*. That same year Roberts also exhibited with the London Group. In 1918, he took part in an exhibition by Group X and became a member of the London Artists' Association. After the experiences of the First World War, Roberts returned to figurative painting. In 1965 the Tate Gallery honoured Roberts with a large retrospective.

William Roberts, The Vortex Pamphlets 1956–1958, London 1958. William Roberts R. A.. Paintings, Drawings and Watercolours, 1910–1978, exh. cat. Albemarle Gallery, London 1989.

HELEN SAUNDERS
(born in London, 1885, died 1963)

Helen Saunders is one of the few women whose art attracted attention in the world of the avantgarde prior to the First World War. The daughter of a company solicitor with the Great Western Railway, she came from a secure, though not wealthy, middle-class background. She received most of her training as a painter from 1903–06 in a teaching studio in Ealing, from a former Slade School student, Rosa Waugh, though she also attended the Slade School itself part-time for a period of three months at the beginning of 1907, and then the Central School of Art. In 1914, she became a member of the Rebel Art Centre and took part in the exhibition *British Sculpture in the Twentieth Century* at the Whitechapel Art Gallery in London. Saunders signed the Vorticist Manifesto that appeared in *Blast*, no. 1, and contributed a poem and illustrations to the second issue of *Blast* in 1915, as well as taking part in various activities of the group for the next few years. Her artistic production of this period is dominated by colourful abstractions inspired by Cubism and Futurism. After 1918, Saunders withdrew from the art world and rarely exhibited again. The main subjects of her late figurative works are landscapes, portraits and still lifes.

Helen Saunders, 1885–1963, exh. cat. Ashmolean Museum, Oxford 1996.

TIM SCOTT
(born in London, 1937)

Tim Scott trained as an architect from 1954–59, before studying sculpture under Anthony Caro at St. Martin's School of Art, and he worked for a while in Le Corbusier's office in Paris. He first attracted attention in the early 1960s with a group of unusual sculptures, in which his experience as an architect and his work with space played a significant role. His works of the 1960s and early 1970s were characterised by a fascination with technology and with creating a sculptural equilibrium of disparate forms and materials, such as fibreglass constructions and flat, coloured Plexiglas sheets, metal tubes and painted wood. The

Counterpoint series, in steel and acrylic glass, which were reminiscent of Constructivist sculpture, were followed around 1974 by a long series of the *Natarajas* and *Mudras*, which were created by fusing massive geometric chunks of raw steel into a form of sculptural montage. These works continued into the 1980s and formed the bulk of a retrospective exhibition of Scott's work at the Galerie Wentzel in Cologne, which toured a number of German museums in 1988. In addition to his activities as an artist, Scott has achieved distinction as a university teacher. He directed the Department of Fine Art at Birmingham Polytechnic from 1975 to 1978 and the Department of Sculpture at St. Martin's School of Art from 1980 to 1987.

Tim Scott. Skulpturen, 1961–1979, exh. cat. Kunsthalle Bielefeld, Bielefeld 1979. Tim Scott. Skulpturen, exh. cat. Kunstverein Braunschweig, Brunswick 1988.

WILLIAM SCOTT
(born in Greenock, Scotland, 1913, died 1989)

While still a student in Cornwall in 1935, William Scott was impressed by the exhibitions of the Seven and Five Society and Unit One. After completing his studies at the Royal Academy Schools in London in 1936, he travelled to France and Italy, spending much of the time from 1937–39 in Pont-Aven in Brittany. From 1946 to 1956, Scott was a lecturer at the Bath Academy of Art in Corsham, where he formed close contacts with the painters of St. Ives, including Bryan Wynter, Peter Lanyon and Patrick Heron. Scott had his first solo exhibitions at the Leger Gallery in London in 1942 and the Martha Jackson Gallery in New York in 1954, where he met Jackson Pollock and Mark Rothko, though he returned to England more convinced than before of his "European-ness". Under the influence of the American Abstract Expressionists, which he communicated to his fellow artists in Corsham and St. Ives, Scott's paintings became larger in format and more abstract, though he never relinquished his thematic concern with the human figure and the still life, both of which frequently took on metaphorical associations with the landscape. William Scott was one of three artists chosen to represent Britain at the Venice Biennale in 1958 and took part in *documenta 2* in Kassel in 1959, as well as winning the John Moores Prize in Liverpool in the same year.

William Scott, exh. cat. Tate Gallery, London 1972. William Scott. Paintings and Drawings, exh. cat. Irish Museum of Modern Art, London 1998.

RICHARD SMITH
(born in Letchworth, Hertfordshire, 1931)

Richard Smith completed his education at the Royal College of Art in 1957. In he same year, he paid his first of many visits to New York, where he achieved artistic recognition earlier than in his native land. Although he had studied with Peter Blake, Smith was only loosely connected to Pop Art. In his painting he showed great talent as a colourist, combined with an interest in new forms of three-dimensional painting, as in his "dragon paintings" of the early 1970s, in which the canvas is freed from the frame and held in place by string, tape and other materials. In 1970 Smith was chosen to represent Britain at the Venice Biennale, after winning the Robert C. Scull Prize there in 1966, and the Grand Prix at the São Paolo Bienal in 1967. In 1975 he moved to New York. In the same year, the Tate Gallery in London organised a retrospective of his work, which Smith designed as a documentation of six solo exhibitions, from 1961 onwards, in order to emphasise the serial nature of his work.

Richard Smith. Retrospective Exhibition of Graphics + Multiples, exh. cat. Arnolfini Gallery, Bristol 1970. Richard Smith, Seven Exhibitions 1961–1975, exh. cat. Tate Gallery, London 1975.

STANLEY SPENCER
(born in Cookham-on-Thames, Berkshire, 1891, died 1959)

The central themes of Stanley Spencer's artistic oeuvre derive from Christian mysticism and the experiences of two world wars. After completing his studies at the Slade School of Art in London in 1912, where his fellow students included Christopher Nevinson, David Bomberg, Paul Nash and Edward Wadsworth, he served in the infantry in Macedonia during the First World War. His impressions of the war are reflected in a series of monumental mural paintings (1927–32) for the memorial chapel in Burghclerc, Berkshire, which presents a visionary interpretation of the daily life of a soldier. A later cycle of works treats the Glasgow dockyards and the workers there in large-scale, strongly schematised compositions in a style which bears some affinity to East European Socialist Realist painting of the period. Spencer's paintings, however, are always permeated by religious motifs. All his life he believed in the connection between divine and earthly love; thus, his native village of Cookham became the imaginary scene for the events of the New Testament. Some of the most powerful and unsparing images he painted were of himself and his family in the 1930s. This was also the period when he achieved international recognition, with the inclusion of his work at the Venice Biennale in 1932 and his first sale to a foreign museum, when the Stedelijk Museum in Amsterdam purchased his *Self-Portrait* (1936), in 1938. Spencer was knighted in 1958, shortly before his death.

Keith Bell, *Stanley Spencer. A Complete Catalogue of the Paintings*, London 1992.

Stanley Spencer. Letters and Writings, ed. Adrian Glew, exh. cat. Tate Gallery, London 2001.

Stanley Spencer, eds. Timothy Hyman and Patrick Wright, exh. cat. Tate Gallery, London 2001.

GRAHAM SUTHERLAND
(born in London, 1903, died 1980)

Graham Sutherland, who was trained at Goldsmiths' College in London, developed a formal language which employed intense colours and was inspired by the works of Samuel Palmer and William Blake. The drama and mystery of the landscape were the central themes in his work, and his anthropomorphised Welsh landscapes, in particular, conveyed a sense of foreboding. In 1936, Sutherland took part in the *International Surrealist Exhibition*, although he was not so interested in their ideas and maintained a certain distance from artists on the European continent. The drawings and paintings that Sutherland produced as an official War Artist depicted the devastation caused by the Blitz on British cities and the existential struggle with elemental forces of tin miners and foundry workers. Other paintings dealing with religious motifs were influenced by the experiences of the Second World War. *Thorn Tree* (1945–46) and *Crucifixion* (1946), for example, were inspired by newspaper photographs of the horrors of the concentration camps in Germany. Sutherland's reputation grew quickly after the War, and he settled in southern France in 1947, where he painted many portraits of the rich and famous, including Somerset Maugham and Sir Winston Churchill. In the final years of his life he concerned himself primarily with the relationship between painting and literature.

John Hayes, *The Art of Graham Sutherland*, Oxford 1980.

Roger Berthoud, *Graham Sutherland. A Biography*, London 1982.

JOE TILSON
(born in London, 1928)

In an oeuvre that now spans more than forty years, Joe Tilson has worked with the widest variety of themes and materials. A graduate of St. Martin's and the Slade School, Tilson developed a reputation as a Pop artist, in particular, for the silk screens he produced between 1964 and 1969, that treated the symbols and landscapes of American metropolises in images inspired by books of postcards. Symbols from the world of advertising, codes, numbers and popular icons like Malcolm X also appear in Tilson's works. He combines painting with woodcuts and collage and relief work in wood. Tilson has travelled extensively in southern Europe, and his late work is archaic and full of mystical symbols.

Joe Tilson. Works 1961–1991, exh. cat. Waddington Galleries, London 1992.

Isabel Carlisle and Norman Rosenthal, *Joe Tilson (1950–2002)*, exh. cat. Royal Academy of Arts, London 2002.

JULIAN TREVELYAN
(born in Leith Hill near Dorking, 1910, died 1988)

Julian Trevelyan, who was one of the most important graphic artists of his time, initially studied English literature in Cambridge from 1928 to 1930. His circle of friends there included Humphrey Jennings, who introduced him to French painting and the ideas of the Surrealists. In 1931, Trevelyan left Cambridge and went to Paris. In Stanley William Hayter's Atelier 17, he studied etching techniques. His fellow students included Max Ernst, Oskar Kokoschka, Joan Miró and Pablo Picasso. In 1932 he began to exhibit his works at the Bloomsbury Gallery. In 1935 he purchased Durham Wharf on the Thames near Hammersmith, where he would live and work for the rest of his life. Trevelyan associated with the Surrealists in London and exhibited at the *International Surrealist Exhibition* in 1936. In 1938 he broke with Surrealism, took part in pacifist demonstrations and created several works in support of the Popular Front in the Spanish Civil War. During the Second World War he worked as a camouflage expert for the Royal Engineers. From 1955 to 1963 he taught graphic arts at the Royal College of Art and influenced a younger generation of artists, including David Hockney. In 1987 Trevelyan was elected to the Royal Academy of Arts.

Julian Trevelyan, *Indigo Days*, Aldershot 1996.

Silvie Turner (ed.), *Julian Trevelyan. Catalogue of Prints*, Aldershot 1998.

WILLIAM TUCKER
(born in Cairo, 1935)

In 1937 William Tucker came to England with his family. From 1955 to 1958 he studied history at Oxford and then sculpture at Martin's School of Art, where Anthony Caro was teaching at the time, and his fellow students inluded David Annesley, Phillip King and Isaac Witkin. Tucker's early sculptures were abstract, geometric compositions, made of assemblages of steel or wood, cast in plaster or concrete. Issues of weight and gravity were important factors in his work. His exhibitions at the Tate Gallery, in 1987 and his retrospective at the Storm King Art Center, resulted in sales to three musems in New York and laid the basis for Tucker's reputation in the USA. In 1974 Tucker published his influential book, *The Language of Sculpture*. In 1978 he moved to New York and taught at Columbia University until 1982. Tucker represented Britain at the Venice Biennale in 1972.

William Tucker. Detwiller Visiting Artist, exh. cat. Williams Center for the Arts Lafayette College, Easton, Pennsylvania 1992.

JOHN TUNNARD
(born in Sandy, Bedfordshire, 1900, died 1971)

The painter John Tunnard studied textile design at the Royal Academy of Arts in London from 1919 to 1923 and in the 1920s worked as a designer in the textile industry. In 1930 he moved to Cornwall, where he started a company for hand-printed silk fabrics and also turned to painting, under the influence of Surrealism. He had his first solo exhibition at the Redfern Gallery in 1933 and joined the London Group the following year. He spent the war with the Coast Guard in Cornwall. The British American Art Center in New York had a solo exhibition of Tunnard's work in 1941. In 1942 the Tate Gallery purchased his painting *Construction*, and two years later the Museum of Modern Art in New York purchased the painting *Fugue*, from 1938. From 1948 to 1964 Tunnard taught design at the Penzance School of Art.

John Tunnard, 1900–1971, exh. cat. Royal Academy of Arts, London, and Kettle's Yard Gallery, Cambridge, London 1977.

Alan Peat and Brian A. Whitton, *John Tunnard: His Life and Work*, Aldershot 1997.

WILLIAM TURNBULL
(born in Dundee, Scotland, 1922)

After two years of study at the Slade School in London, the sculptor and painter William Turnbull, together with his friend Eduardo Paolozzi, visited Jean Dubuffet's Foyer de l'art brut in Paris in 1947. From then on, he showed an intense interest in foreign and past cultures. In the late 1940s Turnbull spent two years in Paris, where he was able to establish contacts with Jean Hélion, Fernand Léger, Alberto Giacometti and Constantin Brancusi. Following his return to London, Turnbull joined the Independent Group, to which Richard Hamilton and Paolozzi also belonged and which organised a series of debates and exhibitions. In 1952, Turnbull exhibited at the Venice Biennale, together with Kenneth Armitage, Henry Moore, and others, under the slogan "New Aspects of British Sculpture". In 1956, Turnbull was greatly impressed by a roomful of Abstract Expressionist paintings in the Tate Gallery's exhibition *Fifty Years of American Art*. The following year, he saw the work of Rothko and Still in New York. The large-scale paintings he exhibited with the Situation Group in 1960 showed the impact of this experience. Turnbull's subsequent paintings and sculpture have increasingly reflected his involvement with oriental art and philosophy.

Richard Morphet, *William Turnbull*, exh. cat. Tate Gallery, London 1973.

William Turnbull. Sculpture and Paintings, exh. cat. Serpentine Gallery, London 1995.

EDWARD WADSWORTH
(born in Cleckheaton, Yorkshire, 1889, died 1949)

Edward Wadsworth is considered a pioneer of abstract art. On leaving school, he studied engineering in Munich for one year, in 1906–07, where he attended the atelier of Heinrich Knirr in his spare time. Shortly after completing his studies in art at the Slade School in London in 1911, Wadsworth was invited by Roger Fry to join the Omega Workshops and the Bloomsbury Group. Soon afterwards, he broke with the artists and writers who belonged to these groups and joined Percy Wyndham Lewis in setting up the Rebel Art Centre. Thus, he was one of the artists who signed the Vorticist Manifesto, and whose work showed the strong stamp of Cubist and Futurist influences. Wadsworth's knowledge of German enabled him to contribute to *Blast*, no. 1, his own translations (with illustrations) from Wassily Kandinsky's *Über das Geistige in der Kunst*, under the heading *Inner Necessity*. Only in the 1930s did Wadsworth's highly geometric and abstract style begin to change, and his later works show the influence of Surrealism. Together with Paul Nash, Edward Burra, Barbara Hepworth, Henry Moore and Ben Nicholson, he was a co-founder of the London-based group Unit One. In 1940, his work was selected for the Venice Biennale, and he was elected a member of the Royal Academy in 1943.

Barbara Wadsworth, *Edward Wadsworth. A Painter's Life*, Salisbury 1989.

Jeremy Lewison (ed.), *A Genius of Industrial England. Edward Wadsworth, 1889–1949*, London 1990.

ALFRED WALLIS
(born in Devon, 1855, died 1942)

Alfred Wallis spent most of his life in the coastal town of St. Ives in Cornwall, where he worked as a fisherman and later had his own small shop on the harbour front. Wallis only began to paint at the age of seventy, after the death of his wife. In his characteristically naïve style, he concentrated mainly on views of the Cornish coastline, with its stormy seas, ships and lighthouses. As a self-taught artists, he readily made use of whatever materials came to hand, from ships' paint to pieces of flotsam and cardboard from washing powder boxes. In 1928 the painters Ben Nicholson and Christopher Wood discovered the old man's work whilst on a visit to St. Ives, and from then on included his paintings in numerous exhibitions in London. Up to the time of his death, at a ripe old age, Wallis continued to paint works that evoke the atmosphere of a bygone age of seafaring and fishing.

Sven Berlin, *Alfred Wallis. Primitive*, Bristol 1992.

RICHARD WENTWORTH
(born on Samoa, 1947)

Richard Wentworth started working for Henry Moore before completing his degree at the Royal College of Art in London in 1970. Since the late 1970s, his objects, installations and sculptures have played an important role in the British art scene. Wentworth's original and sometimes humorous works transform everyday objects, endow them with many layers of meaning and usually incorporate an element of mystification. Simple ceramic plates are arranged in a circular installation that has a mystical effect, and the writing desk of the French philosopher and linguist Roland Barthes is spiked with nails. Wentworth's sculptures are displayed in museums and galleries of contemporary art throughout the world. Since the 1970s, he has also been active as a lecturer – most notably, at Goldsmiths' College, in London (1971–87). In 1993–94, he stayed in Berlin under the auspices of the German Academic Exchange Service (DAAD) programme. In 2002, he was appointed Master of Drawing at the Ruskin School of Art, Oxford.

Richard Wentworth, exh. cat. Serpentine Gallery, London 1993.

Richard Wentworth's Thinking Aloud, exh. cat. Hayward Gallery, London 1998.

RACHEL WHITEREAD
(born in London, 1963)

In her sculptures of plaster, resin or rubber, the sculptor Rachael Whiteread seeks to make the invisible visible and to see, grasp and preserve the space around us. She produces casts of empty living-spaces that are threatened with demolition, of unnoticed interstices and of hollow spaces in the everyday objects that surround us; in the process, she creates new forms and sculptures from what is actually an absence. Rachel Whiteread graduated from the Slade School in London in 1987. Her work *House* was awarded the Turner Prize in 1993. For this, she took a concrete impression of the interior of one of the last remaining nineteenth-century houses on Grove Road in East London, thus temporarily preserving the memory of a building that would shortly be demolished. In 1997, she represented Great Britain at the Venice Biennale. In 2000, her Holocaust Memorial for the Judenplatz in Vienna was finally unveiled, after some five years of controversy and delays.

Rachel Whiteread, exh. cat. Kunsthalle Basel, Basel 1994.

James Lingwood (ed.), *House. Rachel Whiteread*, London 1995.

STEPHEN WILLATS
(born in London, 1943)

By the age of sixteen, Stephen Willats had already met conceptual artists through his gallery jobs in London at the Drian Gallery and the New Vision Centre Gallery and recognised the distance that separated them from the public. Thereafter, he always took a close interest in the relationship between the artist and the viewer, and between the work of art and the public. After completing his studies at Ealing School of Art, he learned about "systems research" while working as a junior assistant to a group of psychologists and cyberneticists and used their socio-political analyses to develop his own, socially orientated, artistic concepts.

Willats taught at Ipswich School of Art for a period from 1964–67, before going on to found *Control Magazine*, in 1967. Through this publication, he developed a system of interaction with local residents that helped them to express views about the community in which they lived. For his projects on high-rise dwellings in London and Berlin in the 1970s, Willats also took on the role of a social worker. He would feed the visual results of his collaboration with residents into his artwork, in the form of photographs, plans, diagrams and interviews. From the 1980s onwards Willats has expanded his system of signs and signals to include fashion and the popular music scene. *Multiple Clothings*, made of plastic, serve as bearers of meaning for verbal expressions and may be understood in the context both of conceptual art and of the crossover between art and fashion.

Stephen Willats, *Intervention and Audience*, London 1986.

Stephen Willats. Häuser und Menschen, Berlin 1979–1993, exh. cat. Berlinische Galerie, Landesmuseum für Moderne Kunst, Photographie und Architektur, Berlin 1993.

BILL WOODROW
(born in Henley-on-Thames, 1948)

Like Richard Deacon, Antony Gormley and Tony Cragg, Bill Woodrow was one of the protagonists of the "New British Sculpture", which brought the formal purism of Minimal Art closer to the everyday world through the addition of real objects. After graduating from the Chelsea School of Art in London in 1972, Woodrow produced complex assemblages of discarded household appliances and other objects, in keeping with a junk aesthetic. He cut into objects to create intersections, layerings and complicated areas of overlap. In the late 1970s, under the impact of a visit he had paid to the fossil collections in the Natural History Museum, he also began to imbed objects in plaster or concrete and then break open the cast, so that the impressions left by the objects would remain visible after the objects themselves had been removed. But his working method did not stop short at creating an archaeology of the everyday: his sculptures have a poetic, narrative quality that is derived from the often surprising combination of objects. In the late 1980s Woodrow largely abandoned cutting for welding and casting in bronze, and this has enabled him to create large topographies, animals and objects and to explore a wide range of dialectical themes, such as nature versus culture and the human anatomy versus power. Woodrow took part in the ground-breaking exhibition *Objects and Sculpture* at the Institute of Contemporary Arts (ICA) in London in 1981 and in *documenta 8* in Kassel in 1987. In 1991 he represented Britain at the São Paulo Bienal.

Sculpture, 1980–86, exh. cat. The Fruitmarket Gallery, Edinburgh 1986.

John Roberts, *Bill Woodrow. Fool's Gold*, London 1996.

BIBLIOGRAPHY

compiled by Simon Ford

GENERAL WORKS

Anderson, Perry, *English Questions*, London 1992.

Appleyard, Brian, *The Pleasures of Peace. Art and Imagination in Postwar Britain*, London 1989.

Avant-Garde British Printmaking, 1914–1960, exh. cat. British Museum, London 1990.

Archer, Michael, *Art Since 1960*, London 1997.

Beattie, Susan, *The New Sculpture*, New Haven 1983.

Bloom, Clive (ed.), *Literature and Culture in Modern Britain*, London 1993–2000.

Booker, Christopher, *The Neophiliacs. A Study of the Revolution in English Life in the Fifties and Sixties*, London 1969.

Bowness, Sophie and Phillpot, Clive (eds.), *Britain at the Venice Biennale, 1895–1995*, London 1995.

Bradbury, Malcolm, *The Social Context of Modern English Literature*, Oxford 1971.

Bradbury, Malcolm and MacFarlane, James (eds.), *Modernism, 1890–1930*, Harmondsworth 1976.

Brighton, Andrew and Morris, Lynda (eds.), *Towards Another Picture*, Nottingham 1977.

Britannica: 30 ans de sculpture, exh. cat. Le Havre Musée, Centre Régional d'Art, Le Havre 1988.

British Art in the 20th Century, ed. Susan Compton, exh. cat. Royal Academy of Arts, London 1986.

British Painting 1910–1945, exh. cat. Tate Gallery, London 1967.

British Painting Since 1945, exh. cat. Tate Gallery, London 1964.

British Sculpture of the Twentieth Century, eds. Sandy Nairne and Nicholas Serota, exh. cat. Whitechapel Art Gallery, London 1981.

British Sculpture Since 1945, exh. cat. Tate Gallery, London 1965.

Button, Virginia, *The Turner Prize*, London 1997.

Cairncross, Alec, *The British Economy Since 1945*, Oxford 1992.

Causey, Andrew, *Sculpture Since 1945*, Oxford 1998.

A Century of Art Education, 1882–1982, London 1982.

Cohen, Stanley, *Folk Devils and Moral Panics. The Creation of the Mods and Rockers*, Oxford 1987.

Colls, Robert, and Dodd, Philip (eds.), *Englishness, Politics and Culture, 1880–1920*, London 1996.

A Continuing Process. The New Creativity in British Art Education, exh. cat. Institute of Contemporary Arts, London 1981.

Corbett, David Peters, *The Modernity of English Art, 1914–30*, Manchester 1997.

Coutts-Smith, Kenneth, *The Dream of Icarus. Art and Society in the Twentieth Century*, London 1970.

Curtis, Penelope, *Sculpture 1900–1945*, Oxford 1999.

Davey, Kevin, *English Imaginaries. Six Studies of Anglo-British Modernity*, London 1999.

Donaldson, Frances, *The British Council. The First Fifty Years*, London 1984.

Dworkin, Dennis, *Cultural Marxism in Postwar Britain. History, the New Left, and the Origins of Cultural Studies*, Durham and London 1997.

The Other Story. Afro-Asian Artists in Post-War Britain, exh. cat. South Bank Centre, Hayward Gallery, London 1989.

Easthope, Anthony, *British Post-Structuralism Since 1968*, London 1988.

The Edwardians and After. The Royal Academy, 1900–1950, exh. cat. Royal Academy, London 1988.

Etats spécifiques. 11 artistes anglais, exh. cat. Musée des Beaux-Arts André Malraux, Le Havre 1992.

Farr, Dennis, *English Art, 1870–1940*, Oxford 1978.

Finch, Christopher, *Image As Language. Aspects of British Art 1950–1968*, Harmondsworth 1969.

Frith, Simon and Horne, Howard, *Art into Pop*, London 1987.

From Blast to Pop. Aspects of Modern British Art, 1915–1965, exh. cat. David and Alfred Smart Museum of Art, Chicago 1997.

Gage, Edward, *The Eye of the Wind. Scottish Painting Since 1945*, London 1977.

Garlake, Margaret, *New Art, New World. British Art in Postwar Society*, London and New Haven 1998.

Garlake, Margaret (ed.), *Artists and Patrons in Post-War Britain*, Aldershot 2001.

Hammacher, Abraham Marie, *Modern English Sculpture*, London 1967.

Harrison, Charles, *English Art and Modernism, 1900–1939*, London and New Haven 1994.

Havighurst, Alfred F., *Britain in Transition. The Twentieth Century*, Chicago and London 1979.

Hebdige, Dick, *Subculture. The Meaning of Style*, London 1979.

Herbert Read. A British Vision of World Art, eds. Benedict Read and David Thistlewood, exh. cat. Leeds City Art Galleries, Leeds, London 1993.

Hewison, Robert, *Culture and Consensus. England, Art and Politics Since 1940*, London 1995.

Hobsbawm, Eric, *Age of Extremes. The Short Twentieth Century 1914–1991*, London 1994.

Hunt, Leon, *British Low Culture. From Safari Suits to Sexploitation*, London 1998.

Hutchinson, Robert, *The Politics of the Arts Council*, London 1982.

Jeffrey, Ian, *The British Landscape. 1920–1950*, London 1984.

Johnson, Jane and Gruetzner, A., *The Dictionary of British Artists, 1880–1940*, Suffolk 1976.

Johnson, Paul, *Twentieth-Century Britain. Economic, Social and Cultural Change*, London 1994.

Knowles, Rodney (ed.), *Contemporary Irish Art*, Dublin 1982.

Levin, Bernard, *The Pendulum Years*, London 1970.

Lucie-Smith, Edward, *Movements in Art Since 1945*, London 1984.

MacDonald, Stuart, *The History and Philosophy of Art Education*, London 1970.

Morgan, Kenneth, *The People's Peace. British History 1945–89*, Oxford 1990.

Minihan, Janet, *The Nationalization of Culture. The Development of State Subsidies to the Arts in Great Britain*, London 1977.

Nairne, Sandy, *State of the Art. Ideas and Images in the 1980s*, London 1987.

Nava, Mica and O'Shea, Alan, *Modern Times. Reflections on a Century of English Modernity*, London 1996.

Nehring, Neil, *Flowers in the Dustbin. Culture, Anarchy, and Postwar England*, Ann Arbor 1993.

New Beginnings. Postwar British Art From the Collection of Ken Powell, exh. cat. Scottish National Gallery of Modern Art, Edinburgh 1992.

Newburn, Tim, *Permission and Regulation. Law and Morals in Post-War Britain*, London 1992.

Pevsner, Nikolaus, *The Englishness of English Art*, London 1956.

Pugh, Martin, *Women and the Women's Movement in Britain 1914–59*, Basingstoke 1992.

A Quiet Revolution. British Sculpture Since 1965, ed. Terry A. Neff, exh. cat. Museum of Contemporary Art, Chicago, and San Francisco Museum of Modern Art, San Francisco 1987.

Rothenstein, John, *British Art Since 1900. An Anthology*, London 1962.

Rothenstein, John, *Modern English Painters*, London 1984.

Sampson, Anthony, *Changing Anatomy of Britain*, London 1982.

Shone, Richard, *The Century of Change. British Painting Since 1900*, Oxford 1977.

Sinclair, Andrew, *Arts and Cultures. The History of the 50 Years of The Arts Council of Great Britain*, London 1977.

Sinfield, Alan, *Literature, Politics and Culture in Postwar Britain*, Berkeley 1989.

Spalding, Frances, *British Art Since 1900*, London 1986.

Spalding, Frances, *The Tate. A History*, London 1998.

Taylor, Brandon, *Art for the Nation. Exhibitions and the London Public 1747–2001*, Manchester 1999.

Taylor, Roger L, *Art, an Enemy of the People*, Sussex 1978.

Thistlewood, David, *Herbert Read. Forcefulness and Form – An Introduction to His Aesthetics*, London 1984.

Tillyard, Stella, *The Impact of Modernism. Early Modernism and the Arts and Crafts Movement in Edwardian England*, London 1988.

Turner, Graeme, *British Cultural Studies. An Introduction*, Boston 1990.

Un siècle de sculpture anglaise, exh. cat. Galerie Nationale du Jeu de Paume, Paris 1996.

Walker, John A., *Cultural Offensive. America's Impact on British Art Since 1945*, London 1999.

Walker, John A., *Art and Outrage. Provocation, Controversy, and the Visual Arts*, London 1999.

The War Artists. British Official War Art of the Twentieth Century, exh. cat. Imperial War Museum and Tate Gallery, London 1983.

Waters, Grant M., *Dictionary of British Artists, Working 1900–1950*, Eastbourne 1975.

Waugh, Patricia, *The Harvest of the Sixties. English Literature and Its Background 1960 to 1990*, Oxford 1995.

White, Eric W., *The Arts Council of Great Britain*, London 1975.

Wiener, Martin J., *English Culture and the Decline of the Industrial Spirit, 1850–1980*, Harmondsworth 1985.

Windsor, Alan, *Handbook of Modern British Painting and Printmaking 1900–1990*, Aldershot 1998.

Witts, Richard, *Artist Unknown. An Alternative History of the Arts Council*, London 1998.

Young, Alan, *Dada and After. Extremist Modernism and English Literature*, Manchester 1981.

1910–20 VORTICISM, FIRST WORLD WAR AND ITS AFTERMATH

Abstract Art in England, 1913–1915, exh. cat. D'Offay Couper Gallery, London 1969.

Art Made Modern. Roger Fry's Vision of Art, ed. Christopher Green, exh. cat. Courtauld Galleries, London 1999.

Baron, Wendy, *The Camden Town Group*, London 1979.

Bell, Clive, *Art*, London 1914.

Bell, Michael (ed.), *1900–1930. The Context of English Literature*, London 1980.

Corbett, David Peters (ed.), *Wyndham Lewis and the Art of Modern War*, Cambridge 1998.

Cork, Richard, *A Bitter Truth. Avant-Garde Art and the Great War*, London and New Haven 1994.

Dynamism. The Art of Modern Life Before the Great War, exh. cat. Tate Gallery, London 1991.

Easton, Malcolm, "Camden Town into London, Some Intimate Glimpses of the Transition and Its Artists, 1911–1914",

in *Art in Britain, 1890–1914*, Hull 1967, p. 60–75.
The Edwardian Era, exh. cat. Barbican Art Gallery, London 1987.
Eksteins, Modris, *Rites of Spring. The Great War and the Birth of the Modern Age*, London 1990.
Exhibition of Works By the Italian Futurists, exh. cat. Sackville Gallery, London 1912.
Ferguson, John, *The Arts in Britain in World War One*, London 1980.
Fry, Roger, *Vision and Design*, London 1920.
The Great British Vortex. Modern Drawings From the Collection of Mr. and Mrs. Michael W. Wilsey, exh. cat. San Francisco Museum of Modern Art, San Francisco 1993.
Howlett, Jana, and Mengham, Rod, *The Violent Muse. Violence and the Artistic Imagination in Europe, 1910–1939*, Manchester 1994.
Hynes, Samuel, *A War Imagined. The First World War and English Culture*, London 1990.
Kenner, Hugh, *The Pound Era. The Age of Ezra Pound, T. S. Eliot, James Joyce and Wyndham Lewis*, London 1972.
Lewis, Wyndham, *Blasting and Bombardiering*, London 1937.
Lewis, Wyndham, *Wyndham Lewis on Art. Collected Writings 1913–1956*, London 1969.
Materer, Timothy, *Vortex. Pound, Eliot and Lewis*, Ithaca and London 1979.
Meyers, Jeffrey, *The Enemy. A Biography of Wyndham Lewis*, London 1980.
Michel, Walter, *Wyndham Lewis. Paintings and Drawings*, London 1971.
Modern Art in Britain 1910–1914, exh. cat. Barbican Gallery, London 1997.
Morgan, Kenneth O., *Consensus and Disunity. The Lloyd George Coalition Government 1918–1922*, Oxford 1979.
Nevinson, Christopher Richard Wyne, *Paint and Prejudice*, London 1937.
Normand, Tom, *Wyndham Lewis the Artist. Holding the Mirror Up to Politics*, Cambridge 1992.
Orchard, Karin (ed.), *Blast. Vortizismus – Die erste Avantgarde in England 1914–1918*, Berlin 1997.
Pound's Artists. Ezra Pound and the Visual Arts in London, Paris and Italy, exh. cat. Tate Gallery, London 1985.
Sillars, Stuart, *Art and Survival in First World War Britain*, Basingstoke 1987.

Stansky, Peter, *On or About December 1910. Early Bloomsbury and Its Intimate World*, Cambridge/Mass. 1996.
Tickner, Lisa, *Modern Life and Modern Subjects. British Art in the Early Twentieth Century*, London and New Haven 2000.
Vorticism and Abstract Art in the First Machine Age, exh. cat. Gordon Fraser Gallery, London 1976.
Vorticism and Its Allies, London, exh. cat. Hayward Gallery, London 1974.
Watney, Simon, *English Post-Impressionism*, London 1980.
Wees, William C., *Vorticism and the English Avant-Garde*, Manchester 1972.

1920–40 PRIMITIVISM, ABSTRACTION AND SURREALISM

Art and Power. Europe Under the Dictators 1930–45, exh. cat. South Bank Centre, London 1995.
Barbara Hepworth, exh. cat. Tate Gallery, London 1998.
Barbara Hepworth. Works in the Tate Gallery Collection and the Barbara Hepworth Museum, St. Ives, exh. cat. Tate Gallery, London 1999.
Blythe, Ronald, *The Age of Illusion. England in the Twenties and Thirties, 1919–40*, London 1963.
Branson, Noreen, *Britain in the Nineteen Twenties*, London 1975.
Britain's Contribution to Surrealism of the '30s and '40s, exh. cat. Harnet Gallery, London 1971.
British Surrealism. Fifty Years On, exh. cat. Mayor Gallery, London 1986.
Cardinal, Roger, *The Landscape Vision of Paul Nash*, London 1989.
Carvings By Barbara Hepworth. Paintings By Ben Nicholson, exh. cat. Arthur Tooth & Sons Galleries, London 1932.
Circle. Constructive Art in Britain 1934–40, ed. Jeremy Lewison, exh. cat. Kettle's Yard Gallery, Cambridge 1982.
Esposito, Carla, *Hayter e l'Atelier 17*, Milan 1990.
Festing, Sally, *Barbara Hepworth. A Life of Forms*, New York 1995.
Gascoyne, David, *A Short Survey of Surrealism*, London 1935.
Graves, Robert, and Hodge, Alan, *The Long Week-End. A Social History of Great Britain, 1918–1939*, Harmondsworth 1971.
Green, Martin, *Children of the Sun. A Narrative of "Decadence" in England After 1918*, London 1992.

Hammacher, Abraham Marie, *Barbara Hepworth*, London 1987.
Hampstead in the Thirties. A Committed Decade, exh. cat. Camden Arts Centre, London 1974.
Harrison, Charles et al., *Primitivism, Cubism, Abstraction. The Early Twentieth Century*, New Haven and London 1993.
Higginbottom, W. Hugh, *Frightfulness in Modern Art*, London 1928.
Hiller, Susan (ed.), *The Myth of Primitivism. Perspectives on Art*, London 1991.
Hoskins, Katharine Bail, *Today the Struggle. Literature and Politics in England During the Spanish Civil War*, Austin 1969.
Isherwood, Christopher, *Lions and Shadows. An Education in the Twenties*, London 1996.
James, Philip (ed.), *Henry Moore on Sculpture*, London 1966.
Light, Alison, *Forever England. Femininity, Literature and Conservatism Between the Wars*, London 1991.
Lucie-Smith, Edward, *Art of the 1930s. The Age of Anxiety*, London 1985.
Lye, Len, *Figures of Motion. Selected Writings*, Auckland and Oxford 1984.
Lynton, Norbert, *Ben Nicholson*, London 1993.
Martin, Leslie et al. (eds.), *Circle. International Survey of Constructive Art*, London 1937.
Metamorphose. British Surrealists and Neo-Romantics, 1935–55, New York 1992.
Modern Britain, 1929–1939, eds. James Peto and Donna Loveday, exh. cat. Design Museum, London 1999.
Mowat, Charles Loch, *Britain Between the Wars, 1918–1940*, London 1956.
Nash, Paul, *Outline. An Autobiography and Other Writings*, London 1949.
Penrose, Roland, *Scrapbook 1900–1981*, London 1981.
"Primitivism" in 20th Century Art. Affinity of the Tribal and the Modern, ed. William Rubin, exh. cat. Museum of Modern Art, New York 1984.
Ray, Paul C., *The Surrealist Movement in England*, Ithaca 1971.
Rea, Betty (ed.), *Five on Revolutionary Art*, London 1935.
Read, Herbert, *The Meaning of Art*, London 1931.
Read, Herbert (ed.), *Unit 1. The Modern Movement in English Architecture, Painting and Sculpture*, London 1934.

Read, Herbert (ed.), *Surrealism*, London 1936.
Real Surreal. British & European Surrealism, exh. cat. Wolverhampton Art Gallery, Wolverhampton 1995.
Recording Britain. A Pictorial Domesday of Pre-War Britain, exh. cat. Victoria & Albert Museum, London 1990.
Remy, Michel, *Surrealism in Britain*, Aldershot 1999.
Renzio, Tony del, *Incendiary Innocence*, London 1944.
Renzio, Tony del and Scott, Duncan, *Surrealism in England, 1936 and After*, Canterbury 1986.
Rutter, Frank, *Art in My Time*, London 1933.
Rutter, Frank, *Evolution in Modern Art. A Study of Modern Painting*, London 1932.
Saler, Michael T., *The Avant-Garde in Interwar England. Medieval Modernism and the London Underground*, Oxford 1999.
Stokes, Adrian, *Colour and Form*, London 1937.
Surrealism in Birmingham 1935–1954, exh. cat. Birmingham Museums and Art Gallery, Birmingham 2000.
Surrealism in Britain in the Thirties, Angels of Anarchy and Machines for Making Clouds, exh. cat. Leeds City Art Gallery, Leeds 1986.
Thirties. British Art and Design Before the War, exh. cat. Hayward Gallery, London 1979.
Unit One. Spirit of the 30s, exh. cat. Mayor Gallery, London 1984.
Walter Sickert, exh. cat. Tate Gallery, London 2001.
Wilcox, Denys J., *The London Group 1913–1939. The Artists and Their Works*, Aldershot 1995.

1940–50 SECOND WORLD WAR, ISOLATION AND EXISTENTIAL CONCERNS

Addison, Paul, *Now the War Is Over. A Social History of Britain 1945–51*, London 1995.
AIA. The Story of the Artists' International Association, 1933–1953, exh cat. Museum of Modern Art, Oxford 1983.
Alphen, Ernst van, *Francis Bacon and the Loss of Self*, London 1992.
Art in Exile in Great Britain, 1933–45, exh. cat. Camden Arts Centre, London 1986.
Banham, Mary and Hillier, Bevis (eds.), *A Tonic to the Nation. The Festival of Britain*, London 1976.

Barnett, Correlli, *The Audit of War. The Illusion and Reality of Britain As a Great Nation*, London 1986.
Berger, John, *Permanent Red*, London 1960.
The British Neo-Romantics, 1935–1950, London 1983.
British Preliminary Exhibition for the Unknown Political Prisoner Competition, exh. cat. New Burlington Galleries, London 1953.
Calder, Angus, *The Myth of the Blitz*, London 1991.
Davies, Hugh Marlais, *Francis Bacon. The Early and Middle Years, 1928–1958*, New York 1978.
Farr, Dennis (ed.), *Francis Bacon. A Retrospective*, New York 1999.
Farson, Daniel, *Soho in the Fifties*, London 1993.
The Forgotten Fifties, exh. cat. Sheffield City Art Galleries, Sheffield 1984.
Gombrich, Ernst, *The Story of Art*, London 1950.
Grigson, Geoffrey, *Samuel Palmer. The Visionary Years*, London 1947.
Guilbaut, Serge, *How New York Stole the Idea of Modern Art. Abstract Expressionism, Freedom, and the Cold War*, Chicago 1983.
Hennessy, Peter, *Never Again. Britain 1945–51*, London 1992.
Hewison, Robert, *Under Siege. Literary Life in London 1939–45*, London 1977.
Hewison, Robert, *In Anger. Culture in the Cold War 1945–60*, London 1981.
Jenkins, David Fraser, *John Piper. The Forties*, London 2000.
The Kitchen Sink Painters, exh. cat. Mayor Gallery, London 1991.
Klingender, Francis, *Marxism and Modern Art. An Approach to Social Realism*, London 1943.
The Last Romantics. The Romantic Tradition in British Art, Burne-Jones to Stanley Spencer, ed. John Christian, exh. cat. Barbican Art Gallery, London 1989.
Lichtenstein, Claude and Schregenberger, Thomas (eds.), *As Found. The Discovery of the Ordinary. British Architecture and Art of the 1950s*, Baden 2001.
Lindey, Christine, *Art in the Cold War. From Vladivostok to Kalamazoo, 1945–1962*, London 1990.
Mellor, David Alan, *A Paradise Lost. The Neo-Romantic Imagination*

in Britain 1935–1955, London 1987.

Mellor, David Alan, "Existentialism and Post-War British Art", in *Paris Postwar, Art and Existentialism 1945–55*, ed. Frances Morris, exh. cat. Tate Gallery, London 1993, p. 53–61.

Michael Ayrton. An Illustrated Commentary, exh. cat. City Museums and Art Gallery, Birmingham 1978.

Paul Nash. Aerial Creatures, exh. cat. Imperial War Museum, London 1996.

Osborne, John, *Look Back in Anger*, London 1956.

Radford, Robert, *Art for a Purpose. The Artists' International Association, 1933–1953*, Winchester 1987.

Shaw, Tony, *British Cinema and the Cold War. The State, Propaganda and Consensus*, London 2001.

Sissons, Michael and French, Philip (eds.), *The Age of Austerity 1945–51*, Harmondsworth 1964.

Stansky, Peter and Abrahams, William. *London's Burning: Life, Death and Art in the Second World War*, Stanford 1994.

Soho in the Fifties and Sixties, exh. cat. National Portrait Gallery, London 1998.

Sutherland. The War Drawings, exh. cat. Imperial War Museum, London 1982.

Sylvester, David, *The Brutality of Fact. Interviews with Francis Bacon*, London 1987.

Tassi, Roberto, *Sutherland. The Wartime Drawings*, London 1980.

Transition. The London Art Scene in the Fifties, exh. cat. Barbican Art Centre, London 2002.

Wilson, Colin, *The Outsider*, London 1956.

Yorke, Malcolm, *Spirit of Place. Nine Neo-Romantic Artists and Their Times*, London 1988.

1950–60
BRAVE NEW WORLDS, ABSTRACTION AND THE AESTHETICS OF PLENTY

21 From 51. Paintings From the Festival of Britain, exh. cat. Sheffield City Art Galleries, Sheffield 1978.

Alloway, Lawrence, *Nine Abstract Painters*, London 1954.

An Exhibit, exh. cat. Institute of Contemporary Arts, London 1957.

Baker, Denys Val, *Britain's Art Colony By the Sea*, London 1959.

Banham, Reyner, *Theory and Design in the First Machine Age*, London 1960.

Bann, Stephen (ed.), *The Tradition of Constructivism*, London 1974.

Biederman, Charles, *Art As the Evolution of Visual Knowledge*, Red Wing/Minnesota 1948.

Cornwall 1945–1955, exh. cat. New Art Centre, London 1977.

Cross, Tom, *Painting the Warmth of the Sun. St. Ives Artists, 1939–1975*, London 1984.

Denis Bowen, exh. cat. Drian Gallery, London 1961.

The Developing Process, exh. cat. Institute of Contemporary Arts, London 1959.

Dimensions. British Abstract Art 1948–1957, exh. cat. O'Hana Gallery, London 1957.

Gardiner, Juliet, *From the Bomb to the Beatles*, London 1999.

Growth and Form, exh. cat. Institute of Contemporary Arts, London 1951.

Hall, Stuart and Whannel, Paddy, *The Popular Arts*, London 1964.

Heron, Patrick, *The Changing Forms of Art*, London 1955.

Hoggart, Richard, *The Uses of Literacy*, London 1957.

Hopkins, Harry, *The New Look. A Social History of the Forties and Fifties in Britain*, London 1963.

MacInnes, Colin, *Absolute Beginners*, London 1959.

Man, Machine and Motion, exh. cat. Hatton Gallery, Newcastle 1955.

Massey, Anne, *The Independent Group. Modernism and Mass Culture in Britain 1945–59*, Manchester 1995.

Matter Painting, exh. cat. Institute of Contemporary Arts, London 1960.

Metavisual, Tachiste, Abstract, exh. cat. Redfern Gallery, London 1957.

Metzger, Gustav, *Manifesto: Auto-Destructive Art*, London 1960.

The New American Painting. As Shown in Eight European Countries, 1958–1959, exh. cat. Museum of Modern Art, New York 1959.

New Trends in Painting, London 1956.

Nigel Henderson. Paintings, Collages and Photographs, exh. cat. Anthony d'Offay Gallery, London 1977.

Parallel of Life and Art, exh. cat. Institute of Contemporary Arts, London 1953.

Robbins, David (ed.), *The Independent Group. Postwar Britain and the Aesthetics of Plenty*, Cambridge/Mass. and London 1990.

St. Ives 1939–64. Twenty-five years of Painting, Sculpture and Pottery, ed. David Brown, exh. cat. Tate Gallery, London 1996.

Statements. A Review of British Abstract Art in 1956, exh. cat. Institute of Contemporary Arts, London 1957.

Stoner Saunders, F., *Who Paid the Piper? The CIA and the Cultural Cold War*, London 1999.

Taylor, Richard, *Against the Bomb. The British Peace Movement, 1958–1965*, Oxford 1988.

This Is Tomorrow, exh. cat. Whitechapel Art Gallery, London 1956.

Walker, John A., *Cultural Offensive. America's Impact on British Art Since 1945*, London 1998.

Woollcombe, Tamsyn. (ed.), *The Fifties. Art From The British Council Collection*, London 1998.

1960–65
POP, OP AND HARD EDGE

Aitken, Jonathan, *The Young Meteors*, London 1967.

Alley, Ronald, *New Paintings 61–64*, London 1964.

Alloway, Lawrence et al., *Modern Dreams. The Rise and Fall and Rise of Pop*, Cambridge/Mass. and London 1988.

Amaya, Mario, *Pop As Art. A Survey of the New Super Realism*, London 1965.

Barrett, Cyril, *An Introduction to Optical Art*, London 1971.

Bowness, Alan (ed.), *Recent British Painting. The Peter Stuyvesant Foundation Collection*, London 1968.

Brett, Guy, *Kinetic Art*, London 1968.

Compton, Michael, *Pop Art*, London 1970.

Contemporary British Art, exh. cat. National Museum of Modern Art, Tokyo 1970.

Gablik, Suzi and Russell, John (eds.), *Pop Art Redefined*, London 1969.

Hyman, James, *The Battle for Realism. Figurative Art in Britain During the Cold War, 1945–60*, London and New Haven 2001.

Jacob, Jürgen, *Die Entwicklung der Pop Art in England*, Frankfurt on Main 1986.

London, The New Scene, exh. cat. Walker Art Center, Minneapolis 1965.

Melly, George, *Revolt Into Style. The Pop Arts in Britain*, London 1970.

Mellor, David Alan and Laurent, Gerveau (eds.), *The Sixties. Britain and France, 1962–1973. The Utopian Years*, London 1996.

New Vision 56–66, exh. cat. Bede Gallery, Jarrow 1984.

New Generation: 1964, exh. cat. Whitechapel Art Gallery, London 1964.

New Generation: 1965, exh. cat. Whitechapel Art Gallery, London 1965.

Pop Art, ed. Marco Livingstone, exh. cat. Royal Academy of Arts, London 1991.

Pop Art in England. Beginnings of a New Figuration, 1947–1963, exh. cat. Kunstverein in Hamburg, Hamburg 1976.

Pop Art. U. S./U. K. Connections, 1956–1966, exh. cat. The Menil Collection, Houston 2001.

Pop Design. Modernism to Mod, exh. cat. Design Council, London 1987.

Ralph Rumney, exh. cat. New Vision Centre Gallery, London 1956.

Ralph Rumney. Constats: 1950–1988, London 1989.

Ready, Steady, Go. Painting of the Sixties from the Arts Council Collection, exh. cat. South Bank Centre, Hayward Gallery, London 1992.

Richard Smith, Paintings 1958–1966, exh. cat. Whitechapel Art Gallery, London 1966.

Seago, Alex, *Burning the Box of Beautiful Things. The Development of a Postmodern Sensibility*, Oxford 1995.

Sculpture. The New Generation: 1968 Interim, exh. cat. Whitechapel Art Gallery, London 1968.

Situation, exh. cat. RBA Galleries, London 1960.

The Sixties Art Scene in London, exh. cat. Barbican Art Gallery, London 1993.

Two Young Figurative Painters. Howard Hodgkin and Allen Jones, exh. cat. Institute of Contemporary Arts, London 1962.

Whiteley, Nigel, *Reyner Banham. Historian of the Immediate Future*, Cambridge/Mass. 2002.

William Green, London 1993.

Wilson, Simon, *Pop*, London 1974.

Woods, Alan, *Ralph Rumney. The Map is Not the Territory*, Manchester 2000.

1965–80
COUNTERCULTURE AND THE "NEW ART"

1965 to 1972. When Attitudes Became Form, ed. Hilary Gresty, exh. cat. Kettle's Yard Gallery, Cambridge 1984.

Arte inglese oggi, 1960–1976, exh. cat. British Council, 2 vols., Milan 1976.

Arts Council of Great Britain. *The Arts in Hard Times. Arts Council of Great Britain, 31st Annual Report and Accounts Year Ended 31 March 1976*, London 1976.

Archiving My Own History. Documentation of Works 1969–1994, exh. cat. Cornerhouse, Manchester, and South London Gallery, London 1994.

Auty, Giles, *The Art of Self-Deception. An Intelligible Guide*, Bedford 1977.

Battock, Gregory (ed.), *The New Art. A Critical Anthology*, New York 1966.

Beale, Philippa and Swinson, James (Producers), *From Wilson to Callaghan. Documents 1964–1979*, [Videotape] London, 1999.

Berger, John, *Ways of Seeing*, London 1972.

Berke, Joseph (ed.), *Counter Culture*, London 1969.

Braden, Sue, *Artists and People*, London 1978.

Burgin, Victor, *Work and Commentary*, London 1973.

Burgin, Victor, *The End of Art Theory. Criticism and Postmodernity*, London 1986.

Un certain art anglais. Sélection d'artistes britanniques 1970–1979, exh. cat. Musée d'Art Moderne de la Ville de Paris, Paris 1979.

Cork, Richard, *The Social Role of Art. Essays in Criticism for a Newspaper Public*, London 1979.

Curtis, David (ed.), *A Directory of British Film & Video Artists*, London 1996.

Ford, Simon, *Wreckers of Civilisation. The Story of COUM Transmissions and Throbbing Gristle*, London 1999.

Francis, Richard (ed.), *Hayward Annual 1979*, London 1979.

Fuller, Peter, *Beyond the Crisis in Art*, London 1980.

Greer, Germaine, *The Female Eunuch*, London 1970.

Hadjinicolaou, Nikos, *Art History and Class Struggle*, London 1970.

Hannema, Sjoerd, *Fads, Fakes and Fantasies. The Crisis in the Art Schools*, London 1970.

Happening & Fluxus, exh. cat. Kölnischer Kunstverein, Cologne 1970.

Henri, Adrian, Environments and Happenings, London 1974.

Hewison, Robert, Too Much. Art and Society in the Sixties 1960–75, London 1986.

Hornsey College of Art Students and Staff, The Hornsey Affair, London 1969.

Howell, Anthony, The Analysis of Performance Art. A Guide to Its Theory and Practice, Amsterdam 1999.

John Latham. Early Works, 1954–1972, exh. cat. Lisson Gallery, London 1987.

Keeler, Paul, Planted, London 1968.

Kelly, Mary, Post-Partum Document, London 1983.

Kelly, Owen, Community, Art and the State, London 1984.

Latham, John, Event-Structure. Approach to Basic Contradiction, Bracknell 1981.

Latham, John, Report of a Surveyor, London and Stuttgart 1984.

Lippard, Lucy, Six Years. The Dematerialization of the Art Object from 1966 to 1972, London 1973.

Live in Your Head. Concept and Experiment in Britain, 1965–75, exh. cat. Whitechapel Art Gallery, London 2000.

Lord Redcliffe-Maud, Support for the Arts in England and Wales. A Report to the Calouste Gulbenkian Foundation, London 1976.

Lucie-Smith, Edward and White, Patricia, Art in Britain, 1969–1970, London 1970.

Mayor, David (ed.), Fluxshoe, Cullompton 1972.

Moore-Gilbert, Bart, The Arts in the 1970s. Cultural Closure? London 1994.

Neville, Richard, Play Power, London 1970.

The New Art, exh. cat. Hayward Gallery, London 1972.

Newman, Michael and Bird, Jon, Rewriting Conceptual Art, London 1999.

Nuttall, Jeff, Bomb Culture, London 1971.

Nyman, Michael, Experimental Music. Cage and Beyond, New York 1974.

Out of Actions. Between Performance and the Object, 1949–1979, ed. Paul Schimmel, exh. cat. The Museum of Contemporary Art, Los Angeles, and London 1998.

Popper, Frank, Art: Action and Participation, London 1975.

Reichardt, Jasia, The Computer in Art, London 1971.

Roberts, John (ed.), The Impossible Document. Photography and Conceptual Art in Britain 1966–1976, London 1997.

Sabin, Roger, Punk Rock. So What? The Cultural Legacy of Punk, London 1999.

Savage, Jon, England's Dreaming. Sex Pistols and Punk Rock, London 1991.

Stansill, Peter and Mairowitz, David Zane, BAMN. Outlaw Manifestos and Ephemera, 1965–1970, Harmondsworth 1971.

When Attitudes Become Form, exh. cat. Institute of Contemporary Arts, London 1969.

Willats, Stephen, The Artist As an Instigator of Changes in Social Cognition and Behaviour, London 1973.

Wittgenstein, Ludwig, Philosophical Investigations, Oxford 1974.

1980–90
PAINTING, OBJECTS AND INSTALLATIONS

About Vision. New British Painting in the 1990s, exh. cat. Museum of Modern Art, Oxford 1996.

Antony Gormley, Five Works, London 1987.

Artist and Model, exh. cat. Whitworth Art Gallery, Manchester 1986.

The Artist's Eye. An Exhibition Selected By Howard Hodgkin, exh. cat. National Gallery, London 1979.

Arts Council of Great Britain, The Glory of the Garden. The Development of the Arts in England: A Strategy for a Decade, London 1984.

Bacon-Freud. Expressions, exh. cat. Foundation Maeght, Paris 1985.

Baldry, Henry, The Case for the Arts, London 1981.

Bickers, Patricia, The Brit Pack. Contemporary British Art, The View From Abroad, Manchester 1995.

"Brilliant!". New Art From London, exh. cat. Walker Art Center, Minneapolis 1995.

Broken English, exh. cat. Serpentine Gallery, London 1991.

Burrows, David (ed.), Who's Afraid of Red White and Blue, Birmingham 1998.

Causey, Andrew, Sculpture Since 1945, Oxford 1998.

Collins, Matthew, Blimey. From Bohemia to Britpop. The London Artworld From Francis Bacon to Damien Hirst, Cambridge 1997.

Collins, Matthew, Art Crazy Nation. The Post Blimey Art World, London 2001.

Current Affairs. British Painting and Sculpture in the 1980s, exh. cat. Museum of Modern Art, Oxford 1987.

East Country Yard Show, eds. Henry Bond and Sarah Lucas, exh. cat. East Country Yard, London 1990.

L'Ecole de Londres: de Bacon à Bevan, exh. cat. Fondation Dina Vierny-Musée Maillol, Réunion des Musées Nationaux, Paris 1998.

Edward Allington. In Pursuit of a Savage Luxury, exh. cat. Midland Group Gallery, Nottingham 1984.

Emotion. Young British and American Art From the Goetz Collection, ed. Zdenek Felix, exh. cat. Deichtorhallen Hamburg, Ostfildern-Ruit 1998.

Entre el objeto y la imagen: escultura británica contemporánea, Madrid 1986.

Englische Plastik heute/British Sculpture Now, ed. Martin Kunz, exh. cat. Kunstmuseum Luzern, Lucerne 1982.

Freeze, exh. cat. Surrey Docks, London 1988.

Frank Auerbach. Recent Paintings and Drawings, London 1987.

From London, Bacon, Freud, Kossoff, Andrews, Auerbach, Kitaj, eds. Richard Calvocoressi and Philip Long, exh. cat. Scottish National Gallery of Modern Art, London 1995.

Fuller, Peter, Seeing Berger, London 1981.

Fuller, Peter, Peter Fuller's Modern Painters. Reflections on British Art, London 1993.

Gamble, Andrew, The Free Economy and the Strong State. The Politics of Thatcherism, London 1988.

Gambler, exh. cat. Building One, London 1990.

General Release. Young British Artists at Scuola di San Pasquale, Venice, 1995, London 1995.

The Hard-Won Image. Traditional Method and Subject in Recent English Art, exh. cat. Tate Gallery, London 1984.

Hatton, Rita and Walker, John A., Supercollector. A Critique of Charles Saatchi, London 2000.

Hewison, Robert, Future Tense. A New Art for the Nineties, London 1990.

Hicks, Alistair, New British Art in the Saatchi Collection, London 1989.

Hicks, Alistair, The School of London, The Resurgence of Contemporary Painting, Oxford 1989.

Hirst, Damien, Pictures From the Saatchi Gallery, London 2001.

Hirst, Damien and Burn, Gordon, On the Way to Work, London 2001.

Howard Hodgkin. Forty Paintings, 1973–84, ed. Nicholas Serota, exh. cat. Whitechapel Art Gallery, London 1984.

Hyman, Timothy, Figurative Paintings. Figurative Art of Two Generations, Bristol 1979.

The Image As Catalyst. The Younger Generation of British Figurative Painters, exh. cat. Ashmolean Museum, Oxford 1984.

Intelligence. New British Art 2000, exh. cat. Tate Gallery, London 2000.

Julian Opie, exh. cat. Lisson Gallery, London 1985.

Kapoor, Anish, British Pavilion, XLIV Venice Biennale, London 1990.

Keens, W. et al. (eds.). Arts and the Changing City. An Agenda for Urban Regeneration, London 1989.

Kearton, Nicola (ed.), British Art. Defining the 90s, London 1995.

Kent, Sarah, Shark Infested Waters. The Saatchi Collection of British Art in the 90s, London 1994.

Kitaj, R. B., The Human Clay. An Exhibition, London 1976.

Life/Live. La Scène artistique au Royaume-Uni en 1996. De nouvelles aventures, exh. cat. Musée d'Art Moderne de la Ville de Paris, Paris 1996.

Lingwood, James (ed.), Rachel Whiteread. House, London 1995.

Lucian Freud. Paintings, London 1987.

Market, exh. cat. Building One, London 1990.

Material Culture. The Object in British Art of the 1980s and '90s, exh. cat. South Bank Centre, Hayward Gallery, London 1997.

McCorquodale, Duncan et al. (eds.). Occupational Hazard. Critical Writing on Recent British Art, London 1998.

Modern Medicine, exh. cat. Building One, London 1990.

Moving Targets 2. A User's Guide to British Art Now, exh. cat. Tate Gallery, London 2000.

Myerscough, J., The Economic Importance of the Arts in Britain, London 1988.

New British Sculpture, exh. cat. Air Gallery, London 1986.

A New Spirit in Painting, eds. Christos Joachimides and Norman Rosenthal, exh. cat. Royal Academy of Arts, London 1981.

Objects and Sculpture, exh. cat. Institute of Contemporary Arts, London and Bristol 1981.

Picturing People. British Figurative Art Since 1945, London 1989.

The Proper Study. Contemporary Figurative Painting From Britain, London 1984.

Renton, Andrew and Gillick, Liam (eds.), Technique Anglaise. Current Trends in British Art, London 1991.

Richard Wentworth. Sculptures, exh. cat. Lisson Gallery, London 1986.

Schiller, Herbert I., Culture Inc. The Corporate Takeover of Public Expression, New York and Oxford 1989.

A School of London, Six Figurative Painters, London 1987.

Sensation. Young British Artists From the Saatchi Collection, exh. cat. Royal Academy of Arts, London 1998.

Seven British Painters. Selected Masters of Post-War British Art, London 1993.

Signs of the Times. A Decade of Video, Film and Slide-Tape Installation in Britain, 1980–1990, exh. cat. Museum of Modern Art, Oxford 1990.

Some Went Mad, Some Ran Away, exh. cat. Serpentine Gallery, London 1994.

Stallabrass, Julian, High Art Lite. British Art in the 1990s, London 1999.

Starlit Waters. British Sculpture, an International Art 1968–1988, exh. cat. Tate Gallery, Liverpool 1988.

This Knot of Life. Paintings and Drawings By British Artists, exh. cat. L. A. Louver Gallery, Venice/California 1979.

Thompson, Jon, "The Economics of Culture. The Revival of British Art in the 80s", in Howard Singerman (ed.), Public Offerings, New York 2001, p.219–208.

Tony Cragg. British Pavilion. XLIII Biennale di Venezia, London 1988.

The Turner Prize 1985, exh. cat. Tate Gallery, London 1985.

Tony Cragg. Winner of the 1988 Turner Prize, exh. cat. Tate Gallery, London 1988.

An Urban Renaissance. The Role of the Arts in Urban Regeneration, The Case for Increased Public and Private Sector Cooperation, London 1988.

Woodrow, Bill and Richard
  Deacon, *Only the Lonely and
  Other Shared Sculptures*,
  exh. cat. Chisenhale Gallery,
  London 1993.
*Young British Artists. John Green-
  wood, Damien Hirst, Alex Landrum,
  Langlands & Bell, Rachel
  Whiteread*, exh. cat. Saatchi
  Collection, London 1992.
Wu, Chin-tao, *Privatising Culture.
  Corporate Art Intervention
  Since the 1980s*, London 2002.
Young British Art. The Saatchi Decade,
  London 1999.

AUTHORS' BIOGRAPHIES

ANDREW CAUSEY

Andrew Causey is Professor of Modern Art History at Manchester University. He has published extensively on (mainly British) twentieth-century art. His early publications include monographs on Paul Nash (1980) and Edward Burra (1986), and he has done extensive research into the works of Percy Wyndham Lewis and Stanley Spencer. His most recent book is *Sculpture Since 1945* (1998). He was Chair of the selection committee for the exhibition *British Art in the Twentieth Century* at the Royal Academy, London, and the Staatsgalerie Stuttgart, 1987.

RICHARD CORK

Dr. Richard Cork is an art critic, historian, broadcaster and exhibition organiser. He has been art critic of *The Evening Standard* and *The Listener* and Chief Art Critic of *The Times*. He was the Slade Professor of Fine Art at Cambridge from 1989 to 1990 and served as Chair of the Visual Arts Panel of the Arts Council of England from 1995 to 1998. His exhibition *A Bitter Truth. Avant-Garde Art and the Great War* was shown at the Altes Museum, Berlin, and the Barbican Art Gallery London in 1994. His books include a two-volume study of *Vorticism* (1976), *David Bomberg* (1987), *Art Beyond the Gallery* (1994) and *Jacob Epstein* (1999). Four volumes of his selected critical writings are due to appear with Yale University Press, in autumn 2002.

DAVID CURTIS

David Curtis was involved in the British experimental film scene in the 1960s and 1970s before becoming Senior Visual Arts Officer at the Arts Council of England from 1977 to 1999, with responsibility for funding artists' films and video. He is currently Senior Research Fellow at Central St. Martin's, the London Institute, where he has established a British Artists' Film and Video Study Collection (www.bftv.ac.uk/avantgarde). He has also designed programmes of artists' films for BBC2 and Channel 4 television. His publications include *Experimental Cinema* (1971) and a directory of *British Avant-Garde Film & Video Artists* (1996).

PENELOPE CURTIS

Dr. Penelope Curtis is Curator of the Henry Moore Institute in Leeds, where she runs a programme devoted to the study of sculpture from the historic to the contemporary. For the Tate Gallery she has written *Modern British Sculpture from the Collection* (1988), *Barbara Hepworth. A Retrospective* (1994) and *Barbara Hepworth* (1998). She has published an international survey, *Sculpture 1900–1945* (1999).

MARGARET GARLAKE

Dr. Margaret Garlake is an art historian, teacher and former editor of *Art Monthly*, who specialises in twentieth-century British art and has a particular interest in patronage. Her publications include *Britain and the São Paulo Bienal 1951–1991* (1991) and *New Art, New World. British Art in Postwar Society* (1998), and she has just completed a book on the drawings of Peter Lanyon. Dr. Garlake is the editor of the *Sculpture Journal*.

CHARLES HARRISON

Charles Harrison has been associated with the practice of Art & Language since 1971. He is the author of *English Art and Modernism 1900–1939* (1981 and 1984), *Modernism* (1997), *Essays on Art & Language* (1991 and 2001) and *Conceptual Art and Painting* (2001). He is co-editor of *Art in Theory 1900–2000*, *Art in Theory 1815–1900* and *Art in Theory 1648–1815*. He has held visiting professorships at the Universities of Chicago and Texas at Austin and was a Getty Scholar at the Getty Research Institute, Los Angeles, in 2001–2. He is currently Professor of the History and Theory of Art and Staff Tutor at the Open University.

ROBERT HEWISON

Robert Hewison is a cultural historian who has written widely on aspects of nineteenth- and twentieth-century British culture. He also writes on the arts and the politics of the arts for the London weekly newspaper *The Sunday Times*. His publications include *The Heritage Industry. Britain in a Climate of Decline* (1987), *Future Tense. A New Art of the Nineties* (1990) and *Culture and Consensus. England, Art and Politics Since 1940* (1995). An authority on the work of John Ruskin, he was Slade Professor of Fine Arts at Oxford in 2000, Ruskin's centenary year, and co-curated the Ruskin centenary exhibition at Tate Britain. He is an Honorary Professor at Lancaster University.

ANTHONY HOWELL

Anthony Howell trained as a dancer and joined the Royal Ballet by the time he was twenty. Soon after, he turned to writing and performance art and went on to found The Theatre of Mistakes, which created pieces for the Stedelijk Museum in Amsterdam, the Paris Biennale and the Paula Cooper Gallery in New York. Howell has published many collections of poetry and *The Analysis of Performance Art* (1999). In 1995 he performed a *Commentary on Yves Klein* at the Hayward Gallery. In 2001–02 he spent three months in Argentina studying tango on a Live Art Development Agency Bursary.

JAMES HYMAN

James Hyman received his doctorate from the Courtauld Institute, University of London, and is a writer, lecturer, curator and art dealer. Recent publications include *The Battle for Realism. Figurative Art in Britain During the Cold War, 1945–60* (2001), as well as complete catalogues of the prints of Tony Bevan (1995), the woodcuts of Anselm Kiefer (1997), and the lithographs of Henri Cartier-Bresson (1998). Exhibitions he has curated include *British Figurative Painting of the Twentieth Century* (The British Council 1992) and *Picasso. Artist of the Century* (Kunsthal Rotterdam 1999).

JEREMY LEWISON

Jeremy Lewison is a freelance curator, writer and consultant. He spent five years as Curator of Kettle's Yard, University of Cambridge, before joining the Tate Gallery as Assistant Keeper, eventually rising to the position of Director of Collections, from 1998 to 2002. Exhibitions he organised at the Tate Gallery include *Ben Nicholson* (1993) and *Jackson Pollock* (1999), both of which were accompanied by major publications. In 2002 he organised a Ben Nicholson retrospective at the IVAM Centre Julio González, Valencia. He has also written extensively about graphic work by artists including Sol LeWitt, Anish Kapoor and Brice Marden, and about David Smith's *Medals of Dishonor 1937–40* (1991).

MARCO LIVINGSTONE

Marco Livingstone is an art historian and independent curator. He has organised retrospectives of the work of Allen Jones (1979), Patrick Caulfield (1981), Peter Phillips (1982), David Hockney (1989 and 1994), Jim Dine (1990 and 1996), Tom Wesselmann (1993), Duane Hanson (1994), George Segal (1997) and R. B. Kitaj (1998), and a number of major Pop Art exhibitions (Royal Academy of Arts, London, 1991 and Centro Cultural de Belém, Lisbon, 1997). His publications include Pop Art. A Continuing History (1990) and monographs and major exhibition catalogues on Hockney, Dine, Kitaj, Caulfield, Jones, Tony Bevan, Tim Head, Michael Sandle, Edward and Nancy Reddin Kienholz and Duane Michals.

NORBERT LYNTON

Norbert Lynton, Professor Emeritus of the University of Sussex, is an art historian and experienced teacher, who was the London correspondent for Art International from 1961 to 1966 and art critic for The Guardian from 1970 to 1975. He was also the Arts Council's Director of Exhibitions from 1970 to 1975. Since then, he has served as an advisor to many public organisations, including the Arts Council, the British Council and the National Portrait Gallery (as Trustee) and is currently Chairman of the Charleston Trust. His survey The Story of Modern Art (1980) is still widely admired. He has published books on Paul Klee, Ben Nicholson, Victor Pasmore and Jack Smith, and his monograph on William Scott is due to appear shortly.

TIM MARLOW

Tim Marlow is a writer, critic and broadcaster. Until recently, he was editor of Tate magazine, which he founded in 1993. He is the author of numerous television and radio arts programmes, including a four-part series on Tate Modern for Channel 5 and a documentary on William Turner for BBC1 in 2002. He is currently Creative Director of Sculpture for Goodwood, and his most recent book is Great Artists. From Giotto to Turner (2001).

ANNE MASSEY

Professor Anne Massey is Director of the School of Design at the Arts Institute at Bournemouth. After studying for a first degree in the history of art, she completed a PhD on the Independent Group at the University of Northumbria in 1984. Her book The Independent Group. Modernism and Mass Culture, 1945–59 (1995) is the standard work on the subject. Her most recent book is Hollywood Beyond the Screen. Design and Material Culture (2000). She is currently working on the myth of Cinderella.

DAVID ALAN MELLOR

Dr. David Alan Mellor is Professor of Art History at the University of Sussex. He has published widely and curated several exhibitions on twentieth-century British art and visual culture, including Cecil Beaton (1986), A Paradise Lost/Neo-Romantic Art and Culture in Britain, 1935–45 (1987), The Sixties Art Scene in London (1993), Les Années soixante (1997); Chemical Traces. Photography and Conceptual Art (1998), The Art of Robyn Denny (2002), Interpreting Lucian Freud (2002) and Van Gogh vu par Bacon (2002).

HENRY MEYRIC HUGHES

Henry Meyric Hughes is an independent curator and writer on art in Britain and Central Europe. He has worked for the British Council in several countries and as Director of its Visual Arts Department, in London and British Commissioner for the Venice Biennale and Bienal de São Paulo from 1986 to 1992. From 1992 to 1996 he was Director of the Hayward Gallery, London. He was Commissioner of the XXIII Council of Europe exhibition Europe Under the Dictators 1930–45 (1995–56) and Associate Curator of The Age of Modernism in Berlin 1997. He is a past President of the British Section of AICA and a founder and current President of the International Foundation Manifesta in Amsterdam.

RICHARD SHONE

Richard Shone is the author of several books on French and modern British art, most recently, The Art of Bloomsbury (1999) and has been an Associate Editor of The Burlington Magazine since 1979. He has written frequently on artists such as Damien Hirst, Rachel Whiteread, Michael Landy, Julian Opie and Fiona Rae and contributed a history of the Freeze generation of artists to the catalogue of the exhibition Sensation at the Royal Academy in 1997.

CHRISTOPHER STEPHENS

Dr. Christopher Stephens is an art historian and Senior Curator at Tate Britain. He is a specialist in mid-twentieth century British art, with particular interests in St. Ives and in sculpture. He has published widely in these areas, including books on Barbara Hepworth (with Matthew Gale), Peter Lanyon, Bryan Wynter, Terry Frost and Hubert Dalwood. He is currently writing a critical history of St. Ives.

GIJS VAN TUYL

Dr. Gijs van Tuyl was curator of Painting and Sculpture from 1969 to 1976 at the Stedelijk Museum in Amsterdam. He was Director of the Office for Fine Arts Abroad from 1976 to 1985 and Director of Exhibitions at the Netherlands Office for Fine Art from 1985 to 1992; also the Permanent Commissioner for the Netherlands for the Venice Biennale and São Paulo Bienal from 1978 to 1991. Van Tuyl was art critic of Vrij Nederland from 1977 to 1980 and editor of Dutch Art & Architecture Today from 1977 to 1988. Since 1992 he has been the Director of the Kunstmuseum Wolfsburg. He has been Honorary Professor at Brunswick School of Art since 2000. He is also a Board member of the Conseil International des Musées d'Art Moderne (CIMAM).

NICK DE VILLE

Nick de Ville is the Professor of Visual Arts at Goldsmiths' College, University of London. His research is focused on contemporary art and its relation to the wider culture. He both curates and writes. His most recent exhibition as curator was Small Truths. Repetition and the Obsessional in Contemporary Art (1996). Recent books include Space Invaders. Issues of Presentation, Context and Meaning in Contemporary Art (1993) and The Artist & The Academy. Issues in Fine Art Education and the Wider Cultural Context (1994). He is currently writing a book on the twentieth-century history of design for music – particularly the album sleeve design and its reflection of its cultural context.

ANDREW WILSON

Dr. Andrew Wilson is an art historian, critic and curator living in London. He is the Deputy Editor of Art Monthly. He has researched British art of the 1920s and 1930s for the last fifteen years and curated a major exhibition of the British Surrealists Dr. Grace Pailthorpe and Reuben Mednikoff at Leeds City Art Gallery in 1998. Recent publications include contributions to Art & Language. Too Dark to Read (Musée d'Art Moderne Lille Métropole, Villeneuve d'Ascq, 2002), Hamish Fulton (Tate Britain, London, 2002), and Grayson Perry (Stedelijk Museum, Amsterdam, 2002). He is currently working on a major study on the counterculture in London in the 1960s and 1970s.

PHOTO CREDITS

p. 21/fig. 10, p. 22/fig. 11, p. 23/fig. 12, p. 27/fig. 1,
p. 28/fig. 3, p. 31/fig. 9, p. 62/fig. 10, 11, p. 64/fig. 14,
p. 67/fig. 2, p. 68/fig. 5, p. 71/fig. 11–13, p. 72/fig. 14,
p. 142/fig. 11, p. 171/fig. 9, p. 282/fig. 6, p. 289/fig. 2, 4,
p. 297/fig. 1, pls. 4, 9, 21, 23, 78, 106
Rodney Todd-White and Son pl. 121
Piotr Tomczyk pls. 127, 139
Tyne and Wear Museums Services p. 110/fig. 9, p. 302/fig. 6
V&A Picture Library pl. 2
Waddington Galleries, London p. 306/fig. 9
Elke Walford pl. 154

John Webb pls. 11, 168, 201
Courtesy John Webb/Karsten Schubert pl. 151
Gareth Winters pls. 167, 166
Edward Woodman pl. 213

Our special thanks go to Boyle Family, David Curtis, Ivor Davies,
Anthony Howell, Dr. Jeffrey and Ruth Sherwin as well as to Ivor
Braka Limited, London, who provided copies for illustrations.

This catalogue is published
on the occasion of the exhibition

BLAST TO FREEZE
BRITISCHE KUNST IM 20. JAHRHUNDERT
Kunstmuseum Wolfsburg
14 September 2002 – 19 January 2003

BLAST TO FREEZE
BRITISH ART IN THE 20TH CENTURY
Les Abattoirs, Toulouse
24 February – 11 May 2003

The exhibition is sponsored by Volkswagen Bank.

EDITED BY
  Kunstmuseum Wolfsburg
GENERAL EDITORS
  Henry Meyric Hughes, Gijs van Tuyl
CO-ORDINATING EDITOR
  Holger Broeker
EDITING ASSISTANTS
  Annelie Lütgens, Anja Westermann,
  Kristin Schrader
COPY EDITING
  Henry Meyric Hughes, Ingrid Nina Bell
TRANSLATION
  Ingrid Nina Bell, Henry Meyric Hughes,
  Steven Lindberg (from German)
  Charles Penwarden (from French)
GRAPHIC DESIGN
  Gerard Hadders, Andreas Tetzlaff,
  Buro Lange Haven, Schiedam
TYPESETTING
  Sabine Pflitsch, Andreas Tetzlaff
REPRODUCTION
  Repromayer, Reutlingen
PRINTED BY
  Dr. Cantz'sche Druckerei,
  Ostfildern-Ruit

PUBLISHED BY
  Hatje Cantz Publishers
  Senefelderstraße 12, 73760 Ostfildern-Ruit, Germany
  Tel. +49/7 11/4 40 50
  Fax +49/7 11/4 40 52 20
  Internet: www.hatjecantz.de

DISTRIBUTION IN THE US
  D.A.P., Distributed Art Publishers, Inc.
  155 Avenue of the Americas, Second Floor
  New York, N.Y. 10013-1507, USA
  Tel. +1/2 12/6 27 19 99
  Fax +1/2 12/6 27 94 84

ISBN 3-7757-1248-8 (English edition)
ISBN 3-7757-1180-5 (German edition)

Printed in Germany

Die Deutsche Bibliothek – CIP-Einheitsaufnahme
Blast to freeze : British art in the 20th century ;
Kunstmuseum Wolfsburg, 14.9.2002 bis 19.1.1003. –
Ostfildern-Ruit : Hatje Cantz, 2002
    Dt. Ausg. u.d.T.: Blast to freeze
    ISBN 3-7757-1248-8

Cover illustration: Jacob Epstein, THE ROCK DRILL,
1913–15 / Reconstruction 1976, polyester resin
(figure), metall (drill), wood (drill bit), 205 x 141.5 cm
Birmingham Museums and Art Gallery

We should like to thank Annette Kulenkampff and her team
at Hatje Cantz Publishers, in particular Anja Breloh,
for their excellent help and collaboration, at all stages in
the production of the English and German catalogues.

EXHIBITION

CONCEPT
  Henry Meyric Hughes, Gijs van Tuyl
EXHIBITION ARCHITECTURE
  David Chipperfield Architects, Berlin
INSTALLATION
  Henry Meyric Hughes, Gijs van Tuyl,
  Veit Görner
DIRECTOR'S OFFICE
  Eveline Welke
PROJECT MANAGEMENT
  Manfred Müller
EXHIBITION OFFICE
  Carmen Müller
CONSERVATION
  Christiane Altmann
ART HANDLING
  Eva Gebhard
COMMUNICATION
  Thomas Köhler (Director), Andrea Bahl (Assist-
  ant), Ute Lefahrt (Visual Literacy), Gudrun
  Kolleck (Assistant), Ilona Schnellecke (Press),
  Nicole Schütze (Press)

KUNSTMUSEUM WOLFSBURG
Porschestraße 53, 38440 Wolfsburg, Germany
Tel. +49/53 61/26 69 0
Fax +49/53 61/26 69 66
E-mail: info@kunstmuseum-wolfsburg.de
Internet: www.kunstmuseum-wolfsburg.de

ORGANISATION OF THE EXHIBITION IN TOULOUSE

DIRECTOR
  Alain Mousseigne
  assisted by Lydia Maurel
ARTWORKS LOGISTICS
  Valentin Rodriguez
COMMUNICATION
  Michel-Paul Monredon
WEB SITE
  Virginie Desrois
DOCUMENTATION
  Gaelle Rageot
PUBLIC PROGRAMMES
  Laurence Darrigrand

Les Abattoirs gratefully acknowledge the support of the
Ville de Toulouse and the Conseil Régional de Midi-Pyrénées.

 BRITISH COUNCIL   The venue in Toulouse is supported
                   by The British Council France.